Theology after Lacan

Theology after Lacan

The Passion for the Real

Edited by
Creston Davis,
Marcus Pound,
and
Clayton Crockett

CASCADE *Books* · Eugene, Oregon

THEOLOGY AFTER LACAN
The Passion for the Real

Cascade Books
An Imprint of Wipf and Stock Publishers
199 W. 8th Ave., Suite 3
Eugene, OR 97401

www.wipfandstock.com

ISBN 13: 978-1-61097-101-0

Cataloguing-in-Publication data:

Theology after Lacan : the passion for the real / edited by Creston Davis, Marcus Pound, and Clayton Crockett.

xiii + 278 pp. ; 23 cm. Includes bibliographical references and index(es).

ISBN 13: 978-1-61097-101-0

1. Lacan, Jacques, 1901–1981. 2. Psychoanalysis and religion. 3. Postmodernism—Religious aspects—Christianity. I. Davis, Creston. II. Pound, Marcus. III. Crockett, Clayton, 1969–. IV. Title.

BD573 .T53 2014

Manufactured in the U.S.A.

Contents

Acknowledgments | vii

Introduction—Traversing the Theological Fantasy | 1
Creston Davis, Marcus Pound, and Clayton Crockett

Part One: Lacan, Religion, and Others

1 *Cogito*, Madness, and Religion: Derrida, Foucault, and Then
Lacan | 19
Slavoj Žižek

2 Nothing Really Matters—Rhapsody for a Dead Queen: A
Lacanian Reading of Thomas Aquinas | 34
Tina Beattie

3 Subjectification, Salvation, and the Real in Luther and
Lacan | 58
Carl Raschke

4 *Lacan avec le Bouddha*: Thoughts on Psychoanalysis and
Buddhism | 71
Mario D'Amato

5 Life Terminable and Interminable: The Undead and the
Afterlife of the Afterlife—A Friendly Disagreement with
Martin Hägglund | 87
Adrian Johnston

6 Solidarity in Suffering with the Non-Human | 125
Katerina Kolozova

Part II: Theology and the Other Lacan

7   There Is Something of One (God): Lacan and Political
    Theology | 150
    Kenneth Reinhard

8   Woman and the Number of God | 166
    Lorenzo Chiesa

9   Secular Theology as Language of Rebellion | 192
    Noëlle Vahanian

10 Making the Quarter Turn: Liberation Theology after
    Lacan | 211
    Thomas Lynch

11 By the Grace of Lacan | 232
    Marcus Pound

12 The Triumph of Theology | 250
    Clayton Crockett

Contributors | 267

Bibliography | 271

Index | 281

Acknowledgments

THIS BOOK IS WAS the initial idea of Creston Davis, without whom this project would not have found fruition; our thanks go to him and the various contributors to the work. In the preparation of the manuscript our thanks especially go to Jacob Martin at Wipf and Stock, Marcus Mayo, and Tyler Harper.

A previous version of chapter 5 was published by Adrian Johnston, "Life Terminable and Interminable: The Undead and the Afterlife of the Afterlife—A Friendly Disagreement with Martin Hägglund," in *New Centennial Review* 9.1 (2009), special issue: "Living On: Of Martin Hägglund," edited by David E. Johnson, 147–89. It is republished with the permission of *New Centennial Review*.

A different version of chapter 6 and under a different title has been published in Katerina Kolozova, *The Lived Revolution: Solidarity with the Body in Pain as the New Political Universal* (Skopje: EvroBalkan, 2010). It is republished here with the permission of EvroBalkan Press.

A previous version of chapter 7 was published by Kenneth Reinhard, "There Is Something of One (God): Lacan and Political Theology," in *Political Theology* 11.1 (2010) 43–60. It is republished here with the permission of Equinox Publishing.

Introduction

Traversing the Theological Fantasy

Creston Davis, Marcus Pound, and Clayton Crockett

The Real Introduction

FYODOR DOSTOEVSKY'S PROTAGONIST IN *Notes from Underground* nicely
identifies the central thesis of this book, namely, that theology in the wake
of Lacanian psychoanalysis is devoid of the "the big Other," i.e., a guarantee
that a system of belief is forever secured by a master-signifier around which
all meaning takes its place. Indeed, this book reverses this thesis: Only after
Lacan can theology mean anything at all. It is precisely by rejecting the idol
of God's necessity (*deus ex machina*) that theology can only make sense in
and through the wild untamable flux and fury of an uncontrollable contingency. Radical contingency grounds the truth of an infinite faith beyond
our primordial drive and instinct to control all things—like Aaron's golden
calf that attempts to hijack the infinite in terms of a master-signifier into
which all our longings and desire can be cast upon ever so easily. With our
hands washed free of faith by controlling the absolute, the desire for living
is denuded and life is substituted by believing in a fake god, the big Other.
In short, Lacanian psychoanalysis diagnoses the symptom inherent in theology, namely, a symptom that relies upon the hidden idol underneath its
golden veneer. Thus the very term *theology* is metonymic in that it refers
to a structure that unconsciously misnames its own truth, the truth of the
infinite that is substituted for a fake reality of a false God of the absolute.

1

One of the principle goals of the psychoanalytic method is to release repressed traumatic experiences so that those experiences can be articulated and desire flows again. It is our contention that traditional theology has been the *raison d'etre* for trauma, (the impossible demands of the Superego, The Paternal Father, the Big Other, God, etc.) which needs to be drained into the symbolic order so that desire once again flows through contingency, otherness, difference, and ultimately love. In treatment, the analyst listens "sideways" for shifts in tone, sounds, words, fixated images, stutters, and metonymic displacement in order to integrate the subject deeper into their fantasy, what Bruce Fink calls "traversing the fantasy."[1] In a way, Post-Lacanian theology traverses the fantasy of an absolute God in order to live into the calling of a radically contingent love; or, that which we have no control over and yet desire. If you like, we want to rename theology as a flow of desire devoid of the big Other, a desire that gives birth to an ethics beyond morals, and to a connection beyond the centered Ego at home with itself.

Traditional theology has never been very good about coming unstuck. Indeed it has a tendency for a bi-polar logic wherein it either raises to a level beyond critique, solidifying in absolute authoritarianism (mania), or else it becomes drained of all authority (depression). We are all too familiar with theological mania, and the 1960s so-called death of God theology gave birth to this depressive form of theology in which God was simply dismissed only to be replaced with the Ego as Absolute devoid of community, difference, and infinite contingency. What we are proposing is a method of traversal, namely, traverse the theological fantasy in a manner that neither slips into mania (pure enjoyment, authoritarianism) nor depression (no enjoyment, depression), but rather the release of desire that won't kill itself, but live in-and-through-itself. But how does one traverse this theological deadlock? The answer this book suggests is through Lacanian psychoanalysis. To this end, we would like to draw on Fyodor Dostoevsky's example about how he proposes to traverse the theological fantasy.

In his powerful novella *Notes from Underground*, Dostoevsky gives a voice to a suppressed language, i.e., the "underground" voice that functions like the unconscious, or in Lacanian terms, the "order of the Real." In the French language, the "Real" (*Reel*) means "to stop short of the actual object"; indeed "the order of the real" for Lacan inherently resists symbolization. The Real is that which cannot be encased in language. "The real is impossible" as Lacan says, in that it cannot be represented in language, but is nevertheless present in its very absence of the act of trying to symbolize it. So the very

---

1. Bruce Fink, *The Lacanian Subject: Between Language and Jouissance* (Princeton: Princeton University Press, 1996) 27.

use of language itself inherently creates a double-bind: language is necessary in order to communicate ideas, concepts, and desires, yet, in the very use of language, something always gets lost, and escapes the grasp of symbolizing those very ideas that we want to communicate. This loss is the presence of the Real in its very absence. In this way, Lacan identifies a paradox at work in the very use of language—in trying to communicate, we can only do so through a necessary *miscommunication*—and the "missing" part is that which haunts every word—it is the hidden *other* found in language itself haunting it like a ghost. So to get to the hidden (otherness) found within language, which is the very process of traversal, Lacan proposes a method not of direct engagement with language, but rather an *indirect* avenue of approach. This approach must therefore look for desire, the hidden otherness, in slips of the tongue, in unlocking trauma, sideways, if you will.

Exposing the Real can thus take on different formulations, genres, and mishaps. One way to attempt to expose the Real is through literature, and one of the great masters of this genre is Dostoevsky and his brilliant novella, *Notes from Underground*. We submit that Dostoevsky represents an extraordinary example of psychoanalytical treatment, that is, traversing the theological fantasy. The title of the work itself, *Zapiski iz podpol'ya* (also translated as *Letters from the Underworld*), immediately splits the world up into two parts: there is your standard "world" or *status quo*, the conscious world, and then there is the "sub-world," the world beneath consciousness, that is, the unconscious world. The main thrust of the novella then is to try to express the unconscious world in the language of the conventional dog-eat-dog world. Interestingly enough, Dostoevsky wrote the novella as an attack both against Nikolai Chernyshevsky's defense of a utopian, utilitarian novel *What Is to Be Done?*, as well as Western European philosophy, especially targeting Kant's purely rational universe. But in his attack against determinism in all its forms, philosophical, traditional and social pressures to conform, he articulates what many consider to be the first existential novel.

What you see in this short novel is a struggle at the most fundamental level of existence; it is a struggle above all in trying to find the language for expressing the inexpressible—the Real. The key term here is *trying* to express the Real, but knowing all the while that it is impossible to do so. It is like Sisyphus, a crowned king condemned to repeating the seamlessly absurd act of rolling a boulder up the side of a mountain only to watch the valley swallow the boulder up again. Sisyphus's punishment was repeating this meaningless act forever. But as Albert Camus masterfully concludes in his *Myth of Sisyphus*, what matters most of all in life is not finding meaning as a fixed thing (the big Other), but living the fullest life possible given the non-existence of fixed meaning itself.

Camus thus echoes Dostoevsky's realization that expressing the Real is impossible; nevertheless one committed to a true, authentic life is compelled to try to express the inexpressible *anyway*. And that is the basic matrix that structures *Notes from Undergound*. Further, the very matrix itself thus gives rise to the enigmatic protagonist, "The Underground Man" who opens the novel in the Imaginary register: "I am a sick man. . . . I am a wicked man. An unattractive man."[2] The very appearance of a self-reflective and conscious ego "I" that appears in the midst of the conscious "everyday" world is deeply disturbing to the reader, and a product of the Symbolic Order itself, for as Dostoevsky himself maintains: ". . . such persons as the writer of such notes (i.e., the Underground Man) not only may but even must exist in our society, taking into consideration the circumstances under which our society (i.e., language) has generally been formed."[3] In other words, what makes the Underground Man so disturbing is that he calls attention to the very sickness of what society and tradition have fashioned, namely, a world without a conscience, a world, if you will, that systematically enacts and socially reproduces[4] repression of the unconscious/Real as such. Said differently, society and tradition, according to the Underground Man, have a vested interest in *not* exposing the absence of a center point of *static* meaning around which all social mores take their place and into which the subject is determined as if they are a fixed, infinite object at home in the house of the "ego."

The Underground Man impolitely deconstructs our assumptions and tacit presupposition about meaning. The act of socially repressing the truth of the void of our existence is precisely what gives rise to boredom and creates action without substance and truth.

> I emphatically repeat: ingenuous people and active figures are active simply because they are dull and narrow-minded . . . [And] . . . as a consequence of their narrow-mindedness, they take the most immediate and secondary causes for the primary ones, and thus become convinced more quickly and easily than others that they have found an indisputable basis for their doings, and so they feel at ease. . . . For in order to begin to act, one must first be completely at ease, so that no more doubts remain.[5]

2. Fyodor Dostoevsky, *Notes from Underground*, trans. Richard Pevear and Larissa Volokhonsky (New York: Vintage, 1993) 3.

3. See ibid., Dostoyevsky's "Author's Note" on the bottom of page 5.

4. This is Louis Althusser's basic question in his famous essay "Ideology and Ideological State Apparatuses" (in *Lenin and Philosophy, and Other Essays*, trans. Ben Brewster [Monthly Review Press, 1971]). Althusser states, "The Ultimate condition of production [i.e., social formation via language] is therefore the reproduction of the conditions of production" (85).

5. Dostoyevsky, *Notes from Underground*, 17–18.

Society thus rests on the notion of fake peace so as to justify their actions that are morally acceptable to do. Doubt itself is repressed out of existence so one's social actions are not based on the truth of our radical contingency, but rather on a false sense of a master-signifier that neutralizes risk, openness, and real personality, even love. To this problem, the Underground Man asks a series of disturbing but necessary questions about our subjective contingency: "Well, and how am I, for example, to set myself at ease? Where are the primary causes on which I can rest, where are my bases? Where am I going to get them?" And his answer reveals less a stability than a continual and infinite growth, for he ". . . exercises thinking, and, consequently, for me [the Underground Man] every primary cause immediately drags with it yet another, still more primary one, and so on *ad infinitum.*"[6]

The honesty with which the Underground Man penetrates beyond the social crust of consciousness reveals a contradiction: everyday social consciousness is false consciousness because it rests on a premise that cannot hold up under the conditions of "thinking" that is, living a true and authentic life in the face of the void. This is the traumatic act of "traversing the fantasy." Dostoevsky's Underground Man unveils a deeper more profound logic operating beneath the surface (like the unconscious) that society projects and maintains. This unveiling by no means captures the Real (this is impossible), but it does challenge the categorical social—desire to control human beings by means of a purely rational, mathematical measurement. However, as the Underground Man says, "All man needs is independent volition, whatever that independence might cost and wherever it might lead."[7]

It is not new knowledge that what the Underground Man is pointing out with regard to social logic is intimately related to the highs and lows of bi-polar disorder in general as discussed above. Theology in the twentieth century has reached an apex of both authoritarianism and fundamentalism in absolute terms (mania), as well as being reduced to a nominalist disinterestedness (depression), i.e., the death of God theology as well as a general laziness that collapses into an indifference toward all possibility of meaning making. What this book is proposing above all an attempt to traverse the theological fantasy by one's own life lived in the wake of an infinite power beyond the purely rational on the one hand and apathy on the other. The psychoanalytic structure of Lacan's through, we surmise, gives us the matrix of traversing the theological fantasy.

---

6. Ibid., 18.

7. Dostoyevsky, *Notes from Underground*, 24 (different translation—Penguin Classics).

The Symbolic Introduction

How then does this collection sit within the current of scholarship on Lacan and theology? In many respects this collection is both a tribute *to* and critique *of* the first such collection to expressly treat the work of Lacan and theology in tandem: *Lacan and Theological Discourse* (1989).[8] For those intellectual pioneers, including Carl Raschke, Mark C. Taylor, Charles Winquist, and Edith Wyschogrod, the chief import of Lacan was his critique of the ego as an alienating form of defense against desire (i.e., lack). Their orientation was distinctly Heideggerian, but they took their cue from Derrida and Levinas as well. In the eyes of these authors Lacan was a thinker of "Otherness," forcing theology, in the words of Charles Winquist, "to seriously assess the problematic of its own textuality"; Lacan reminds us that all theological discourse is a form of speech and it therefore speaks a lack.[9]

Derrida had already made connection between his philosophy of *différance* and negative theology, as had Lacan concerning his own work,[10] and it was a short step from there on the part of theologians to couple postmodern "Otherness" with the biblical injunction against idolatry. As Catherine Clément put it: a Lacanian theology would be a

> miss-tical *a*/theology, [is] one that would involve real risks. . . . For Lacanian analysis "does not provoke any triumph of self-awareness," as Roudinseco rightly points out. "It uncovers, on the contrary, a process of decentering, in which the subject delves . . . into the loss of his mastery."[11]

By ceding mastery theology could become less concerned with defending existing doctrine to become instead an "ethical experiment in letting things be in their otherness."[12]

Given that the barb of Lacan's critique was aimed at American ego-psychology, it is understandable that the American contributors to *Lacan and Theological Discourse* made the critique of the ego their central point. Through attenuation of desire, reified theological forms are opened out into the uncertain play of the symbolic. In this sense their work may be

---

8. *Lacan and Theological Discourse*, ed. Edith Wyschogrod et al. (Albany: State University of New York Press, 1989).

9. Charles Winquist, "Lacan and Theological discourse," in ibid., 26–38, 32.

10. Jacques Lacan, "Seminar XIV, Logic of Phantasy," trans. Cormac Gallagher (unpublished manuscript), 25.1.67, lecture ix, 3.

11. Catherine Clément, *The Lives and Legends of Jacques Lacan*, trans. Arthur Goldhammer (New York: Columbia University Press, 1983) 144.

12. Winquist, "Lacan and Theological Discourse," 31.

characterized in terms of discourse formation; i.e., their concern is the way theology is falsely unified through institutional forms when desire is lost sight of.

However, such an approach could easily become drained of all authority or institutional mooring, pushing a Lacanian theology into a very private space, a point succinctly put by David Crownfield in the collection when he says that these theologians "locate theological discourse in the . . . imaginary, in the isolation of the solitary and marginal wanderer without context or community."[13]

Part of the problem was material: the accessibility of the primary sources themselves. One notes in the first instance, and with few exceptions, the range of primary material consulted in *Lacan and Theological Discourse* amounts to little more than Alan Sheridan's selections from *Ecrits*; Jacqueline Rose's selections and translations from *Seminar XX*, published under the title *Feminine Sexuality*; *Seminar XI*, the first edited and published Seminar; and Anthony Wilden's critical edition of "The Function and Field of Speech and Language in Psychoanalysis."[14]

The impact of this limited selection is acutely felt in Mark C. Taylor's contribution. He pits Lacan against Lacan, reading the later seminar "God and ~~Woman~~'s *jouissance*" against Lacan's early work on law and the name-of-the-father.[15] In the later work, Lacan suggests there must be a specifically female *jouissance* not prey to the economy of patriarchy, which Taylor identified with the early work.[16] However, missing from the debate is any reference to the formulas of sexuation around which discussion of gender revolves in the later Lacan.

If part of the problem was the lack of texts, this was further compounded by the texts that were available. To take *Écrits* as an initial example, first: even in the French original the text only covered the period up to 1966; second: neither the French nor English editions showed much regard for any chronological order—the French edition starts with an essay from 1966, followed by one from 1955. All of this conspired to offer up, as David Macey has argued, a neatly homogenous picture of Lacan.[17]

---

13. David Crownfield, "Summary of Chapter 1," in Wyschogrod et al., *Lacan and Theological Discourse*, 38.

14. A. Wilden, *Speech and Language in Psychoanalysis* (Baltimore: Johns Hopkins University Press, 1981).

15. Jacques Lacan, *Seminar XX, Encore: Feminine Sexuality: The Limits of Love and Knowledge* (New York: Norton, 1999) 64–77.

16. Mark C. Taylor, "Refusal of the Bar," in Wyschogrod et al., *Lacan and Theological Discourse*, 50.

17. David Macey, *Lacan in Contexts* (London: Verso, 1988) 10.

This picture was aided by the inclusion of a glossary and index of concepts. These additions to the text, written and compiled by Jacques-Alain Miller, played a crucial role for an earlier generation determining how the text was read, selectively navigating the reader around the text, shutting out some influences while privileging others.

As Miller himself tells us in a series of pointers in which he justifies his inclusion of an index: "in the index, it is the concept that must be looked for, not the word,"[18] and arguably this was his self-stated aim: "forming a system" for the training of analysts. Nonetheless, as Macey argued, *Écrits* appeared a "conceptually homogenous text rather than a collection of papers written over a considerable period of time, with all the shifts and modifications that implies,"[19] and in this way the presentation flattened out the "polysemic complexity" of the work.[20]

However, chiefly, the case to be made is that the lack of easy available *Seminars* and a lack of critical attention to reception of the texts also meant that many of Lacan's most profound discussions on theology remained out of reach. A case in point, as noted by Cormac Gallagher, is the way that Lacan's fundamental concepts are often accompanied by a major text or paradigmatic point within the history of thought: Love in transference is accompanied by Plato's *amalga* from *Symposium*; the o-object in relation to the gaze is accompanied by Velasquez's *Las Meninas; Antigone* serves as the paradigm for sublimation in tragedy. Yet as Gallagher points out, none of these figures, literary or otherwise, are accorded the importance Lacan gave to Pascal, who remains curiously absent from discussions on the relation of the subject to Other.

What the *Seminars* have brought into view is the way religious and theological traditions are a constant source of reference for Lacan, and in particular, the degree to which theology plays a central structuring role in Western subjectivity for Lacan.

By contrast what we find in the early theological appropriation is a formalisation of Lacan's work into a central philosophical critique of onto-theology, but little on the central place theological discourse plays within his texts, or the way they later develop. So where early debates about his status were branded in terms of "structuralist," "post-structuralist," or "surrealist," we now increasingly find "Catholic," "Reformed," or "Buddhist" versions of Lacan.

18. Jacques Lacan, *Écrits: The First Complete English Translation*, trans. Bruce Fink (New York: Norton, 2005) 893.

19. Macey, *Lacan in Contexts*, 13.

20. Elizabeth Roudinesco, *Jacques Lacan: An Outline of a Life and a History of a Thought*, trans. Barbara Bray (Cambridge: Polity, 1999) 305.

Žižek

Central to some of the contributors to this volume is the subsequent reception of Lacan by Slavoj Žižek. Arguably part of Žižek's success has also been, like Miller, to synchronise Lacan's work as a whole into a formal logic, but also and more startlingly, the direct way in which he has brought the later Lacan, by way of Hegel and German idealism, to bear directly on theology, politics, and culture with often surprising results.

Hegel understood the Christian passion in terms of a Godhead who dies absolutely on the cross, kenotically pouring himself out, only to be resurrected both in and as the material world. Henceforth Spirit names not some ethereal animating power, but quite simply the corporal body of the church. All of this makes for a transition from a traditional transcendental framework from which God might be said to participate in reality, to an immanent and dialectical framework according to which God is continually reborn into the things of this world; *traversing the fantasy.*

Speaking of the passion in this way eliminates the need of God to serve as an external guarantor of meaning. In place of the Big Other we get a God who fully abandons himself into his own creation, "fully engaging himself in it up to dying, so that we, humans, are left with no higher Power watching over us, just with the terrible burden of freedom and responsibility for the fate of divine creation, and thus of God himself."[21]

For Žižek, as Cyril O'Regan puts it, the logic of kenosis signals an end to "obfuscation and fetishization, and a liberation into the inexplicable joy and suffering of the world."[22] In this way he links both psychoanalysis and theology with revolutionary praxis. Indeed, he goes as far as to suggest that theology offers the very first critique of ideology in the Biblical figure of Job. Faced with unending suffering, Job refuses the solace offered by the theologians according to which his suffering is given meaning by way of recourse to a metaphysical answer (e.g., you suffer in this life because . . .); rather he asserts the very meaninglessness of suffering to the extent that even God cannot supply an answer. And because Žižek reads Job as the precursor to Christ, he is able to push the consequences of this logic a little further. Christ's cry of dereliction upon the cross is the point at which God faces up to his own powerlessness: God is an atheist.

As Adam Kotsko has noted, Žižek's approach is in accord with the Protestant death-of-God theology out of which many of the contributions to

21. Slavoj Žižek and John Milbank, *The Monstrosity of Christ: Paradox or Dialectic?*, ed. Creston Davis (Cambridge: MIT Press, 2009) 25.

22. Cyril O'Regan, "Žižek and Milbank and the Hegelian Death of God," *Modern Theology* 26 (2010) 278–86.

the first collection arose.[23] Consider, for example, Mark C. Taylor's heralding in of postmodernism as a "carnivalesque comedy" in which God is dead, and the incarnated Christ becomes ceaselessly disseminated.[24] Indeed, more recently both Žižek and Thomas Altizer—the father of Protestant death-of-God theology—have mutually endorsed each other's work.[25]

However, unlike his theological contemporaries Žižek does not take the death of God as an event that opens the field up for the "reassertion of the true abyss of Divinity as a spectral promise."[26] Rather, what dies is the "very structuring principle of our entire universe." The logic of kenosis offers a "properly apocalyptic shattering power."[27] And this traumatic power names the event or monstrosity of Christ: the cry of dereliction upon the cross. Žižek's Christology is therefore both orthodox (Christ must actually be God to push the consequences of the logic to its extreme); and exemplary: God's kenotic outpouring becomes the subjective task, emptying the subject of the illusion of a substantial self. In short, Žižek enlists for his emancipatory project all the "perverse twists of redemption through suffering, the death of God, etc., but without God."[28]

What are the implications of this shift in focus? In the first instance this makes for a more subversive edge. If the earlier contributors were seeking to disrupt imaginary identifications in the name of the symbolic through attenuation to desire, Žižek wants to disrupt the symbolic in the name of the Real through attenuation to the Drive (to which we shall return. Second, because Žižek equates the real with religion it follows that his work develops into what may be termed more broadly a political theology. So, while the former thinkers remain largely critical of institutional religion they rarely touch on political theology. By contrast, not only does Žižek critique institutional religion, he critiques the wider social order, albeit by way of theology. To take an example, while Taylor critiques traditional theology in the name of a return to the "goddess," seen from the perspective of Žižek such a return amounts to reinstating the Big Other; instead Žižek makes the

23. Adam Kotsko, "The 'Christian Experience' Continues: On Žižek's Work since *The Parallax View,*" *IJŽS Special Issue: Žižek's Theology* 4.4 (2010). http://zizekstudies.org/index.php/ijzs/article/view/272/365.

24. Mark C. Taylor, *Erring: A Postmodern A/Theology* (Chicago: University of Chicago Press, 1984) 163.

25. Žižek spoke on the same platform with Altizer at the AAR Annual Meeting 2009 and affirmed his similarity with Altizer's Hegelian position on the death of God.

26. Žižek and Milbank, *Monstrosity of Christ,* 260.

27. Ibid.

28. Slavoj Žižek, *Less Than Nothing: Hegel and the Shadow of Dialectical Materialism* (New York: Verso, 2012) 119.

case for the traumatic perversity contained within incarnational logic as the means to a wider social critique.

One may frame the difference Žižek introduces into the reception of Lacan in terms of the shift in Lacan's own work from desire to drive, and their relative object—the o-object or *objet petit a*. As Žižek explains, "in the shift from desire to drive, we pass from the *lost object*, to *loss itself as an object*." Desire strives for an impossible fullness which, forced to renounce, becomes stuck on a partial object; drive however represents more radically the "drive" "to break the All of continuity in which we are embedded."[29]

To put this in theological terms, when God is treated under the rubric of desire, God is taken simply as the impossible object, forever pursued, but also that which forever eludes the subject. This is the God of negative theology in which God's impossible fullness forces the subject to renounce in one way or another any positive predication of God. By contrast, it is precisely the bizarre passionate attachments of faith that highlight for Žižek the point at which "human life is never "just life": humans are not simply alive, they are possessed by a strange drive to enjoy life in excess, passionately attached to a surplus which sticks out and derails the ordinary run of things."[30]

As the above quote highlights, related to the economy of the drive is the coterminous question of enjoyment. From the perspective of desire, enjoyment is endlessly deferred, pertaining as it does to the lost object; however from the perspective of Drive, enjoyment is "satisfied," or rather, a satisfaction is generated from the very repetition of failure experienced *qua* desire. One of the key points Žižek takes from this transition is the transformation that occurs between a failure (desire) and the ability to translate a failure into a success (drive). Žižek's point here is that the shift from desire to drive is of itself a paradigmatic example of the way in which, socio-politically speaking, we can transform "failure into triumph."[31]

Taken together then, it might be said that where earlier theologians took the eccentricities of theology as outmoded, to be jettisoned in favour of the normative ("post-structualist") discourse on language and the self, Žižek takes the eccentricities of theology, and Christianity in particular, as the very "lost" cause which as such, might save the world.[32]

In his "Extraduction" to *Lacan and Theological Discourse*, David Crownfield closes the book by opening up a future discussion. He points to the relation between Lacan and Kierkegaard: "Lacan's radical diagnosis

29. Ibid., 498.
30. Ibid., 499.
31. Ibid., 498.
32. Ibid., 1010.

of the self as split, decentred, imaginary, unachievable is reminiscent of Kierkegaard's."[33] However, Kierkegaard is seen to offer a resolution of sorts to the extent that the fractured self is unified through a decision, specifically the "decision of faith [or love] in the God of Jesus Christ."[34]

If, as Alain Badiou has argued, Lacan is "our Hegel,"[35] then Žižek may well, despite Hegelian leanings, be "our Kierkegaard" (a reveller of paradox, and a pugnacious, astute commentator on cultural life)[36]—hence the prescience of David Crownfield's concluding remarks. However, Žižek sees in the passionate attachment of faith, not a resolution as such—anymore than Kierkegaard would have—but rather, after Lacan, a perverse attachment of enjoyment to a kernel of revolutionary thought.

The Imaginary Introduction

This volume is divided into two parts. Part One is titled "Lacan, Religion and Others," and productively puts Lacan's work in conversation with other philosophers, theologians, and religious figures around the question of religion. Part Two, "Theology and the Other Lacan," more explicitly and intensively imagines what theology might mean or become after traversing the fantasy of its own identity by way of an engagement with Lacan.

The first chapter is by Slavoj Žižek, the most influential philosopher writing today. Žižek's contribution, "*Cogito*, Madness and Religion: Derrida, Foucault and Then Lacan," shows how Kant's reading of Descartes gets repeated and amplified in different ways in Foucault and Derrida. There is an intrinsic madness of the subject, and this madness is religious in an important sense. Lacan's work provides Žižek a vantage point from which to appreciate and critique both Foucault and Derrida's reflections on madness and the Cartesian *cogito*.

From Žižek, we step back to consider Thomas Aquinas, and Tina Beattie gives us a provocative constructive re-reading of Aquinas avec Lacan, mediated by the rock group Queen's famous song "Bohemian Rhapsody." For Beattie, "Nothing Really Matters," and yet, strangely enough, everything matters for a Lacanian-inspired theology that returns to the Middle Ages. This return to Aquinas is not intended to become handmaiden to a

33. David Crownfield, "Extraduction," in Wyschogrod et al., *Lacan and Theological Discourse*, 162.

34. Ibid.

35. Alain Badiou, *Theory of the Subject* (London: Continuum, 2009) 132.

36. Slavoj Žižek, "Kierkegaard as a Hegelian," in Žižek, *The Parallax View* (Cambridge: MIT Press, 2006) 75–80.

sovereign King, but to adopt a position as the "queen" that queers or makes strange all the sciences in the name of theology. Beattie's essay also helps open up the terrain that is engaged in Part Two.

Shifting from Aquinas to Luther, Carl Raschke's essay, "Subjectivation, Salvation, and the Real in Luther and Lacan," shows a strange affinity between Lacan and Luther despite the evident and much-documented Catholic elements of Lacan's work. Raschke suggests that there is a structurally similar undecidability between law and gospel in Luther's theology that corresponds to the undecidable tension between the symbolic and the Real in Lacan's psychoanalysis. Raschke suggests that theological discourse concerns the speech of God, and we must understand this in psychoanalytic terms as speech of the Other that insists upon a truth which is not objective but is subjective truth, *our* truth.

Chapter 4 focuses on the Buddha; Mario D'Amato in *"Lacan avec le Bouddha"* provides an analysis of some of the overlapping concepts shared by Lacanian psychoanalysis and Buddhism, particularly the Yogacara tradition. Both traditions focus on the limits and the possibilities of language, and how language connects paradoxically (or parallactically) with the Real.

After this engagement with Buddhism we turn to atheism, in the form of Martin Hägglund's radical atheism, which is the subject of a friendly critique by Adrian Johnston. In "Life Terminable and Interminable," Johnston demonstrates how a Lacanian perspective complicates Hägglund's straightforward affirmation of life as infinite temporal survival. He suggests that Hägglund confuses prescription with description, and that Hägglund prescribes the radical atheism he pretends to describe in Derrida's work. Johnston suggests that both Derrida's and Lacan's thinking about ghosts opens up a perspective on the complex and fantastic nature of human desire in its unconscious effects that Hägglund neglects.

In her essay "Solidarity in Suffering with the Non-Human," Katerina Kolozova develops a provocative understanding of Judith Butler's thought by crossing it not only with Lacan but also the non-philosophy of François Laruelle. She suggests that Butler and Donna Haraway offer resources for a universal definition of humanity as a creature that is capable of identifying with suffering. We become human by directly identifying with the Real of the suffering body, rather than being caught up in the transcendental and symbolic mediations of language. This becoming human is also an overcoming of the essential limits of philosophical humanism and a way to embrace our solidary existence as a human animal, a non-human in the sense of Laruelle's non-philosophy. Here both Christ and Oedipus serve as exemplary figures of the non-human. Kolozova's rich account opens up

Lacan to a kind of non-Lacan, and this political and ethical matrix provides resources to reconceive and reconfigure theology itself.

Part Two, "Theology and the Other Lacan," more explicitly and intensively reworks Lacan in theological terms that deform our understanding of theology and reconfigure our understanding of Lacan. In his essay "There Is Something of One (God): Lacan and Political Theology," Ken Reinhard rereads Lacan's formulas of sexuation in a political theological context over against Carl Schmitt. Reinhard reads Lacan from the standpoint of Alain Badiou, and suggests that Lacan offers not only a political theology of sovereignty based on a masculine logic of exception, which accords with Schmitt's political theology, but also a political theology of the neighbor based on a feminine logic of not-all. In the latter case, a "something of One" is the product rather than the agent of discourse. Here the "subject" of political theology is not God or the self but the neighbor.

From the idea of the One in Lacan, we turn to the question of "Woman and the Number of God." Lorenzo Chiesa provides a magisterial interpretation of *Seminar XX*. Chiesa, perhaps the most careful contemporary reader of Lacan, distinguishes not only between a masculine and a feminine *jouissance*, but also and more importantly between two forms of a feminine *jouissance*, one that is phallic and one that is mystical or non-phallic. The non-phallic female *jouissance* subtracts from the more general phallic *jouissance*, and the status of this mystical *jouissance* has implications for how we think about God, including the number of God, which is not One but also not simply two.

In her contribution, "Secular Theology as Language of Rebellion," Noelle Vahanian inhabits this complex space opened up by Reinhard's political theology of the neighbor to suggest that Lacan's psychoanalytic desire is an intrinsically "rebellious desire to no end." For Vahanian, a secular theology of language in the wake of the death of God as sovereign subject takes up the task of what Julia Kristeva calls rejection in *Revolution in Poetic Language*. What Kristeva calls rejection or revolt, Vahanian names rebellion, and it is this rebellion that drives secular theology in its restlessness. She expresses a rich interpassivity in which "I am active through the Other" that she finds in the jazz music of Louis Armstrong, and this is a profoundly religious experience.

In "Making the Quarter Turn," Thomas Lynch reclaims liberation theology in light of Lacan's work as well as Žižek's political recuperation of it. For Lynch, a Lacanian interpretation of liberation theology produces a new form of discourse that emerges out of the split subject of the hysteric's discourse, one of the four forms of discourse Lacan analyzes in *Seminar XVII*. What begins as a hysterical discourse then opens up to become a new analyst's discourse by traversing the fantasy of traditional theological discourse.

For Marcus Pound, theology begins and ends with grace, and grace is an underappreciated theme of Lacan's work. Pound traces Lacan's understanding of grace in his readings of Pascal in *Seminar XIII* and *Seminar XVI*. Grace is not simply a theological problem, but the very locus of subjectivity for Lacan because it mediates the encounter with the Real. Grace refers us to a God or Other that structures our subjectivity and our experiences. Pound attends to the theological framework that underlies Lacan's thought as the very possibility of psychoanalysis.

Clayton Crockett concludes by wrestling explicitly with Lacan's proclamation of the triumph of religion, which is referenced by other contributors. He suggests that we distinguish theology in Hegelian terms into theology in itself, which is ideology, theology for itself, which is energy, and theology in and for itself, which is psychoanalysis. Crockett offers readings of how the question of God is related to the status of the Other in Lacan's work, and he analyzes the shift in Lacan's work from the Other to the other, the *objet petit a*, in *Seminar XVII*. This shift is coincident with an extraordinary transformation of global capitalism, and Crockett traces some of the political and theological implications. Altogether, these essays develop some of the most important theological results of engaging with Lacan's work, as theology struggles with the task of traversing its own fantasy to arrive, however fleetingly, at the Real.

Part One

Lacan, Religion, and Others

1

Cogito, Madness, and Religion

Derrida, Foucault, and Then Lacan

Slavoj Žižek

THE "ANTAGONISM" OF THE Kantian notion of freedom (as the most concise expression of the antagonism of freedom in the bourgeois life itself) does not reside where Adorno locates it (the autonomously self-imposed law means that freedom coincides with self-enslavement and self-domination, that the Kantian "spontaneity" is *in actu* its opposite, utter self-control, thwarting of all spontaneous impetuses), but "much more on the surface":[1] for Kant as for Rousseau, the greatest moral good is to lead a fully autonomous life as a free rational agent, and the worst evil subjection to the will of another; however, Kant has to concede that man does not emerge as a free mature rational agent spontaneously, through his/her natural development, but only through the arduous process of maturation sustained by harsh discipline and education which cannot but be experienced by the subject as imposed on his/her freedom, as an external coercion:

> Social institutions both to nourish and to develop such inde-
> pendence are necessary and are consistent with, do not thwart,
> its realization, but with freedom understood as an individual's
> causal agency this will always look like an external necessity that
> we have good reasons to try to avoid. This creates the problem
> of a form of dependence that can be considered constitutive of

1. Robert Pippin, *The Persistence of Subjectivity: On the Kantian Aftermath* (Cambridge: Cambridge University Press, 2005) 118.

independence and that cannot be understood as a mere com-
promise with the particular will of another or as a separate,
marginal topic of Kant's dotage. This is, in effect, the antinomy
contained within the bourgeois notions of individuality, individuality responsibility . . .[2]

One can effectively imagine here Kant as an unexpected precursor on
Foucault's thesis, from his *Discipline and Punish*, of the formation of the
free individual through a complex set of disciplinary micro-practices—and,
as Pippin doesn't wait to point out, this antinomy explodes even larger in
Kant's socio-historical reflections, focused on the notion of "unsocial socia-
bility": what is Kant's notion of the historical relation between democracy
and monarchy if not this same thesis on the link between freedom and
submission to educative dependence applied to historical process itself? In
the long term (or in its notion), democracy is the only appropriate form of
government; however, because of the immaturity of people, conditions for a
functioning democracy can only be established through a non-democratic
monarchy which, through the exertion of its benevolent power, educates
people to political maturity. And, as expected, Kant does not fail to mention the Mandevillean rationality of the market in which each individual's
pursuit of his/her egotistic interests is what works best (much better than
direct altruistic work) for the common good. At its most extreme, this
brings Kant to the notion that human history itself is a deployment of an
inscrutable divine plan, within which we, mortals, are destined to play a role
unbeknownst to us—here, the paradox grows even stronger: not only is our
freedom linked to its opposite "from below," but also "from above," i.e., not
only can our freedom arise only through our submission and dependence,
but our freedom as such is a moment of a larger divine plan—our freedom
is not truly an aim-in-itself, it serves a higher purpose.

A way to clarify—if not resolve—this dilemma would have been to
introduce some further crucial distinctions into the notion of "noumenal"
freedom itself. That is to say, upon a closer look, it becomes evident that, for
Kant, discipline and education do not directly work on our animal nature,
forging it into human individuality: as Kant points out, animals cannot be
properly educated since their behavior is already predestined by their instincts. What this means is that, paradoxically, in order to be educated into
freedom (qua moral autonomy and self-responsibility), I already have to be
free in a much more radical, "noumenal" sense, monstrous even.

Daniel Dennett draws a convincing and insightful parallel between an
animal's physical environs and human environs; not only human artefacts

2. Ibid., 118–19.

(clothes, houses, tools), but also the "virtual" environs of the discursive cob-web: "Stripped of [the 'web of discourses'], an individual human being is as incomplete as a bird without feathers, a turtle without its shell."[3] A naked man is the same nonsense as a shaved ape: without language (and tools and . . .), man is a crippled animal—it is this lack which is supplemented by symbolic institutions and tools, so that the point made obvious today, in popular cul-ture figures like Robocop (man is simultaneously super-animal and crippled), holds from the very beginning. How do we pass from "natural" to "symbolic" environs? This passage is not direct, one cannot account for it within a con-tinuous evolutionary narrative: something has to intervene between the two, a kind of "vanishing mediator," which is neither Nature nor Culture—this In-between is not the spark of logos magically conferred on homo sapiens, en-abling him to form his supplementary virtual symbolic environs, but precisely something which, although it is also no longer nature, is not yet logos, and has to be "repressed" by logos—the Freudian name for this monstrous freedom, of course, is death drive. It is interesting to note how philosophical narratives of the "birth of man" are always compelled to presuppose a moment in human (pre)history when (what will become) man, is no longer a mere animal and simultaneously not yet a "being of language," bound by symbolic Law; a mo-ment of thoroughly "perverted," "denaturalized," "derailed" nature which is not yet culture. In his anthropological writings, Kant emphasized that the hu-man animal needs disciplinary pressure in order to tame an uncanny "unruli-ness" which seems to be inherent to human nature—a wild, unconstrained propensity to insist stubbornly on one's own will, cost what it may. It is on account of this "unruliness" that the human animal needs a Master to disci-pline him: discipline targets this "unruliness," not the animal nature in man.

In Hegel's *Lectures on Philosophy of History*, a similar role is played by the reference to "negroes": significantly, Hegel deals with "negroes" before history proper (which starts with ancient China), in the section titled "The Natural Context or the Geographical Basis of World History": "negroes" stand there for the human spirit in its "state of nature," they are described as a kind of perverted, monstrous child, simultaneously naive and extremely corrupted, i.e., living in the pre-lapsarian state of innocence, and, precisely as such, the most cruel barbarians; part of nature and yet thoroughly de-naturalized; ruthlessly manipulating nature through primitive sorcery, yet simultaneously terrified by the raging natural forces; mindlessly brave cow-ards . . .[4] This In-between is the "repressed" of the narrative form (in this

---

3. Daniel C. Dennett, *Consciousness Explained* (New York: Little, Brown, 1991) 416.

4. G. W. F. Hegel, *Lectures on the Philosophy of World History, Introduction: Reason in History*, trans. H. B. Nisbet (Cambridge: Cambridge University Press, 1975) 176–90.

case, of Hegel's "large narrative" of world-historical succession of spiritual forms): not nature as such, but the very break with nature which is (later) supplemented by the virtual universe of narratives. According to Schelling, prior to its assertion as the medium of the rational Word, the subject is the "infinite lack of being" (*unendliche Mangel an Sein*), the violent gesture of contraction that negates every being outside itself. This insight also forms the core of Hegel's notion of madness: when Hegel determines madness to be a withdrawal from the actual world, the closing of the soul into itself, its "contraction," the cutting-off of its links with external reality, he all too quickly conceives of this withdrawal as a "regression" to the level of the "animal soul" still embedded in its natural environs and determined by the rhythm of nature (night and day, etc.). Does this withdrawal, on the contrary, not designate the severing of the links with the *Umwelt*, the end of the subject's immersion into its immediate natural environs, and is it, as such, not the founding gesture of "humanization"? Was this withdrawal-into-self not accomplished by Descartes in his universal doubt and reduction to *Cogito*, which, as Derrida pointed out in his "*Cogito* and the History of Madness,"[5] also involves a passage through the moment of radical madness?

This brings us to the necessity of Fall: what the Kantian link between dependence and autonomy amounts to is that Fall is unavoidable, a necessary step in the moral progress of man. That is to say, in precise Kantian terms: "Fall" is the very renunciation of my radical ethical autonomy; it occurs when I take refuge in a heteronomous Law, in a Law which is experience as imposed on me from the outside, i.e., the finitude in which I search for a support to avoid the dizziness of freedom is the finitude of the external-heteronomous Law itself. Therein resides the difficulty of being a Kantian. Every parent knows that the child's provocations, wild and "transgressive" as they may appear, ultimately conceal and express a demand, addressed at the figure of authority, to set a firm limit, to draw a line which means "This far and no further!", thus enabling the child to achieve a clear mapping of what is possible and what is not possible. (And does the same not go also for the hysteric's provocations?) This, precisely, is what the analyst refuses to do, and this is what makes him so traumatic—paradoxically, it is the setting of a firm limit which is liberating, and it is the very absence of a firm limit which is experienced as suffocating. *This* is why the Kantian autonomy of the subject is so difficult—its implication is precisely that there is nobody outside, no external agent of "natural authority," who can do the job for me and set me my limit, that I myself have to pose a limit to my natural "unruliness."

---

5. Jacques Derrida, "*Cogito* and the History of Madness," in *Writing and Difference*, trans. Alan Bass (Chicago: University of Chicago Press, 1978) 31–63.

Although Kant famously wrote that man is an animal which needs a master, this should not deceive us: what Kant aims at is not the philosophical commonplace according to which, in contrast to animals whose behavioral patterns are grounded in their inherited instincts, man lacks such firm coordinates which, therefore, have to be imposed on him from the outside, through a cultural authority; Kant's true aim is rather to point out how the very need of an external master is a deceptive lure: man needs a master in order to conceal from himself the deadlock of his own difficult freedom and self-responsibility. In this precise sense, a truly enlightened "mature" human being is a subject who no longer needs a master, who can fully assume the heavy burden of defining his own limitations. This basic Kantian (and also Hegelian) lesson was put very clearly by Chesterton: "Every act of will is an act of self-limitation. To desire action is to desire limitation. In that sense every act is an act of self-sacrifice."[6]

The lesson here is thus Hegelian in a very precise sense: the external opposition between freedom (transcendental spontaneity, moral autonomy and self-responsibility) and slavery (submission, either to my own nature, its "pathological" instincts, or to external power) has to be transposed into freedom itself, as the "highest" antagonism between the monstrous freedom qua "unruliness" and the true moral freedom. However, a possible counter-argument here would have been that this noumenal excess of freedom (the Kantian "unruliness," the Hegelian "Night of the World") is a retroactive result of the disciplinary mechanisms themselves (along the lines of the Paulinian motif of "Law creates transgression," or of the Foucauldian topic of how the very disciplinary measures that try to regulate sexuality generate "sex" as the elusive excess)—the obstacle creates that which it endeavors to control. Are we then dealing with a closed circle of a process positing one's own presuppositions?

Madness and (in) the History of *Cogito*

This paraphrase of the title of Derrida's essay on Foucault's *Histoire de la folie* has a precise stake: madness is inscribed into the history of *Cogito* at two levels. First, throughout entire philosophy of subjectivity from Descartes through Kant, Schelling and Hegel, to Nietzsche and Husserl, *Cogito* is related to its shadowy double, *pharmakon*, which is madness. Second, madness is inscribed into the very (pre)history of *Cogito* itself; it is part of its transcendental genesis.

6. G. K. Chesterton, *Orthodoxy* (New York: John Lane, 1909) 70.

In "*Cogito* and the History of Madness" (*Writing and Difference*), Derrida states that

> the *Cogito* escapes madness only because at its own moment,
> under its own authority, it is valid *even if I am mad*, even if my
> thoughts are completely mad.... Descartes never interns mad-
> ness, neither at the stage of natural doubt nor at the stage of
> metaphysical doubt.
>   ... Whether I am mad or not, *Cogito, sum*.... [E]ven if the
> totality of the world does not exist, even if nonmeaning has in-
> vaded the totality of the world, up to and including the very
> contents of my thought, I still think, I am while I think.[7]

Derrida leaves no doubt that "as soon as Descartes has reached this extremity, he seeks to reassure himself, to certify the *Cogito* through God, to identify the act of the *Cogito* with a reasonable reason."[8] This withdrawal sets in
"from the moment when he pulls himself out of madness by determining
natural light through a series of principles and axioms."[9] The term "light" is
here crucial to measure the distance of Descartes from German Idealism, in
which, precisely, the core of the subject is no longer light, but the abyss of
darkness, the "Night of the World."
    This, then, is Derrida's fundamental interpretive gesture: the one of
"separating, within the *Cogito*, on the one hand, hyperbole (which I maintain cannot be enclosed in a factual and determined historical structure,
for it is the project of exceeding every finite and determined totality), and,
on the other hand, that in Descartes's philosophy (or in the philosophy
supporting the Augustinian *Cogito* or the Husserlian *Cogito* as well) which
belongs to a factual historical structure."[10]
    Here, when Derrida asserts that "the historicity proper to philosophy
is located and constituted in the transition, the dialogue between hyperbole and the finite structure, ... in the difference between history and
historicity,"[11] he is perhaps too short. This tension may appear very "Lacanian": is it not a version of the tension between the Real—the hyperbolic
excess—and its (ultimately always failed) symbolization? The matrix we
thus arrive at is the one of the eternal oscillation between the two extremes,
the radical expenditure, hyperbole, excess, and its later domestification
(like Kristeva, between Semiotic and Symbolic ...). Both extremes are il-

7. Ibid., 55–56.
8. Ibid., 58.
9. Ibid., 59.
10. Ibid., 60.
11. Ibid.

lusionary: pure excess as well as pure finite order would disintegrate, cancel themselves. . . . This misses the true point of "madness," which is not the pure excess of the Night of the World, but the madness of the passage to the Symbolic itself, of imposing a symbolic order onto the chaos of the Real. (Like Freud, who, in his Schreber analysis, points out how the paranoiac "system" is not madness, but a desperate attempt to *escape* madness—the disintegration of the symbolic universe—through an ersatz, as if, universe of meaning.) If madness is constitutive, then *every* system of meaning is minimally paranoiac, "mad."

Recall Brecht's "what is the robbing of a bank compared to the founding of a new bank?"—therein resides the lesson of David Lynch's *Straight Story*: what is the ridiculously pathetic perversity of figures like Bobby Perou in *Wild at Heart* or Frank in *Blue Velvet* compared to deciding to traverse the U.S. central plane in a tractor to visit a dying relative? Measured with this act, Frank's and Bobby's outbreaks of rage are the impotent theatrics of old and sedate conservatives.

This step is the properly "Hegelian" one—Hegel, who is the philosopher who made the most radical attempt to *think together* the abyss of madness at the core of subjectivity *and* the totality of the System of meaning. This is why, for very good reasons, "Hegel" stands for the common sense for the moment at which philosophy gets "mad," explodes into a "crazy" pretense at "absolute knowledge".

So: not simply "madness" and symbolization—there is, in the very history of philosophy (of philosophical "systems"), a *privileged* point at which the hyperbole, philosophy's ex-timate core, directly inscribes itself into it, and this is the moment of *Cogito*, of transcendental philosophy. "Madness" is here "tamed" in a different way, through a "transcendental" horizon, which does not cancel it in an all-encompassing world view, but maintains it.

> In the serene world of mental illness, modern man no longer communicates with the madman: . . . the man of reason delegates the physician to madness, thereby authorizing a relation only through the abstract universality of disease.[12]

However, what about psychoanalysis? Is psychoanalysis not precisely the point at which the "man of reason" reestablishes his dialogue with madness, rediscovering the dimension of truth in it? And this is not the same ("hermeneutic"-mantic) truth as before, in the pre-modern universe. Foucault deals with this in his *History of Sexuality*, where psychoanalysis as the culmination of "sex as the ultimate truth" has a confessionary logic.

12. Michel Foucault, *Madness and Civilization* (London: Tavistock, 1967) x.

In spite of the finesse of Foucault's reply, he ultimately falls prey to the trap of historicism which cannot account for its own position of enunciation; this impossibility is redoubled in Foucault's characterization of his "object," madness, which oscillates between two extremes. On the one hand, his stategic aim is to make madness itself talk, as it is in itself, outside the (scientific, etc.) discourse on it: "it is definitely not a question of a history of ideas, but of the rudimentary movements of an experience. A history not of psychiatry, but of madness itself, in its vivacity, before knowledge has even begun to close in on it."[13] On the other hand, the (later) model deployed in his *Discipline and Punish* and *History of Sexuality* compels him to posit the absolute immanence of the (excessive, transgressive, resisting) object to its manipulation by the dispositif of power-knowledge: in the same way that "the carceral network does not cast the unassimilable into a confused hell; there is no outside";[14] in the same way that the "liberated" man is itself generated by the dispositif that controls and regulates him; in the same way that "sex" as the unassimilable excess is itself generated by the discourses and practices that try to control and regulate it; madness is also generated by the very discourse that excludes, objectivizes and studies it, there is no "pure" madness outside it—Foucault here "effectively acknowledges the correctness of Derrida's formulation,"[15] namely, of *il n'y a pas de hors-texte*, providing his own version of it.

Foucault writes, "Perhaps one day [transgression] will seem as decisive for our culture, as much part of its soil, as the experience of contradiction was at an earlier time for dialectical thought."[16] Does he not thereby miss the point, which is that this day has already arrived, that permanent transgression already *is* the feature of late capitalism? His final reproach to Derrida's *il n'y a pas de hors-texte*:[17] textual analysis, philosophical hermeneutics, no exteriority:

> Reduction of discursive practices to textual traces; elision of the
> events which are produced in these practices, so that all that

13. Michel Foucault, *Folie et deraison: Histoire de la folie à l'age classique* (Paris: Plon, 1961) vii.

14. Michel Foucault, *Discipline and Punish*, trans. Alan Sheridan (Harmondsworth: Penguin, 1977) 301.

15. Robert Boyne, *Foucault and Derrida: The Other Side of Reason* (London: Unwin Hyman, 1990) 118.

16. Michel Foucault, *Language, Counter–Memory, Practice*, trans. Donald F. Bouchard and Sherry Simon (Oxford: Blackwell, 1977) 33.

17. "Reading . . . cannot legitimately transgress the text toward something other than it. . . . There is nothing outside the text." Jacques Derrida, *Of Grammatology*, trans. Gayatri Chakravorty Spivak (Baltimore: Johns Hopkins University Press, 1976) 158.

remains of them are marks for a reading; inventions of voices behind the texts, so that we do not have to analyze the modes of the implication of the subject in the discourses; the assignation of the originary as [what is] said and not-said in the text, so that we do not have to locate discursive practices in the field of transformations in which they effectuate themselves.[18]

Some Marxists even presume this, as if Foucault/Derrida = materialism/idealism. Textual endless self-reflexive games versus materialist analysis. *But*: Foucault: remains *historicist*. He reproaches Derrida his inability to think the exteriority of philosophy—this is how he designates the stakes of their debate:

Could there be something prior or external to the philosophical discourse? Can the condition of this discourse be an exclusion, a refusal, an avoided risk, and, why not, a fear? A suspicion rejected passionately by Derrida. *Pudenda origo*, said Nietzsche with regard to religious people and their religion.[19]

However, Derrida is much closer to thinking this externality than Foucault, for whom exteriority involves simple historicist reduction which cannot account for itself (to which Foucault used to reply with a cheap rhetorical trick that this is a "police" question, "who are you to say that"—*again*, combining it with the opposite, that genealogical history is "ontology of the present"). It is easy to do *this* to philosophy, it is much more difficult to think its *inherent* excess, its ex-timacy (and philosophers can easily dismiss such external reduction as confusing genesis and value). These, then, are the true stakes of the debate: ex-timacy or direct externality.

Foucault versus Derrida, or Foucault on Descartes

Cogito, madness and religion are interlinked in Descartes (*génie malin*), in Kant (despite his distance from Swedenborg, who stands for madness, etc.). Simultaneously, *Cogito* emerges through differentiation from (reference to) madness, *and Cogito* itself (the idea of *Cogito* as the point of absolute certainty, "subjective idealism") is perceived by common sense as the very epitome of the madness of philosophy, crazy paranoiac system-building (philosopher as madman—[not only] late Wittgenstein). And, also simultaneously,

18. Michel Foucault, "Mon corps, ce papier, ce feu," in *Histoire de la folie à l'age classique* (Paris: Gallimard, 1972) 602.

19. Ibid., 584.

religion (direct faith) is evoked as madness (Swedenborg for Kant, or radical Enlightenment rationalists, up to Dawkins), *and* religion (God) enters as the solution from (solipsistic) madness (Descartes).

Foucault and Derrida's polemic is one in which they share the key underlying premise: that *Cogito* is inherently related to madness. The difference is that for Foucault, *Cogito* is grounded in the exclusion of madness, while, for Derrida, *Cogito* itself can only emerge through a "mad" hyperbole (universalized doubt), and remains marked by this excess. Before it stabilizes itself as *res cogitans*, the self-transparent thinking substance, *Cogito* as a crazy punctual excess.

In Foucault there is a fundamental change in the status of madness that took place in the passage from Renaissance to the classical Age of Reason (the beginning of seventeenth century). In the Renaissance (Cervantes, Shakespeare, Erasmus, etc.), madness was a specific phenomenon of human spirit which belonged to the series of prophets, possessed visionaries, those obsessed by demons, saints, comedians, etc. It was a meaningful phenomenon with a truth of its own. Even if madmen were vilified, they were treated with awe, like messengers of sacred horror. With Descartes, however, madness is excluded: madness, in all its varieties, comes to occupy a position that was the former location of leprosy. It is no longer a phenomenon to be interpreted, searched for its meaning, but a simple illness to be treated under the well-regulated laws of a medicine or a science that is already sure of itself, sure that it cannot be mad. This change does not concern only theory, but social practice itself: from the Classical Age, madmen were interned, imprisoned in psychiatric hospitals, deprived of the full dignity of a human being, studied and controlled like a natural phenomenon.

In his *Histoire de la folie*, Foucault dedicates three to four pages to the passage in *meditations* in which Descartes arrives at *Cogito, ergo sum*. Searching for the absolutely certain foundation of knowledge, Descartes analyses the main forms of delusions: delusions of senses and sensible perception, illusions of madness, dreams. He ends with the most radical delusion imaginable, the hypothesis that all that we see is not true, but a universal dream, and illusion staged by an evil God (*Malin Génie*). From here, he arrives at the certainty of *Cogito* (I think): even if I can doubt everything, even if all I see is an illusion, I cannot doubt that I think all this, so *Cogito* is the absolutely certain starting point of philosophy. Foucault's reproach is that Descartes does not really confront madness, but avoids thinking it. *He excludes madness* from the domain of reason: "Dreams or illusions are surmounted within the structure of truth; but madness is inadmissible for the doubting subject." In the Classical Age, Reason is thus based on the exclusion of madness: the very existence of the category "madness" is historically determined, along with its opposite "reason"; that is, it is determined, through power relations. Madness in the modern sense is not directly a phenomenon that we can observe, but a discursive construct which emerges at a certain historical moment, together with its double, Reason, in the modern sense.

In his reading of *Histoire de la folie*, Derrida focuses on these four pages about Descartes which, for him, provide the key to the entire book. Through a detailed analysis, he tries to demonstrate that Descartes does not *exclude* madness, but brings it to *extreme*: the universal doubt, where I suspect that the entire world is an illusion, is the strongest madness imaginable. Out of this universal doubt, *Cogito* emerges: even if everything is an illusion, I can still be sure that I think. Madness is thus not excluded by *Cogito*: it is not that the *Cogito* is not mad, but *Cogito* is true even if I am totally mad. The extreme doubt, the hypothesis of universal madness, is not external to philosophy, but strictly internal to it. It is the hyperbolic moment, the moment of madness, which *grounds* philosophy. Of course, Descartes later "domesticates" this radical excess: he presents the image of man as thinking substance, dominated by reason; he constructs a philosophy which is clearly historically conditioned. But the excess, the hyperbole of universal madness, is not historical. It is the excessive moment which grounds philosophy, in all its historical forms. Madness is thus not excluded by philosophy: it is internal to it. Of course, every philosophy tries to control this excess, to repress it—but in repressing it, it represses its own innermost foundation: "Philosophy is perhaps the reassurance given against the anguish of being mad at the point of greatest proximity to madness."[20]

In his reply, Foucault first tries to prove, through a detailed reading of Descartes, that the madness evoked by Descartes does not have the same status of illusion as sensory illusions and dreams. When I suffer sensory illusions of perception or when I dream, I still *remain normal and rational*, I only deceive myself with regard to what I see. In madness, on the contrary, I myself am no longer normal, I lose my reason. So madness has to be excluded if I am to be a rational subject. Derrida's refusal to exclude madness from philosophy bears witness to the fact that he remains a philosopher who is unable to think the Outside of philosophy, who is unable to think how philosophy itself is determined by something that escapes it. Apropos the hypothesis of universal doubt and the Evil Genius, we are not dealing with true madness here, but with the rational subject who feigns to be mad, who makes a rational experiment, never losing his control over it.

Finally, in the very last page of his reply, Foucault tries to determine the true difference between himself and Derrida. He attacks here (without

20. Foucault, *Discipline and Punish*, 59.

naming it) the practice of deconstruction and textual analysis, for which "there is nothing outside the text" and we are caught in the endless process of interpretation. Foucault, on the contrary, does not practice textual analysis, but analyses of *discourses*. He analyses "dispositifs," formations in which texts and statements are interlinked with extra-textual mechanisms of power and control. What we have to look for are not deeper textual analyses, but the way discursive practices are combined with practices of power and domination.

. . . and Then Lacan

The philosopher who stands for one of the extremes of "madness" is Nicholas Malebranche, his "occasionalism." Malebranche, a disciple of Descartes, drops Descartes's ridiculous reference to the pineal gland in order to explain the coordination between the material and the spiritual substance, i.e. body and soul; how, then, are we to explain their coordination, if there is no contact between the two, no point at which a soul can act causally on a body or vice versa? Since the two causal networks (that of ideas in my mind and that of bodily interconnections) are totally independent, the only solution is that a third, true Substance (God) continuously coordinates and mediates between the two, sustaining the semblance of continuity: when I think about raising my hand and my hand effectively raises, my thought causes the raising of my hand not directly but only "occasionally"—upon noticing my thought directed at raising my hand, God sets in motion the other, material, causal chain which leads to my hand effectively being raised. If we replace "God" with the big Other, the symbolic order, we can see the closeness of occasionalism to Lacan's position: as Lacan put it in his polemics against Aristotle in "Television,"[21] the relationship between soul and body is never direct, since the big Other always interposes itself between the two. Occasionalism is thus essentially a name for the "arbitrary of the signifier," for the gap that separates the network of ideas from the network of bodily (real) causality, for the fact that it is the big Other which accounts for the coordination of the two networks, so that, when my body bites an apple, my soul experiences a pleasurable sensation. This same gap is targeted by the ancient Aztec priest who organizes human sacrifices to ensure that the sun will rise again: the human sacrifice is here an appeal to God to sustain the coordination between the two series, the bodily necessity and the concatenation of symbolic events. "Irrational" as the Aztec priest's sacrificing may appear, its underlying premise is far more insightful than our commonplace

21. Jacques Lacan, "Television," *October* 40 (1987) 7–50.

intuition according to which the coordination between body and soul is direct, i.e., it is "natural" for me to have a pleasurable sensation when I bite an apple since this sensation is caused directly by the apple: what gets lost is the intermediary role of the big Other in guaranteeing the coordination between reality and our mental experience of it. And is it not the same with our immersion into Virtual Reality? When I raise my hand in order to push an object in the virtual space, this object effectively moves—my illusion, of course, is that it was the movement of my hand which directly caused the dislocation of the object, i.e., in my immersion, I overlook the intricate mechanism of computerized coordination, homologous to the role of God guaranteeing the coordination between the two series in occasionalism.[22]

It is a well-known fact that the "Close the door" button in most elevators is a totally disfunctional placebo, which is placed there just to give the individuals the impression that they are somehow participating, contributing to the speed of the elevator journey—when we push this button, the door closes in exactly the same time as when we just pressed the floor button without "speeding up" the process by pressing also the "Close the door" button. This extreme and clear case of fake participation is an appropriate metaphor of the participation of individuals in our "postmodern" political process. And this is occasionalism at its purest: according to Malebranche, we are all the time pressing such buttons, and it is God's incessant activity that coordinates between them and the event that follows (the door closing), while we think the event results from our pushing the button.

For that reason, it is crucial to keep open the radical ambiguity of how cyberspace will affect our lives: this does not depend on technology as such but on the mode of its social inscription. Immersion into cyberspace can intensify our bodily experience (new sensuality, new body with more organs, new sexes), but it also opens up the possibility for the one who manipulates the machinery which runs the cyberspace literally to steal our own (virtual) body, depriving us of the control over it, so that one no longer relates to one's body as to "one's own." What one encounters here is the constitutive ambiguity of the notion of mediatization:[23] originally this notion designated the gesture by means of which a subject was stripped of its direct, immediate right to make decisions; the great master of political mediatization was Napoleon, who left to the conquered monarchs the appearance of power, while they were effectively no longer in a position to exercise it. At a more general level, one could say that such a "mediatization" of the monarch

22. The main work of Nicolas Malebranche is *Recherches de la vérité* (1674-75), the most available edition Paris: Vrin, 1975.

23. As to this ambiguity, see Paul Virilio, *The Art of the Motor*, trans. Julie Rose (Minneapolis: University of Minnesota Press, 1995).

defines the constitutional monarchy: in it, the monarch is reduced to the point of a purely formal symbolic gesture of "dotting the i's," of signing and thus conferring the performative force on the edicts whose content is determined by the elected governing body. And does not, mutatis mutandis, the same not hold also for today's progressive computerization of our everyday lives in the course of which the subject is also more and more "mediatized," imperceptibly stripped of his power, under the false guise of its increase? When our body is mediatized (caught in the network of electronic media), it is simultaneously exposed to the threat of a radical "proletarization": the subject is potentially reduced to the pure $ (the divided subject), since even my own personal experience can be stolen, manipulated, regulated by the machinical Other.

One can see, again, how the prospect of radical virtualization bestows on the computer the position which is strictly homologous to that of God in the Malebrancheian occasionalism: since the computer coordinates the relationship between my mind and (what I experience as) the movement of my limbs (in the virtual reality), one can easily imagine a computer which runs amok and starts to act like an Evil God, disturbing the coordination between my mind and my bodily self-experience—when the signal of my mind to raise my hand is suspended or even counteracted in (the virtual) reality, the most fundamental experience of the body as "mine" is undermined . . . It seems thus that cyberspace effectively realizes the paranoiac fantasy elaborated by Schreber, the German judge whose memoirs were analyzed by Freud: the "wired universe" is psychotic insofar as it seems to materialize Schreber's hallucination of the divine rays through which God directly controls the human mind. In other words, does the externalization of the big Other in the computer not account for the inherent paranoiac dimension of the wired universe? Or, to put it in a yet another way: the commonplace is that, in cyberspace, the ability to download consciousness into a computer finally frees people from their bodies—but it also frees the machines from "their" people . . . This brings us the Wachowski brothers' *Matrix* trilogy: much more than Berkeley's God who sustains the world in his mind, the *ultimate* Matrix is Malebranche's occasionalist God.

What, then, is the Matrix? Simply the Lacanian "big Other," the virtual symbolic order, the network that structures reality for us. This dimension of the "big Other" is that of the constitutive alienation of the subject in the symbolic order: the big Other pulls the strings, the subject doesn't speak, he "is spoken" by the symbolic structure. In short, this "big Other" is the name for the social Substance, for all that on account of which the subject never fully dominates the effects of his acts, i.e., on account of which the final outcome of his activity is always something else with regard to what he aimed at or anticipated. However, it is here crucial to note that, in the key chapters of *The Four Fundamental Concepts of Psycho-Analysis*, Lacan struggles to delineate the operation that follows alienation and is in a sense its counterpoint, that of separation: alienation IN the big Other is followed by the separation *from* the big Other. Separation takes place when the subject takes note of how the big Other is in itself inconsistent, purely virtual, "barred," deprived of the Thing—and fantasy is an attempt to fill out this lack of the Other, not of the subject, i.e., to (re)constitute the consistency of the big Other. For that reason, fantasy and paranoia are inherently linked: paranoia is at its most elementary a belief in an "Other of the Other," into another Other who, hidden behind the Other of the explicit social texture, programs (what appears to us as) the unforeseen effects of social life and thus guarantees its consistency: beneath the chaos of market, the degradation of morals, etc., there is the purposeful strategy of the Jewish plot. This paranoiac stance acquired a further boost with today's digitalization of our daily lives: when our entire (social) existence is progressively externalized-materialized in the big Other of the computer network, it is easy to imagine an evil programmer erasing our digital identity and thus depriving us of our social existence, turning us into non-persons.

Following the same paranoiac twist, the thesis of *The Matrix* is that this big Other is externalized in the really existing Mega-Computer. There is—there *has* to be—a Matrix because "things are not right, opportunities are missed, something goes wrong all the time," i.e., the film's idea is that it is so because there is the Matrix that obfuscates the "true" reality that is behind it all. Consequently, the problem with the film is that it is *not* "crazy" enough, because it supposes another "real" reality behind our everyday reality sustained by the Matrix. One is tempted to claim, in the Kantian mode, that the mistake of the conspiracy theory is somehow homologous to the "paralogism of the pure reason," to the confusion between the two levels: the suspicion (of the received scientific, social, etc. common sense) as the formal methodological stance, and the positivation of this suspicion in another all-explaining global para-theory.

2

Nothing Really Matters—
Rhapsody for a Dead Queen

A Lacanian Reading of Thomas Aquinas

TINA BEATTIE[1]

THEOLOGY WAS ONCE THE Queen of the Sciences, this discipline above all disciplines that claimed philosophy as her handmaid in order to enact a marriage of desire between grace and nature, revelation and reason. This marriage may look somewhat queer from the perspective of modernity, but it was no gay science. In the *Summa theologiae* of Thomas Aquinas it was a plodding and pedantic attempt to show that the straight and narrow path of reason leads to a blinding encounter with the mystery of God, shining through and beyond all the things of this world and illuminating them from within by way of a dazzling darkness that Christians call grace. Aristotle provided the maps, scripture provided the compass, and desire for God provided the motivation. By way of these guides, Thomas and his scholastic contemporaries led theology into the throne room of the medieval university where she remained until a scientific revolution (Galileo, Galileo) overthrew the queen and prepared the way for her handmaid to usurp her place. The monarchical kingdom of truth was becoming a democratic republic, and today theology is not so much a queen as a court jester amidst the disciplines.

Lacan is a little silhouetto of a man doing the fandango with Thomas in the graveyard of the saint's unconscious God. He tears up the maps, sends

1. The themes in this essay are developed at much greater length in my *Theology after Postmodernity: Divining the Void—A Lacanian Reading of Thomas Aquinas* (Oxford: Oxford University Press, 2013).

34

the needle of the compass spinning, and shows us that, even if Thomas was not given to dancing, he understood something about the nature of being and desire. Unlike many of his postmodern contemporaries—and, as François Regnault points out, unlike Freud[2]—Lacan also understands a little theology. A sometimes critical analysis of Lacan's medievalism among scholars such as Amy Hollywood,[3] Bruce Holsinger,[4] Erin Labbie[5] and others has raised awareness of the extent to which Lacan was influenced by his encounters with French Thomists, particularly Étienne Gilson, in the 1950s,[6] so that it is possible to discern a pervasive Thomism (or sometimes an anti-Thomism) running through his ideas. Malcolm Bowie refers to Lacan's "truth-intoxicated writings."[7] My own inclination is to read Lacan's pursuit of truth as a futile endeavour to escape the God of his early Catholicism who pursued him relentlessly through the labyrinths of the soul: Never let you go—let me go, Never let me go—ooo.

Scaramouch, Scaramouch Will You Do the Fandango

Lacan opens the way for theology to become a nomad among the disciplines. Contrary to the endeavors of some modern theologians to restore theology to its place of pre-eminence in the ivory towers of academia and indeed to confer upon it the normative status that it once had, I am proposing a bohemian theology—a nomadic gypsy doing a wild Lacanian fandango among the disciplines so as to disrupt and unsettle all claims to knowledge, including the claims of theology itself.

The time has come to leave it all behind and face the truth, and Lacan, speaking as the voice of truth, tells us that this means following a tangled path through the labyrinths of language, desire and knowledge. Shunning the men of God, truth allows herself to be hijacked by a scaramouch who

2. See François Regnault, *Dieu est Inconscient: Études Lacaniennes autour de Saint Thomas d'Aquin* (Paris: Navarin, 1985).

3. Amy Hollywood, *Sensible Ecstasy: Mysticism, Sexual Difference, and the Demands of History* (Chicago: University of Chicago Press, 2002).

4. Bruce W. Holsinger, *The Premodern Condition: Medievalism and the Making of Theory* (Chicago: University of Chicago Press, 2005).

5. Erin Felicia Labbie, *Lacan's Medievalism* (Minnesota: University of Minnesota Press, 2006).

6. Cf. Marcus Pound, "Lacan's Return to Freud: A Case of Theological *Ressourcement?*," in *Ressourcement: A Movement for Renewal in Twentieth-Century Catholic Theology*, ed. Gabriel Flynn and Paul D. Murray (Oxford: Oxford University Press. 2012).

7. Malcolm Bowie, *Lacan* (London: HarperCollins, 1991) 116.

prances before us, exposing himself for all to see that he's not all there, something's missing from the perspective of his manhood, even though he covers the horror of his hole with a magnificent dildo that sends feminists wild and makes other men want one too. Here, then, if we follow this gnomic figure, is where we might have to go:

> Whether you flee me in deceit or think you can catch me in error, I will catch up with you in the mistake from which you cannot hide. . . . I wander about in what you regard as least true by its very nature: in dreams, in the way the most far-fetched witticisms and the most grotesque nonsense of jokes defy meaning, and in chance—not in its law, but rather in its contingency.[8]

Theology has become too straight in its pursuits. It needs to be queered, to rediscover that it is the gay science, queen indeed in relation to all that appears by way of the straight and narrow path of rationalism. Taking Lacan as my unreliable guide, I go anyway the wind blows, following an overgrown and abandoned path towards the Catholic God of Thomas and Lacan, for by that word "God" they mean the same no-thing/the Thing. The question is one of performative hermeneutics not signification: is that empty signifier related to all or nothing, an unsayable plenitude which invites a bodily response of love, or an unspeakable abyss which lures the self towards annihilation? Are we sure we can tell the difference?

My Lacanian quest is motivated by the obscure realization that nothing really matters for the angelic Doctor, though to confess that would be an absurdity beyond all absurdities. So I want to wander about in what Thomas and his postmodern heirs regard as least true by its very nature, the monstrosity of matter from which no human life is spared and which has always haunted the dreams of the men of God. Every time they attempt to look up to the skies and see, this boggy stuff rises up and threatens to swamp them with its viscous fleshiness.

In order to embark upon this bohemian quest, I begin where Lacan says it is both necessary and impossible to begin—at the beginning, creation *ex nihilo.* In what follows, I consider questions of being, form, and matter in the context of creation and the Tetragrammaton—the self-revelation of God in Exodus 3:15 as YHWH, "I am that I am" or "I will be what I will be," rendered in Latin as "*qui est.*" First, I focus briefly on Lacan's *Seminar VII,*[9]

8. Jacques Lacan, "The Freudian Thing, or the Meaning of the Return to Freud in Psychoanalysis," in *Écrits,* trans. Bruce Fink (New York: Norton, 2006) 341–42.

9. Jacques Lacan, *The Ethics of Psychoanalysis 1959–1960: The Seminar of Jacques Lacan, Book VII,* trans. Dennis Porter (London: Routledge, 1999).

before turning to look more closely at *Seminar XX*,[10] in which he discusses questions of being, form, sexuality and embodiment in relation to the One of Western philosophy and the Other of the Christian God. Then I ask how Thomas understands the relationship between creation, form and matter, focusing on the *Summa Theologiae*,[11] and finally I consider the theological implications of following Lacan beyond the philosophical fantasy of the sexual relationship to a new appreciation of the non-copulative potency of the incarnate God.

This is a highly selective theological reading of these ancient and postmodern masters, which seeks a place amidst and not over and against multiple other possible readings of both. Easy come, easy go—I forego mastery in order to "have a fling with the philosophers,"[12] though it sends shivers down my spine when I think of how those who claim mastery might try to stop me and spit in my eye.

Mama, Life Had Just Begun

How does life begin? We think we know. Aristotle thought he knew too. It's all a matter of copulation. Eternal matter/mother encounters eternal form/father in copulative fractals that repeat themselves at every level of being. But Lacan, like Thomas, takes his beginnings from the book of Genesis, not from Aristotle, and this introduces an abysmal void where the sexual relationship ought to be. The Hebrew story of creation is an act of *coitus interruptus*. It suspends the eroticism of pagan accounts of being, condemns the sexuality of the pagan gods and their orgiastic cults, and evacuates the Judaeo-Christian soul and its modern secular derivatives of their sexual consolations.

Jewish monotheism and its Christian refigurations open up in the Western imaginary a possibility that was unthinkable, even for a mind as great as Aristotle's, by rejecting the idea that matter is eternal, and by

10. Jacques Lacan, *Le Séminaire Livre XX: Encore* (Paris: Éditions du Seuil, 1975); Jacques Lacan, *The Seminar of Jacques Lacan, Book XX: On Feminine Sexuality, the Limits of Love and Knowledge, 1972–1973 (Encore)*, ed. Jacques-Alain Miller, trans. Bruce Fink (New York: Norton, 1999). I refer to the French text for this seminar, with references to Bruce Fink's translation in parentheses. This is because the Thomist nuances of Lacan's discussion are sometimes lost in Fink's translation. See also Cormac Gallagher's translation at Lacan in Ireland: http://www.lacaninireland.com/web/?page_id=123.

11. I have used the online parallel text of the translation by the Fathers of the English Dominican Province: Thomas Aquinas, *The Summa Theologica*, trans. the Fathers of the English Dominican Province (Benziger Bros. ed., 1947): http://josephkenny. joyeurs.com/CDtexts/summa/index.html.

12. Luce Irigaray, *This Sex Which Is Not One*, trans. Catherine Porter (Ithaca: Cornell University Press, 1985) 150.

asserting that something is created from nothing—*ex nihilo*.[13] Like the potter who creates a vase in order to enclose emptiness (Lacan finds the biblical metaphor of the potter particularly apt), God shapes creation around
the void. Matter and the temporal order enclose and conceal an abysmal
emptiness, for a creation that emerges out of nothing retains that nothingness within itself, and is subject to fundamental contingency and existential
facticity. For the linguistic species that we are, this is not a question of a pre-
discursive reality, but an insight into how the order of language that forms
us is predicated upon an unspeakable abyss at the heart of things.

Christianity introduces the obscenity of a fleshy and crucified God
into this religion of lack, so that bodiliness intrudes upon the divine and
lures the Western subject towards a horizon in which eternity is presided
over by the tortured body on the cross, arousing an unfathomable *jouissance*
in the soul. In *Seminar VII*, Lacan associates this with the female sex organs
which, stripped of their linguistic veils of seductive femininity, arouse in
the subject the primal horror of the void—the Freudian "horror of nothing
to see"—luring him towards the womb/tomb of his origins and endings.
Where once a pagan *jouissance* might have been discovered in the fantasized
divinization of the sexual relationship, in Christianity the body is deprived
of its sacred sexuality and bears instead the encryptions of an endless and
sublime torment that seduces the subject towards death.

The focus of this essay, however, is not *Seminar VII* but *Seminar XX*,
which can be read as a feminized reinterpretation of *Seminar VII*. Here,
Lacan takes us to the edge of a new way of speaking of the relationship
between desire, embodiment and God, associated with the language of the
medieval mystic and the modern hysteric. "Woman" shifts and some mur-
mured intimation of bodily ecstasy and anguish emerges from the shadows
and silence to which Lacan consigned her in *Seminar VII*.

Is This the Real Life? Is This Just Fantasy?

The soul (*l'âme*) is the focus of Lacan's attention in *Seminar XX*—the masculine soul of Aristotelian philosophy and modern romanticism that appropriates the body of woman as its other, and the carnal soul of female
mysticism and hysteria that deconstructs the Cartesian subject through the
invocation of an elusive material/maternal otherness. This leads Lacan to
suggest—cryptically and enigmatically as always—that attentiveness to the
immediacy of language that emanates from the body as the feminized other
of the Cartesian "I" gestures towards an obscure linguistic path of longing

13. See Lacan, *Ethics of Psychoanalysis*, 121.

for Christianity's incarnate and unknowable God, who is the Other of the One of Greek philosophy.

In *Seminar XX*, Lacan suggests that Christianity is "the true religion,"[14] because it exposes the mythical nature of Greek philosophical accounts of being as a copulative encounter between paternal form and maternal matter. It reveals instead the lack that constitutes the subject and the impossibility of the sexual relationship:

> Let us only consider the terms of active and passive, for example, which dominate all that has been cogitated about the relationship between form and matter, so fundamental a relationship, to which each step of Plato refers, then of Aristotle, concerning the nature of things. It is visible, palpable, that these utterances support only a fantasy by way of which they have tried to make up for that which can in no way express itself, to know the sexual relationship.[15]

The sexual relationship constitutes the quest for fantasized fusion and union that copulative accounts of being arouse in the Western soul, but it is a futile quest because by its very nature the sexual encounter is located in the ephemerality of the body and its *jouissance*. Any attempt to project sexual identities and imagined copulations beyond that epiphanic and episodic encounter is a symptom of the unbearable lack that the castrated subject bears within himself.

Christianity is true insofar as it is the only religion that might explain the topology of the Western soul that psychoanalysis discovers, and the relationship of this to the question of being which belongs within the matrix of the culture that Christianity helped to create. In removing copulation from the order of being, Christianity unveils the falsehood of Greek ontology and modern romanticism, and it expresses the truth of human reality by exposing the hole that constitutes the absent Other at the heart of desire. For Thomas, this was the unspeakable mystery of Christianity's self-revealing God beyond all language and conceptualization, knowable only in the unknowing of contemplative prayer. For Lacan, it is the soul's turbulent undertow that remains when scientific rationalism renders God unconscious. Lacan's God is unconscious rather than dead, because the lingering effects of Christianity's God on the Western soul manifest themselves in the yearnings and horrors that leak through the ruptures and gaps in language to which psychoanalysis pays heed.

14. Ibid., 137 (107).
15. Lacan, *SXX*, 104 (82).

Spare Him His Life from This Monstrosity!

However, Christians, like psychoanalysts, "are disgusted by what has been revealed to them."[16] This is the only explanation as to why "the philosophy of Aristotle was reinjected by Saint Thomas into what one could call Christian consciousness, if that meant anything." Lacan says he rolls about laughing when he reads Saint Thomas, because "it's awfully well put together."[17] By introducing the logic of Greek philosophy with its divinized One and its copulative relationships of form and matter into theology, Thomas allows Christians to hide from themselves the obscenity of their faith behind the linguistic masks of philosophical rationalism. In *Seminar XX*, Lacan sets about disentangling these two Gods that have formed the gendered Christian soul in their image—the divinized masculine One of theological rationalism, and the incarnate, maternal Other of mystical *jouissance*—by addressing questions of being, otherness, sexuality, the body, and love.

Lacan addresses the question of being from the perspective of the copulative function of the verb "to be." Ontology, he says, "is what highlighted in language the use of the copula, isolating it as a signifier."[18] He asks what it means to believe and to know with regard to the question of being— "*ce qu'il en est de l'être*"[19]—in the context of the idea of the One that has shaped Western philosophy since the time of Parmenides, whether it is the Platonic form, the Aristotelian unmoved mover, or the Hegelian absolute. This leads him to return to a theme he first addressed in *Seminar XIX* the year before—the claim that "there is something of the One" (*Y a d'l'Un*).[20] In his translator's footnote, Bruce Fink explains that Lacan's emphasis is not "on the 'thing' or on quantity": "Lacan is *not* saying 'there's some One' (in the sense of some quantity of One) since he is talking about *the One of 'pure difference.*'"[21] This is a crucial insight that Lacan gleans from Étienne Gilson, about the difference between a Platonic and a Thomist approach to the question of being.

In Lacan's reading of Plato, knowledge of the form constitutes the singular totality of all that there is to know. The *a priori* One of form sets itself over and against the ephemeral multitude of material beings and the flux of desire. The masculine subject made in the image of this One also

16. Ibid., 145 (114).

17. Ibid., "*Parce que c'est rudement bien foutu.*" One might suggest a more Lacanian innuendo by translating this as "it's fuckingly well put together."

18. Ibid., 43 (31).

19. Ibid., 11 (3).

20. Ibid., 13 (5).

21. Ibid., n. 19 (5), my italics.

sets himself over and against the materiality of the body, nature and desire because of their resistance to the unity and rationality of form. However, Lacan posits an alternative interpretation of the One—*Y'a d'l'Un*—"The One happens." Here we we are very close to Lacan's Gilsonian Thomism.

Open Your Eyes, Look Up to the Skies and See

Gilson argues that, in Thomas's mind, "the notion of being underwent a remarkable transformation," away from the idea of "entity" (*essentia*) to the idea of being as "the act pointed out by the verb 'to be.'" Gilson continues:

> In the doctrine of Thomas Aquinas, being has received the full-ness of its existential meaning. . . . [B]ecause it is to act, "to be" is something fixed and at rest in being: *esse est aliquid fixum et quietum in ente*. . . . As Thomas Aquinas understands him, God is the being whose whole nature it is to be such an existential act. This is the reason why his most proper name is, HE IS. After saying this, any addition would be a subtraction. To say that God "is this," or that he "is that," would be to restrict his being to the essences of what "this" and "that" are. God "is," absolutely.[22]

We should note that the translation of the non-gendered Latin "*qui est*" as "*he is*" already constitutes such a subtraction by addition, but we'll come back to that. Gilson provides the context in which to situate Lacan's exploration of the question of being in *Seminar XX*. In God, the word "is" loses its copulative function, just as creation itself is liberated from all copulative ne-cessity and conflict in order to become an expression instead of the dynamic being as doing of God, who creates freely, out of nothing, as an expression of unfathomable and gratuitous love, but also against a terrifying hinterland of damnation and eternal bodily torment. I do not refer to Thomas's account of demons, hell and pre-destination here, but it is vital for a more developed account of Lacan's Thomism.

In the debates of his time, Thomas opposed the philosophical argu-ment put forward by Avicenna and others that reality adds something to being.[23] For Thomas, such an assertion would violate the absolute simplic-ity of God, and therefore oneness must be understood as something other than a mathematical principle by way of which something is added to something else. Over and against such a definition of singularity, Thomas

22. Étienne Gilson, *History of Christian Philosophy in the Middle Ages* (London: Sheed & Ward, 1955) 368–69, quoting Aquinas, *SCG* I: 20, 4.

23. Aquinas, *ST* I, 11, 2.

posits the concept of one as synonymous with being, by way of which nothing can possibly be added to the divine being. Lacan's "One of 'pure difference'" alludes to this. In Thomist terms, it is the perfect simplicity of the divine being as pure act—*actus purus*—with no predicate, copula, distinction or complexity.

This leads Thomas to reject a dualistic interpretation of the one as opposed to the many, in favour of a less polarized duality in which the multitude, being divided, lacks the undivided fullness of the oneness of being. In other words, for anything to become other than God, there must be some limit and boundary to its being—it must be not-all—if it is to exist as different from other beings and as distinct from the fullness of God's being. Otherwise, there would be no created beings at all—the divine plenitude would be all in all.

In one section of the first part of the *Summa Theologiae,* Thomas represents lack as the condition by way of which each species in its own created perfection reveals something of the divine perfection, so that the fullness of God's being is better revealed by plurality and diversity than by singularity:

> For God brought things into being in order that His goodness might be communicated to creatures, and be represented by them; and because His goodness could not be adequately represented by one creature alone, He produced many and diverse creatures, that what was wanting to one in the representation of the divine goodness might be supplied by another. For goodness, which in God is simple and uniform, in creatures is manifold and divided and hence the whole universe together participates in the divine goodness more perfectly, and represents it better than any single creature whatever.[24]

From this perspective, as Lacan recognizes, lack becomes the condition of there being any beings at all other than God's being, and the totality of all beings will never amount to the fullness of God's being. In this account, Thomas's God is not the philosophical One of ancient philosophy and modern theism, but "the One of pure difference." Lack is not the fantasized deprivation and prohibition associated with the Oedipus complex, but the primordial condition for intelligent, linguistic beings to enjoy a certain freedom in relation to the things around them. If I were to be more than I am, I would cease to be the particular being that I am and become a different being, not a more perfect or complete version of my own being. The relationship between the being of God and other beings is not quantitative but qualitative, not relative but relational—all beings

24. Aquinas, *ST* I, 47, 1.

participate in God, but the divine being participates in no other being for there is no lack or distinction within the being of God that would allow for such participation in a lesser being.

Got to Leave You All Behind and Face the Truth

This harmonious difference between the simplicity of the divine being and the complexity of created beings is altogether other than the philosophical conflict between the One and the many, in which the One/the Absolute requires the conquest and destruction or assimilation of otherness. This is why, in *Seminar XX*, Lacan insists that woman, belonging on the side of the philosophical not-all, reveals the Christian Other of the philosophical One. She never attains to the (illusory) universality of the One that man claims for himself. She is always one plus one plus one, in a series of infinite exceptions to the oneness of being that is the condition for anything else to become. Because of this, it is woman rather than man who reveals what it means to be in the context of Christianity's understanding of God.

Here, Lacan is at his most provocative from the perspective of his feminist interlocuters, particularly those in the post-Protestant tradition of English-speaking academia, who are tone-deaf to the theological nuances in Lacanian theory. Lacan situates the question of subjectivity and otherness in terms of the philosophical distinction between paternal form and maternal matter, masculine perfection and feminine lack. A woman lacks the definite article, because her otherness derives from the fact that she is on the side of the not-all, matter in relation to form, lack in relation to perfection, as the excluded other of the universal One of the form: "The Woman can only be written with a line through The. There is no Woman with the definite article designating the universal. There is no Woman because . . . of her essence, she is not all."[25] But it is in this "not-all" that Thomas's God can be purged of his Aristotelian distortions, and revealed anew as the Other of woman's *jouissance*, which expresses an incarnate desire for that which is beyond all knowing, naming and possessing. This is a surplus *jouissance*, supplementary to anything that can be said of the sexual relationship in terms of desire and otherness.

Lacan detects a double deception in Thomas's Christian appropriation of Aristotelianism. First, Aristotle defies the logic of his own philosophy when he privileges the soul over the body, because in the Aristotelian/ Thomist order of being there is no *a priori* knowledge. All that we are is formed by way of our sensory interactions with the material world. So, says

25. Lacan, *SXX*, 93 (72–73).

Thomas, "The proper act is produced in its proper potentiality. Therefore since the soul is the proper act of the body, the soul was produced in the body."[26] Second, in Christianity the emphasis is not on Christ's soul but on his body—a body that, like every human body, has a beginning but no end in the order of being. So not only does Christianity introduce the obscenity of the flesh into the purity of the Greek philosophical form, it also condemns the human to the unbearable *jouissance* of eternal bodily life. We come into being from a void but we can never escape from being back into the void. Let's bear these points in mind, for they haunted Lacan's Catholic soul.

Christianity's God as Other must be differentiated from "the idea of a God that is not that of the Christian faith, but that of Aristotle—the unmoved mover, the supreme sphere."[27] Over and against this Aristotelian concept of God, Lacan posits the Other of woman's bodily desire:

> The whole foundation of the idea of the Good in Aristotle's ethics is that there is a being such that all other beings with less being than him can have no other aim than to be the most being they can be. . . . [I]t is in the opaque place of the jouissance of the Other, this Other as being which might be the woman, if she existed, that the Supreme being, manifestly mythical in Aristotle, is situated, the unmoved sphere from which there proceed all movements whatever they may be. . . .
>
> It is insofar as her jouissance is radically Other that woman has more of a relationship to God than all that could have been said in ancient speculation following the pathway of that which manifestly articulates itself only as the good of the man.[28]

Lacan is both deconstructing the Aristotelian/Thomist order of knowledge, and appropriating it as potentially offering a more truthful account of reality than Platonic and later Cartesian and Kantian accounts of the subject. With Thomas/Aristotle, he is insisting that the soul is empty of content except insofar as this is provided by the experiencing body. Against Thomas/Aristotle, he is refusing to ontologize the reproductive/sexual relationship as fundamental to the order of being.

Referring to Aristotle's *De Anima*, Lacan points out that "if there is something that grounds being, it is assuredly the body."[29] But according to Lacan, Aristotle fails to link this to "his affirmation . . . that man thinks *with*—instrument—his soul." This means, says Lacan, that "man thinks with

26. *ST* I, 90, 4.
27. Lacan, *SXX*, 104 (82).
28. Ibid., 104–5 (82–83).
29. Ibid., 140 (110).

Aristotle's thought. In that sense, thought is naturally on the winning side."[30] Through the influence of Aristotle, mediated by way of Thomas, the mind has displaced the body as a source of knowledge, so that man/form/mind is "on the winning side" over woman/matter/body. But this is an illusion, because in saying that the man thinks with his soul, Aristotle denies that the source of thought is the body. So, says Lacan, "He animates nothing, he (mis)takes the other for his soul" (*il prend l'autre pour son âme*).[31]

Lacan seeks to expose this inverted order of truth that constitutes intellectual mastery in the Western ordering of knowledge, by bringing into view the excluded other of the body as the locus wherein the God of Christian desire is to be discovered, beyond all the myths and frustrations of the sexual relationship. Language (*le langage*) constitutes the conceptualized and rationalized sphere of the symbolic, but this conceals the body's mother tongue (*la langue*), the voice of the unconscious with its visceral and unformed expressions of lack and longing, horror and ecstasy, love and loss. There is an inversion in the order of reality, when Western philosophy privileges soul over body and mind over matter, for in fact, without the medium of the body the soul would know nothing.

Didn't Mean to Make You Cry

In modernity, God as the One of form mutates into the absent lawgiver of the symbolic order, purged of the contaminating otherness of the imaginary as it shades towards the real (flesh, matter, nature, the drives). This translates into the modern scientific quest for the accumulation of facts, statistics, and proofs. It secures being against an incremental horizon of knowledge that will eventually add up to all there is to know about everything. The philosophical formlessness of prime matter becomes the swarm of phonemes that the non-subject enunciates within the bodily immediacy and transience of the here and now (the mystical rapture or the psychoanalytic session), before the abstract Cartesian "I" of the enunciated subject takes control to give written form to these verbal ejaculations of love and longing, delight and torment. The modern linguistic subject masters and orders these rapturous carnal utterances in the same way that the soul of the ancient master took control of the body of his feminized other, filtering the body's delight and anguish in its unknown God through the conceptualizing and rationalizing grids of Aristotelian theology. The ancient copulative relationship between form and matter is perpetuated within the linguistic order of modern

30. Ibid., 141 (111).

31. Ibid., 104 (82).

secular culture, and it foments within itself a sexual turmoil of frustration and longing which psychoanalysis discovers in the haunted caverns of the modern soul. Here, a viscous ooze leaks from the abandoned body of Christianity's unconscious God, manifesting itself as the turbulent undercurrent of dread and desire that emanates from the conflict between the paternal philosophical One and the maternal incarnate Other.

As the man of reason begins his postmodern disintegration, an overgrown path begins to open up through psychoanalytic discourse, leading back to the future in the company of this elusive and awesome Other—an Other which, insofar as it is other than the philosophical One, must have something to do with the other sex. Psychoanalysis seeks to reanimate the lost order of corporeal knowledge, which Lacan describes as "the very backbone of my teaching":

> I speak with my body and I do so without knowledge. So I always say more than I know of it.
>
> That is where I arrive at the meaning of the word "subject" in analytic discourse. What speaks without knowledge makes me "I," subject of the verb. That is not enough to make me be. That has nothing to do with what I am forced to put in being—enough knowledge for it to hold up, but not one drop more.
>
> That is what used to be called form. According to Plato, the form is the knowledge that fills being. The form doesn't know any more about it than it says. It is real in the sense that it holds being in its glass, but full to the brim. It is the knowledge of being. The discourse of being presumes that being is, and that is what holds it.
>
> There is some relationship of being that cannot be known.[32]

This relationship can only be discovered by attending to the feminized voice of bodily otherness that emanates from the abjected site of body/matter/mother which is subordinated by Aristotelian Thomism, and finally rejected altogether in the rise of modern rationalism. This calls for patient attentiveness to bodily expressiveness, for there are, says Lacan, "miracles of the body."[33] As an example, he refers to the lachrymal gland which must produce tears in order for the eye to function, but which also expresses emotion and grief from which the subject shies away.

This expressive capacity of the body can be illustrated by quoting a short exchange from Peter Carey's novel *The Chemistry of Tears*, where he describes how even the chemical composition of tears marks this difference between functionality and expressiveness:

32. Ibid., 150–51 (119).
33. Ibid.

He told me that tears produced by emotions are chemically different from those we need for lubrication. So my shameful little tissues, he said, now contained a hormone involved in the feeling of sexual gratification, another hormone that reduced stress; and finally a very powerful natural painkiller.

"What is that one called?" I asked.

"Leucine enkephalin," he smiled. I wrote it down.[34]

This is an exquisite cameo to illustrate what Lacan means. Tears have a subtlety of language all of their own. They know a truth about the self that the "I" who claims to know does not know. When the subject enters the scene, the immediacy of the body's language yields to naming and writing, and thereby it loses its eloquent capacity to express a truth beyond what we think we know.

In order to appreciate the far-reaching implications of this for Christian theology, let me turn now to Thomas's Aristotelian account of the relationship between form, matter, and the God who creates *ex nihilo*. How far can Lacan help theology to expose the cracks and gaps in Thomas's theological system, in order to allow the body of God to speak? This is a vast question, and elsewhere I show that a maternal Trinity haunts the pages of Thomas's theology with an elusive but persistent otherness. Here, I focus on questions of form and matter, but this maternal Trinitarian hinterland needs to be borne in mind.

Bismillah!

Gilson points to the crucial importance of Exodus 3 in enabling Thomas to reconcile philosophical metaphysics with scriptural revelation, so that the "pure act-of-being which St Thomas the philosopher met at the end of metaphysics, St Thomas the theologian had met too in Holy Scripture."[35] This, argues Gilson, constitutes the genius of Thomas's thought. In recognizing that "*He Who Is* in Exodus means the *Act-of-Being*," Thomas brings to light not only the compatibility between philosophical reason and scriptural revelation, but also the balanced unity of his own thought. Gilson refers to "this sublime truth—*hanc sublime veritatem*—whose light illumines the whole of Thomism."[36]

---

34. Peter Carey, *The Chemistry of Tears* (London: Faber & Faber, 2012) 265.

35. Étienne Gilson, *The Christian Philosophy of St. Thomas Aquinas* (London: Victor Gollancz, 1961) 93.

36. Ibid., 95.

Thomas discusses Exodus 3 in Question 13 of Part I of the *Summa theologiae*. I leave *"qui est"* untranslated, because its translation as "He Who Is" deprives the Latin of its semantic freedom to signify the simple act of being prior to the attribution of any other quality, predicate or concept, including that of gender.

Thomas offers three reasons as to why "this name *qui est* is the most appropriate name of God."[37] First, it signifies existence itself and not any kind of form.[38] Second, by virtue of its indeterminacy it is universal in its application. Thomas quotes John Damascene (*De Fide Orth.* i): "*Qui est* is the principal of all names applied to God; for comprehending all in itself, it contains being itself as an infinite and indeterminate sea of substance."[39] Third, "It signifies being in the present; and this above all properly applies to God, whose being knows neither past nor future."[40] Thomas goes on to argue that the Tetragrammaton is most properly applied to God: "And the Tetragrammaton is an even more appropriate name, because it is imposed to signify the incommunicable and, if one may so speak, singular substance itself of God."[41]

We should note here that Thomas affirms that the being of God is "not any kind of form." His use of John Damascene's oceanic metaphor—"an infinite and indeterminate sea of substance"—is evocative of Plato's *khora*. Analogically speaking, it tends more towards the philosophical imagery of matter than form. Thomas is also cautious in his attribution of singularity to God—"if one may so speak"—because, as we have seen, he wants to guard against any suggestion that this is a quantitative or mathematical singularity. So far, it would seem that Thomas denies both form and matter to God, so that Thomas's God is not the One of Greek philosophy.

However, here we encounter a persistent ambiguity in Thomas's attempt to wed the incarnate, Trinitarian God of Christian revelation to the Supreme Being and Prime Mover of Aristotelian philosophy. Rather than affirming that God is neither form nor matter, Thomas is repeatedly seduced by the divinized form of Greek philosophy. So he claims that "whatever is primarily and essentially an agent must be primarily and essentially form.

37. Aquinas, *ST* I, 13, 11, "*hoc nomen qui est . . . est maxime proprium nomen Dei.*"

38. "*Non enim significat formam aliquam, sed ipsum esse.*"

39. "*principalius omnibus quae de Deo dicuntur nominibus, est qui est, totum enim in seipso comprehendens, habet ipsum esse velut quoddam pelagus substantiae infinitum et indeterminatum.*"

40. "*Significat enim esse in praesenti, et hoc maxime proprie de Deo dicitur, cuius esse non novit praeteritum vel futurum.*" Thomas cites Augustine (*De Trin.* v).

41. "*Et adhuc magis proprium nomen est tetragrammaton, quod est impositum ad significandam ipsam Dei substantiam incommunicabilem, et, ut sic liceat loqui, singularem.*"

Now God is the first agent, since He is the first efficient cause. He is therefore of His essence a form; and not composed of matter and form."[42] This would suggest that God is form, and creation involves prime matter but not form, so that an eternity of form would be posited over and against the creation of matter *ex nihilo*. But Thomas does not want to allow this either, for he argues that "Creation does not mean the building up of a composite thing from pre-existing principles; but it means that the 'composite' is created so that it is brought into being at the same time with all its principles."[43] He goes on to reject the suggestion that "the thing supposed in natural generation is matter. Therefore matter, and not the composite, is, properly speaking, that which is created." To this he responds, "This reason does not prove that matter alone is created, but that matter does not exist except by creation; for creation is the production of the whole being, and not only matter."

Nothing Really Matters

If God creates *ex nihilo*, then God creates forms along with matter. As Gilson argues, neither forms nor matter actually exist for Thomas except insofar as they exist in composite beings—they are theories that function to explain the otherwise inexplicable continuity of beings and the diversity of individuals and species that emerge as different forms from within the flux of matter.[44] There is therefore no "form" as such for Thomas—there are only forms. So, says Thomas, "being [*esse*] is that which makes every form or nature actual,"[45] and later he says that "nothing has actuality except so far as it exists. Hence being itself [*ipsum esse*] is that which actuates all things, even their forms."[46] Gilson argues that "form is a nobler element of substance than is matter,"[47] but that Thomas went beyond the "metaphysical heights" achieved by Plato and Aristotle, by recognizing that

> Since neither matter nor form can exist apart, it is not difficult to see that the existence of their composite is possible. But it is not so easy to see how their union can engender actual existence. How is existence to arise from what does not exist? It is therefore necessary to have existence come first as the ultimate term to which the analysis of the real can attain. When it is thus related

42. Aquinas, *ST* I, 3, 2.

43. Aquinas, *ST* I, 45, 4.

44. See Gilson, *Christian Philosophy of St. Thomas Aquinas,* 31–34.

45. Aquinas, *ST* I, 3, 4.

46. Aquinas, *ST* I, 4, 1.

47. Gilson, *Christian Philosophy of St. Thomas Aquinas,* 32.

to existence, form ceases to appear as the ultimate determination of the real.[48]

By now, it should be clear how deeply Thomist Lacan's *Seminar XX* is. The Lacanian real bears the closest possible resemblance to Thomas's God, but like the real, this God is neither form nor matter and therefore it occupies that deep well of the unconscious where the symbolic and the real bleed into one another beyond the far horizons of language. God is beyond form and matter is below form, but both are ultimately formless, and that means that the human mind cannot think them except as an infinite other beyond what we know. But because man is culturally conditioned to think of himself as closer to God and therefore as nobler than woman, he begins to equate himself with form, which in turn he equates with God, while woman is the "below" of matter in relation to both.

If Thomas is ambivalent about form, he is adamant about matter in relation to God: there is no matter in God.[49] The human is made in the image of God not in terms of the body but in terms of the incorporeal faculties of intelligence and reason. David Dinant's teaching that God is primary matter is "most absurd."[50] In seeking to distinguish between God and primary matter, Thomas appeals to Aristotle's distinction in *Metaphysics*: "'things which are diverse are absolutely distinct, but things which are different differ by something.' Therefore, strictly speaking, primary matter and God do not differ, but are by their very being, diverse. Hence it does not follow they are the same."[51]

This claim should bring any Thomist up short. Thomas's doctrine of creation teaches that all being that is not God participates in and is conditional upon the perfect simplicity of being that is God. If so, then prime matter—created by God out of nothing—is not "absolutely distinct" from God. It is at least as distinct from and related to God as forms. If it is "absolutely distinct," then Thomas has subtly reinscribed the eternity of matter within Christian theology in a way which does away with creation *ex nihilo* and contradicts some of his most central arguments about the nature of creation in relation to God. This is not consistent with the more general direction of Thomas's theology. Prime matter cannot be "absolutely distinct" from God, for it is created by God and participates in the divine being along with its forms. At the very least, if it is "most absurd" to equate God with prime matter, it is surely no less absurd to equate God with form?

48. Ibid., 33.
49. The relevant discussion here is in Aquinas, *ST* I, 3.
50. Aquinas, *ST* I, 3, 8.
51. Ibid.

Meister Eckhart said that we must pray God to free us from God. Without dissolving theological revelation into psychoanalytic theory, I believe that Lacan can free us from Thomas's Aristotelian God of a pagan order of law and knowledge, in order to let Thomas's God become the God of incarnate Christian desire. In order to do this, we must liberate Thomas's theology from its own docetic tendencies, in order to bring onto the scene the fleshy, bloody matter of the God who was born, crucified and bodily resurrected in Jesus Christ, in such a way that all human flesh was divinized. Thomas himself provides the resources for this liberation of God into the body and of matter into God.

I See a Little Silhouetto of a Man

In Part III of the *Summa theologiae*, Thomas addresses the question of the incarnation and resurrection. The incarnation is a union of two natures in the one person of Christ, but it is, insists Thomas, a real union of body and soul:

> It belongs essentially to the human species that the soul be united to the body, for the form does not constitute the species, except inasmuch as it becomes the act of matter, and this is the terminus of generation through which nature intends the species. Hence it must be said that in Christ the soul was united to the body; and the contrary is heretical, since it destroys the truth of Christ's humanity.[52]

Later, in the discussion of Christ's resurrection,[53] Thomas insists that Christ is really risen corporeally in his glorified flesh, so that he is risen in the same uncorrupted flesh and blood that he assumed on his conception: "All the blood which flowed from Christ's body, belonging as it does to the integrity of human nature, rose again with His body."[54] Quoting Damascene (*De Fide Orth.* iv), Thomas says that "the son of God existing before ages, as God and consubstantial with the Father, sits in His conglorified flesh; for, under one adoration the one hypostasis, together with his flesh, is adored by every creature."[55]

In the person of Christ, there is matter in God—there is no other possible conclusion in the context of Thomas's theological orthodoxy. To say

52. Aquinas, *ST* III, 2, 5.
53. Aquinas, *ST* III, 54.
54. Aquinas, *ST* III, 54, 3.
55. Aquinas, *ST* III, 5, 8, 3.

otherwise is to make the docetist claim that Christ only appeared to be a human body—he was an avatar of the divine, not God incarnate.

Christianity seeks refuge in the myths of philosophy and romance to hide from itself what it knows to be true—that there is no sexual relationship. Yet it also embodies the truth within its forgotten relationship to the body and God as the Other of the philosophical One, and (according to Lacan) it is the task of psychoanalysis to rediscover that truth and relocate it where it belongs—within the human soul. This means recognizing that "what makes up for the sexual relationship is, quite precisely, love."[56] I want to conclude this essay by asking what Lacan means by this love that exceeds and renders redundant the sexual relationship.

So You Think You Can Love Me and Leave Me to Die?

To the acknowledged consternation of his audiences—those who belong within the "pure philosophical tradition"[57]—Lacan reintroduces the question of God into the relationship between man and woman, "this God of whom I said that he has dominated every philosophical debate about love."[58] This is, Lacan claims, a way of "exorcising" the "good Old God" by way of showing in what sense this God exists.[59]

Let me turn briefly to Lacan's discussion of the transference in *Seminar XI*. Here, he suggests that the analyst must accompany the analysand through and beyond the transference which projects onto the other the narcissistic demand of and for an all-sustaining love, to a renunciation of the object. Only by accepting lack through a recognition of the limits of desire and its capacity for gratification does love become possible: "Love . . . can be posited only in that beyond, where, at first, it renounces its object."[60] This entails acceptance of the necessary act of separation, acceptance of lack as the condition by way of which love might mediate between desire and the drive:

> Any shelter in which may be established a viable, temperate re-
> lation of one sex to the other necessitates the intervention . . . of

56. Lacan, *SXX*, 59 (45).

57. Ibid., 88 (68).

58. Ibid.

59. Ibid., 89 (68).

60. Jacques Lacan, *The Four Fundamental Concepts of Psychoanalysis: The Seminar of Jacques Lacan, Book XI*, trans. Alan Sheridan (New York: Norton, 1981) 276.

that medium known as the paternal metaphor. The analyst's desire is not a pure desire. It is a desire to obtain absolute difference, a desire which intervenes when, confronted with the primary signifier, the subject is, for the first time, in a position to subject himself to it. There only may the signification of a limitless love emerge, because it is outside the limits of the law, where alone it may live.[61]

In *Seminar XX*, Lacan recognizes that this description of love is too conformist. It conforms the desire of the hysteric to the symbolic order. The "paternal metaphor" remains in place, and the analysand is reconciled to the lack that it represents. It retains its universality, and makes of her the symptom as the excluded other. The One of form prevails in the symbolic, and the inchoate desire of the other retains its subordinated position.

Lacan introduces a more radical possibility when he makes the symbolic itself a symptom, for this drains it of its overarching power—its formative power over desire. In *Seminar XX*, the phallus loses its mastery and becomes a symptom among symptoms. The mystic/hysteric is interpreted in the context of an Other that violates the phallic prohibition, not in terms of a transgressive and ultimately futile desire for the all to which the phallus forbids access, but in terms of a *jouissance* that delights in the impossibility of the Other, that makes absolute lack the site of an ecstasy of joy and suffering that knows neither prohibition nor expectation.

Lacan refers to Kierkegaard who, beyond reason and resignation, cuts himself off from love in the paradoxical conviction that only thereby will he gain access to it. In Marcus Pound's interpretation, "Kierkegaard's God is not invoked as a neurotic defence against difference, but is instead the very principle of difference. . . . [T]he embrace of law need not be construed as a resignation to lack, but the very opposite: we are entertained by the plenitude of God's difference."[62]

Lacan relates this to what he sees as the orgasmic quality of female mysticism, in which the experience of joy is not conditional upon knowledge of its object but, on the contrary, derives its intensity from the impossibility of knowing its object. Nineteenth-century attempts to interpret this in terms of sexuality miss the point (and so does Lacan, when he interprets Bernini's statue of St. Teresa of Avila in terms of sexual orgasm).[63] The mystic's delight flows from the radical otherness and difference of God, not from any pro-

---

61. Ibid.

62. Marcus Pound, *Theology, Psychoanalysis and Trauma* (London: SCM, 2007) 85.

63. For more on this, see Hollywood's critique of Lacan's interpretation of medieval mysticism in *Sensible Ecstasy*.

jection into that relationship of sexual otherness and desire. Although shot through with eroticism, mystical language expresses a surplus *jouissance* that cannot be reduced to the sexual relationship. The linguistic location of woman marks a position of supplementarity—of excess—rather than of complementarity—of completion—in relation to that of man.

I'm Easy Come, Easy Go

The difference constituted by Christianity's God as Other is altogether other than the difference between form and matter that constitutes the philosophical account of being. It is a difference so radical that it is, we could say, full to the brim of the joy of being empty, for it is only in the utter abandonment of knowledge that the body is capable of experiencing the Other. Yet because this is obscene from the perspectives of both reason and romance, Christianity too falls prey to the fictions of philosophy and the sexual romance. It reintroduces God as "the third party in this business of human love," and by way of what Lacan refers to as Saint Thomas's "physical theory of love," it adopts the Aristotelian idea that the Supreme Good— God's *jouissance*—is somehow related to the human good: "The first being we have a sense of is clearly our being, and everything that is for the good of our being must, by dint of this very fact, be the Supreme Being's jouissance, that is, God's. To put it plainly, by loving God, we love ourselves, and by first loving ourselves—'well-ordered charity,' as it is put—we pay the appropriate homage to God."[64]

This, suggests Lacan, constitutes a confusion between love and knowledge. The love of God becomes confused with philosophical accounts of knowledge, in a way that inevitably diminishes its radical otherness and domesticates it within the copulative relationships of form and matter, male and female.

This philosophical shift that confuses the absolute alterity of God with the continuum of philosophical being also interrupts Christianity's ties to the God of the Jewish tradition. To rediscover the Other of God— the Other of mystical/hysterical *jouissance*—the God of Exodus must be posited as a contradiction or an exception to the Aristotelian concept of being, not as the greatest and most sublime expression of that being. Lacan suggests that, if this can be approached from an Aristotelian perspective, it might be by way of Aristotle's obscure concept of *enstasis*—the obstacle or exception by way of which the universality of the symbolic is shown to be false. There is an exception that uses language to say that it cannot

64. Lacan, *SXX*, 91 (70–71).

be spoken of, and this exposes the failure of language to encompass the totality of being. To explore this further, let me turn to an essay in which Slavoj Žižek discusses *Seminar XX*.

Žižek suggests that, in opening up questions of otherness and desire from the perspective of woman, Lacan's interpretation of the Christian God might be interpreted as "the very passage from Judaism to Christianity" which "ultimately obeys the matrix of the passage from the 'masculine' to the 'feminine' formulas of sexuation."[65] He refers to Lacan's engagement with the Pauline dialectic of transgression and the Law in *Seminar VII*, and he suggests that *Seminar XX* can be read in the context of Saint Paul's passage on love in 1 Corinthians 13. According to Žižek, this constitutes the feminized corollary to the dialectic between law and transgression—a dialectic that is "clearly 'masculine' or phallic: it involves the tension between the All (the universal Law) and its constitutive exception. Love, on the other hand, is 'feminine': it involves the paradoxes of the non-All."[66] Here is the famous passage from Corinthians to which Žižek refers, as quoted by him:

> If I speak in the tongues of mortals and of angels, but do not have love, I am a noisy gong or a clanging cymbal. And if I have prophetic powers, and understand all mysteries and all knowledge, and if I have all faith, so as to remove mountains, but do not have love, I am nothing. If I give away all my possessions, and if I hand over my body so that I may boast [alternative translation: "may be burned"], but do not have love, I gain nothing. . . .
>
> Love never ends. But as for prophecies, they will come to an end; as for tongues, they will cease; as for knowledge, it will come to an end. For we know only in part, and we prophesy only in part; but when the complete comes, the partial will come to an end. . . . For now we see in a mirror, dimly, but then we will see face to face. Now I know only in part; then I will know fully, even as I have been fully known. And now faith, hope, and love abide, these three; and the greatest of these is love.

Love here is paradoxically the only eternally enduring condition of the fullness of knowing, but it is also a condition of the partiality of knowledge. The limitation of knowledge is the necessary condition within which we experience the abiding reality of love. As not-all, we discover what love is, for it shows us that even the totality of knowledge is nothing compared to what truly is. Between love and knowledge there is an unbridgeable gap. The

---

65 Slavoj Žižek, "The Real of Sexual Difference," in *Reading Seminar XX: Lacan's Major Work on Love, Knowledge, and Feminine Sexuality*, ed. Suzanne Barnard and Bruce Fink (Albany: State University of New York Press, 2002) 57–76, 59.

66. Ibid., 61.

order of knowledge—the complete knowledge of everything that adds up to One that is the quest of philosophy and science—is altogether different from the fullness of being known and being loved within which I become not One but an ecstatic Nothing. To quote Žižek again,

> the point of the claim that even if I were to possess all knowledge, without love, I would be nothing, is not simply that with love, I am "something." For in love, I also am a nothing, but as it were a Nothing humbly aware of itself, a Nothing paradoxically made rich through the very awareness of its lack. Only a lacking, vulnerable being is capable of love: the ultimate mystery of love is therefore that incompleteness is in a way higher than completion.[67]

This is the context in which mystical *jouissance* finds its voice, in Catherine of Siena's ecstatic cry that "I am she who is not"[68] and her bold claim that she herself has become Christ, for he makes of her another himself.

Oh Mama Mia

Yet Lacan is wrong about the body that Christianity introduces into God, for he equates it with the baroque.[69] Here, he sees evidence of Christianity's sublime non-copulative carnality, but these baroque bodies come too late to express the *jouissance* of the incarnate Christ, whom Luce Irigaray describes as "the fragile little brother of the god of Greek desire."[70] Christ was not a Greek god, and those muscular baroque bodies do not celebrate the incarnation but mask its vulnerability and pathos behind the same pagan masks that Aristotle provided to Thomas. Moreover, as Irigaray suggests in her mimetic feminine critique of Lacan, his Christ remains primarily associated with sacrifice and death, so that there is no sense of the maternal body and the joy of fecundity and birth in his representation of the incarnation.[71] Lacan's Christ suffers and dies, but it is far less clear that he is also born of a woman's body and nurtured at a woman's breasts.

· 67. Ibid.

68. Catherine of Siena, *The Dialogue*, trans. Suzanne Noffke (New York: Paulist, 1980) 273.

69. Lacan, *SXX*, 105 (116).

70. Luce Irigaray, *Marine Lover of Friedrich Nietzsche*, trans. Gillian C. Gill (New York: Columbia University Press, 1991) 184.

71. See Tina Beattie, *God's Mother, Eve's Advocate: A Marian Narrative of Women's Salvation* (London: Continuum, 2002).

Virgo Lactans

If we want to see the incarnate *jouissance* of Christianity's non-copulative God, we must look to the smiles and tears of the Virgin Mother of God, for she wears the face of our ecstasy and anguish. In her we see the sublime obscenity of the fleshy embrace of God from which the man who believes himself to be made in the image of the Greek God turns his face in disgust.

Lacan opens up a strange path that theology might follow, without following him all the way. In the end, Lacan ventriloquizes the Catholic faith that he never quite managed to escape from or surrender to. He projects it into the body of the mystic and the hysteric, and therefore keeps his own body insulated against its sacramental practices and its lush bodily demands.

Roettgen Pieta

Will You Do the Fandango?

Yet Lacan can help theology to discover a path out of the disciplinary ghetto to which secularism has consigned it and away from the Aristotelian nostalgia that infects a growing number of Catholic theologians today. If we are to rediscover the bodies that theology has abandoned along the way—including the body of its incarnate God—theologians need to become bohemians among the disciplines. What does it matter if we find ourselves homeless, if we discover that we have no place to lay our heads among the sacred groves of academe?

We need to queer the straight and narrow path, and become the gay queens of an ancient science. We must park our gypsy caravans in the fields of history's green and pleasant lands, where we are unwelcome intruders. We must splice our voices into the secularized discourses of film studies, and daub our graffiti in the godless galleries of history of art. We must become anarchists in the study of the law and bodies of resistant visceral diversity confounding the social sciences. We must even venture into the deconsecrated soul of Lacanian psychoanalysis, and fill its unspeakable abyss with the unsayable plenitude of the incarnate God, so that it becomes brimful with the joy of the emptiness of its own being. All this we must do, to show that nothing really matters. For if nothing really matters, then everything really matters—even, and especially, God.

3

Subjectification, Salvation, and the Real in Luther and Lacan[1]

Carl Raschke

I AM HONORED TO be invited to give a presentation at this important work-shop which links the thought of the German theologian Martin Luther, the burning brand that ignited the Protestant Reformation of the sixteenth century, and the French psychoanalyst/philosopher Jacques Lacan, that smoldering bed of embers from which flamed the intellectual revolution of the late twentieth century we now know as "postmodernism," and to which I myself in a book published not quite a decade ago referred as "the next Reformation." While the connection between Luther and Lacan was not obvious to me before I was invited to participate in this workshop, on months of reflection and actual writing I have now come to the conclusion that Prof. Westerink's idea for a topic is amazingly prescient, to say the least.

I will not bore you in this presentation with a lot of technical analysis and exploration of what Lacan meant, or what people believe he meant, with his many operative terms and turns of phrase with which many of, at least in the academic world, are now quite familiar. Nor will I spend too much time on the particulars and historical situatedness of Luther's theo-logical sayings and writings. I have to confess that at one time in graduate school I had fantasies about becoming a Reformation scholar with special attention to Luther, not only because I was baptized as a baby in a German Lutheran church in Philadelphia attended by my great aunt, the last living

1. Paper presented at an international workshop on Luther and Lacan at the University of Vienna, Vienna, Austria, 11 November 2011.

58

descendant of the generation that emigrated to the United States in the 1870s. But because as a uniquely American *indignado*—the term currently in fashion in Europe for protesters—in the 1960s, I devoured the writings of Luther and identified with his personality and his cause. We all know that Luther did not really write "theology" in the sense that the term is used in the academic context today. What he did was defend a stance that came to be known in Latin as *sola fide*, "by faith alone," and undertook this defense through the development of a "theological language," or a *facon parler*, that spoke decisively from the standpoint of faith and embodies the voice of the faithful believer, who responds to the "word of faith" we know as Scripture. Faith was what Lacan would call Luther's "place" from which his speech (*parole*) begins. Likewise, Lacan was not a psychoanalyst in the professional sense any more than Luther was a theologian. His "place" was what could be summed up as the truth of "becoming a subject," not exactly in the way Kierkegaard meant it, but close enough.

But my task here is not to compare Luther and Lacan overall as towering intellectual figures that rightfully have a place now in our own Western legacy. I want to concentrate on what is common among these two giants, but at the same time unique within the "tradition," as we call it. And what is common is the way in which they both challenge our habit of talking about God, which common religious believers and professional theologians routinely do, rather than our understanding "God" not so much as a noun, but as a form of address, an address to "the Other."

One of the cardinal elements of both Lutheran and what is broadly called "Reformation Theology" is the doctrine of *pro me*, namely, that the Incarnation of God in Christ expresses not God's aseity but his *essentially* relational character. This relational nature of God is expressed in the very Hebraic representation of humanity itself. God created us "in his image," and the image itself is ultimately relational. Like *theos*, *anthropos* is ontologically constituted as a relationship, an intimate relationship between the sexes which expresses their intimate relationship to God. "And man created human beings in the image of God; male and female he created them." As Karl Barth famously observed, the phrase *imago Dei* signifies an *analogia relationalis* rather than an *analogia entis*.[2] For Luther, however, the intimacy of the God-humanity relationship—not to mention the intimacy of the man-woman relationship—is compromised by sinfulness. Following Paul in Romans, Luther stresses how the relationship is exacerbated by the seemingly insurpassable distance between a Holy God and an unrighteous subject revealed through the Law. It is only the Gospel, disclosing dialectically

---

2. Karl Barth, *Church Dogmatics*, III.2 (New York: T. & T. Clark, 1958) 323–24.

that Christ died for us on the cross rather than allowing us to be annihilated in the presence of God on account of sin, that allows us to experience the full sense of a restored primordial relationship. In other words, Christ *as* God did not "die" in himself, but singularly "for me," in order to re-establish my participation in the ontological relationship that is humanity as *imago Dei*. Both the Christian God and the Christian idea of the essential nature of humanity is predicated on a "subject-object split" presenting us with a profound dialectical dilemma. In Continental philosophy we term such a dilemma an *aporia*, an "undecidable." This aporia amounts to what John Calvin called the "incapacity" (*non capax*) of the finite for the infinite. As Luther essentially argues in his *Commentary on Galatian* (while) again citing Paul, the Pharasaic way beyond this aporia is to privilege the language of the infinite, the revelation of the Law that articulates "righteousness" in terms of an impossible canon of measure. But the language of the gospel affirms that the dialectic of the possible and impossible has now been resolved in Christ's death and satisfaction for sin.

What is the "Gospel" (*Evangelium* in German, *evangelion* in Greek), according to Luther? The tendency of Luther's theological interpreters has been to reify it. Furthermore, this tendency itself is supported by Luther's own predilection, exceeding the original meaning in Paul's text, toward contrasting "law" and "gospel" as if they were simple semiotic , or conceptual, antitheticals. However, In the commentary Luther shows that he is attuned to the original set of significations for the word, and that he understands it as a mode of discourse concerning salvation, a form that constitutes in its syntactical intricacy a coming-to-truth of the "revelation" that we are saved by "faith alone" in the final efficacy of Christ's death on the cross. In the opening portions of the commentary Luther focuses on Paul's grounding of his own authority in the "revelation" of Christ he received on the road to Damascus and its ramifications in his concomitant "call" to serve as an apostle. Luther underscores how Paul's "call," or "appointment," by God to become the "apostle to the Gentiles" is integrally associated with the trajectory of his testimony that manifests the "truth" of the Gospel of Christ Jesus itself. "The call is not to be taken lightly. For a person to possess knowledge is not enough. He must be sure that he is properly called. Those who operate without a proper call seek no good purpose."[3] Luther compares every divine calling in Christ with this authorization of the trajectory of truth in Scripture. "We exalt our calling, not to gain glory among men, or money, or

---

3. Martin Luther, *Commentary on the Epistle to the Galatians*, e-book (Boston: MobileReference, 2009) 71.

satisfaction, or favor, but because people need to be assured that the word we speak are the words of God."[4]

Later in the commentary Luther exalts the "truth" of the Gospel over doctrine and traditions, which he compares to the Pauline reading of "law." "I too may say that before I was enlightened by the Gospel, I was as zealous for the papistical laws and traditions of the fathers as ever a man was. I tried hard to live up to every law as best I could."[5] How do we construe, then, the difference between Law and Gospel, so far as they function semantically and not as simple, familiar, Protestant theological word pairings?" The New Testament expression "false apostle" epitomizes that discourse which purports to parallel the compact, singular truth contained in Paul's original "revelation," but on consideration and methodical exposition turns out to betray its own promise. In contemporary parlance we can say that if we read both discourses "deconstructively," we end up with one that returns to the singular semantics of the Damascus road experience and the other that discloses itself as idle and empty. Luther recounts his own life as the ultimate testament to the fecklessness of the "law" of doctrine and the saving power of the gospel. "I crucified Christ daily in my cloistered life, and blasphemed God by my wrong faith. Outwardly, I kept myself chaste, poor, and obedient. I was much given to fasting, watching, praying, saying of masses, and the like. Yet under the cloak of my outward respectability I continually mistrusted, doubted, feared, hated, and blasphemed God. My righteousness was a filthy puddle."[6] As those who are familiar with Luther's life, he is referencing here his prior way of approaching the content of scripture, informed by the quasi-scholastic , exegetical procedures that derived in many respects from Aristotle's *Topics* and *Prior Analytics*. Scholastic exegesis relied on several approaches. However, the most important one was the so-called *collationes*, "talks" or "conferences" on the meaning of certain passages by a learned doctor, who took Scripture itself and explained it in light of what had been said before. The output was what Aquinas called "sacred doctrine," an enhanced version of the Biblical text with normative commentary, similar but not necessarily comparable to the formation of the Jewish Talmud.

As historians of Christian exegesis routinely note, the Schoolmen rarely distinguished between the original text and what the authorities, ancient or more recent, said about the text.[7] Indeed, the *scholia* carried equal weight

4. Ibid., 84.

5. Ibid., 433.

6. Ibid., 446.

7. See Eduard Reuss, *History of the Sacred Scriptures of the New Testament*, trans. Edward L. Houghton (Boston: Houghton, Mifflin, 1884) 2:555ff.

to the originals. Furthermore, the relevance of the text—whether original or annotated—to an individual's own personal faith concerns or struggles, as became the litmus test of later "Reformed" theology, was utterly inconsequential. Biblical texts were treated exegetically in almost in the same way as ancient, pagan philosophical texts (though regarded as having a "sacrality" the others lacked). The *scholia* were resource material for the learned *collationes*, which in turn could be integrated sometimes as commentaries themselves that clarified the content of the evolving texts. The *collationes*, of which Peter Abelard's are perhaps the most famous, often used a combination of argumentation that followed Aristotle's rules of logic and rhetoric. However, they did not seek at all to bring forth what the later Reformation tradition would designate generically as the "plain" sense of Scripture, as it could be appropriated by a believer.

Luther, in setting a new precedent for interpretation of texts based on his own experiences, turns the ancient project of Christian hermeneutics into an existential challenge. While observing the Augustinian principle of Scriptural interpretation through *inward illumination*, Luther however sets up a dualistic, or dialectical, tension between the reading of the text as either "law" and as "gospel." The transposition of the legalistic reading into an emancipatory reading of Scripture as the word of salvation, or what we might call a "salvation event," depends on whether comes to the text with a humble attitude of faith that seeks God's wisdom (*sapientia*) or through the arrogant presumption of a mainly rational understanding that can be parsed, disputed, and settled through the kind of computative inference (*scientia*) that depends on doctrinal subtlety and established authorities as well as intellectual precedents. Only when one approaches the mysteries of the text with the innocence and openness of faith can the Holy Spirit truly operate, and illumination take place. The work of the Spirit also allows for "law" to be fulfilled, although from the realization that one is already made right, or "justified," before God through faith. "The real doers of the Law are the true believers. The Holy Spirit enables them to love God and their neighbor." The "Galatians," those who turn gospel into law and law into gospel, are the same, like the curia, who "take liberties" with the meaning of Scripture. Truth lies in the realization of language as transformative of the subject. That is the fundamental implication of the statement that God can only be comprehended in his nature as the crucified Christ, as the semantic fulcrum of the gospel as *theologia crucis*, as *pro me*.

But we are concerned here not so much with the intimate particulars of a theology with which every scholar familiar with the history of Protestantism knows at some level. Our task is to give an account, as we indicated at the beginning, of how the transformations that took place in the general semantic field of seventeenth-century theological discourse as a result of the Lutheran "revelations" on the road from Rome to Wittenberg eventuated in the postmodernist revolution. And we suggested that the decoding mechanism for transposing the message from theology to secular philosophy in the postmodern era is the innovations in psychoanalysis carried through with the work of Lacan. The analogy is not perfect, but the correlations are strong enough to justify this claim. In the same way that Luther's *sola fide* served to reconfigure the very context of theological discourse by refusing the legitimacy of an exegetical strategy founded on the coherence of propositional reasoning derived from previous clarifications and commentaries, so Lacan's replaced Freud's hydraulic model of the instincts with a post-Saussurian adaptation of the *langue/parole* distinction to an analysis of the patient's discourse. Lacan's "linguistic turn" was comparable in Heidegger's "overcoming" (*Überwindung*) of the metaphysical tradition. At the same time, it heralded the kind of "theological turn" we saw in Continental—or at least French—philosophy as early as the late 1980s. In many important respects this latter-day theological turn has amounted to a "turn to the subject," recapitulating Kierkegaard's early—and shall we say Lutheran?—dictum of *truth as subjectivity* with minimal differences. Kierkegaard's rendering of truth as the sidebar of "becoming a subject" parallels Lacan's "subjectification" through a discourse to the Other stabilized through the skillful intervention of the analyst.

We cannot, and we cannot pretend to, translate Luther's dialectical theologizing directly into what we might call *Lacan-speak*. But we should observe that the critical Lutheran undecidable of law versus gospel amounts to a curious kind of Lacanian undecidable concerning whether the symbolic order, to which all theology belongs, shall be decipherable psychoanalytically as a discourse that productively results in a truthfulness which the subject acknowledges. In his *Ecrits*, especially in the long and well-known essay entitled "The Function and Field of Speech in Language and Psychoanalysis" that was originally presented as a paper in 1953 and published in 1956, Lacan treats "speech" (*parole*) in much the same manner as Luther regarded the reading of Scripture. As overdetermining symbolic frameworks, both Scripture and language—(*langue*) in the sense of what Wittgenstein had in mind with the expression *Lebensform* ("form of life")—consist in complex conditions of experience and self-understanding that must be slowly and strenuously worked out through elaboration, dialectical interposition, and the difficult interpretations of life's many twists and pitfalls. As we say in linguistics, every paradigmatics requires not merely a syntagmatics, but its own distinctive *pragmatics*. Both analysis in Lacan and a faithful dedication to the reading of the Word in Luther comprise parallels types of such a pragmatics. Both also lead not to a *scientia* that masters "structurally" and systematically the text but to an existentially grounded *sapientia* that only the "spirit" can bring forth. The significance of the word "post-structuralism," which Lacan's philosophical musings along with his psychoanalytic insights pioneered, hinges on this key distinction.

Interestingly, in the "Function of Speech" Lacan refers to his own redesign of what Freud called "the talking cure" as a form of "exegesis." Just as Lutheran exegesis leads to the disclosure of the word of the text as the *Word* of assurance and salvation—the transformation of the text as law into the word as gospel—so Lacanian "exegesis" *as* analytical procedure results in the redemption of the patient from the compulsion of his or her symptoms through an emancipatory revaluation of one's own discourse as the language of truth. Lacan describes such a symptom as "the signifier of a signified that has been repressed from the subject's consciousness. A symbol written in the sand of the flesh and on the veil of Maia, it partakes of language by the semantic ambiguity . . . highlighted in its constitution."[8] But its symbolic functioning conceals "the other's discourse in the secret of its cipher [*chiffré*]." The other's discourse is coded into "hieroglyphics of hysteria, blazons of phobia, and the labyrinths of *Zwangneurose* [obsessive neurosis]," and so forth. "These are the hermetic elements," Lacan writes, "that our exegesis resolves, the equivocations that our invocations dissolves, and the artifices that our dialectic absolves, by delivering the imprisoned meaning in ways that run the gamut from revealing the palimpsest to providing the solution [*mot*] of the mystery and to pardoning speech."[9] True *parole* is "pardoning" *parole*.

It is here that we should raise a question that stalks not only any contemporary appropriation of Lacan, but also the kind of strategic comparison we are undertaking here. It is similar to Nietzsche's famous question "who speaks?" which is also the question the whole of Lacanian analysis poses consistently, if only at times indirectly. The question of "who speaks?" embeds the problem of the production of truth in discourse, because if all unconscious discourse, as Lacan asserts, is the other's discourse, then the aim of analysis—or "exegesis"—is to reconstitute speech as the *discourse of the subject*, and thereby as "true" discourse. But at the same time this transition to true discourse demands that one pose the further question "who pardons?" In the Lacanian venue the pardoning becomes evident through the unfolding, emancipatory discovery of the subject who speaks his way to the site we might designate as "truthfulness." Speech liberates for Lacan, because it relativizes the pseudo-objectivity of language along with the "law

8. Jacques Lacan, *Écrits*, trans. Bruce Fink (New York: Norton, 2006) 280.
9. Ibid., 281.

of the father," while nurturing a space for *one's own speech* to construct its own rules and protocols, a kind of "grammar of authenticity". In the Lacanian framework we have too the passage from the hypnotic power of the symbolic order and its various imaginary codings to the recognition of the perdurance and presence of the Real. The words of the Big Other are "deconstructed" and "disseminated" (as Derrida would say) as the heterogeneous, but self-authenticating, genuine words of "true speech."

In Luther—and generally in Reformation praxis—everything of this order seems perhaps more obvious, though that sense of self-evidence may be more of a mirage than we care to admit. Our first response would be, "well, in theology God pardons." Not exactly. Luther's struggle with a "holy and righteous" God who could only condemn us to eternal suffering because of our sin is the fulcrum of the same kind of "dialectic" Lacan outlines. Ironically, this same kind of dialectic is endlessly repeated every Sunday morning in evangelical Christian churches around the world. For Luther, however, it is not God so much as it is "Gospel" *that pardons.* Allow me to make this point by constructing a kind of Lacanian quasi-algebraic, notational function for illustration. The following chain of substitutions among signifiers—the type of device which Lacan repeatedly employs to amplify his dictum that *parole* is primarily metonymy rather than synonymy and which corresponds not just to the Lutheran formula as well as to the core "evangelical" message—is as follows: $f(S) \approx$ God $\rightarrow$ Gospel $\rightarrow$ Death on Cross $\rightarrow$ Christ $\rightarrow$ Justification $\rightarrow$ Assurance of Salvation, where S equals "salvation." Note that "gospel" comes second in the metonymic chain and Christ "as" God comes fourth. Although from a theological standpoint the order would normally be reversed, Luther himself is quite explicit. It is the reading of the Gospel—and the transformation of the inner person through a recognition that we are "justified" *sola fide* despite our inherent sinfulness—that activates our salvation. Christ has already "accomplished" this work through his sacrifice on the Cross—that is, from the standpoint of both history and eternity is already done, *telestai.* But it is only when we become cognizant of this eternal deed through the reading of Scripture and the illumination of the Holy Spirit as to its essential import and significance that we can say confidently that "justification" in its thoroughly personal and inward sense has taken place.

Thus it is the *language* of the Gospel, not the Gospel as *res ipsa,* that provides us with the theological, if not the philosophical, index to the event of salvation. In Luther's theology of the Word, summarized in the Reformation doctrine of *sola Scriptura* as the semiotic equivalent for a *theologia crucis,* we have both a *prototype* and a *precursor* for the Lacanian reinvention of Freud's "talking cure" through the struggle of language toward speech, of discourse in the direction of *truth*. Subjectification and truth-telling are intimately associated with each other in Lacan. Similarly, in Luther the appropriation of the justifying, and thereby "saving," text of Scripture—the transmutation of Scriptural and theological *langue* into its therapeutic counterpart as *parole*—becomes the basis for an event of subjective appropriation that corresponds to Lacan's "advent of true speech."

As Lacan writes, "the function of language in speech is not to inform but to evoke." Furthermore, "what I seek in speech is a response from the other."[10] Luther's biography, especially during the years 1513–1517, demonstrated strongly this Lacanian precept. His overzealousness in utilizing the monastic confessional and penitential system in order to secure a minimal security that might somehow equilibrate God's "righteousness" with his own led to a personal spiritual crisis that would not only turn his own life upside down but European history as well as thought. For Luther, the abysmal gap between God's unmeasurable holiness and his own sinful human nature—what would later be encapsulated in the Reformation principle of *finitus non capax infiniti*—stamped on to his own sense of self what Hegel would call the "unhappy consciousness," the inherent inability to reconcile the balance the equation psychologically as well as theologically.[11]

10. Ibid., 299.

11. Luther's well-known dilemma is, of course, the same as Paul's dilemma, and Paul's dilemma ultimately, Lacan suggests, serves as a template for modern epistemology starting with Kant. Lacan develops this argument, albeit in his typically allusive vein, in the section of the seminar he calls "On the Moral Law" conducted from 1959–60. That seminar has come to be characterized as an exploration of his "ethics" so far as psychoanalysis is concerned. However, Lacan's ethics turns out to be more Levinasian than Kantian, insofar as it turns on the question not simply of the kind of "representation" (*Vorstellung*) that can be considered valid as an object of pure reason, but the kind of representation that arises when my desire is confronted with the desire of the Other. Lacan calls this object *das Ding* ("The Thing"), which has not so adventitious resonances with Kant's *Ding an sich*. *Das Ding* has a certain conjugal connection with Lacan's *objet petit a*. Briefly stated, the latter can be described as the fantastical (albeit arbitrary) source of desire, the former as the representational locus for all the operations of the symbolic in constructing an imaginary space in perception where the desire of the I (Freud's *Ich-Lust*) and the desire of the Other can somehow be seen to converge. *Das Ding*, therefore, performs what we might term a "salvific" operation in the conflict of the pleasure and reality principles. It performs the role of "assurance" (Lacan employs the German term *Sicherung*), as the Gospel does for Luther. "It is not just a matter of drawing close to das Ding, but also to its effects, to its presence at the core of human activity, namely, in that precarious existence in the midst of the forest of desires and compromises that these very desires achieve with a certain reality, which is certainly not as confused as one might imagine." Jacques Lacan, *The Seminar of Jacques Lacan, VII*, ed. Jacques-Alain Miller, trans. Dennis Porter (New York: Norton, 1997) 105.

In the same way, Lacan views the question of *das Ding* as one that arises, as it does for Luther, out of the Pauline paradox of the law and sin. The law that is meant to

This inherent "imbalance" in Luther's own theological rhetoric, buttressed as biographers have repeatedly pointed out by a combination of his peasant mannerisms and personality and his private revolt against the excesses of the church in its late medieval efforts to inflame the religious imagination with the threat of hell. Luther was also upset at the way in which church had carefully constructed an absurd "economy" of penance through the doctrine of indulgences. Luther's meticulous reading of the letters of the apostle Paul, therefore, is more than an historical eccentricity. It is pure grist for psychoanalysis.

The pre-eminence among twentieth-century Luther biographies of *Young Man Luther* by the neo-Freudian Harvard clinician Erik Erikson in the late 1950s testifies to this fact. Erikson first published the book in 1958, about the same time Lacan was transitioning from his many early academic essays collected in the Écrits to the famous "seminars" that would foster a whole generation of French "post-structuralists" that, in turn, would launch the "postmodernist" revolution in philosophy. Its complete lack of the Lacanian sensibility concerning the role of language in psychoanalysis and its

---

save creates consciousness of sin. For Lacan explicitly, and for Luther implicitly, it is a question of language. Both "solutions" to the problem revolve around the fact that law (Greek=*nomos*) depends on the *nomothetic* function of language as a system of discursive codings, codings that do not belong within the subjective matrix of desire and its struggle for representation, codings that are *nicht-Ich*, that "condemn," especially in the negative form that are the Ten Commandments. This "condemnation" of desire through the enforcement of linguistic—and by extension moral—codes forces desire to be "repressed," that is, as the more precise meaning of Freud's term *Verdrängni*s implies, to be dislocated, to be partially hidden, to be unable to be enunciated by the subject. In other words, language and lying (just as legalism and hypocrisy) go hand in glove. "The point is that speech doesn't itself know what it is saying, when it lies, and that, on the other hand, in lying it also speaks some truth" (ibid., 82). For both Luther and Lacan, it is the impossibility of reconciling the representations of desire (what Lacan riffing on Freud calls *Vorstellungsrepräsentanz*) with the "universalizing" requirements of discourse. Hence, the inevitability of the "law" revealing sin, which Lacan in the same section identifies with *das Ding*, which in effect is the "emptiness" of all moral significations of desire. That is why Lacan concludes the opening discussion of *das Ding* with the following observation: "Whatever some may think in certain milieu, you would be wrong to think that the religious authors aren't a good read. I have always been rewarded whenever I have immersed myself in their works. And Saint Paul's Epistle is a work that I recommend to you for your vacation reading" (ibid., 83).

For Luther, the Pauline "aporia" vanishes when the "language" that "speaks" is my own (Luther=*meine eigene*), when it becomes the redemptive speech of the Gospel that is now within my own "conscience." It becomes the liberating act of a "sinner" who is not only *peccator* as in a former time, but now a "new person" as *iustus*. For Lacan, the "partial" truth of the speech that is caught up in the lie of the language of the law is emancipated as well through the *Sprachkur*, as a fully enunciating subject. That is why Lacan describes the trajectory that traces the intimate intertwinings of language and desire as "rediscovering the relationship to *das Ding*" as "somewhere beyond the law" (ibid., 84).

focus on a direct psychobiography that simply imposes the classic Freudian topology of id, ego, and superego—or the developmental model of oral, anal, and genital stages—on the life of Luther renders it now intellectually outdated. Yet it is the book's profound contextualization of Luther within the general history of ideas that makes it exceptionally relevant here.

Early in the biography Erikson focuses on the manner in which Ockhamist nominalism played a truly formative role in the shaping of Luther's later philosophical, not to mention his theological, outlook. "Ockham had taught," writes Erikson, "that concepts are only symbols of things and exist only in the act of giving meaning, *in significando*" (that is, in the "act of signifying").[12] Furthermore, according to Erikson, Luther employed this thoroughly anti-Aristotelian and anti-metaphysical theory of signification in undertaking what today we would term the "deconstruction" of the broad Medieval "text" of the salvation process. The result was that Luther himself transitioned from the inherent late Medieval theological habit of reifying God's infinite "justice" as one who wreaks "horrible and accusatory wrath, with man prostrate in his sight," to a Deity who "imputes" his own righteousness to the simple believer reading Scripture and responding in faith. In the "word" that evokes faith, Erikson says, the believer encounters God "face to face, recognizing Him as He would be recognized" and "learning to speak to Him directly."[13] Here we have the Lacanian characterization without Lacan of the psychoanalytical transaction that lifts language from its pure formality, or status as *langue*, to the spoken response of the subject as one's own "truth," the personal sense of actuality that suddenly emerges from the intersubjective process, which Lacan himself employs as a paradigm of intervention and transference. "The speech value of a language is gauged by the intersubjectivity of the 'we' it takes on."[14]

Here, therefore, the ultimate question of the relationship between Luther and Lacan comes to the fore. Both the Lacanian "we" and the Lutheran *testamentum* are marked by the Reformation sign of the *non capax*. The dissymmetrical relationship between discourse and the "other," who also possesses discourse, is made even more extreme by the fact that the speech *de l'autre* constitutes the speech of God, the self-revealer of the divine *logos*, the infinitely productive source of all signification against which "my speech" always measures itself. But it must also inevitably measure itself not only in terms of "distance," but also in terms of *difference*. So if the "subject" of faith

---

12. Erik Erikson, *Young Man Luther: A Study in Psychoanalysis and History* (New York: Norton, 1958) 89.

13. Ibid., 165.

14. Lacan, *Écrits*, 299.

in the Lutheran language world can arrive at its own truth—its *angeeignete Wahrheit*—through speech, it must also "appropriate"—as Kierkegaard would say—God's self-revelation. What significance does this transaction therefore confer on the infinite Signifier "God"? Luther's God is both *Deus revelatus* and *Deus absconditus*. In Lutheran terms we might say that God is both the God whose speech becomes "my speech" , that is when he is "revealed" to me because he is always God *für mich* as a subject, and the God who remains "hidden" to me because his signifying capacity outstrips both the finite givenness of the language, or languages, I speak, and the limits of my performance within that language. God is always a cipher for the impossible Pentecost moment. However, for Luther, salvation does not require Pentecost. Salvation only requires that I learn to speak as "my truth" his revealed truth.

In Lacanian psychoanalysis the Lutheran faith-function of standing ready and willing to appropriate God's truth as my truth corresponds to the *desire-causing function* of the symbolic form that evokes my willingness to talk and eventually arrive at what is "my own." This desire-causing "object," always framed within a signifying or symbolized structure of desire itself Lacan refers to as the *objet petit a*. I will not take time here to explore all the vicissitudes of Lacan's discussion of the meaning of the *objet petit a*, which he refused to specify as a concept, only to formalize as what he termed a pure "algebraic sign" that inscribes a kind of semiotic operation within the movement of subjectification itself. But if there is anything we can say about the *objet petit a*, or "object little a" where a stands for both *autre* in French and *ander* in German, is that it is the most streamlined or most mobile of all Lacanian "sliding signifiers." In "desiring God" we desire all the shifting and confusing "abductive" (C.S. Peirce's term) *differentia* within the semiotic structure of how we articulate the desire for salvation. We are reminded of Augustine's question of what we desire when desire God. To put the matter less philosophically as well as psychoanalytically, and perhaps more "theologically," we can thus say that God is the ultimate *objet petit a*. God can never be "object Big A" because the pure *jouissance*—in Lacan's phrasing—of "becoming God" is impossible. We can never have such a God, even if we desire such a God.

Henceforth, all our theological musings and reflections, from Paul to the present, in some ways constitute one extended, two-thousand-year Lacanian session, or seminar. I am not trying to be flippant in this context. If there is anything we can really say about the theological enterprise, especially after Luther, is that it is not about "speaking the truth" but "speaking *our* truth." That truth is spoken as the assurance of our salvation, which the Holy Spirit illuminates in our souls as both the general and *singular truth of*

Scripture. We tend to believe theology is about language, but is really about speech. That is what we learned from Luther. We can learn much better how to concretize as well as "deconstruct" the entire text of that truthfulness by finally comprehending why truth must always be *said*, not demonstrated. It is not mere happenstance that Lacan regarded himself as an admirer of Heidegger. But that alone is another topic to take up some day. Suffice it to say at this point that we must study Lacan, psychoanalysis, linguistics, and of course post-structuralist explorations of the way in which the sign itself signifies, in order to better comprehend how, as Heidegger says, *die Sprache spricht* ("language speaks").

4

Lacan avec le Bouddha

Thoughts on Psychoanalysis
and Buddhism

Mario D'Amato

In Hegel's conception, the fundamental aim of religion is relating oneself to the divine, to the infinite. But while for Hegel this relation to the infinite may be understood as a process of unfolding or disclosing what is already there,[1] for psychoanalysis things are different: there is, rather, a gradual unfolding or disclosing of what is precisely *not* there—namely, the subject. And so we may be led to consider Buddhism, the religion of "no self" (*anātman*), wherein the purported self is interpreted as a sign without a referent. Returning to Hegel, in his philosophical analysis of Buddhism, he points out that the conception of the divine in Buddhism is also negative, and that the goal of Buddhism "consists in uniting oneself, by this negation, with nothingness, and so with God, with the absolute."[2] But insofar as Buddhism is considered to be a *religion* (and Hegel certainly considers it so), how is it possible for there to be a relation to the infinite, when there are no relata? Reflecting on this question may then lead us to reflect on language, and the role of language in Buddhism. I would suggest that the most interesting points of connection between Buddhism and

1. Hegel states: "In all higher religions, but particularly in the Christian religion, God is the one and absolute substance; but at the same time God is also subject, and that is something more." G. W. F. Hegel, *Lectures on the Philosophy of Religion: The Lectures of 1827*, ed. Peter C. Hodgson, trans. R. F. Brown, P. C. Hodgson, and J. M. Stewart (Berkeley: University of California Press, 1988) 263.

2. Ibid., 254.

Lacanian psychoanalytic theory are in the domain of theorizing language. In this essay, I will attempt to elucidate some of these points. But first it may be helpful to situate our thoughts in relation to some of the broader connections between Buddhism and psychoanalysis.

Interactions between Buddhism and Psychoanalysis: A Brief Overview

While Freud himself did not conduct any researches on Buddhism, other psychoanalysts did investigate Buddhism even in the 1920s and 1930s. The psychoanalyst Joseph C. Thompson (under the pseudonym "Joe Tom Sun") published an essay on "Psychology in Primitive Buddhism" in *The Psychoanalytic Review* in 1924, which is the earliest known publication examining the connections between Buddhism and psychoanalysis. Less than a decade later, Franz Alexander published a psychoanalytic study of Buddhist meditation, titled "Buddhistic Training as an Artificial Catatonia," in the same journal in 1931. Thompson's brief essay stays at the surface of things, and emphasizes (indeed, exaggerates) the "affinities between the Buddhist philosophy and Freudian psychoanalysis."[3] Alexander's essay, however, plumbs the depths of Buddhist meditation theory, specifically the system of *jhānas*— sometimes translated as states of "absorption," and considered in Buddhist theory to be a form of *samādhi*, or "concentration." In the essay, Alexander argues that the ultimate effect of Buddhist meditation is to produce "a complete psychic regression," and that "the end goal of Buddhistic absorption is an attempt at psychological and physical regression to the condition of intra-uterine life."[4] It is notable that Alexander interprets the condition of nirvana as "alibidinous," since there is no distinction between subject and object in the intrauterine state; rather, alluding to the "Nirvana principle" discussed by Freud in "Beyond the Pleasure Principle,"[5] Alexander states that Buddhist meditation "serves to free psychic processes from every tone

3. Joe Thompson, "Psychology in Primitive Buddhism," *The Psychoanalytic Review* 11 (1924) 47.

4. Franz Alexander, "Buddhistic Training as an Artificial Catatonia," *The Psychoanalytic Review* 18 (1931) 137–38.

5. "The dominating tendency of mental life, and perhaps of nervous life in general, is the effort to reduce, to keep constant or to remove internal tension due to stimuli (the 'Nirvana principle' . . .)—a tendency which finds expression in the pleasure principle; and our recognition of that fact is one of our strongest reasons for believing in the existence of death instincts." Sigmund Freud, "Beyond the Pleasure Principle," in *The Standard Edition of the Complete Psychological Works of Sigmund Freud*, ed. James Strachey (London: Hogarth, 1957–1974) 18:55–56.

of emotion, pleasurable as well as painfull."[6] It is also interesting to note that Alexander is not entirely disapproving of the techniques of Buddhism, and even goes so far as to make the following claim: "The overcoming of affective resistance and of narcissism, so that one is able to recollect instead of repeat the extension of consciousness in a regressive direction toward the past, this is the doctrine common to Freud and Buddha."[7] We will return to the topic of Buddhist meditation below.

Another important phase in the dialogue between Buddhism and psychoanalysis occurred in the 1950s, a decade which saw a surge of interest in Buddhism by psychoanalytic thinkers such as Karen Horney;[8] the famous conversation between C. G. Jung and Shin'ichi Hisamatsu, a disciple of Kitarō Nishida, founder of the Kyōto School of philosophy; and the workshop on Zen Buddhism and Psychoanalysis, held by the Department of Psychoanalysis of the Medical School of the Autonomous National University of Mexico, and attended by the Zen Buddhist scholar D. T. Suzuki and the psychoanalyst Erich Fromm.[9]

In a recent essay by Anthony Molino, "Zen, Lacan, and the Alien Ego," Molino begins by tracing out a few similarities between the thought of Lacan and the interpretation of Zen offered by Richard De Martino.[10] Molino points out that for both, "a primordial break with an undifferentiated 'natural' state is posited," and that a "split likewise inheres in the formation and function of the *ego*."[11] However, Molino goes on to state that for Lacan, "there is no room for the proposed unity of self and subject that Zen envisions," and that "Lacan's 'truth' is the Zen position turned upside down."[12] In other words, while both begin with a primordial split—a sense that the "subject's profoundest desire is to be 'One' again"[13]—Lacan does not hold that this desire for unity can finally be fulfilled. In "The Finger Pointing at the Moon: Zen Practice and the Practice of Lacanian Psychoanalysis," Raul

6. Alexander, "Buddhistic Training," 138–39.

7. Ibid., 144.

8. In fact, Karen Horney had already referred to Zen Buddhism in her work *Our Inner Conflicts* published in 1945.

9. Papers from this workshop were published under the title of *Zen Buddhism and Psychoanalysis* in 1960.

10. D. T. Suzuki, Erich Fromm, and Richard De Martino, *Zen Buddhism and Psychoanalysis* (New York: Harper & Row, 1960).

11. Anthony Molino, "Zen, Lacan, and the Alien Ego," in *The Couch and the Tree: Dialogues in Psychoanalysis and Buddhism*, ed. Anthony Molino (New York: North Point, 1998) 292–93.

12. Ibid., 297.

13. Ibid., 300.

Moncayo—himself a Lacanian-trained psychoanalyst—offers a complex analysis of various themes in Lacanian and Zen Buddhist thought. Moncayo states that both traditions "could be said to converge on the Zen formula that 'true self is no-self' or the Lacanian-informed formula that 'true subject is no ego.'"[14] Moncayo argues that he is "in favor of a marriage of the Lacanian concept of the Real with the Buddhist notion of the Real in terms of emptiness,"[15] and highlights the similarity between the "sudden perceptual realization beyond language and logic into the empty essence of reality" in Zen, and the psychoanalytic "act of autopoiesis, or *se parere*, as Lacan called it, of self-creation or self-realization."[16] Thus Moncayo is much more optimistic than Molino regarding the convergence between Buddhism and Lacanian psychoanalysis even in terms of their goals.

Lacan himself is known to have referred to Buddhism at various points in his works. While I have not made an exhaustive examination of every mention of Buddhism in Lacan's entire corpus, I will indicate all the references to Buddhism found in the Écrits. In "The Function and Field of Speech and Language in Psychoanalysis," in the context of a discussion of transference, Lacan states, "We need but consider the traditional facts—which Buddhists provide us with, although they are not the only ones—to recognize in this form of transference the characteristic error of existence, broken down by Buddhists into the following three headings: love, hate, and ignorance."[17] Later in the same essay, in discussing his analytic technique of the variable-length session ("short sessions"), he states, "And I am not the only one to have remarked that it bears a certain resemblance to the technique known as Zen, which is applied to bring about the subject's revelation in the traditional ascesis of certain Far Eastern schools."[18] In "Kant with Sade," Lacan critiques some analysts by pointing out that they "have been unable to learn from the technique they owe Freud, or from his teachings, that language has effects that are not simply utilitarian"; he then further states that for such analysts who do not properly understand Freud (the precise phrase here is "In the eyes of such puppets"!), Buddhism will incorrectly be seen as "underdeveloped."[19] Thus Lacan here draws attention to a connection between Buddhism and language. Later in the same essay, Lacan makes a passing reference to a traditional Buddhist

14. Raul Moncayo, "The Finger Pointing at the Moon: Zen Practice and the Practice of Lacanian Psychoanalysis," in *Psychoanalysis and Buddhism: An Unfolding Dialogue*, ed. Jeremy D. Safran (Boston: Wisdom, 2003) 349.

15. Ibid., 346.

16. Ibid., 349.

17. Ibid., 254.

18. Ibid., 260.

19. Jacques Lacan, Écrits, trans. Bruce Fink (New York: Norton, 2006) 655.

narrative in which the Buddha in a previous rebirth (as a bodhisattva on the way to becoming enlightened) offers his life to a tigress, to prevent her from devouring her own cubs out of hunger.[20] In the essay "The Subversion of the Subject and the Dialectic of Desire in the Freudian Unconscious," in discussing the very notion of a "state of consciousness," Lacan briefly refers to "the degrees of samādhi in Buddhism."[21] Later in the same essay, he states that one "who really wants to come to terms with this Other has open to him the path of experiencing not the Other's demand, but its will," and that one route to this is to "realize himself as an object, turning himself into the mummy of some Buddhist initiation."[22] And finally, in the essay "Science and Truth," Lacan states that Lévi-Strauss "conceives of Buddhism as a religion of the generalized subject, that is, as involving an infinitely variable stopping down of truth as cause," and that insofar as Lévi-Strauss conceives of Buddhism in this way, he inappropriately believes that "it concords with the universal reign of Marxism in society."[23] From these comments we may note that Lacan demonstrates a rather sophisticated understanding of Buddhism, and that the judgments he offers, whether explicitly or implicitly, are not easily reducible to simple "positive" or "negative" terms. Of course none of this seems surprising in any way.

Theoretical Points of Convergence

As indicated above, the earliest known publication on Buddhism and psychoanalysis points to similarities between Buddhist philosophy and psychoanalytic theory. This comparative approach has continued into the present century, and I will not attempt to summarize all of the ways in which Buddhist and psychoanalytic theorizing have been thought to converge. What I will do, however, is highlight three significant aspects of Buddhist thought, in order to convey some sense of why these two traditions have so often been presented in comparative terms. The three aspects of Buddhism I will consider are the doctrine of "no self" (*anātman*), the doctrine of the Buddhist unconscious (*ālaya-vijñāna*, lit. "store consciousness"), and the practice of meditation.

1. A central doctrine of Buddhism—indeed, *the* central doctrine of Buddhism—is that there is no eternal, unchanging self. This is the doctrine of "no self" or "absence of self" (*anātman*). According to

20. Ibid., 658.
21. Ibid., 673.
22. Ibid., 700.
23. Ibid., 742.

the Buddhist account, what is conventionally taken to be the "self" should be understood as a series of interrelated processes of momentary events comprised of the categories of form, feeling (or more precisely, stimulus-response), conceptualization, dispositions, and consciousness. The Buddhist account does not of course deny that there is a *person* in the conventional sense, but rather emphasizes that there is no underlying permanence, essence, or intrinsic nature to the conventionally posited person. According to the doctrine of *anātman*, the self is an imaginary construction (*parikalpita*) that is not ultimately real, and through attachment to the view of self (through being fixated on the self and its demands), sentient beings become mired in the cycle of conditioned existence.

Epstein emphasizes that the aim of Buddhism is not to eliminate the conventional "sense of I, which remains a necessary and useful concept," but rather to come to view this ego-sense "as a *representation*, as an image or simulacrum devoid of *inherent* existence."[24] He further points out that the self which is negated in the Buddhist doctrine of *anātman* should be understood in psychoanalytic terms as the "ideal ego," which Hanly defines as "the ego in so far as it believes itself to have been vouchsafed a state of perfection."[25] Epstein also draws a connection between the ideal ego and Lacan's notion of the "specular I," i.e., the "tendency to identify with an idealized image of the self"; rather than holding on to this idealized image, one must instead realize "the manner in which the self-concept has been constructed out of internalized images of self and other."[26] So the Buddhist doctrine of *anātman* and the psychoanalytic interpretation of the self are notable in their emphasis on the constructedness of what is often taken to be a stable and enduring self-concept. In lieu of a definitive point of reference for subjectivity, one instead finds an *effect*, an effect of various mental processes, both conscious and unconscious.

2. While the doctrine of "no self" (*anātman*) analyzes the conventional self into processes of form, feeling, conceptualizations, dispositions, and consciousness, further analyses would break consciousness itself down into six subtypes, including five forms of consciousness

24. Mark Epstein, "Beyond the Oceanic Feeling: Psychoanalytic Study of Buddhist Meditation," in *The Couch and the Tree: Dialogues in Psychoanalysis and Buddhism*, ed. Anthony Molino (New York: North Point, 1998) 125.

25. Charles Hanly, "Ego Ideal and Ideal Ego," *International Journal of Psychoanalysis* 65 (1984) 253.

26. Epstein, "Beyond the Oceanic Feeling," 125.

corresponding to the bodily senses (i.e., visual, auditory, olfactory, gustatory, and tactile consciousness) and "mental consciousness," which cognizes mental objects as well as data from the other five consciousnesses. One school of Buddhist philosophy, the Yogācāra (lit., "practice of spiritual discipline"), would then offer a further innovative analysis of the functioning of mind, through adding two underlying subliminal forms of consciousness to the standard subtypes of consciousness, viz., the "afflicted mind" (*kliṣṭa-manas*) and the "store consciousness" (*ālaya-vijñāna*). The function of the afflicted mind, according to this school of Buddhism, is to construct the delusion of an underlying self. This subliminal mental process operates as a form of unconscious ego-awareness that arises concomitantly with all other conscious processes; hence it might be understood as analogous to the unconscious dimensions of the ego, as well as the super-ego, insofar as the latter is considered to be the locus of ego-ideals. The more fundamental subliminal form of consciousness, however, is the "store consciousness" (*ālaya-vijñāna*), which is referred to as such insofar as it is considered to be a repository or "store" of mental tendencies and dispositions, both positive and negative. Furthermore, this store consciousness is understood to function as the substratum or basis of all other forms of consciousness, including the six supraliminal forms of consciousness and the subliminal ego-awareness of the afflicted mind.

The relations between the subliminal store consciousness and the six supraliminal active forms of consciousness may be explained in terms of mutually interacting process in three stages, whereby the subliminal store consciousness accumulates tendencies and dispositions as a result of previous karmic activity, conditions the functioning of the six supraliminal forms of consciousness which themselves lead to further karmic activity, and is thus in turn further perpetuated by the functioning of these six supraliminal consciousnesses. So in adding the store consciousness to the analysis of mind, the Yogācāra articulates a model of mind in which subliminal and supraliminal forms of consciousness interact with one another—a model that resonates with Freud's model of the psyche. Waldron states that according to the Yogācāra model, "the simultaneous processes of mind are best conceived, much as Freud once put it, by 'dividing them between two separate but interrelated component parts or systems' . . . —that is, into the *ālaya-vijñāna* [store consciousness] and manifest cognitive awareness—and then describing the synchronic, reciprocal relations between them."[27] Waldron also points out that the store consciousness is intended to account for "the multifarious physiological and mental structures and processes subserving emotion, perception, language, memory, and so on . . . For what the *ālaya-vijñāna* [store consciousness] effectively represents . . . is *all aspects of vijñāna* [consciousness] *excluding supraliminal cognitive processes*"[28]—in other words, the store consciousness may be aptly referred to as the "Buddhist unconscious."

3. Finally, turning to the role of meditation in Buddhism, we may point out that the discipline of meditation has been considered to be the most important form of Buddhist practice, as may be seen from the primary statement of Buddhist doctrine, viz., the four noble truths (suffering, arising, cessation, path). The fourth noble truth specifies the eightfold path leading to the cessation of suffering, and the final three limbs of this eightfold path are identified as right effort, right mindfulness, and right concentration, each of which concerns mental cultivation; in fact, Buddhist tradition groups these three limbs together under the general rubric of the practice of meditation. Fundamental to ending suffering, on the Buddhist account, is removing mental factors which contribute to the arising of suffering, and the practice of meditation is thought to be of central importance in this regard because of its efficacy in identifying negative mental factors which lead to the arising of suffering, and in breaking the hold of these negative tendencies through creating a degree of distance or detachment from them: it is one thing to be immersed in impassioned states of mind, and another to be mindfully aware of the bodily and mental processes signaling the arising, occurrence, and abatement of such states. Indeed, it might not be too far off the mark to consider the aim of certain forms of Buddhist meditation to be similar to the psychoanalytic goal of bringing unconscious processes to consciousness, at least insofar as one is to become aware of the often unconscious negative mental tendencies which give rise to suffering. Furthermore, we might also point out that a number of scholars have noted the similarity between the Buddhist practice of mindfulness and Freud's recommendation for psychoanalysts to cultivate an "evenly-suspended attention"[29] as a crucial dimension of the analytic practice of listening.[30]

27. William S. Waldron, *The Buddhist Unconscious: The Ālaya-vijñāna in the Context of Indian Buddhist Thought* (New York: Routledge Curzon, 2003) 134.

28. Ibid., 100.

29. Sigmund Freud, "Recommendations to Physicians Practicing Psycho-Analysis," *SE* 12:109–20.

30. For a review and assessment of the comparison of these techniques, see Jeffrey

There is, interestingly enough, even some support from Freud for noting a similarity between the practice of psychoanalysis and "certain mystical practices." Freud points out that such practices "may succeed in upsetting the normal relations between the different regions of the mind, so that, for instance, perception may be able to grasp happenings in the depths of the ego and in the id which were otherwise inaccessible to it."[31] And while Freud of course doubts whether mystical practices can truly disclose the ultimate nature of reality, he goes on to state, "Nevertheless it may be admitted that the therapeutic efforts of psycho-analysis have chosen a similar line of approach. Its intention is, indeed, to strengthen the ego, to make it more independent of the super-ego, to widen its field of perception and enlarge its organization, so that it can appropriate fresh portions of the id. Where id was, there shall ego be [Wo Es war, soll Ich werden]."[32] Given such a remark from the master himself, it is perhaps not surprising that so many have attempted to elucidate points of convergence between psychoanalytic theory and Buddhist philosophy.

Language

Reflecting on the role of language in Buddhism and Lacanian psychoanalysis is perhaps the most fruitful direction in which to extend the conversation between these two traditions. The points of connection between Buddhist and Lacanian theory may be seen more clearly if we consider Buddhist thought on language in semiotic terms, especially since Lacan explicitly drew from the seminal work of Ferdinand de Saussure, one of the key figures (along with Charles Sanders Peirce) in modern semiotic discourse.[33] We should begin with an understanding of how language functions according to Buddhism, and the role it plays in constructing conditioned existence. In concise terms, a Buddhist account of semiotic processes would include a three-stage process of noting the sign, recognizing the object to which the sign refers, and becoming volitionally engaged with the object; and in terms

---

B. Rubin, "Meditation and Psychoanalytic Listening," in *Psychotherapy and Buddhism: Toward an Integration* (New York: Plenum, 1966).

31. Sigmund Freud, *New Introductory Lectures on Psycho-Analysis*, SE 22:79–80.

32. Ibid., 80.

33. I have begun to develop an interpretation of Buddhist philosophy in semiotic terms in two previous papers, and in this section I will draw from those two papers in places. See Mario D'Amato, "The Semiotics of Signlessness: A Buddhist Doctrine of Signs," *Semiotica* 147.1 (2003) 185–207; Mario D'Amato, "Buddhism, Apophasis, Truth," *Journal for Cultural and Religious Theory* 9.2 (2008) 17–29.

of the Buddhist analysis of semiosis, the "task is to bring the process back to the initial point, before any 'superimpositions' have distorted the actual and initial datum."[34] According to Buddhist semiotics, there is a significant sense in which semiosis itself is systematically deceptive, further binding one to cyclic existence. This is because conditioned phenomena—phenomena that comprise "the world," including whatever we refer to as "the self"—are radically impermanent and without inherent nature or essence. Signs, on the other hand, function to posit stable entities where there are none, affixing inherent natures onto hypostatized existents. While phenomena are in flux, signs posit enduring objects. While phenomena are without essence, signs posit essential natures. Signs point to a realm of stable referents, but the purported "objects" to which they refer are always on the move. So coming to a proper understanding of semiosis, and bringing about its end or terminus through a radical transformation, is understood to be the path to liberation. This is consistent with the fact that certain strands of Buddhist thought emphasize that the fundamental cause of suffering is some form of conceptualization, conceptual discrimination (*vikalpa*), conceptual imagination (*parikalpa*), or conceptual proliferation (*prapañca*)—in short, the fundamental problem is some form of semiosis.

With this basic understanding of semiotic processes in Buddhism, we may consider the Buddhist account of different registers of meaning. The significant theory here is the three-nature (*trisvabhāva*) theory, which, like the doctrine of the "store consciousness," is specific to the Yogācāra school. According to the Yogācāra school, the three-nature theory is the key to disclosing the way things really are, or the lens through which the fundamental Buddhist doctrine of emptiness (*śūnyatā*) is properly brought into focus. As such, the three-nature doctrine should be understood as the central element of the Yogācāra path of spiritual practice. The theory is directed towards effecting a shift in one's overall perspective on reality, altering the terms in which reality is interpreted or envisioned.

The three natures are the imagined nature (*parikalpita-svabhāva*), the dependent nature (*paratantra-svabhāva*), and the perfected nature (*pariniṣpanna-svabhāva*). Briefly, the imagined nature refers to reality as it appears to ordinary, deluded sentient beings: the world seen in terms of subject-object duality, as it has been constructed through language and conceptualization; as Williams points out, the imagined nature encompasses "the falsifying activity of language . . . the realm of words which attribute

34. Edward Conze, *Buddhist Thought in India* (Ann Arbor: University of Michigan Press, 1962) 65.

inherent existence to things."[35] The dependent nature, on the other hand, refers to the causally interdependent nature of reality: the causally dependent flow of representations, or the "dependent origination of phenomena."[36] Finally, the perfected nature refers to the true vision of reality: reality as it truly is, unmediated by conceptualization; Buddhist texts describe the perfected nature as "'thusness' (*tathatā*), the true nature of things, which is discovered in meditation."[37] While these general definitions of the three natures remain important for the Yogācāra tradition, there are some differences regarding how the three natures are further elucidated by different Buddhist thinkers, though here we will stay within the bounds of what may be referred to as the "progressive model," wherein each of the three natures refers to a different level of semiotic awareness.

The progressive model lays out the three natures in terms of gradual stages of gnosis, moving from the deluded to the fully awakened, as follows. Deluded sentient beings confront reality in terms of a dualism between subject and object, and use the superimpositions of language and concepts to construct an interpretation of the constant flow of appearances; this is the level of the imagined nature. Then through spiritual practice, one comes to the realization that conceptually imagined entities do not actually exist, but are simply the effects of a causally interdependent flow of illusory appearances; this is the level of the dependent nature. Finally, when the termination of the illusion is achieved, when the basis of the matrix of conceptual construction is abandoned, enlightenment is attained, an attainment which is interpreted in the Yogācāra tradition as a nonconceptual awareness (*nirvikalpa-jñāna*) of thusness (*tathatā*); this is the level of the perfected nature. In this interpretation, each of the stages entails a distinct mode of semiosis, and the movement through the stages is progressive, with each stage superseding the previous stage. The focus of the three-nature theory, on this reading, is the relation between mind and signs (language, concepts): one must move from a deluded mode of semiosis, wherein objects posited by language are taken as really existent things; through a more refined mode of semiosis, wherein everything is viewed as a causally dependent flow of signs, as representation-only (*vijñapti-mātra*); and ultimately to a perfected mode of semiosis (actually the end or terminus of semiosis), which is realized as a nonconceptual awareness of thusness.

35. Paul Williams, *Mahāyāna Buddhism: The Doctrinal Foundations* (New York: Routledge 1989) 83.

36. *Wisdom of Buddha*, trans. John Powers (Berkeley: Dharma, 1995) 83.

37. Williams, *Mahāyāna Buddhism*, 84.

Since the three-nature theory is directed towards a spiritual goal, we might characterize the "technique" entailed by the Yogācāra three-nature theory as a technique of shifting perspectives. This may be seen in that the three natures do not refer to three distinct realities, but rather to reality viewed under different descriptions: viewed in terms of the fixed constructs of language and conceptualization, phenomena are imagined; viewed as dependently originating, they are dependent; and viewed as they truly are, they are perfected. So while the technique of the Madhyamaka school—another important school of Mahāyāna Buddhist philosophy—entails statements such as "it is not the case that x is F, and it is not the case that x is not F," the Yogācāra technique entails statements such as "x is F, and x is not F." However, in each statement x is viewed from a different perspective, e.g., from the perspective of the imagined or the perfected. Since the value of x differs in each statement, there is no real contradiction. The Yogācāra technique, then, implies that one must shift perspectives—that a kind of decentering must occur—in order to envision reality from an enlightened point of view.

Buddhism's analysis of language as constituting a stable realm of referents is mirrored to some extent by Lacan's own thoughts on language, especially as articulated in "The Function and Field of Speech and Language in Psychoanalysis." In this essay, Lacan states, "Through the word—which is already a presence made of absence—absence itself comes to be named in an original moment," thus calling attention to the dialectic between presence and absence that is fundamental to the function of language.[38] He points out that through the bringing together of presence and absence, "a language's [langue] world of meaning is born, in which the world of things will situate itself"[39]—hence objects are constituted as such by the function of language, a thesis which is also affirmed in the Buddhist analysis of language discussed above. Lacan goes on to state, "Through what becomes embodied only by being the trace of a nothingness . . . concepts, in preserving the duration of what passes away, engender things,"[40] which sounds almost like a Lacanian formulation of the central Buddhist doctrines of emptiness (śūnyatā) and impermanence (anityatā)—that all phenomena are without intrinsic nature and in a constant state of flux. So both Buddhism and Lacan emphasize the fundamental role that language plays in constituting the very objects that are taken to comprise reality.

38. Lacan, Écrits, 228.
39. Ibid.
40. Ibid.

Lacan's approach to language also involves an analysis of the three registers of the imaginary, the symbolic, and the real. Following Fink's account, we may understand the imaginary as a register that is "dominated by the analysand's self-image and the image he or she forms of the analyst";[41] given such constructed images of self and other, the analysand then proceeds to measure himself or herself vis-à-vis these images. Hence, as Fink points out, "*Imaginary relations are dominated by rivalry*": Is one superior to or inferior to the image one has of the other?[42] The symbolic, on the other hand, encompasses "one's relation to the Law"; hence symbolic relations may be understood as the ways in which individuals relate to the "*ideals* that have been inculcated in them by their parents, schools, media, language, and society at large."[43] The symbolic register is intrinsically connected to language, since the Law can only be formulated with language. As Moncayo points out, the symbolic pertains to the functioning of "the laws of language—the rules of syntax, metaphor, and metonymy," which serve to "determine how something can and cannot be said."[44] Finally, the real "is what has not yet been put into words or formulated"; Fink states that the real may be thought of "as the connection or link between two thoughts that has succumbed to repression and must be restored," and thus he interprets the real in relation to Freud's conception of trauma.[45] Moncayo indicates that the real is the "dimension of experience existing outside or beyond language and experience."[46] And Lacan himself states that the "ultimate real"—that is, "the real lacking any possible mediation"—is "the essential object which isn't an object any longer, but this something faced with which all words cease and all categories fail, the object of anxiety *par excellence.*"[47] So here we see that the fundamental dimensions of the real are its inability to be expressed in language, and, in connection with that, its power to induce anxiety.

41. Bruce Fink, *A Clinical Introduction to Lacanian Psychoanalysis: Theory and Technique* (Cambridge: Harvard University Press, 1997) 32.

42. Ibid.

43. Ibid., 33.

44. Moncayo, "Finger Pointing at the Moon," 343.

45. Fink, *Clinical Introduction to Lacanian Psychoanalysis*, 49.

46. Raul Moncayo, "True Subject Is No-subject: The Real, Imaginary, and Symbolic in Psychoanalysis and Zen Buddhism," *Psychoanalysis and Contemporary Thought* 21 (1998) 395.

47. Jacques Lacan, *The Seminar of Jacques Lacan, Book II: The Ego in Freud's Theory and in the Technique of Psychoanalysis, 1954–1955*, ed. Jacques-Alain Miller, trans. Sylvana Tomaselli (New York: Norton, 1991) 161.

Here it might be interesting to consider a possible way of correlating the Yogācāra three natures with the Lacanian three registers. While this can only be an experimental attempt, insofar as there are differing interpretations of each of these tripartite doctrines, this should not deter us from seeing whether any insight might be gained from an attempt at relating the Buddhist and Lacanian accounts. I would suggest that the imagined nature can be correlated with the imaginary, insofar as both are based on a fundamental distinction between subject and object, an image of self and other; the dependent can be correlated with the symbolic, insofar as the Buddhist understanding of the causally interdependent nature of reality in the dependent might be viewed in relation to the Lacanian understanding of the symbolic as pertaining to the interdependent functioning of the rules of syntax, metaphor, and metonymy; and the perfected can be correlated with the real, insofar as both are domains which are unable to be symbolized through language.

However, this attempt at aligning the Yogācāra Buddhist three natures with the Lacanian three registers should not occlude the significant differences between the two, and indeed may bring into greater relief the fundamental disjunction between the Buddhist perfected nature and the Lacanian real: for Buddhism, the perfected nature is the domain of awakened awareness, and it is certainly not understood to be "the object of anxiety *par excellence.*"[48] To put the point in more straightforward terms: for Lacanian psychoanalytic theory, the non-linguistic domain of the real is viewed in terms of trauma and anxiety; while for Buddhist philosophy, the non-linguistic domain of the perfected nature is interpreted as the perfection of awakening and buddhahood. Does this Buddhist aim of reaching the non-linguistic domain represent a position which is semiotically regressive? Is it the case that, as Alexander states, "the end goal of Buddhistic absorption is an attempt at psychological and physical regression,"[49] the return to a state absent of all stimulus, which might be interpreted as an expression of the Freudian death drive? As I have indicated elsewhere, my sense is that the goal of Buddhism is not to completely *eliminate* semiosis, but rather to *change one's relation to it*, which is evidenced by the fact that models of buddhahood in Yogācāra texts characterize a buddha-mind as "reengaging with conceptual thought, although in a way that has somehow been fundamentally transformed through the attainment of a nonconceptual awareness"[50]

48. Ibid., 164.

49. Alexander, "Buddhistic Training as an Artificial Catatonia," 137.

50. Mario D'Amata, "Why the Buddha Never Uttered a Word," in *Pointing at the Moon: Buddhism, Logic, Analytic Philosophy*, ed. Mario D'Amato, Jay L. Garfield, and Tom J. F. Tillemans (New York: Oxford University Press, 2009) 49.

Returning again to a consideration of the similarities between the Buddhist doctrine of the three natures and the Lacanian account three registers, I would offer the following two further observations regarding Buddhist and Lacanian theory: (1) both traditions entail a parallax view of reality;[51] and (2) both traditions articulate their respective goals in terms of effecting a systematic shift in perspective, a shift involving their respective three registers.

Terminating the Analysis:
Some Concluding Remarks

Perhaps the most poignant question in any discussion of Buddhism and Lacanian psychoanalysis is the question regarding what fundamental position one should adopt vis-à-vis desire. Put in its most basic terms: *What are we to do?* While I will not pretend to offer an answer here, I will suggest that perhaps Buddhism and Lacanian psychoanalysis are not necessarily in opposition in their responses to this question. Of course, one could imagine a number of possible options: viz., that Buddhism and psychoanalysis ultimately reduce to the same formula, or that each is in some sense the negation of the other, or perhaps that each is a distinct moment in the unfolding of something higher. For my part, I am most intrigued by the last option. Perhaps we might imagine Buddhism and Lacanian psychoanalysis as regions of discourse that are somewhat adjacent to one another, in the way that, say, chemistry (which, of course, began in traditions of alchemy) is adjacent to physics and to biology. But unlike the natural sciences (that address entities that are not themselves semiotic), the domains of philosophico-religious discourse and psychoanalytic discourse fall within the purview of the semiotic sciences (wherein the study of linguistics would be most fundamental, in the way that particle physics is most fundamental to the natural sciences; and the general study of theoretical semiotics might be considered analogous to the study of abstract mathematics for the natural sciences). We can at least note that philosophico-religious discourses and psychoanalytic theorizing are both similarly engaged in understanding the

51. "The standard definition of parallax is: the apparent displacement of an object (the shift of its position against a background), caused by a change in observational position that provides a new line of sight. The philosophical twist to be added, of course, is that the observed distance is not simply 'subjective,' due to the fact that the same object which exists 'out there' is seen from two different stances, or points of view. It is rather that, as Hegel would have put it, subject and object are inherently 'mediated,' so that an 'epistemological' shift in the subject's point of view always reflects an 'ontological' shift in the object itself." Slavoj Žižek, *Parallax View* (Cambridge: MIT Press, 2006) 17.

construction of *meaning*. And perhaps the way to the religion of the future might be made clearer through more nuanced and self-reflexive understandings of how human beings construct meaning.

Finally, to return again to the question with which we began this essay: how is it possible for there to be a relation to the infinite, when there are no relata? Or when the relata are ever-changing and inexpressible through language—since any sense of the stability of the self always eludes us, and since the "ultimate real" may simply be beyond symbolization? Language must play a role here, insofar as it allows us to represent—to creatively imagine—how we might engage with whatever lies beyond our capacity for engagement. So perhaps while language is in some sense always inhibiting, in another sense it may be a condition for the possibility of moving beyond the barriers it has itself raised.

5

Life Terminable and Interminable

The Undead and the Afterlife
of the Afterlife—A Friendly Disagreement with
Martin Hägglund

ADRIAN JOHNSTON

§1 From the Religion of Survival to the Survival of Religion—The Difficulties of Atheism

JACQUES LACAN'S 1974 INTERVIEW with Italian journalists in Rome, entitled "The Triumph of Religion," implicitly addresses what has come to appear, with the benefit of hindsight, as a failure of vision on Freud's part. In his 1927 text *The Future of an Illusion*, one of the greatest manifestos of atheism in history, the founder of psychoanalysis predicts the inevitable demise of religion, allegedly doomed to wither away in the face of the steadily accelerating advances of the sciences; in accordance with a well-established Enlightenment narrative, Freud has faith that the progress of knowledge is bound to drive an increasing secularization of human societies through its relentless insistence on propagating the desacralizing insights of reason.[1] By the time Lacan gives his interview in Rome—and this has become ever-

---

1. Sigmund Freud, *The Future of an Illusion*, in *The Standard Edition of the Complete Psychological Works of Sigmund Freud*, ed. and trans. James Strachey (London: Hogarth, 1957–74) 21:38, 49–50, 53–56.

more evident since then—religion obviously seems to continue enjoying a vibrant afterlife on the world stage in the wake of the Enlightenment emergence of the naturalist and materialist discourses integral to the scientific *Weltanschauung*.[2] Indeed, the potent forces of modernizing techniques and technologies, fuelled by the massive economic energies unleashed by capitalism, have continued to prove themselves to be powerless to liquidate thoroughly the specters of idealisms, spiritualisms, and theisms. Simply put, the problem with the atheism Freud anticipates and celebrates is that it severely underestimates the resilience and persistence of religiosity[3] (borrowing the title from Oskar Pfister's 1928 article responding to *The Future of an Illusion*, one could fault Freud for succumbing to "the illusion of a future"[4]). When asked how he explains the triumph of religion over psychoanalysis, Lacan, speaking with an acute awareness of post-Freudian history's resounding verdict regarding Freud's 1927 prophecy, responds, "If psychoanalysis will not triumph over religion, it is that religion is eternally tireless (*increvable*). Psychoanalysis will not triumph—it will survive or not."[5] Associating from Lacan's recourse here to notions of eternity and survival to Martin Hägglund's *tour de force* manifesto pleading for a "radical atheism" inspired by the philosophy of Jacques Derrida, one might be led to ask whether and how religion will survive in the shadow of Derridean-Hägglundian analyses concerning the very concept of survival itself. Without spending too much precious time recapitulating the main lines of argumentation of Hägglund's book in the form of an exegetical summary, suffice it to note a few of its key ideas focused on by the reflections to follow in this response to his work. Hägglund defines radical atheism through contrasting it with familiar varieties of traditional atheism. The latter negates the existence of the divine and everything connected with it (immortality, indestructibility, fullness, flawlessness, etc.) without calling into question whether everything whose existence it denies is desirable. Such pre-Derridean atheism simply takes it for granted that those things vanishing with the renunciation of the transcendent beyond of an unscathed afterlife obviously are *prima facie* desir-

2. Sigmund Freud, *New Introductory Lectures on Psychoanalsysis*, SE 22:34, 160–61, 167–69, 171–74.

3. Adrian Johnston, "A Blast from the Future: Freud, Lacan, Marcuse, and Snapping the Threads of the Past," *Umbr(a)—A Journal of the Unconscious: Utopia* (2008) 67–84.

4. Oskar Pfister, "The Illusion of a Future: A Friendly Disagreement with Prof. Sigmund Freud," ed. Paul Roazen, trans. Susan Abrams, *International Journal of Psycho-Analysis* 74 (1993) 574.

5. Jacques Lacan, "Le triomphe de la religion," in *Le triomphe de la religion, précédé de Discours aux catholiques*, ed. Jacques-Alain Miller (Paris: Éditions du Seuil, 2005) 78–79.

able. By contrast, Derridean-Hägglundian radical atheism not only negates what traditional atheism negates—it even contests the assumed desirability of the ostensible "paradise lost" produced by the denials of traditional atheism,[6] thereby refusing perpetually to wallow in the pathetic *pathos* of a position stuck forever pining after disappeared gods and withdrawn heavens. The slogan of radical atheism, apropos the lack jointly posited by both traditional atheism and its religious opponents (specifically, a lack in this material world of a wholly immune eternal life), might be the hopeful declaration that, "You have nothing to lose but this loss itself!" In several significant ways, Hägglund offers readers a chance to reject melancholic atheism as a depressing, self-deceiving *doxa* hankering after an Elsewhere modeled on false promises of stagnant, lifeless security and stability.

Hägglund goes so far as to invoke a "law of survival" brooking absolutely no exceptions whatsoever.[7] Viewed from Hägglund's perspective, nobody can and does ever really desire everlasting life *qua* timeless, unchanging being. Rather, the lively kinesis of temporal "survival" (i.e., "living on" in time), and not the deathly stasis of atemporal immortality, is what all desires, without exception, truly desire.[8] One of the justifications for this surprising assertion is the argument that "everlasting life" is a contradiction in terms—and this insofar as the essential temporality of life renders the insatiable thirst for more life, often (mis)represented as a craving for an eternal life transcending time, a yearning for remaining open to the perpetually renewed alterity of time *à venir*, with the incalculable numbers of dangers and risks this openness to futurity necessarily and unavoidable entails.[9]

Ultimately, Hägglund's case for radical atheism rests on a theory of desire (hence the relevance of bringing psychoanalysis into this discussion). He directly avows this in stating that, "Radical atheism proceeds from the argument that everything that can be desired is mortal in its essence."[10] Or, as he reiterates a few pages later, "the radically atheist argument is that *one cannot want* absolute immunity and that it has never been the aim of desire."[11] But, regardless of whether Hägglund is justified in maintaining that what looks to be a desire for immortality is, in truth, a desire for survival in the strict Derridean sense, it's certainly undeniable that neither traditional theists nor

---

6. Martin Hägglund, *Radical Atheism: Derrida and the Time of Life* (Stanford: Stanford University Press, 2008) 111–12.

7. Ibid., 122.

8. Ibid., 2, 8, 28, 32–34, 44, 48–49, 130, 132.

9. Ibid., 121, 129.

10. Ibid., 111.

11. Ibid., 119.

their equally traditional atheist adversaries (i.e., the vast bulk of humanity past and present) experience their desire as such. The least one can say along these lines—Hägglund acknowledges this—is that the fiction of the infiniteness of a transcendent immortality, and not the fact of the finitude of an immanent survival, is an enduring mirage which, in its misleading guises, attracts humanity's hopes and aspirations. One doesn't have to be a practicing psychoanalyst steeped in intricate and subtle metapsychological conceptualizations of unconscious fantasy life to know that illusions are not without an influence on desire. Similarly, time spent between the four walls of the clinical consulting room isn't requisite for grasping that desire is far from reasonable, willing and able to be downright unreasonable. Thus, any comprehensive, faithful account of desire cannot be limited to external critical assessments of its object, dismissing the illusions shaping desire itself as mere illusions *qua* ineffective epiphenomena, as unreal by virtue of being irrational when measured by the standards of directed, self-conscious reasoning. One could surmise that this is an aspect of what Lacan is getting at when he warns analysts that "desire must be taken literally,"[12] namely, at its word as well as to its letter.

In this vein, Hägglund notes, "A radical atheism cannot simply denounce messianic hope as an illusion. Rather, it must show that messianic hope does not stem from a hope for immortality (the positive infinity of eternity) but from a hope for survival (the negative infinity of time)."[13] However, at this precise juncture, questions proliferate: Even if "messianic hope" (as an apparent wishing for the saving grace of deliverance from mortal time) can be shown fundamentally somehow to "stem from" the Derridean-Hägglundian "hope for survival," does such a demonstration prove that the passion for salvation is wholly reducible to its finite ground or origin, the "ultra-transcendental"[14] Ur-source from which it stems? What does it mean to claim that a desire doesn't genuinely desire what it takes itself to desire? Are there crucial differences between an atheism, be it traditional or radical, embraced consciously and one internalized unconsciously? Is the unconscious discovered by Freudian psychoanalysis capable of digesting radical atheism? Has this unconscious ever been radically atheist? Will it ever be?

Freud claims that humanity eventually will become atheist. Hägglund claims that humanity always has been atheist. Freud's prediction has failed the test of subsequent history, at least thus far at first glance. Hägglund's

12. Jacques Lacan, "The Direction of the Treatment and the Principles of Its Power," in *Écrits*, trans. Bruce Fink (New York: Norton) 518.

13. Hägglund, *Radical Atheism*, 136.

14. Ibid., 27–29, 31–32, 38, 46, 51, 73, 210–11, 220.

thesis has yet to be as thoroughly tested. Its unpredictable, unforeseeable tomorrows await it.

For the sake of contributing to what hopefully will be the long and prosperous future of radical atheism, this response to Hägglund's theses will put forward a set of three inter-linked proposals (i.e., criticisms/counterarguments) to be defended below. To being with, the problem with radical atheism is not that it is unreasonable, warranting critique due to certain defects or shortcomings in the reasoning supporting it. On the contrary, from a psychoanalytic standpoint, it's too reasonable. Ironically enough, although professional philosophers frequently accuse Derrida of indulging in anything but philosophy by engaging in something (whatever it is) that's purportedly beneath the proper dignity of authentic, respectable philosophy, Hägglund's Derrida turns out to be too much of a philosopher for psychoanalysis (a comparable, related irony is that Derridean thought displays the armchair philosopher's penchant for challenging psychoanalytic hypotheses, hypotheses informed by far-from-purely-theoretical endeavors, with *apriori* assertions without firm anchoring in any sort of empirical and/ or practical discipline apart from the rarified textual and ideational ethers in which the philosophical tradition has moved comfortably since its inception in ancient Greece). Despite deconstruction supposedly eschewing classical, bivalent logic by questioning the law of non-contradiction as the fundamental principle on which this logic is based,[15] many of the manners in which Hägglund argues for a radically atheist vision of desire exhibit reasoning impeccable by the standards of classical logic (one imagines that logic professors would be quite pleased with the argumentative acumen displayed by Hägglund's writing). If, as Freud adamantly insists, the unconscious thinks in fashions utterly different than consciousness—the former disregards the rules of bivalent logic and linear chronology generally adhered to be the latter—then can Hägglund reason his way to conclusions about the real nature of unconscious desire (conclusions maintaining that the desire for immortality unknowingly is a desire for survival) using premises chained together according to the conventions of the logic molding conscious cognition?

Hägglund's reasoning is too reasonable for the unconscious, his logic too logical. One might remark that he's much too clever for both the unconscious as well as the bulk of people believing themselves to desire things Hägglund valiantly tries to prove they cannot desire and never have desired. He seeks to force rational constraints upon desire that desire, as generated and sustained in part by unconscious processes, tends to ignore, for better or worse. This isn't to be denounced and dismissed as a failure of desire to be

---

15. Ibid., 24–25.

true to itself by not experiencing itself as radically atheist. Instead, it's to be diagnosed as a failure of radical atheism to take stock of how and why desire fails to experience itself as radically atheist. There are precise metapsychological reasons for these failures.

A second and related line of counter-argumentation to be formulated is that, judged by the standards of the classical logic on which much of his reasoning rests, Hägglund employs a false dilemma affecting the very core of his radically atheist theory of desire. The mutually exclusive, either/or opposition he thrusts forward between life and death—the former is equated with living on as the time of mortal survival, while the latter is associated with eternity as possible only through the cadaverizing cancellation of life[16]—serves as the basis for his claim that desire always fantasizes about having more (mortal) time, rather than, as with an immortal, no time (and, hence, no life, given the equation of being alive with being-in-time, since "there cannot even in principle be anything that is exempt from temporal finitude").[17] Departing from Hägglund's related characterization of temporal life as "infinite finitude,"[18] a third possibility in excess of the bivalent binary distinction between mortal life and immortal death is thinkable: the "finite infiniteness" of "undeath" *à la* the horror-fiction category of the undead as neither alive nor dead in the standard senses of these terms (Slavoj Žižek, among others, effectively utilizes this fictional category in elucidating the fundamental psychoanalytic concepts of drive [*Trieb*] and repetition).[19] That which is undead neither heeds the linear, chronological time of survival nor languishes in the frozen immobility of timeless death, these being the only two options allowed for by Hägglund: "If to be alive is to be mortal, it follows that to *not* be mortal—to be immortal—is to be

16. Ibid., 33–34.

17. Ibid., 3.

18. Ibid., 110, 131, 144, 214, 220, 227.

19. Slavoj Žižek, *The Sublime Object of Ideology* (London: Verso, 1989) 4–5; Slavoj Žižek, *The Plague of Fantasies* (London: Verso, 1997) 89; Slavoj Žižek, *The Ticklish Subject: The Absent Centre of Political Ontology* (London: Verso, 1999) 66, 293–94; Slavoj Žižek, "Death and the Maiden," in *The Žižek Reader*, ed. Elizabeth Wright and Edmond Wright (Oxford: Blackwell, 1999) 211; Slavoj Žižek, *On Belief* (New York: Routledge, 2001) 104; Slavoj Žižek, "'I do not order my dreams,'" in *Opera's Second Death*, ed. Slavoj Žižek and Mladen Dolar (New York: Routledge, 2002) 106–7; Slavoj Žižek, *The Parallax View* (Cambridge: MIT Press, 2006) 182; Slavoj Žižek, *In Defense of Lost Causes* (London: Verso, 2008) 54; Adrian Johnston, *Time Driven: Metapsychology and the Splitting of the Drive* (Evanston: Northwestern University Press, 2005) 368–69; Adrian Johnston, *Žižek's Ontology: A Transcendental Materialist Theory of Subjectivity* (Evanston: Northwestern University Press, 2008) 37, 52.

dead. If one cannot die, one is dead."[20] If a satisfactory case can be made for there being a third dimension to the temporality of the libidinal economy, a dimension irreducible to either pole of the dichotomy between the chronological temporality of life and the timeless eternity of death, then some of the load-bearing components of the argumentative architecture supporting the Derridean-Hägglundian radical atheist conception of desire will be weakened and in need of reconstruction.

Not only does Hägglund's deconstructive logic remain, on multiple levels, indebted to classical, non-deconstructive logic—however much the recto of the law of identity (i.e., "A = A") is attacked here,[21] its verso, the law of non-contradiction (i.e., "A ≠ A"), clearly continues to be operative at select junctures—his, as it were, chrono-logic remains strangely mute with respect to the innovative, non-traditional theorizations of temporality advanced by both psychoanalysis and deconstruction (for example, in his criticisms of this respondent's first book, *Time Driven: Metapsychology and the Splitting of the Drive*,[22] he pays too little attention to the role therein of retroactive temporality [as Freud's *Nachträglichkeit* and Lacan's *après-coup*] in the dynamics of the drives, tending instead to think through problems in drive theory via a developmental perspective that privileges linear, chronological time, a perspective closer to phenomenological psychology than Freudian-Lacanian psychoanalysis).[23] The sole form of temporality Hägglund seems to rely upon in pursuing his purposes is a conception that's at least as old as the ancient Greeks, that is, the idea of time as the continuous, ceaseless succession of ever-self-dividing now-points with a past behind them and a future ahead of them. If there's one thing that Freud, Lacan, and Derrida share in common, it's the problematization of thinking time in these terms alone.[24] Additionally, glancing back at the first difficulty articulated above (i.e., the one proposing that radical atheism is too reasonable for unconscious desire), one can see that the duel staged between classical and deconstructive logics likewise involves the false dilemma of leaving out alternatives over and above the two logics thus pitted against each other. At a minimum, what about the logic upon which psychoanalysis bases not only its theory of the psychical apparatus, but also its practice as centered on the "fundamental rule" of free association, namely, the, so to speak, methodical madness of

20. Hägglund, *Radical Atheism*, 8.

21. Ibid., 24–25.

22. Johnson, *Time Driven*.

23. Martin Hägglund, "Chronolibidinal Reading: Deconstruction and Psychoanalysis," *The New Centennial Review* 9 (2009) 1–43.

24. Johnson, *Time Driven*, 6.

primary process mentation characteristic of the signifying unconscious? Can this "logic" be reduced to classical logic, deconstructive logic, or some combination of these latter two alone? If not, then further detours lie along the road ahead for Derridean-Hägglundian radical atheism.

The third and final thread of criticism to be unfurled in this response has to do with the familiar but crucial difference between description and prescription. Hägglund himself is quite cognizant of the importance of this distinction, deftly employing it to devastating effect in raising a plethora of serious objections to various well-known attempts to interpret Derrida's writings as marshaling ethical and political prescriptions (on Hägglund's highly persuasive reading, Derrida is to be understood as primarily pronouncing a descriptive discourse stating how things are, instead of a prescriptive one proclaiming how things should be). As will be substantiated here later, despite his very effective critical deployment of the description-prescription distinction against depictions of Derrida as the preacher of a theosophical ethics of alterity, Hägglund sometimes sounds as though he succumbs to confusion apropos this difference between "is" and "ought." To be specific, the argument will be made that Hägglund's radical atheism is more prescriptive than descriptive, despite him presenting it as the reverse.

This respondent is extremely sympathetic to the atheism envisioned by Hägglund—albeit sympathetic to it as a vision of what thought hopefully can become in the future, rather than as a picture of what it was in the past and is in the present (like the best of philosophers measured by Nietzschean standards, Hägglund could be characterized as marvelously "untimely"). Succinctly asserted, authentic atheism is a hard-won accomplishment, not an insurmountable, default subjective setting. For Hägglund, the conscientious faithful are nonetheless unwitting atheists. For this respondent, by contrast, even many professed atheists are unconscious believers (a point already made by Lacan through references to both the purportedly atheistic materialists of eighteenth-century France as well as certain features of evolutionary theory).[25] Consciously believing oneself to be rid of religiosity once and for all is one easy thing—another, much harder, matter is the dual-aspect labor of working through one's atheism past the initial point of its mere intellectual acceptance. This arduous *Durcharbeiten* has

25. Jacques Lacan, *The Seminar of Jacques Lacan, Book VII: The Ethics of Psychoanalysis, 1959–1960*, ed. Jacques-Alain Miller, trans. Dennis Porter (New York: Norton, 1992) 213–14; Jacques Lacan, *Le Séminaire de Jacques Lacan, Livre XVII: L'envers de la psychanalyse, 1969–1970*, ed. Jacques-Alain Miller (Paris: Éditions du Seuil, 1991) 66; Lorenzo Chiesa and Alberto Toscano, "Ethics and Capital, Ex Nihilo," *Umbr(a)— A Journal of the Unconscious: The Dark God* (2005) 10; Adrian Johnston, "Conflicted Matter: Jacques Lacan and the Challenge of Secularizing Materialism," *Pli: The Warwick Journal of Philosophy* 19 (2008) 166, 168–70.

two aspects insofar as it entails simultaneously both internalizing atheism at non-conscious levels beyond superficial self-consciousness as well as unmasking hidden, unacknowledged vestiges of beliefs subsisting below the threshold of explicit recognition. Even if, as is sadly unlikely, Hägglund miraculously manages to convince the masses that they are not and never have been faithful to their religions, even this doesn't amount to succeeding at ridding them of religious revenants, revenants that enjoy defying would-be exorcists and have show themselves to be devilishly cunning survivalists over the course of recent history, rebelliously lingering on after all atheist eulogies pronounced before. Atheism, including radical atheism, certainly has its work cut out for it. May it triumph against the odds!

§2 The Fantasy of Logic—Thought and Time in the Unconscious

In the spirit of Lacan, a brief return to Freud promises to be productive at this point. Hägglund himself zeros in on one of Freud's texts of the greatest degree of topicality in this context: the short 1916 piece "On Transience." Therein, Freud succinctly addresses issues and themes at the very heart of Hägglund's undertakings (both in *Radical Atheism* as well as the article "Chronolibidinal Reading: Deconstruction and Psychoanalysis"). Without exhaustively summarizing the various details contained in this three-page Freudian text, suffice it to say for now that the discoverer of the unconscious, himself burdened by a persistent, obsessive concern over his own mortality,[26] here confronts (through two other people as interlocutors) the fleeting, transitory nature of all things, the condemnation of each and every being, without exception, to the cycles of generation and corruption, growth and decay. In response to this undeniable fact, Freud resists falling into a depressive refusal to engage with the world under the shadow of this world's transience. Disputing a contention voiced by one of his walking companions, a poet, that transience, like an inverse Midas touch, lessens the value of everything it envelops, Freud retorts in quasi-economic terms, "On the contrary, an increase! Transience value is scarcity value in time. Limitation in the possibility of an enjoyment raises the value of the enjoyment."[27] Basing himself on this statement by Freud, which he takes to support his radical atheist theory of desire, Hägglund concludes that, "Indeed, temporal

26. Adrian Johnston, "Intimations of Freudian Mortality: The Enigma of Sexuality and the Constitutive Blind Spots of Freud's Self-Analysis," *Journal for Lacanian Studies* 3 (2005) 224–26, 243–45.

27. Sigmund Freud, "On Transience," *SE* 14:305.

finitude—far from being a privation—is the reason why anything is desirable in the first place."[28] Or, as he puts it in *Radical Atheism*, in which he calls for a temporalized conception of enjoyment,[29] *"temporal finitude is the condition for everything that is desirable."*[30]

Already, there are several problems plaguing the conclusions Hägglund draws from this 1916 essay by Freud. To begin with, Freud doesn't maintain that transience (i.e., temporal finitude) is the ultimate underlying reason or source (in Hägglund's parlance, the ultra-transcendental condition) for the desirability of anything and everything. Rather, he merely observes that scarcity in/of time need not, as is the case for his friend the poet in particular, be bemoaned as a wretched stain indelibly tainting objects and experiences that, in the absence of ubiquitous transience, supposedly would be worthy of committed love and enthralled esteem (or, so this melancholic writer imagines). Freud responds to this poetic pessimism in a very analytic manner, inquiring whether it's obvious and self-explanatory that one necessarily must construe scant time, with its constraining parameters, as poisoning and devaluing all that one might otherwise invest with one's desires. He proposes, to himself, his interlocutors, and his readers, that another attitude toward temporal limits is possible. This is a (self-)analyzed analyst offering those with ears to hear an alternate interpretation, one that opens up the affirmative potential for embracing a superabundant reality full to overflowing with finite things, rather than defensively retreating from this fluctuating existence into a rigid, lifeless pseudo-safety toiling in vain to fend off feeling losses (i.e., neurotically attempting to lose feelings of attachment to temporally finite beings so as to avoid inevitable feelings of loss).[31] Hence, Freud is prescribing another way of positioning oneself *vis-à-vis* transience, and not describing how transience is an ultra-transcendental condition for each and every instance of desiring something (with this being Hägglund's earlier-mentioned misapplication of the description-versus-prescription distinction). Along these lines, Freud, in "On Transience," doesn't claim that temporal "scarcity" (i.e., finitude) creates desirable values. Instead, he merely maintains that such scarcity/finitude can become a supplement augmenting or enhancing (i.e., increasing, rather than decreasing) what is already enjoyable in things happening to be transient. All things are temporally finite, including all things desired. This temporal finitude either can decrease or increase the ability to desire one's desire, to enjoy one's enjoyment, of these

28. Hägglund, "Chronolibidinal Reading."

29. Hägglund, *Radical Atheism*, 157.

30. Ibid., 32.

31. Freud, "On Transience," 305–6.

transient things. But, neither of these two premises leads to and licenses the conclusion that temporality and the fleeting, ephemeral fragility it brings with it are the ultimate causal origins of desirability *tout court*.

To the extent that Hägglund brings Freudian psychoanalysis into the picture of his Derrida-inspired radically atheist theory of desire, additional problems multiply once one turns to the bundle of roughly contemporaneous texts with which 1916's "On Transience" is inextricably intertwined: "On Narcissism: An Introduction" (1914), the 1915 papers on metapsychology ("Drives and Their Vicissitudes," "Repression," and "The Unconscious"), "Thoughts for the Times on War and Death" (1915), and "Mourning and Melancholia" (1917). To reduce several very long narratives to one very short story—obviously, there can be no attempt here at an exhaustive engagement with this dense cluster of immensely rich slices of the Freudian corpus—these writings, spanning a critical four-year period of Freud's intellectual itinerary, all present ideas cutting against the grain of the Derridean-Hägglundian account of desire. In particular, these essays by Freud contain assertions that, on the one hand, point to deeply engrained patterns of affectively motivated cognition in the psychical apparatus obeying neither classical nor deconstructive logic, and, on the other related hand, cast into doubt whether the unconscious, with its fundamental fantasies, ever was, is, and/or will be radically atheist. Freud's psychoanalytic metapsychology outlines a psyche whose ways and means of thinking, including the thinking (or, alternately, constitutive inability to think) time, must appear to be quite irrational and unreasonable, in a resistant and refractory manner, to a radical atheist equipped with his/her arguments, objections, proofs, and so on (in line with Lacan's warnings against practicing analysis as a knee-jerk hermeneutics of suspicion always on the lookout for intricate, complex hidden meanings of profound significance—he indicates that the truth is sometimes superficially "stupid"[32]—one could say that the unconscious is simultaneously both surprisingly clever as well as unbelievably stupid when measured against the standards of conscious thinking). Will this analytic unconscious listen to these proselytizing efforts at atheistic persuasion? Can conversion take place in this case?

During the conversation in which condemnation to never-enough time is under discussion, neither of Freud's companions are convinced by

---

32. Jacques Lacan, *Le Séminaire de Jacques Lacan, Livre XV: L'acte psychanalytique, 1967–1968*, unpublished typescript, 11, 22, 67; Jacques Lacan, *Le Séminaire de Jacques Lacan, Livre XVI: D'un Autre à l'autre, 1968–1969*, ed. Jacques-Alain Miller (Paris: Éditions du Seuil, 2006) 41; Jacques Lacan, *Le Séminaire de Jacques Lacan, Livre XXIII: Le sinthome, 1975–1976*, ed. Jacques-Alain Miller (Paris: Éditions du Seuil. 2005) 72.

his rationalizations to the effect that temporal finitude adds to, instead of detracts from, the desire-worthiness of transient beings. Freud notes:

> These considerations appeared to me to be incontestable; but I noticed that I had made no impression either upon the poet or upon my friend. My failure led me to infer that some powerfulemotional factor was at work which was disturbing their judgment, and I believed later that I had discovered what it was. What spoilt their enjoyment of beauty must have been a revolt in their minds against mourning. The idea that all this beauty was transient was giving these two sensitive minds a foretaste of mourning over its decease; and, since the mind instinctively recoils from anything that is painful, they felt their enjoyment of beauty interfered with by thoughts of its transience.[33]

He continues:

> Mourning over the loss of something that we have loved or admired seems so natural to the layman that he regards it as self-evident. But to psychologists mourning is a great riddle, one of those phenomena which cannot themselves be explained but to which other obscurities can be traced back. We possess, as it seems, a certain amount of capacity for love—what we call libido—which in the earliest stages of development is directed towards our own ego. Later, though still at a very early time, this libido is diverted from the ego on to objects, which are thus in a sense taken into our ego. If the objects are destroyed or if they are lost to us, our capacity for love (our libido) is once more liberated; and it can then either take other objects instead or can temporarily return to the ego. But why it is that this detachment of libido from its objects should be such a painful process is a mystery to us and we have not hitherto been able to frame any hypothesis to account for it. We only see that libido clings to its objects and will not renounce those that are lost even when a substitute lies ready to hand. Such then is mourning.[34]

If the desires of Freud's companions are grounded upon temporal finitude as an ultra-transcendental condition, they certainly aren't willing and able to acknowledge this and make it their own. Additionally, one can see in these passages connections lead back to 1914's "On Narcissism" and forward to 1917's "Mourning and Melancholia." In the former essay, Freud distinguishes between "narcissistic ego-libido" (i.e., libidinal cathexes of

33. Freud, "On Transience," 306.
34. Ibid., 306–7.

one's own ego as a love-object) and "anaclitic object-libido" (i.e., libidinal cathexes of another as a love-object). In certain instances, ego-libido resists being converted into object-libido (in terms of the Freudian economics of psychical-libidinal energy, a zero-sum relation obtains between the narcissistic and the anaclitic).[35] Freud proceeds to speculate that a general resistance to other-oriented sexuality might exist, specifically insofar as sexual reproduction confronts the ego with something injurious to its own sense of itself: its status as a "mortal vehicle of a (possibly) immortal substance"[36] (interestingly for Hägglund's account of desire, it's here not the beloved object's temporal finitude that's the focus, but the lover's own self as mortal). In "On Transience," a preemptive recoiling before loss, an aversion-in-advance to mourning, is said to be operative in Freud's two interlocutors. At least in these two individuals, desire seems to be dampened or turned off by the scarcity of time, by the temporal finitude of all things. Moreover, in both this text and "Mourning and Melancholia," Freud indicates that anaclitic libidinal attachments, once established, are stubbornly sticky; more specifically, in light of mourning, he observes that the psyche is incredibly slow to concede that the loved object is truly gone, that the beloved has departed and is never coming back again.[37] In short, the psyche's desires for others, rather than being aroused by the finite, mortal status of each and every other, persevere in protracted denials of the transient, evanescent quality of whatever can be and is desired, even when faced with the gaping holes of irrevocable loss. Lacan drops similar hints about mourning couched in his own terminology (in the sixth seminar [1958–1959], he characterizes mourning as the inverse of his notion of "foreclosure" as per the third seminar [1955–1956], that is, as a process in which the void of a Real absence [i.e., the loss of an actual object] is filled in with seemingly indestructible Symbolic signifier-traces of the vanished entity).[38]

Thus, the shadow of death glaringly looms large in the background of "On Narcissism," "On Transience," and "Mourning and Melancholia." It would be neither possible nor productive, in the time-limited format of

35. Sigmund Freud, "On Narcissism: An Introduction," *SE* 14:76.

36. Ibid., 78.

37. Sigmund Freud, "Mourning and Melancholia," *SE* 14:255.

38. Jacques Lacan, *The Seminar of Jacques Lacan, Book III: The Psychoses, 1955–1956*, ed. Jacques-Alain Miller, trans. Russell Grigg (New York: Norton, 1993) 81, 190–91, 321; Jacques Lacan, "Desire and the Interpretation of Desire in *Hamlet*," ed. Jacques-Alain Miller, trans. James Hulbert, *Yale French Studies* 55/56 (1977) 37–39; John P. Muller, "Psychosis and Mourning in Lacan's *Hamlet*," *New Literary History* 12.1 (1980) 147, 156; Slavoj Žižek, *The Fright of Real Tears: Krzysztof Kieślowski Between Theory and Post-theory* (London: British Film Institute, 2001) 100; Johnston, *Žižek's Ontology*, 37–38.

this response to Hägglund's project, to dwell at length on the numerous intricacies, inconsistencies, tensions, and contradictions plaguing Freud's conflicted, multi-faceted relation to the topic of mortality. However, what Freud has to say about death in two other papers contemporaneous and associated with these three already-mentioned papers (these two being "The Unconscious" and "Thoughts for the Times on War and Death") is highly relevant to the issues at stake in this context. The metapsychological essay "The Unconscious," in seeking to delineate the essential contours of the unconscious as the proper object of psychoanalysis as a discipline, is careful to spell out why the unconscious is not simply a "subconscious" *qua* split-off double of consciousness, a second consciousness hidden from first-person consciousness. The unconscious must not be thought of as akin to consciousness precisely because it itself doesn't think like conscious thought. The unconscious thinks differently, engaging in mental maneuvers unfamiliar relative to the ideational patterns manifested and recognized by conscious cognition; conscious and unconscious thinking are not the same thing differentiated solely by whether or not there is an accompanying first-person awareness of thinking.[39] In particular, Freud stipulates that the unconscious is not bound by the logical and chronological principles upon which conscious thought generally bases itself. More precisely, the Freudian unconscious disregards both the logical law of non-contradiction (by virtue of the absence of negation in its mental operations) as well as the chronological law of temporal finitude (by virtue of its "timelessness" when measured by the standards of linear time).[40] If psychoanalysis is right that desires fundamentally are informed by the primary process mentation of an unconscious inherently incapable of obeying classical, bivalent logic (as grounded on the function of negation and the corresponding law of non-contradiction) and congenitally blind to the passage of chronological time (with the finitude this incessant movement entails), then, without utterly contradicting and discarding psychoanalysis altogether, how can one maintain not only that desire can become radically atheist, but that it always has been? Don't Freud's metapsychological axioms pertaining to unconscious psychical life indicate that indissoluble residues of religiosity (with "religiosity" understood in the broad Derridean-Hägglundian sense as centered on ideas of an immunity unscathed by time and everything time brings with it) cling to subjects' thoughts and desires thanks to the primary process underpinnings of these subjects' libidinal economies?

39. Adrian Johnston, "Sigmund Freud," in vol. 3 of *The History of Continental Philosophy*, ed. Alan Schrift (Durham: Acumen, 2010).
40. Sigmund Freud, "The Unconscious," *SE* 14:186–87.

In "Thoughts for the Times on War and Death," dating from the same year as "The Unconscious," Freud draws the obvious conclusion from the metapsychological premises according to which the unconscious lacks cognizance of both logical negation and chronological time: The unconscious is therefore also unaware of its own mortality (at least to the extent that the conscious concept of mortality, one relied upon by Hägglund too, combines the ideational components of the negation of the notion of life [i.e., death as "not-life"] and the sense of the limited nature of lived, linear time [i.e., the chronology of life]). The second section of Freud's essay, titled "Our Attitude Towards Death," repeatedly stresses this imperviousness to the idea of death of those sectors of the psyche lying beyond the circumscribed sphere of consciousness. At the start of this section, Freud remarks:

> To anyone who listened to us we were of course prepared to maintain that death was natural, undeniable and unavoidable. In reality, however, we were accustomed to behave as if it were otherwise. We showed an unmistakable tendency to put death on one side, to eliminate it from life. We tried to hush it up; indeed we even have a saying [in German]: 'to think of something as though it were death.' That is, as though it were our own death, of course. It is indeed impossible to imagine our own death; and whenever we attempt to do so we can perceive that we are in fact still present as spectators. Hence the psycho-analytic school could venture on the assertion that at bottom no one believes in his own death, or, to put the same thing in another way, that in the unconscious every one of us is convinced of his own immortality.[41]

Freud is far from the first German-speaking thinker to put forward these proposals apropos death (Kant and Schelling make identical claims).[42] Additionally, twelve years later, Heidegger famously articulates similar propositions in his well-known discussion of "being-towards-death" in *Being and Time*.[43]

But, Freud's arguments regarding mortality and immortality in psychical life don't rest on private phenomenological thought-experiments alone. Rather, his clinical and cultural observations of unconsciously influenced thought processes as well as the metapsychological framework with

41. Sigmund Freud, "Thoughts for the Times on War and Death," *SE* 14:289.

42. Immanuel Kant, *Anthropology from a Pragmatic Point of View*, trans. Victor Lyle Dowdell (Carbondale: Southern Illinois University Press, 1978) 55–56; F. W. J. Schelling, "Philosophical Letters on Dogmatism and Criticism," in *The Unconditional in Human Knowledge: Four Early Essays (1794–1796)*, trans. Fritz Marti (Lewisburg: Bucknell University Press, 1980) 181–82; Johnston, *Žižek's Ontology*, 25–26.

43. Martin Heidegger, *Being and Time*, trans. John Macquarrie and Edward Robinson (New York: Harper & Row, 1962) 280–81.

which these observations maintain a dialectical relationship of reciprocally determining co-evolution lead him to surmise that, at least unconsciously, people can't shake a "childish," "primitive" belief that they're somehow immortal. Later on in the second section of "Thoughts for the Times on War and Death," he transitions from an analysis of human perspectives on death evidently pervasive in earlier historical periods (i.e., beliefs of "prehistoric men" in "primaeval history")[44] to the contemporary, "civilized" psyche's *rapport* with mortality (he obviously is relying here on the speculation according to which "ontogeny recapitulates phylogeny," a speculation he entertains in the contemporaneous metapsychological paper on phylogenetic heritage he destroyed unpublished [but a copy of which was found amongst Sándor Ferenczi's possessions]).[45] Freud states:

> Let us now leave primaeval man, and turn to the unconscious in our own mental life. Here we depend entirely upon the psycho-analytic method of investigation, the only one which reaches to such depths. What, we ask, is the attitude of our unconscious towards the problem of death? The answer must be: almost exactly the same as that of primaeval man. In this respect, as in many others, the man of prehistoric times survives unchanged in our unconscious. Our unconscious, then, does not believe in its own death; it behaves as if it were immortal. What we call our 'unconscious'—the deepest strata of our minds, made up of instinctual impulses—knows nothing that is negative, and no negation; in it contradictories coincide. For that reason it does not know its own death, for to that we can give only a negative content. Thus there is nothing instinctual in us which responds to a belief in death.[46]

A few pages later, he adds, "To sum up: our unconscious is just as inaccessible to the idea of our own death, just as murderously inclined towards strangers, just as divided (that is, ambivalent) towards those we love, as was primaeval man."[47] However, despite the unsubtle allusions to the theory of phylogenetic heritage, Freud's 1915 statements concerning death don't rest on shaky appeals to Haeckel, Lamarck, and/or Darwin. Instead, modern individuals' (unconscious) attitudes to death resemble those of earlier people because, in the view of Freudian (and Lacanian) psychoanalytic metapsy-

44. Freud, "Thoughts for the Times on War and Death," 292–96.

45. Sigmund Freud, "Overview of the Transference Neuroses," in *A Phylogenetic Fantasy: Overview of the Transference Neuroses*, ed. Ilse Grubrich-Simitis, trans. Axel Hoffer and Peter T. Hoffer (Cambridge: Harvard University Press, 1987) 11–12, 20.

46. Freud, "Thoughts for the Times on War and Death," 296.

47. Ibid., 299.

chology, there are certain lowest common denominators structuring the psychical apparatuses of human beings living in various historical epochs. The disregard of primary process cognition for negation and time (and, hence, for death as the negation of life by time) would be something shared by "primeaval" and contemporary psyches alike. And, this trans-historical "logic of the unconscious," freely allowing for the coincidence of contradictories and taking non-chronological liberties with temporal sequences, sounds as though it is a logic closer to a sort of deranged, discombobulated Hegelian dialectics than it is to either classical or deconstructive logical reasoning. Freud subsequently reiterates these assertions, saying of the universal inescapability of death that, "no human being really grasps it."[48] Lacan and Žižek echo him[49] (not to mention Otto Rank,[50] Norman O. Brown,[51] and Ernest Becker,[52] among others).

Having reached this point, it appears that Freudian-Lacanian psychoanalysis and Derridean-Hägglundian radical atheism are directly at loggerheads, diametrically opposed to each other. The former denies that individuals' deepest fantasies and desires can and do acknowledge the fact of mortal/temporal finitude; contradicting this, the latter insists that these fantasies and desires cannot help but envision and stage this finitude again

---

48. Sigmund Freud, "The Uncanny," *SE* 17:242.

49. Jacques Lacan, *The Seminar of Jacques Lacan, Book II: The Ego in Freud's Theory and in the Technique of Psychoanalysis, 1954–1955*, ed. Jacques-Alain Miller, trans. Sylvana Tomaselli (New York: Norton, 1988) 211; Lacan, *SIII*, 179–80; Jacques Lacan, *Le Séminaire de Jacques Lacan, Livre V: Les formations de l'inconscient, 1957–1958*, ed. Jacques-Alain Miller (Paris: Éditions du Seuil, 1998) 465; Jacques Lacan, *Le Séminaire de Jacques Lacan, Livre IX: L'identification, 1961–1962*, unpublished typescript, 5/23/62; Jacques Lacan, *Le Séminaire de Jacques Lacan, Livre XVII: L'envers de la psychanalyse, 1969–1970*, ed. Jacques-Alain Miller (Paris: Éditions du Seuil, 1991) 122–23; Jacques Lacan, *Le Séminaire de Jacques Lacan, Livre XXI: Les non-dupes errent, 1973–1974*, unpublished typescript, 12/18/73; Jacques Lacan, *Le Séminaire de Jacques Lacan, Livre XXII: R.S.I., 1974–1975*, unpublished typescript, 4, 8, 75; Lacan, *SXXIII*: 125; Jacques Lacan, "Radiophonie," in *Autres écrits*, ed. Jacques-Alain Miller (Paris: Éditions du Seuil, 2001) 405; Jacques Lacan, "L'étourdit," in *Autres écrits*, ed. Jacques-Alain Miller (Paris: Éditions du Seuil, 2001) 451; Jacques Lacan, "Aristotle's Dream," trans. Lorenzo Chiesa, *Angelaki: Journal of the Theoretical Humanities*, 11 (2006) 83; Slavoj Žižek, *The Metastases of Enjoyment: Six Essays on Woman and Causality* (London: Verso, 1994) 164; Slavoj Žižek, "Da Capo senza Fine," in *Contingency, Hegemony, Universality: Contemporary Dialogues on the Left*, ed. Judith Butler, Ernesto Laclau, and Slavoj Žižek (London: Verso, 2000) 256; Johnston, *Žižek's Ontology*, 26–29.

50. Otto Rank, *The Trauma of Birth* (New York: Dover, 1993) 23–25, 60–61, 81; Otto Rank, *Beyond Psychology* (New York: Dover, 1958) 55, 116, 119, 124–25, 206–7, 212–13.

51. Norman O. Brown, *Life Against Death: The Psychoanalytical Meaning of History* (Middletown: Wesleyan University Press, 1959) 127–28.

52. Ernest Becker, *The Denial of Death* (New York: Free Press, 1973) 96, 107, 163–64.

and again. In terms of the radical atheist replacement of immortal salvation with mortal survival, Hägglundian Derrideanism relies on a line of argumentation resembling one found in Hobbesian epistemology (this makes for strange bedfellows indeed, given that the British empiricism of which Hobbes is a founding figure is the primary historical ancestor of much of twentieth/twenty-first-century Anglo-American Analytic philosophy, an orientation generally quite hostile to and dismissive of Derrida and other post-war French thinkers). To be precise, Hobbes is critical of philosophers (whether medieval scholastics or Continental rationalists) who participate in endless debates about "absurdities," with an "absurdity" being defined by him as an instance of "senseless speech." Hobbes' empiricist contention is that the sole form of meaningful mental content is that which arises from "sense" (i.e., concrete sensory-perceptual experience). If particular words or phrases seem to refer to things of which no idea (*qua* piece of mental content arising from sense) can be formed in the mind, then they're devoid of a genuine, true referent and, thus, are meaningless (in the parlance of the Saussurean structural linguistics dear to both Lacan and Derrida, Hobbesian absurdities, as instances of senseless speech, are signifiers without signifieds, without corresponding spatio-temporal concepts as ideational materials). One of Hobbes' key examples of an absurdity—the target of his criticism here isn't difficult to guess—is the phrase "incorporeal substance" (i.e., metaphysical, and not physical, stuff). In light of an examination of Hägglund's radical atheism, one shouldn't forget that Descartes links his demonstration of the necessary existence of *res cogitans* as incorporeal substance to the theological doctrine of the soul's immortality.[53] All of the above is to be found in the fourth and fifth chapters ("Of Speech" and "Of Reason, and Science") of the first part ("Of Man") of Hobbes' 1651 *Leviathan*.[54] As Hägglund's Derrida has it, immortality basically is a Hobbesian absurdity to the extent that any supposedly "eternal" life one can imagine as an object-referent of desire (i.e., as a desired afterlife, salvation, etc.) must consist of more-time-for-living—and, therefore, this imagined excess of life-beyond-life is anything but timelessly eternal insofar as temporality is an integral ingredient in its imaginary constitution.[55] As Hobbes would put it, when talking about immortality, one thinks either of a mere extension of mortal life (i.e., living on as survival, instead of immortality strictly speaking) or of nothing at all.

53. René Descartes, *Meditations on First Philosophy*, trans. Donald A. Cress (Indianapolis: Hackett, 1993) 1–2, 4, 9.

54. Thomas Hobbes, *Leviathan*, ed. C. B. Macpherson (New York: Viking Penguin, 1985) 102, 108–9, 112–15.

55. Hägglund, *Radical Atheism*, 43.

Hägglund's arguments are as sober-minded as any reasoning spelled out by the hardest-headed modern empiricists or their contemporary offspring this side of the English Channel. But, what in most cases would be a virtue turns out, where a theory of unconsciously shaped desire in relation to mortality is at issue, to be a bit of a vice. In a subtle discussion of Heidegger's treatment of death inspired, in part, by the writings of Maurice Blanchot,[56] Derrida is deliberately unclear about whether any relation to mortal finitude per se is even a thinkable possibility. Simply put, one's "ownmost" death is aporetic, an "x" that cannot be cleanly and decisively categorized along neatly demarcated logical and linguistic lines.[57] Even if Hägglund is absolutely correct that immortality as such, as tied to the timelessness of eternity, is an impossible, unimaginable *telos* for desire's aspirations, Derrida's musings on the aporia of mortality suggest that temporal finitude is at least as elusive and defiant of envisioning as atemporal infiniteness. Or, as Blanchot elegantly encapsulates this conundrum, "To arrive at presence, to die, two equally enchanted expressions."[58] Perhaps desire is stuck stranded between survival and immortality, vainly wanting both, neither, and/or something else. Maybe Sisyphean desire is unreasonable in this futile way, in a way blindly ignoring the cogent, sensible reasons of both classical and deconstructive logics. If indeed there is a third dimension of "something else" in addition to timeless immortality and temporal survival—Hägglund thrusts forward a forced choice between these two alternatives and nothing more—then Hägglund's radical atheist theory of desire must be reconsidered. Exploring whether such a third possibility is at least thinkable is a task to be undertaken below.

The title of Lacan's fourteenth seminar of 1966–1967 is "The Logic of Fantasy." As has been and will be maintained here, this logic, as reflective of the unconscious, must be worked with on its own terms, terms that conform to neither of the logics marshaled by Hägglund. A descriptive account of desire that measures desire externally by logical standards not its own ends up being either inaccurate and misrepresentative *vis-à-vis* its supposed object of description or tipping over into prescription, into informing desire what it should be instead of expressing what it is in and of itself. In telling desire that it doesn't desire what it takes itself to desire, Hägglund's radical

56. Maurice Blanchot, *The Step Not Beyond*, trans. Lycette Nelson (Albany: State University of New York Press, 1992) 1, 93–95, 123; Maurice Blanchot, *The Infinite Conversation*, trans. Susan Hanson (Minneapolis: University of Minnesota Press, 1993) 34, 184; Jacques Derrida, *Aporias*, trans. Thomas Dutoit (Stanford: Stanford University Press, 1993) 87.

57. Derrida, *Aporias*, 8, 11–12, 14, 17–18, 21–23, 36–37, 76.

58. Blanchot, *Step Not Beyond*, 18.

atheist conception of desire suffers from a defect that readily can be conveyed through an inversion of the title of Lacan's fourteenth seminar: the fantasy of logic—that is to say, fantasizing that classical and/or deconstructive logics hold in/for libidinal mechanisms governed by unconscious primary processes such that what desire appears to desire through its fantasies is epiphenomenal relative to what it really and truly desires despite itself. In this respect, Hägglund is in the best of company. In *The Future of an Illusion*, Freud uncharacteristically indulges himself in a rare bout of utopianism, savoring a tempting intellectualist fantasy (one that flies in the face of much of the rest of his own psychoanalytic insights) in which reason eventually triumphs over religion, establishing an undisputed reign under whose rule unconsciously driven irrationalities are reined in by the patient discipline of the secular sciences.[59] As noted, Hägglund goes further than Freud to the extent that he isn't content hopefully to await the future arrival of an atheism *à venir* (insisting instead that atheism always already has arrived). But, more patience is called for at this moment.

§3 Life, Death, and Undeath in Psychoanalysis—Repetition as Finite Infiniteness

During the course of one of his many musings on the infamous *Todestrieb*, Lacan remarks in passing that, "There is nothing so dreadful as dreaming that we are condemned to live repeatedly [*à répétition*]."[60] The nightmare to which he refers is not so much eternal life in the atemporal sense critically scrutinized by Hägglund, but, rather, unending life, survival as a sort of existential insomnia into which one is thrown with no apparent avenue of escape. There can be something awfully horrifying about the prospect of survival-without-end, an existence from which one cannot wake up into the final, resting oblivion of undisturbed nothingness.[61] And yet, at the same time, the alternate prospect of "the End," of the terminal and terminating void of annihilation borne by mortal-making temporality, can seem equally terrible. Could it be said that desire, desiring to have its proverbial cake and eat it too, desires both and neither simultaneously, wanting an unimaginable synthesis combining what is desirable in the ideas of mortality and immortality? Does it want what might be described as a "spectral" (after) life, living on in a mode of being, unknown as such in this world, that would

59. Johnston, "Blast from the Future," 67–68.
60. Lacan, "Aristotle's Dream," 83.
61. Slavoj Žižek, "Kant as a Theoretician of Vampirism," *Lacanian Ink* 8 (2004) 29.

be neither surviving life nor perishing death, neither kinetic time nor static eternity, strictly speaking?

Before proceeding to speak of ghosts, specters, the undead, repetition, and infinity—this tangled jumble of terms is quite relevant to a psychoanalytic engagement with Hägglund's Derrideanism—a few clarifications regarding Lacan's theory of desire are in order (keeping in mind that a thorough investigation into Lacanian *désir* alone would require at least a sizable book or two). Hägglund, with ample textual support, claims that Lacan grounds desire on lack.[62] He construes Lacan's account of desire as entailing that an impossible-to-realize filling-up of temporally induced lack is the ever-receding horizon of the Lacanian libidinal economy (in the guise of what Lacan calls "the Thing" [*das Ding*]). Consistent with his radical atheist thesis stating that the undivided fullness of an infinite presence unscathed by the ravages of temporal negativity isn't what desire actually desires, Hägglund rejects this psychoanalytic model, claiming that the extinguishing of the desire for immortality in the eternal plenitude of everlasting fulfillment would be tantamount to "absolute death" (as immobility, stasis, etc.), and not the "absolute life" desire desires.[63] Consequently, he concludes, *contra* Lacan, that there simply is no desire for an absent, lacking, impossible fullness. For Hägglundian radical atheism, Lacan's Freudian depiction of desiring remains wedded to a traditional (i.e., non-radical) atheism to the extent that, although Lacan atheistically admits that the "sovereign Good" of "the Real Thing" is intrinsically missing and unattainable,[64] he nonetheless continues to insist that subjects are condemned to long after this always-already departed (non-)being.[65]

Hägglund's reading of Lacan overlooks three crucial, interrelated details: one, the essential, fundamental ambivalence of Lacanian desire; two, the dialectical convergences of opposites incarnated in the figure of *das Ding*; and, three, the positive productivity (i.e., the plus), in addition to the negativity (i.e., the minus), involved with Lacan's "*manqué-à-être*" (lack in/of being). First, desire *à la* Lacan isn't simply a matter of attraction to the impossible-to-attain, forever-absent, always-already missing Thing; it also consists of a simultaneous repulsion from the Real of *das Ding*. Particularly in the course of analyses of the play of desire in hysterical subjects—for Lacanian psychoanalysis, features of hysteria as a subjective structural position epitomize select facets of subjectivity

62. Hägglund, *Radical Atheism*, 192–93; Hägglund, "Chronolibidinal Reading."
63. Ibid.
64. Lacan, *SVII*: 70, 300; Lacan, *SXXI*: 3/19/74.
65. Hägglund, "Chronolibidinal Reading."

in general (as the subject of the unconscious)[66]—Lacan is at pains to emphasize
the unstable oscillations and erratic vacillations of desire. In fact, when claiming that Lacan mistakenly believes desire to desire its own cancellation through
consuming immolation in the fires of the undiluted fullness of the Real *an sich*,
Hägglund neglects those instances in which Lacan posits that desire desires its
own perpetuation as desire,[67] a perpetuation requiring the avoidance or deferral
of any ultimate satisfaction through a direct encounter with the Thing incarnate. Lacanian *désir* is caught between conflicting centrifugal and centripetal
movements, splitting subjectivity (as Lacan's "barred S" [$]) because it itself is
torn between an inconsistent multitude of uncoordinated pushes and pulls. It
isn't nearly as univocally coherent and consistent as Hägglund's radical atheism
makes it out to be. Although not radically atheist in a strict Derridean-Hägglundian sense, the desire of Lacan isn't just traditionally atheist either.

Second, *das Ding*, in Lacanian theory, is a far more paradoxical and
multifaceted thing than Hägglund recognizes—and this apart from the
questionability of construing Lacan's Thing-with-a-capital-*T* as a metapsychological equivalent to or synonym for the libidinal *telos* of traditional theisms and atheisms alike (to resort to a flurry of Lacanian jargon for lack of
time, it has much more to do with the desire of/for the absolute alterity of
the Real Other *qua Nebenmensch*—this Other's desire is what desire desires
over and above the answering of signifier-mediated "demands" through the
gratification of bodily driven "needs"[68]—than with full presence, eternal
life, and so on). Apropos the Lacanian Real, the register to which *das Ding*
belongs, Žižek repeatedly explains how this register exhibits, in a Hegelian

66. Slavoj Žižek, "The Abyss of Freedom," in *The Abyss of Freedom/Ages of the World*, ed. Slavoj Žižek and F. W. J. Schelling (Ann Arbor: University of Michigan Press, 1997) 79; Slavoj Žižek, "'I do not order my dreams,'" 192–93; Slavoj Žižek, *Iraq: The Borrowed Kettle* (London: Verso, 2004) 144.

67. Lacan, *SV*: 407; Jacques Lacan, *Le Séminaire de Jacques Lacan, Livre VI: Le dé-sir et son interprétation, 1958-1959*, unpublished typescript, 6/10/59; Jacques Lacan, *Le Séminaire de Jacques Lacan, Livre VIII: Le transfert, 1960-1961*, ed. Jacques-Alain Miller, 2nd ed. (Paris: Éditions du Seuil, 2001) 294; Lacan, *SXVI*: 12–13; Jacques Lacan, *Le Séminaire de Jacques Lacan, Livre XVIII: D'un discours qui ne serait pas du semblant, 1971*, ed. Jacques-Alain Miller (Paris: Éditions du Seuil, 2007) 156; Lacan, "Direction of the Treatment and the Principles of Its Power," 518, 522–23.

68. Sigmund Freud, *Project for a Scientific Psychology*, SE 1:318, 331; Jacques Lacan, *Le Séminaire de Jacques Lacan, Livre IV: La relation d'objet, 1956-1957*, ed. Jacques-Alain Miller (Paris: Éditions du Seuil, 1994) 168–69; Lacan, *SV*: 381–82, 406, 499; Lacan, *SVI*: 4, 15, 59; Lacan, *SVII*: 39, 51; Lacan, *SIX*: 2/21/62; Lacan, *SXVI*: 224–25; Jacques Lacan, "The Signification of the Phallus," in *Écrits*, trans. Bruce Fink (New York: Norton, 2006) 580; Jacques Lacan, "The Subversion of the Subject and the Dialectic of Desire in the Freudian Unconscious," in *Écrits*, trans. Bruce Fink (New York: Norton, 2006) 690; Adrian Johnston, "Nothing Is Not Always No-One: (a)Voiding Love," *Filozofski Vestnik* 26 (2005) 69, 77–81.

manner, paradoxical intersections of seemingly opposed aspects.[69] Specifically, the Real, in the form of the Thing, simultaneously stands for absent presence and present absence,[70] with these two poles each internally split: the former into a presence both alluring and horrifying and the latter into an absence both painful and energizing. Along these lines, the Real Thing both is and isn't desired at the same time, functioning as a center of libidinal gravity that the desiring subject *qua $ neither can live with nor can live without. In one-sidedly emphasizing the Lacanian subject's want relative to *das Ding* as lacking (so as to portray Lacan as complicit with an all-too-traditional atheist theory of desire), Hägglund passes over in problematic silence the plethora of contexts in which Lacan discusses this Thing (as the *jouissance*-laden end of desire, in both senses of the word *end*) as a frightening excess, as an overwhelming presence to be kept safely at arm's length (Hägglund here would need to devote sustained attention to select Lacanian reflections, especially those contained in the tenth seminar [1962–1963], on anxiety, object *a*, the uncanny, the lack of lack, death drive, and desire's positioning in the face of *jouissance* in particular, intricate motifs/topics into which the present discussion cannot go).[71]

The third flaw in Hägglund's reading of Lacan is closely connected with the second one outlined in the paragraph immediately above. For Hägglund, traditional atheism remains mired wallowing in a bog of mourning for the supposed loss of something never truly loved or possessed in the first place. Such atheism, in negating any exhaustively full presence transcending temporality without correspondingly renouncing its libidinal attachments to what is thereby negated, strands itself in pointless mourning. Lacan is construed as condemning the desiring *parlêtre* to precisely this sad fate. However, Lacanian psychoanalysis doesn't limit itself to singing traditional atheist hymns which monotonously rehearse the *pathos* of (symbolic) castration. Despite Lacan's frequent employment, in connection with his depictions of desire, of various terms with negative connotations, each Lacanian minus, as it were, is also, at the same time, a plus (the quasi-Hegelian logic behind this thought-theme ought to please the sensibilities

69. Slavoj Žižek, *Le plus sublime des hystériques: Hegel passe* (Paris: Points Hors Ligne, 1988) 77; Žižek, *Sublime Object of Ideology*, 169–70; Slavoj Žižek, *Tarrying with the Negative: Kant, Hegel, and the Critique of Ideology* (Durham: Duke University Press, 1993) 36; Johnston, *Time Driven*, 365–66; Johnston, *Žižek's Ontology*, 18–19, 109, 146–48, 159–60.

70. Adrian Johnston, "The Vicious Circle of the Super-Ego: The Pathological Trap of Guilt and the Beginning of Ethics," *Psychoanalytic Studies* 3 (2001) 414–15.

71. Jacques Lacan, *Le Séminaire de Jacques Lacan, Livre X: L'angoisse, 1962–1963*, ed. Jacques-Alain Miller (Paris: Éditions du Seuil, 2004) 53, 58–61, 67, 98, 102, 360; Johnston, *Time Driven*, 280–81.

of a deconstructive logic founded on the contestation of the bivalent law
of identity/non-contradiction). For Lacan, lack is far from being mere lack
and nothing else; it isn't purely negative. Like Hegel, Lacan celebrates the
wonderful productive power of the negative, counter-intuitively viewing
the apparent losses of various types introduced into mediated subjective
existence as actual gains, as openings through which everything exceeding
the stifling, idiotic enclosure of dumb, meaningless being can come to be[72]
(in this fashion, Lacanian theory is quite close to Derridean-Hägglundian
radical atheism). A cigar sometimes might be simply a cigar. But, absence is
never simply absence alone in psychoanalysis.

At the level of the (non-)distinction between presence and absence,
it would be worthwhile at this stage to turn to Derrida's "hauntology" in
conjunction with certain Lacanian-Žižekian ponderings about ghosts and
specters as "the undead." Derrida introduces the neologism "hauntology" in
Specters of Marx,[73] and Hägglund refers to it several times in *Radical Atheism*.[74] Derrida specifies that he coins this word to designate something that
"does not belong to ontology, to the discourse on the Being of beings, or to
the essence of life or death."[75] Lacan's hesitations and reservations as regards
ontology would not be inappropriate to mention here in connection with
Derrida's subsequent deconstructivist take on this domain of philosophy.
As is well known, in his famous eleventh seminar of 1964, Lacan answers
Jacques-Alain Miller's query regarding a specifically Lacanian ontology by
avowing that, in essence, there really isn't one: "the unconscious . . . does
not lend itself to ontology"[76]—and, insofar as Lacan is an analyst theorizing
primarily for other analysts about the unconscious as the definitive concern
of the practice of psychoanalysis, he, Lacan, doesn't espouse a psychoanalytic ontology. Later on, in both the nineteenth and twentieth seminars,
he is critical and dismissive of ontology as a vain philosophical effort at
constructing a seamless, totalizing world view (just as Freud before him
cites Heine's derisive depiction of the comical struggles of the philosopher
to "patch up the gaps in the structure of the universe" with "the tatters of
his dressing-gown"[77]): In the nineteenth seminar (1971–1972), he goes so

72. Johnston, *Žižek's Ontology*, 263.

73. Jacques Derrida, *Specters of Marx: The State of Debt, the Work of Mourning, and
the New International*, trans. Peggy Kamuf (New York: Routledge, 1994) 51.

74. Hägglund, *Radical Atheism*, 82, 84.

75. Derrida, *Specters of Marx*, 51.

76. Jacques Lacan, *The Seminar of Jacques Lacan, Book XI: The Four Fundamental
Concepts of Psycho-Analysis, 1964*, ed. Jacques-Alain Miller, trans. Alan Sheridan (New
York: Norton, 1977) 29.

77. Freud, *New Introductory Lectures*, 160–61.

far as to ridicule the discourse of systematic ontology as laughable in light of implications flowing from his "barring" of the Symbolic big Other;[78] in the twentieth seminar (1972–1973), while sharply distinguishing between philosophy and psychoanalysis, he treats ontology as a philosophical *Weltanschauung* and, resonating with his remarks about it from the previous academic year, mocks it as "the funniest thing going."[79]

Funnier still, Derrida's term for his in-between, out-of-joint, not-entirely-an-ontology might not be an utterly unprecedented coincidence. Playing with the French word for shame as an actually felt negative affect (i.e., *honte*), Lacan admits to having his own "*hontologie.*" He speaks of this sort of shame in the closing session of the seventeenth seminar (1969–1970). At the start of that session, with reference to the notion of "dying of shame" and the fact that people often declare "It's a shame" when someone dies, Lacan appeals to a "(h)ontology" as necessary in order to do justice to the non-arriving, always-to-come, deferred (non-)being of death.[80] A couple of years later, he ambiguously remarks that "ontology is a shame."[81] What is one to make of this? Given the issues at stake in this discussion of Hägglund's radical atheist depiction of desire, attention ought to be paid to a common denominator between Lacan and Derrida apropos ontology: When considering mortality and immortality, both thinkers feel compelled to gesture in the direction of a more/other-than-ontology accounting for a spectral netherworld of non-beings, not-quite-beings, not-wholly-existent-beings, and so on. And, for each of them, ghosts turn out to be ideal figures for imaginarily embodying the strange quasi-entities that would be the objects of a Lacanian *hontologie* and/or a Derridean *hantologie*.

Ghosts, as specters condemned to haunt this world, are neither alive nor dead in any conventional sense. They are incompletely dematerialized spirits wandering about between worlds, languishing in a hazy, indeterminate state as misfits bereft of a proper place. These revenants affect the reality of this world here without fully being a part of it. Along these lines, does Lacan, like Derrida, have a hauntology that isn't a crying shame? In his commentary on Shakespeare's *Hamlet* contained in the sixth seminar on the topic of desire, Lacan invokes the same ghost Derrida summons in *Specters of Marx* so as to address and further develop Freud's psychoanalytic understanding of mourning (specifically as per "Mourning and Melancholia"). He begins with

78. Jacques Lacan, *Le Séminaire de Jacques Lacan, Livre XIX: Le savoir du psychanalyste, 1971–1972*, unpublished typescript, 21, 72.

79. Jacques Lacan, *The Seminar of Jacques Lacan, Book XX: Encore, 1972–1973*, ed. Jacques-Alain Miller, trans. Bruce Fink (New York: Norton, 1998) 30–31.

80. Lacan, *SXVII*: 180, 209.

81. Lacan, *SXIX*: 3, 8, 72.

an observation about mortality: "The one unbearable dimension of possible human experience is not the experience of one's own death, which no one has, but the experience of the death of another."[82] Already, a significant point of contrast with radical atheism surfaces: Whereas Hägglund denies the possibility of one relating to oneself, even in the wildest fantasies, as immortal, Lacan (and, on occasion, Derrida too) denies the possibility of relating to oneself as mortal, save for in a vicarious, displaced manner through the deaths of others. In Lacan's eyes, the void left behind by the absent-because-departed other is the site of mourning. He proceeds to clarify:

> Where is the gap, the hole that results from this loss and that calls forth mourning on the part of the subject? It is a hole in the real, by means of which the subject enters into a relationship that is the inverse of what I have set forth in earlier seminars under the name of *Verwerfung* [repudiation, foreclosure].[83]

Lacan continues:

> Just as what is rejected from the symbolic register reappears in the real, in the same way the hole in the real that results from loss, sets the signifier in motion. This hole provides the place for the projection of the missing signifier . . .[84]

According to the above, mourning is the precise mirror-image inversion of psychosis within the Real-Symbolic-Imaginary register theory of Lacanian metapsychology. Psychosis, as arising from the mechanism of foreclosure (i.e., the absence/rejection of "the Name-of-the-Father"), entails a dynamic wherein "*what has been rejected from the symbolic reappears in the real*"[85] (i.e., seemingly "real" delusions and hallucinations appear "out there" in place of an intra-subjectively missing constellation of key Oedipalizing signifiers).[86] Mourning, by contrast, amounts to a rift in the fabric of the Real (to be comprehended in this context as an actual, factual material loss of someone) being filled in by the Symbolic return of that which was lost (through, for instance, a proliferation of commemorations, markers, memorials, monuments, rituals, etc. devoted to the vanished one being mourned).[87] There-

---

82. Lacan, "Desire and the Interpretation of Desire in *Hamlet*," 37.

83. Ibid., 37–38.

84. Ibid., 38.

85. Lacan, *SIII*: 46.

86. Ibid., 12–13, 45–46, 149–50; Lacan, *SV*: 480; Lacan, "On a Question Prior to Any Possible Treatment of Psychosis," in *Écrits*, trans. Bruce Fink (New York: Norton, 2006) 465–66, 479, 481.

87. Johnston, *Žižek's Ontology*, 37–39.

fore, if psychosis is generated by foreclosure, mourning must be generated by inverse foreclosure. And, in inverse foreclosure, the absences of finite others, absences inevitably and unavoidably brought about by the ravages of temporal negativity, are met with the survivors' stubborn insistences on perpetuating the virtual, spectral presence of those absent through the repetitious incantations of signifier-traces.[88]

From a Lacanian perspective, mourning seems to confirm La Rochefoucauld's maxim according to which "Neither the sun nor death can be looked at steadily."[89] Mixing together Lacan and La Rochefoucauld, it could be maintained that death is a sun that can be stared at only when eclipsed. To be more precise, the work of mourning acknowledges and effaces temporal finitude at one and the same time, bearing witness to mortality through a process that simultaneously struggles to cover over this very same mortality through propping up an ethereal, non-mortal double of the deceased, an enshrined socio-symbolic second body seemingly capable of surviving indefinitely. But, arguably, this work of mourning isn't an occasional labor prompted exclusively at those times when another dies and/or disappears.

Surprisingly, the case can be made that the perpetual ontogenetic construction-in-process of a subjectifying ego-level self-identity is spurred, at least in part, by a sort of generally unrecognized mourning. In a passage from the eleventh seminar that Hägglund himself cites,[90] Lacan claims that subjects are haunted by the fantasmatic loss of an immortality never possessed to begin with, perturbed by a living, vital sexuality testifying to individuals' inescapable mortality[91] (he is echoing comments Freud makes about the intimate *rapport* between sex and death in both biological and psychical life[92]). Incidentally, although Hägglund's radical atheist reading of Lacan as an all-too-traditional atheist emphasizes how Lacan's mortal subjects are left desiring an eternal life radical atheism maintains to be undesirable, Hägglund neglects something very important here: In both the eleventh seminar itself as well as an *écrit* from the same year as this seminar (i.e., 1964's "Position of the Unconscious"), Lacan conjures up a little science-fiction myth of his own making, painting an unsettling portrait of a monstrous entity he christens "the lamella."[93] Without getting into the

88. Lacan, "Desire and the Interpretation of Desire in *Hamlet*," 38–39.

89. François duc de la Rochefoucauld, *Maxims*, trans. Leonard Tancock (New York: Penguin, 1959) 40 (maxim 26).

90. Hägglund, "Chronolibidinal Reading."

91. Lacan, *SXI*: 204–5.

92. Ibid., 150.

93. Ibid., 177, 197–99; Jacques Lacan, "Position of the Unconscious," in *Écrits*, trans. Bruce Fink (New York: Norton, 2006) 717–20; Johnston, *Žižek's Ontology*, 22–23, 52.

specifics of its description, this imaginary lamella is the figurative incarnation of the libidinal as excessive vital being, as interminable life idiotically driven to perpetuate itself repetitively. Lacan's myth of the lamella expresses the notion that sexuality is a point at which the opposites of life and death, mortality and immortality converge (for instance, through sexual reproduction, the mortal individual can live on through transmitting his/her genetic material to subsequent generations of offspring; and yet, sexual reproduction itself is the embodied testimony to the mortality of the individual as the disposable husk carrying this transmissible genetic material). Moreover, the "immortality" embodied by the lamella—this is something Hägglund fails to note—isn't, in conformity with traditional atheism, portrayed as desirable. Instead, it inspires revulsion and terror in the face of being smothered by the claustrophobia-inducing immanence of a thriving, parasitical vitality dripping with oozing, obscene *jouissance*. Lacanian desire is profoundly ambivalent about immortality (and this in the same manner as its ambivalence apropos *das Ding*, the Real Thing).

What do mourning and the psychical dynamics of ego formation have to do with these reflections regarding life and death in Lacanian psychoanalysis? In Lacan's account of ego formation through the mirror stage, the complex intertwining of the mortal and the immortal, an intertwining confounding the straightforward dichotomy between life and death relied upon by radical atheism, easily can be discerned. To cut a long story short, the individual's self-alienation through objectification in the form of an *imago-Gestalt* constituting the nucleus of the *moi* introduces this thus-alienated living proto-subject equally to both mortality and immortality through a single process. In becoming an object for itself through the acquisition of an ego, the subject-as-$ is able to imagine its own disappearance, to gaze in fantasies at scenes from which it is absent (such as one's own funeral). Hence, passing through the mirror stage is, according to Lacan, a pre-requisite for awareness of one's own mortality since this awareness relies on the use of self-objectification to stage scenarios in which one's self is pictured as non-existent[94] (but, just as Hägglund claims that spatio-temporal visions pretending to envision absolutely infinite immortality are self-refuting,[95] so too could it be claimed that visions attempting to envision life's mortal finitude in itself and as such, visions in which the subject persists as a gaze beyond the outer limits of the very finitude it's struggling [in vain] to glimpse

94. Lacan, "On a Question Prior to Any Possible Treatment of Psychosis," 461; Johnston, *Žižek's Ontology*, 47–48.

95. Hägglund, *Radical Atheism*, 43–44, 93.

through the windows of fantasies bearing upon matters of birth and death [i.e., fundamental fantasies],[96] are equally self-refuting).

And yet, the mediating images and words into which trajectories of identification are channeled through the mirror stage—this stage facilitates whatever awareness is possible of one's own finitude and mortality—also have the effect of stamping upon subjectivity an impression of its own indelible, permanent duration. The visual and linguistic elements of identity, made of spectral substances consisting of materialities different from the materials composing decomposable bodies, appear to enjoy a capacity for living on different from the survival (as per Derrida-Hägglund) of the terribly perishable lump of flesh and blood identifying with them. Indeed, Lacanian considerations lead to the hypothesis that images and words, although making it possible for subjects to be self-conscious of their own mortality, are embraced and held onto in part because they simultaneously make it impossible for subjects genuinely to envision their own non-being. To put it in hybrid Heideggerian-Derridean parlance, the visual and linguistic elements of ego-level subjectification are, at one and the same time, conditions of possibility and impossibility for relating to oneself as a being-toward-death. Subjects cast themselves into what Lacan characterizes as the "cadaverizing," "corpsifying" second bodies of self-images, proper names, personal pronouns, and socio-symbolic statuses so as to accomplish, among other aims, a staving off of temporal negativity and the mortal finitude inherent to it.[97] These alienating identities quietly bear witness to a lifelong process of mourning, to a never-finished project of continually recognizing and misrecognizing one's status as a death-bound being.

96. Slavoj Žižek, *For They Know Not What They Do: Enjoyment as a Political Factor*, 2nd ed. (London: Verso, 2002) 197; Žižek, *Tarrying with the Negative*, 64; Žižek, *Metastases of Enjoyment*, 120; Slavoj Žižek, *The Indivisible Remainder: An Essay on Schelling and Related Matters* (London: Verso, 1996) 19, 22; Slavoj Žižek, "'I Hear You with My Eyes'; or, The Invisible Master," in *Gaze and Voice as Love Objects*, ed. Renata Salecl and Slavoj Žižek (Durham: Duke University Press, 1996) 94; Žižek, *Fright of Real Tears*, 71; Johnston, *Žižek's Ontology*, 39–43.

97. Lacan, *SII*: 169, 238; Lacan, *SVIII*: 122, 413; Jacques Lacan, "The Mirror Stage as Formative of the *I* Function as Revealed in Psychoanalytic Experience," in *Écrits*, trans. Bruce Fink (New York: Norton) 76; Jacques Lacan, "Aggressiveness in Psychoanalysis," in *Écrits*, trans. Bruce Fink (New York: Norton) 90; Lacan, "*Radiophonie*," 409; Jacques Lacan, "*Le symbolique, le imaginaire et le reel*," in *Des noms-du-père*, ed. Jacques-Alain Miller (Paris: Éditions du Seuil, 2005) 41–43; Mladen Dolar, "At First Sight," in *Gaze and Voice as Love Objects*, ed. Renata Salecl and Slavoj Žižek (Durham: Duke University Press, 1996) 137; Moustapha Safouan, *Pleasure and Being: Hedonism from a Psychoanalytic Point of View*, trans. Martin Thom (New York: St. Martin's, 1987) 60; Žižek, *Plague of Fantasies*, 94; Johnston, *Žižek's Ontology*, 45–51.

What makes subjectifying images and words seemingly immortalizing is their iterability, the fact that they appear to possess the potential, in principle, to be repeated without end. Admittedly, both Derrida and Hägglund would be perfectly correct at this juncture to raise the objection that visual and linguistic traces, as traces, are always and essentially exposed to future destruction, erasure, forgetting, and so on. This is indeed true. However, both phenomenologically and structurally, the ghostly, quasi-dematerialized avatars of its mediated identity lure desiring subjectivity into not being able wholeheartedly to believe in its own mortality, fully to comprehend and digest the radical implications of facing up to the anonymous facelessness of its temporal finitude (and, as asserted earlier, insofar as illusions of immortality shape desire itself, no defensible theory of desire can dismiss these illusions as merely illusory *qua* epiphenomenal). At the level of its (fundamental) fantasies, the psychoanalytic subject of desire cannot but view itself as surviving without end, as living on interminably. There are two lives, which dialectically interpenetrate each other, corresponding to the two deaths spoken of by Lacan in his seventh and eighth seminars (1959–1960 and 1960–1961):[98] a first, material life (i.e., natural and/or Real being) and a second, more-than-material life (i.e., cultural and/or Imaginary-Symbolic being). The subtitle of Hägglund's book refers to "the time of life" without the contents of this thus-subtitled text going on to distinguish between lives. From a Lacanian vantage point, this presents difficulties. The preceding arguments indicate that, through disproportionately stressing a temporal finitude tied primarily to the first, material life, Hägglund neglects temporalities peculiar to the second, more-than-material life. This latter form of living relates to both itself and the former form of living as involving repetition *qua* finite infiniteness (and not, *à la* Hägglund, infinite finitude).

Following Derridean-Hägglundian radical atheism, if infinite finitude refers to life/mortality and infinite infiniteness refers to death/immortality, then finite infiniteness (a third category absent in Hägglund's framework but arguably present in psychoanalytic theory) refers to undeath as neither mortality nor immortality (following Žižek, one could propose a tripartite distinction between the mortal, the immortal, and the non/not-mortal).[99] To be undead (i.e., non/not-mortal as different from immortal) would be to go on surviving without foreseeable end, living on indefinitely. This fantasmatic prospect splits desire by being simultaneously attractive and repulsive all at once. As mentioned previously here a while ago, Žižek employs the horror-fiction category of the undead in his efforts to elucidate Freudian

98. Lacan, *SVII*: 320; Lacan, *SVIII*: 122.
99. Žižek, "Kant as a Theoretician of Vampirism," 27.

and Lacanian concept-terms such as the lamella, *jouissance*, and the death drive. These three things are each related to the fundamental psychoanalytic concept of repetition (a concept forming a crucial component of another foundational psychoanalytic concept, namely, that of drive [*Trieb*]). As is the case with the temporality of retroactive "deferred action" uncovered by psychoanalysis (i.e., Freud's *Nachträglichkeit* and Lacan's *après-coup*), the temporality of repetition in its analytic conception doesn't fit into either of the temporalities operative in radical atheism as per Hägglund (i.e., the time of life and the timelessness of death). Once could succinctly encapsulate repetition as an intra-temporal resistance to time itself, a negation of time transpiring within time. As Judith Butler expresses it, "repetition is a vain effort to stay, or indeed, to reverse time; such repetition reveals a rancor against the present which feeds upon itself."[100]

At one point in his book, Hägglund refers to an aspect of Derrida's interpretation of Hegel. He appeals to the Derridean version of Hegelian "spurious" or "bad" infinity in his efforts to clarify the ultimate underlying mode of temporality posited by radical atheism.[101] Hägglund indicates that extracting this bad/spurious infinity from the relation Hegel places it in with a good/non-spurious infinity—Derridean-Hägglundian radical atheism treats the latter as yet another designation of the impossible, nonexistent, self-refuting (idea of the) absolute (as a full, eternal presence-to-itself transcending the negativity of the time of finite life)—permits putting bad/spurious infinity to work for deconstruction as a means of further illuminating temporal finitude as the infinitely finite. Putting aside disputes bearing upon Hegel's genuine, true infinity as the *Aufhebung* negation-of-the-negation of the temporal negativity of bad/spurious infinity (today more than ever, there are various serious philosophical and mathematical reasons for re-thinking the infinite), a question must be asked: Is Hegelian bad/spurious infinity, even when deconstructively divorced from its partnership with good/non-spurious infinity, obviously akin or similar (solely) to radical atheist temporal finitude?

One should not forget that Hegel's bad/spurious infinity is still infinite (and not finite), still a mode or variant of infiniteness. With this in mind, a passage from the *Encyclopedia Logic*, in which Hegel discusses bad/spurious infinity, deserves to be quoted:

---

100. Judith Butler, "The Pleasures of Repetition," in *Pleasure Beyond the Pleasure Principle: The Role of Affect in Motivation, Development, and Adaptation*, ed. Robert A. Glick and Stanley Bone (New Haven: Yale University Press, 1990) 272.

101. Hägglund, *Radical Atheism*, 93, 220.

> This Infinity is the wrong or negative infinity: it is only a nega-
> tion of a finite: but the finite rises again the same as ever, and is
> never got rid of and absorbed. In other words, this infinite only
> expresses the *ought-to-be* elimination of the finite. The progres-
> sion to infinity never gets further than a statement of the con-
> tradiction involved in the finite, viz.that it is somewhat as well
> as somewhat else. It sets up with endless iteration the alternation
> between these two terms, each of which calls up the other.[102]

Particularly considering the deconstructive and psychoanalytic background
of this current context in which Hegel is being invoked, a couple of features
of these lines from the *Logic* merit close attention. First of all, the descriptive language mobilized by Hegel audibly evokes associations to the undead
monsters of horror films cited as fantastic explanatory examples by Žižek in
his efforts to elucidate the death-drive-like *jouissance* of the Lacanian Real
(not to mention associations to Lacan's 1964 descriptions of the alien lamella-
creature itself). In horror films, the undead monster (be it a vampire, mummy,
zombie, or, in science-fiction horror, a cyborg, robot, or virus) typically ter-
rifies by being that which nightmarishly "rises again the same as ever, and is
never got rid of"; each time the protagonists appear finally to have succeeded
at killing off the malevolent beings antagonizing them, these beings reanimate
themselves and continue their diabolical pursuits in a tireless, relentless way.
Perhaps the undead are uncanny in a specifically Freudian fashion (remem-
bering that Freud, citing Hegel's German idealist contemporary Schelling, defines the uncanny [*das Unheimliche*] as "that" which "ought to have remained
secret and hidden but has come to light,"[103] and then proceeds to analyze the
appearances, in literature, of doppelgangers and entities eerily between life
and death). That is to say, they are, in Žižekian parlance, "things from inner
space." These figure from myth and fiction both fascinate and disturb people
precisely because they represent a return of the repressed, a surfacing, within
the out-in-the-open spheres of quotidian popular culture, of elements and
aspects of unconscious fantasy life.

Another feature of the above quoted characterization of bad/spurious
infinity from Hegel's *Encyclopedia Logic* enables a bridge to be built between, on the one hand, this Hegelian concept, and, on the other hand, the
here-interlinked notions of the undead and unconscious fantasy life. Hegel
speaks of an "endless iteration" generated by a "contradiction." In a very
general fashion, one could say, apropos Lacan's register theory (especially

102. G. W. F. Hegel, *Logic: Part One of the Encyclopedia of Philosophical Sciences*,
trans. William Wallace (Oxford: Oxford University Press, 1975) 137 (§94).

103. Freud, "The Uncanny," *SE* 17:225.

as it's configured in the later period of Lacan's teachings in the 1960s and 1970s), that the representational constructs of Imaginary-Symbolic reality turn around unrepresentable antagonisms, conflicts, deadlocks, impasses, etc. in the Real (related to this, and *contra* Hägglund's Hobbesian empiricist insistence that the fantasies of desire are always and necessarily reducible to sensible spatio-temporal inscriptions, one ought to recall Lacan's repeated assertion that parts of *objet petit a*, the center of gravity around which fantasizing desire orbits, are "non-specularizable," that is, impossible to inscribe in spatio-temporal forms).[104] As with the inauthentic infinity of Hegelian repetition, the dynamics of Imaginary-Symbolic reality's always-in-process constructions are driven along by Real "contradictions." In an early period of *le Séminaire* (the third seminar on the psychoses), Lacan observes that "the question of death and the question of birth are as it happens the two ultimate questions that have precisely no solution in the signifier."[105] As defined by Lacan and others (such as Jean Laplanche and Jean-Bertrand Pontalis, André Green, Žižek, and Alenka Zupančič), fundamental fantasies are formations of the unconscious straining to stage in fantasy subjectified constellations of images and words answering to the enigmas of birth and death, mysteries lying at the heart of the life of temporally finite beings that nonetheless cannot be answered by images and words in an adequate, satisfactory manner.[106] If, as Hägglund argues, immortality per se (as life-beyond-time) is as unimaginable and self-contradictory as a square circle (and, hence, unable to be a fantasmatic object-referent of desire), so too, might it be argued on psychoanalytic grounds, is mortality as the absolute temporal finitude of a being born to die. In Lacanian locution, the radical negativity of the time of a life-bound-to-death is a Real with "no solution in the signifier," an "x" incapable of proper, appropriate representation by the *Vorstellungen* constituting the contents of the living psyche. Subjects'

---

104. Lacan, *SIX*: 5/30/62, 6/6/62, 6/20/62; Lacan, *SX*: 57, 74, 292–94; Lacan, *SXIII*: 1/12/66, 3/30/66, 6/1/66; Jacques Lacan, *Le Séminaire de Jacques Lacan, Livre XIV: La logique du fantasme, 1966–1967*, unpublished typescript, 5/24/67, 6/7/67; Lacan, *SXVI*: 300–305; Lacan, "Subversion of the Subject and the Dialectic of Desire in the Freudian Unconscious," 693, 699.

105. Lacan, *SIII*: 190.

106. Jean Laplanche and Jean-Bertrand Pontalis, "Fantasy and the Origins of Sexuality," in *Formations of Fantasy*, ed. Victor Burgin, James Donald, and Cora Kaplan (New York: Methuen, 1986) 19, 27; André Green, "*L'originaire dans la psychanalyse,*" in *La diachronie en psychanalyse* (Paris: Les Éditions de Minuit, 2000) 59; Alenka Zupančič, "Philosophers' Blind Man's Buff," in *Gaze and Voice as Love Objects*, ed. Renata Salecl and Slavoj Žižek (Durham: Duke University Press, 1996) 47–48; Johnston, *Žižek's Ontology*, 33–36.

fundamental fantasies arguably are incapable of envisioning them as either immortal *qua* infinitely infinite or mortal *qua* infinitely finite.

Fantasy life is spuriously infinite in two senses: one, its Imaginary-Symbolic formations repeatedly fail to capture the twin Reals of mortality as infinite finitude and immortality as infinite infiniteness; two, thanks to this failure, unconscious fantasizing repeatedly struggles again and again in perpetual futility to (borrowing a turn of phrase from, of all people, Richard Rorty) "eff the ineffable." The result of this is that desiring subjects, with their ego-structures and associated fantasy lives as mediated by images, signifiers, and gazes, relate to themselves as uncanny undead beings, entities unable to leave time in both the Derridean-Hägglundian radical atheist sense (i.e., a true transcendence of time cannot even be imagined) as well as in a psychoanalytic sense (i.e., death, as the only exit from time, also cannot be imagined). If Hägglund is right that people never really have been able to conceive of themselves as immortal strictly speaking, it might additionally be contended that, for analytic reasons, they never really have been able to conceive of themselves as mortal per se either. Making a Kantian gesture, one could stipulate that each and every attempt by the psyche to comprehend mortality and immortality (as finitude and infiniteness *an sich*) lands it in a dialectics of fantasy life, in the pincers of irreconcilable antinomies (specifically apropos mortal finitude, this respondent elsewhere has discussed a "psychical antinomy" in connection with fundamental fantasies).[107] Appropriating a now-familiar articulation Lacan employs, starting in the twentieth seminar (but foreshadowed beginning in the eighteenth seminar),[108] to characterize the Real of the antagonistic, antinomic deadlock of sexuation (*à la* the infamous non-existent *rapport sexuel*), mortal finitude, as belonging to the Real (and not to Imaginary-Symbolic reality), is an impossibility that "doesn't stop not being written" (*ne cesse pas de s'écrire*).[109] More precisely, impossible-to-subjectify mortal finitude cannot be inscribed at the level of the *Vorstellungen* composing the contents of the psyche. And yet, in spite and because of this, the ideational representations forming the formations of the unconscious repeatedly circulate around this hole-without-a-trace. Mortality, as embodied by the living being's birth and death, is "fundamentally foreclosed" from this being's subjective structure(s).[110]

107. Johnston, *Žižek's Ontology*, 30–31, 61, 100.

108. Lacan, *SXVIII*: 65, 67, 105, 107; Lacan, *SXIX*: 11/4/71, 3/3/72; Lacan, *SXXI*: 2/12/74, 5/21/74; Jacques Lacan, *Le Séminaire de Jacques Lacan, Livre XXV: Le moment de conclure, 1977–1978*, unpublished typescript, 11/15/77.

109. Lacan, *SXX*: 93.

110. Johnston, *Žižek's Ontology*, 39.

F. H. Jacobi, a contemporary of Kant and the German idealists, somewhere confesses that he finds the theist idea of everlasting-life-without-end and the atheist idea of death-as-the-final-end equally intolerable and unbearable (a sentiment expressible in Leninist-Stalinist style as "both are worse!"). Jacobi's emotional being feels uneasy with both thoughts, with the infinite (as an unending existential insomnia) as well as the finite (as an eventual nocturnal abyss of nothingness). Anything deeper than superficial conscious lip service paid to the intellectual acceptance of the truth that "all men are mortal" is difficult indeed. Saying that one is a radical atheist is much easier than feeling, in the core fibers of one's being, that one is such.

§4 The Desire of Atheist Desire— Radical Atheism's Future(s)

One of the more opaque of Lacan's many cryptic one-liners is a pronouncement about what real atheism would be. In the eleventh seminar, he claims, "the true formula of atheism is not *God is dead*. . . . the true formula of atheism is *God is unconscious*."[111] A few years later, in the seventeenth seminar, he explains exactly why, from a Freudian perspective, trumpeting the death of God isn't the final act of an accomplished atheism taken to its most extreme, consequent endpoint. This explanation relies upon a reading of Freud's *Totem and Taboo* as a new psychoanalytic twist on the Sophoclean tragedy from which the Oedipus complex takes its name (for Lacan, the tale Freud tells in this exemplary 1913 piece of speculative psychoanalytic anthropology, a story he custom tailors rather than borrows from Sophocles, discloses the true analytic import of the Oedipal).[112] What Lacan highlights is that, in the Freudian myth of the primal horde, the murder of the *Urvater* (i.e., the archaic paternal prototype of the divine, of the gods and God[s] of subsequent religious history)[113] by the band of oppressed, sexually deprived brothers doesn't open the floodgates releasing a liberated, bacchanalian *jouissance* in which the women formerly monopolized by this alpha male freely circulate in an orgy of unfettered enjoyment. As Freud observes, "The dead father became stronger than the living one had been. . . . What had up to then been prevented by his actual existence was thenceforward prohibited by the sons themselves."[114] Lacan resorts to a twist on Dostoyevsky's "If God is dead, then everything is permitted" to encapsulate Freud's insight that the destruction of

---

111. Lacan, *SXI:* 59.
112. Lacan, *SXVIII:* 68–69.
113. Freud, *Totem and Taboo, SE* 13:147–49, 154.
114. Ibid., 143.

an incarnation of authority doesn't automatically and necessarily amount to the liquidation of the rule of this authority's law: "If God is dead, then nothing is permitted."[115] Instead, the living paternal figure murdered returns in the much more potent spectral guise of a guilt-ridden regime of socio-symbolic rules imposing even stricter regulations upon the murderers.

The Lacanian lesson for aspiring atheists is not only that consciously mouthing the words "God is dead" is insufficient for ridding oneself of religiosity once and for all-intoning such a mantra, under the impression that it possesses the power to conjure away the spirits of theism, risks blinding one to the multifarious manners in which ghostly unconscious religious beliefs continue to enjoy a psychical afterlife in the aftermath of a supposed accession to atheism at the level of self-consciousness. In fact, if anything, to be a full-fledged atheist, one must, as Lacan indicates, be warily aware that "God is unconscious"—which, in psychoanalysis, is to be far from dead and gone. In other words, until and unless one is willing and able to accept that theological and quasi-theological residues will subsist in an unconscious that will continue to speak in oneself and despite oneself—this unconscious God doesn't die if and when consciousness declares the divine to be deceased and departed—one is likely to remain in the thrall of religiosity (even more so the less one believes oneself to believe). How many people, perceiving themselves decisively to have abandoned religion and everything associated with it long ago in their personal histories, discover on an analyst's couch just how persistent and pervasive in their present lives are the lingering spectral traces of a never-really-discarded-faith? Like the ghost of Freud's murdered *Urvater*, God can and does return in even more powerful guises in the wake of having been declared dead. Altering a line from the 1995 film *The Usual Suspects*—radical atheism should take this altered line to heart as a word of warning about the risks ahead of it—maybe the greatest trick God can play is convincing the world he doesn't exist. The same might be said of (fantasmatic) immortality too.

On several occasions, Lacan indicates that the experience of a psychoanalysis seen through to a proper conclusion (i.e., an analysis that could be said to have been terminated at the right time in the analytic work) must involve an atheistic dimension, namely, in Lacanese, a loss of faith in any and every figuration of an omnipotent and omniscient big Other (whether God, nature, the analyst, whoever, or whatever).[116] Again in the seventeenth seminar, he forcefully insists that, "The pinnacle of

---

115. Lacan, *SXVII*: 119–20.

116. Lacan, *SX*: 357–58; Lacan, *SXVI*: 280–81; Johnston, "Conflicted Matter," 170–71.

psychoanalysis is well and truly atheism"[117] (proceeding to qualifying this by saying, "provided one gives this term another sense than that of 'God is dead,' where all indications are that far from calling into question what is in play, namely the law, it is consolidated instead"[118]—the paraphrase of Dostoyevsky immediately follows).[119] A truly completed analysis ends with, among other things, witnessing and accepting the fall of all instantiations of the all-powerful and all-knowing.

In closing, to bring the discussion back to Hägglund's admirable struggle to formulate a rigorous atheism that, in its far-reaching implications, is authentically radical in the most genuine sense of the word, one ought to note that Lacan's construal of atheism shares something with Freud's views on temporal finitude. Recall that, in "On Transience," Freud suggests one can come to experience the limited duration of everything that is as enhancing rather than degrading the worthiness of objects and others to be valued. He offers to his walking companions, who are haunted by a libidinally paralyzing foreknowledge of inevitable decay and disappearance, another way to interpret this ever-changing world of transient beings. But, Freud's succinct account of this walk through the shadow of the valley of death hints that turning the scarcity of time from an inhibitor into a catalyst of desire is an accomplishment that hopefully should be achieved by those laboring to work through analytic insights. Likewise, Lacan clearly identifies a non-superficial (i.e., radical) atheism worthy of the name as a prescriptive aim of analyses, and not a descriptive default subjective position from which analysands depart in their journeys into the "extimate."[120]

Speaking of desire in the closing minutes of the opening session of his renowned seminar on *The Ethics of Psychoanalysis*, Lacan maintains that "the essential dimension of desire" is that "it is always desire in the second degree, desire of desire."[121] Relating this to the topic of atheism as addressed by psychoanalysis, what the signifier "God" signifies won't drop dead, at least not in the foreseeable future and without a ferocious fight; it will live on under any number of other signifying banners, surviving as an unconscious spirit even in those ignoring it with sealed lips or loudly dancing on its empty grave. This repressed revenant undoubtedly will continue to exert an influence on desiring subjects for quite some time yet. But, radical atheism, whether Lacanian or Derridean, could justifiably be described as

117. Lacan, *SXVII*: 119.

118. Ibid.

119. Ibid., 119–20.

120. Lacan, *SVII*: 139; Lacan, *SXVI*: 224–25, 249.

121. Lacan, *SVII*: 14.

the best possible outcome of a good analysis, whether this analysis is "good" judged by clinical-therapeutic standards or by conceptual-theoretical ones. For now, the most that can be hoped for is that Hägglund's superlative conceptual-theoretical analysis, although arguably incapable of killing for good the (unconscious) desire for what the signifier "God" signifies, can arouse in others a "second degree" desire not to have this desire, a redoubled desire for other desires. In this resides the promise of the project of radical atheism.

6

Solidarity in Suffering
with the Non-Human

Katerina Kolozova

1. Identifying with Suffering
Stripped of Humanity

Judith Butler makes one of the most inventive and potentially revolutionary claims in political theory today by arguing that grief can be a resource for politics. According to Butler, grief offers the possibility to identify with the "suffering itself" that the Other undergoes. Let us consider the following lines from *Precarious Life*:

> Is there something to be gained in the political domain by maintaining grief as part of the framework within which we think our international ties? . . . To grieve, and to make grief itself into a resource for politics, is not to be resigned to inaction, but it may be understood as the slow process by which we develop a point of identification with suffering itself.[1]

Building on this last point made by Butler in the cited paragraph, I will argue that "identification with suffering itself" could constitute a form of political solidarity which is established independently from and at an

---

1. Judith Butler, *Precarious Life: The Power of Mourning and Violence* (London: Verso, 2006) 30.

instance beyond or anterior to language. If we identify with the "suffering itself" we are identifying with the purely "evental," i.e., with the sheer experience (of subjection to pain) which is a pre-linguistic category. The "suffering itself" is but a taking-place of pain and/or of trauma. Put in Laruellean parlance, it is the "lived" *par excellence*. Thus it is the Real in the Laruellian as well as in the Lacanian sense of the word. Resorting to Lacan's terminology, it can be said that the "suffering itself" is the *Tuché* (the incident and the accident, the Trauma) which interrupts the endless chain of "making sense," which produces rupture into the Automaton, i.e., into the Signifying Chain.

First, the *tuché*, which we have borrowed, as I told you last time, from Aristotle, who uses it in his search for cause. We have translated it as *the encounter with the real*. The real is beyond the *automaton*, the return, the coming-back, the insistence of the signs, by which we see ourselves governed by the pleasure principle. The real is that which always lies behind the automaton, and it is quite obvious, throughout Freud's research, that it is this that is the object of his concern.[2]

The Real lies "beyond" but also "behind" the automation of ceaseless signification. The fact that it is "beyond signification" does not mean that it (the Real) cannot and should not be studied. Quite to the contrary, according to Lacan, it is the central "object of concern" in Freud's oeuvre. In other words, the fact that the Real is not the Language, that it is, by definition, that "other-than-Language," that which is not the Language or the Sign, does not mean that signification of the effects of the Real cannot be produced—that "a language *of* the Real" is impossible. The Language—that signifying automaton—is but a constant, never accomplished tendency to re-present the Real, that desire of possession (over the Real) which aims at establishing absolute control over the unruly Real. The lingual re-creation of the Real which desires to understand it in an absolute way, to fully exhaust the Real's "meaning" (to "make sense" out of the sheer "taking place") is in fact a tendency toward possession of the senseless Real by way of attributing it sense and reducing it to sense. The Real *happens* to the Language and the Language *automatically* produces actions of representing the effects of the Real and becomes engaged in the ever frustrating and always already failed attempt to re-present the Real without a remainder.

We can succeed in unravelling this ambiguity of the reality involved in the transference only on the basis of the function of the real in repetition. What is repeated, in fact, is always something that occurs—the expression tells us quite a lot about its relation to the *tuché—as if by chance* . . . Is it not

2. Jacques Lacan, *The Seminar of Jacques Lacan, Book XI: The Four Fundamental Concepts of Psychoanalysis*, ed. Jacques-Alain Miller, trans. Alan Sheridan (New York: Norton, 1998) 53–54.

remarkable that, at the origin of the analytic experience, the real should have presented itself in the form of that which is *unassimilable* in it—in the form of the trauma, determining all that follows, and imposing on it an apparently accidental origin?[3]

Butler's call for "identification with suffering itself" implies that there is a possibility of identification beyond the Discursive, an identification with the Other which is pre-lingual. The potency (or the revolutionary potential) of this idea consists in the fact that it enables inclusion unlimited by the inclusiveness of the category of Human. The site and the agency of this process of identification would be the body since, according to Butler, it is through the body that the suffering and the sense of vulnerable exposure primarily take place. Butler's argument seems to be that bodily suffering and vulnerability are the generic notions from which one could, for instance, infer the psychic suffering and vulnerability. Or rather, the presupposition about the categorical primacy of the physical suffering and vulnerability over their psychic renditions appears to be one of the premises upon which Butler's entire argument is built.

Let us return to the issue of grief, to the moments in which one undergoes something outside one's control and finds that one is beside oneself, not at one with oneself. Perhaps we can say that grief contains the possibility of apprehending a mode of dispossession that is fundamental to who I am. This possibility does not dispute the fact of my autonomy, but it does qualify that claim through recourse to the fundamental sociality of embodied life, the ways in which we are, from the start and by virtue of being a bodily being, already given over, beyond ourselves, implicated in lives that are notour own.[4]

Grief is a state of sheer suffering which cannot be defined in the last instance as "physical." Nevertheless it is precisely the complex transcendental-real and psychic-physical "purely-experiential-state" which signals that the identity in the last instance of the *location* of suffering is physical. (The Real-of-Suffering, however, is situated beyond the philosophical dichotomy of the bodily and the mental.) Butler writes that grief is a state that unravels "a mode of dispossession that is fundamental." The primacy of this dispossessed mode of existence consists in the fact that "prior to the processes of individuation"[5] one is always already an embodied life, which implies that "by virtue of being a bodily being"[6] we are "already given over, beyond ourselves, implicated in

3. Ibid.
4. Butler, *Precarious Life*, 28.
5. Ibid., 31.
6. Ibid., 28.

lives that are not our own."[7] Understanding the effects of the bodily in the creation of the most rudimentary societal and how it operates as one of the most fundamental political premises necessitates a discourse which situates itself beyond the traditional Body/Mind dichotomy.

The mode of dispossession Butler writes of is one that takes place on the plane of the Real; it is an imprint of the Real and into the Real of the pre-lingual subjection to Trauma. It is "prior to individuation," it is pre-subjective, pre-reflexive—it is (in) the Real. One is always already vulnerably exposed to the potential violence (or Trauma in any form) in its sheer brutality, prior to any making sense. And it is with this primordial instance of vulnerability—with "the suffering itself"—we are called upon identifying. In spite of the fact that the means of identification are always already "transcendental" (in the Laruellian sense of the word) or essentially pertaining to the Language (in the Lacanian sense of the word), what we identify with is an instance which does not require discursive recognition. The sense in which I use the expression "identify with" is that of its literal or etymological meaning: the cognitive process of establishing a sense (a representation which is not purely mental but is also followed by pre-reflexive experience) of "sameness" between the subject of cognition and its object.

Bodily suffering, a body in utter helplessness facing a threat of brutal violence, is an instance we can identify with without any need of conceptual frame that would enable valorization or "making sense" of it, i.e., without the category of humanity. What we share in the "common human suffering" is the suffering itself not humanity. Humanity is a restrictive category: it is the product of signification. Or in Larueallian parlance, it is a category of the Transcendental. It is significance in a double sense of the word: it signifies and also it is significant (it is on the top of the signifying hierarchy).

There is a discourse of humanity—or rather humanity is always already the product of a discourse—and it "establishes the limits of human intelligibility":

> It is not simply, then, that there is a "discourse" of dehumanization that produces these effects, but rather that there is a limit to discourse that establishes the limits of human intelligibility. It is not just that a death is poorly marked, but that it is unmarkable. Such a death vanishes, not into explicit discourse, but in the ellipses by which public discourse proceeds.[8]

Concurring with Butler, and building on her other arguments in the chapter "Violence, Mourning, Politics" of *Precarious Life*, I would like to

7. Ibid.
8. Ibid., 35.

explore the possibility of expanding the discursive category of "humanity" by means of identification with the "suffering itself." Or in different words, let us explore the possibility of identification with suffering itself (with grief as suffering) as the means of expanding inclusiveness of the notion of "humanity."

2. The Broken Figure of Humanity: Jesus and Oedipus

2.1. Jesus: Rereading Donna Haraway

Postmodernist, poststructuralist and deconstructivist critique of the category of Humanity (or of the Man") as a term of impossible monolithitism has left us with the fragmented notion of humanity inviting infinite inclusiveness. We have learned that, just like any other discursive phenomenon, the notion of Humanity is historically and culturally conditioned. In other words, there is a hegemonic notion of humanity and it is one that is still white and male.

In an essay titled "Ecce Homo, Ain't (Ar'n't) I a Woman, and Inappropriate/d Others: The Human in a Post-humanist Landscape,"[9] Donna Haraway has taken this point to its farthest by demonstrating that Humanity is a notion constituted by the perennial split and opposition of two transcendental categories: Technology (=Culture, Mind) and the Organic (=Nature, Body). This binary is one of asymmetry and hierarchy whereby the latter term is always already dominated, controlled and prescribed by the former: this is the chief argument of the entire opus of Haraway, and the philosophical core of the "Manifesto for Cyborgs."[10] What Donna Haraway calls upon in these two texts is embracing this radical constructedness and the constitutive split as our true "nature," i.e., as that which defines the "Human" as Cyborg. Consequently, we are called upon embracing our radical fragmentedness since this universal *topos* of Cyborg is inhabited by a multitude of cultural, social, and gendered positions.[11] This multitude of positions is founded upon the constitutive split between Technology (Culture or Civilization) and the Organic (Body or Nature) and formed by the tension between the two terms of the binary (Technology/Organic). The multitude of gendered cultural positions is endlessly diverse. The underlying

9. Donna Haraway, "Ecce Homo, Ain't (Ar'n't) I a Woman, and Inappropriate/d Others: The Human in a Post-humanist Landscape," in *Feminists Theorize the Political,* ed. Judith Butler and Joan Scott (New York: Routledge, 1992) 86–100.

10. Donna Haraway, "A Manifesto for Cyborgs," *Socialist Review* 80 (1985) 65–107.

11. Ibid.

constitutive split, however, is universally shared. Let us call it a "universal" that draws together the endless fractal web of particularities.

The universal which signifies the split between Language (Culture, Technology) and the Body (Organic, Animal) refers to the problematic raised by Butler with the opening of the question about the possibility of identification with the bodily suffering itself vis-à-vis that of discursive identification with the notion of Humanity. Namely, the central thesis in Butler's "Violence, Mourning, Politics" of *Precarious Life*[12] is that the identification with the bodily suffering of the others can bring about greater solidarity among people of different communities and in fact expand inclusiveness of the category of humanity. By way of identifying with suffering, in its radical, i.e., physical rendition, the universal "humanity" is more firmly grounded. Identification with the body exposed to (a threat of) pain enables the stability of the *universal category* of "Humanity" without excluding the reality of an endless socio-cultural and gendered web of particularities. In "Ecce Homo, Ain't (Ar'n't) I a Woman, and Inappropriate/d Others: The Human in a Post-humanist Landscape," Donna Haraway attempts to establish a universal category of humanity which would be inherently inclusive. Similarly to Judith Butler she argues that it is the identification with sheer suffering that makes the universal of Humanity possible. And this universality is not undermined by the socio-cultural, racial and gendered particularities, but rather enabled and, in its inherent inclusiveness, conditioned by them.

> My focus is the figure of a broken humanity, signifying—in ambiguity, contradiction, stolen symbolism, and unending chains of noninnocent translations—a possible hope.[13]

The figure of broken humanity is the figure of human universality and it is one to be constructed by "intercultural and multicultural feminist theory" in terms of "postcolonial, nongeneric, and irredeemably specific figures of critical subjectivity, consciousness and humanity—not in the sacred image of the same, but in the self-critical practice of 'difference,' of the 'I' and we that is/are never identical to itself."[14] This "critical practice of difference" should take place not only on the level of the Discursive, but also on the level of the Bodily—the generic human figures should be "dismembered," writes Haraway, as both discursive and bodily categories.

> "We," in these very particular discursive worlds, have no routes to connection and to noncosmic, nongeneric, nonoriginal

12. Butler, *Precarious Life.*

13. Haraway, "Ecce Homo," 87.

14. Ibid.

wholeness than through the radical dis-membering and dis-placing of our names and our bodies. So, how can humanity have a figure outside the narratives of humanism; what language should such a figure speak?[15]

The figures of humanity outside the narratives of humanism, the figures that can serve as "routes of connection" to a wholeness of the human multitude which is "nongeneric and nonoriginal" occupy temporarily and successively the place of the empty master signifier of Humanity. They are the "dismembered and displaced names and bodies," they are the broken figures of "the suffering servants" and their "mutants." Haraway suggests Jesus and Sojourner Truth as the two paradigmatic figures of broken humanity, the two paradigmatic figures of suffering servants. Both Jesus and Sojourner Truth are tricksters, figures of mime, mockery and masquerade. They are never original, never generic, never monolithic figures of unequivocal and fixed meaning, but rather always already guised, *always already* miming a different figure of humanity in an endless metonymic chain of irony.

> The suffering servant figure has been fundamental in twentieth-century liberation theology and Christian Marxism. The guises of the suffering servant never cease . . . Jesus appears as a mime in many layers; crowned with thorns and in a purple cloak, he is in the mock disguise of a king before his wrongful execution as a criminal. As a criminal, he is counterfeit for a scapegoat, indeed, *the* scapegoat of salvation history[16]

To always already mime an identity in its fullness is to imply a fundamental disbelief in the possibility of identitary fullness, to express doubt in the possibility for the master-signifier to be filled-up by a lived reality, i.e., for the discursive category of identity to equal the Real (or the Larueallian *Lived*). To mime an identity by way of irony and self-irony is to express the sense of failure to achieve a normalized and normalizing identity in its fullness, to express and to affirm the unavoidability of such failure. Jesus is a mocking, carnivalesque figure of a king signifying the "impossible king," the impossibility of kinghood, the underlying remainder of a broken subject as the common human condition and the reality in which one finds oneself unavoidably even when performing the cultural role of a "king" or a masterful subject.

The brutal irony of wearing a crown of thorns, the cruel mocking with the symbol of the subject position of ultimate mastery, is the painful grin in Jesus' mime of kinghood which tells the story of suffering and vulnerability

15. Ibid., 88.
16. Ibid., 90.

as the universal human position. The farce of Jesus' suffering known as the "Passion" tells of the experience of pain and vulnerability as the only universal in the intra- and inter-subjective human condition.

The ridicule of suffering as the "Truth" of the common human condition speaks of the impossibility of truth in the sense of fullness of meaning reflecting the Real in its totality, or rather of the impossibility of establishing an equation between the Truth and the Real. It speaks of the porosity of truth, of the elusive character of meaning, of the illusive nature of knowledge, of the spectral character of Language and Discourse (or, in Laruellian parlance, the Transcendental). Yet the bodily reaction of pain and laughter this farce provokes is the symptom of the Real—it is the signal that the narrative has touched the traumatic spot of sheer experience (of pain) or of the Lived (of pain).

To mime an identity is not necessarily a strategically conceptualized subversive act of auto-irony. It is also a direct result of an ontological impossibility. And it is a poetic act, i.e., the result of a process of sublimation. The void underlying our identity which exposes but our physical vulnerability is elevated to a meaning, to a truth—the Truth of that sheer negativity inhabited by our vulnerable bodies. It is a tragic truth. The truth that every tragedy prompts is the one of our radically ambivalent existence, and the reaction to it is always physical, consisting in the simultaneity of weeping and laughter.

Ancient farce, comedy and tragedy all tell us of the fundamental lack of essence, of that grounding absence of sense, of the founding ontological inconsistency produced by the fact that it is always two contradictory instances that simultaneously determine the courses of our lives: one which is always already beyond our power (the Gods) and one which is by definition in our power (one's Ethos). The two contradicting instances issue into a single one endowed with radical ambivalence—a person's "Fate." Jean-Pierre Vernant[17] explains that the tragic mode of existence should be understood in the double sense of Heraclitus' fragment 119, "Man's character is his daimon." According to Vernant, it does not merely mean that the "daimon" (gods' will) comes down to the person's character, i.e., that it is only one's character or ethos which decides one's fate but also that one's character or ethos is formed by instances beyond one's control and one's ability to understand them.

The instances always already beyond the Subject's control are what would be called in a Greek tragedy the "laws prescribed by the Gods," and

17. Jean-Pierre Vernant and Pierre Vidal-Naquet, *Myth and Tragedy in Ancient Greece*, trans. Janet Lloyd (New York: Zone, 1990).

they are what we would call today the rules of Normality; our failure to understand them and to observe them, our failure to be normalized is what causes our tragic fall. Our failure to control and to understand the void upon which our subjectivities are founded—or rather, out of which they are born—is what makes us always already tragically fallen. In the last instance, we are always already broken subjects, fallen bodies exposed in our vulnerability.

The spectral and elusive character of normality unravels the Subject's empty form, or rather—it unravels the Subject as a sheer gesture and pure posture of striving to achieve fullness of meaning, completion of the self-imposed task of one's existence making sense, of filling up this void posture with signification. The Sisyphus' work of attaining normality, of achieving subjectivity which is prescribed by Normality as not only required but also desired is marked by the absence of that towards which we strive—fullness of meaning of our existences. When a life "has a meaning," when one's existence "makes sense"—"happiness" is achieved. Happiness is about having a "meaningful" life, having a "fulfilled" life—filled by a sense of meaning. By way of seeing through the spectrality of the "Gods' will" and of one's subject position in the World "ruled by the Gods" (=Normality), one faces the void, the lack of sense, and the only thing one can see at this moment is—himself or herself as a vulnerable, exposed, helpless body.

2.2 Oedipus-the Pharmakon: Rereading Sophocles

The paradigmatic helpless, wounded, vulnerable and homeless body, exposed to the threat of the "Outside," i.e., unsheltered by a polis but rather under ceaseless and brutal menace by it, is that of Oedipus as the paradoxical figure of the transgressor who has become a "saint" (or, in the terminology of classical Greece, a hero), a *hubrist* possessing powers of purification from—and protection against—*hubris*. It is the image of Oedipus the pharmakon (or "the homo sacer") depicted by Sophocles in *Oedipus at Colonus* (407–6 BC).

The figure of the self-blinded, ragged, old and banished Oedipus, deprived of not only his polis and home but of any dwelling in the only thinkable world (that of normality). By way of committing parricide and incest, Oedipus is defiled by treading the threshold of the fullness of reality or the Real itself. The greatest and most disturbing *miasma* he bears, however, is that of having looked into the Real itself, into the primordial trauma conditioning humanity itself—that of the sheer exposure to the Real preceding any symbolization. He looks at the spectrality of all that represents normality, of all that seems to represent the substance of any and all conceivable worlds of humanity and sees it proven to be the product of a mere chance and utter arbitrarity. In other words, normality, the only thinkable "World" (or the symbolic order) is a spectral product—that of a sign, product of human judgment and signification. It is the product of human ruse (intelligence) which is there only to invent ways of avoiding and evading direct encounter with the only stable, substantial "out-there" there is—the brutal, traumatizing Real (or in Laruellian parlance: the Lived). Looking into the Real of his own sheer trauma, of his own groundless existence, gazing at the spectral foundations of the only livable human life is what renders Oedipus blind.

Treading into the domain of the fullness of being—the domain belonging exclusively to the Daimon, never to a mortal—is what causes a tragic fall. He or she becomes defiled, stained, invaded by the *miasma* of such transgression. It is believed that the *miasma* can spread endlessly, contaminate everyone that comes in touch with it.[18] Hence, the *hubrist* must be expelled from the polis. In this way, paradoxically, he or she becomes the source of purification, a *pharmakon*. The case of Oedipus is one of radical transformation from source of defilement into source of purity. Immediately before his death, upon which he will undergo a process of heroization (a form of apotheosis), he arrives at Colonus and with Apollo's blessing enters and seats down for some rest in the forbidden space of the shrine of the Erinyes (or the Eumenides)—the *abaton* into which no mortal can set foot. His stain of contact with the domain of the Unthinkable accessible only to the Immortal (i.e., his direct encounter with the Real) has already turned from defilement into sacredness. The *abaton*, the inaccessible space is accessible to Oedipus. In the very opening scene of the tragedy through a dialogue between Oedipus and an Athenian we learn that Oedipus feels no fear of punishment by the Goddesses for whom this inaccessible space is reserved:

> STRANGER: First quit that seat, then question me at large:
> The spot thou treadest on is holy ground.
> OEDIPUS: What is the site, to what god dedicate?
> STRANGER: Inviolable, untrod; goddesses,
> Dread brood of Earth and Darkness, here abide.
> OEDIPUS: Tell me the awful name I should invoke?
> STRANGER: The Gracious Ones, All-seeing, so our folk
> Call them, but elsewhere other names are rife.
> OEDIPUS: Then may they show their suppliant grace, for I
> From this your sanctuary will ne'er depart.
> (Sophocles, *Oedipus at Colonus*, lines 36–45)[19]

18. Robert Parker, *Miasma* (Oxford: Clarendon, 1983).
19. Ξένος

Oedipus is no longer a *hubrist* who dares violate the holy space of the Furies—it is following God's advice (Apollo's prophecy) that he dears set foot in it. Stepping into the holy space reserved for the Erinyes is precisely the condition for his apotheosis, or rather, inauguration into the status of a demigod, a hero.

The broken figure of Oedipus-the Pharmakon is quite similar to that of the "broken figure of humanity" the Christ is. The pure suffering Oedipus-the Pharmakon (of Sophocles' *Oedipus at Colonus*) is made of and conditioned by inaugurates him as the universal figure of humanity in a similar way to that of the Christ as analyzed by Donna Haraway, and also, in a similar way, by Slavoj Žižek. Both Oedipus and Christ are the incarnation and the impossible symbolization of the Real (underlying and repetitively begetting human existence) of pure pain and of the universal human state of always already being (tragically) "fallen."

They are the tragic sublime, or—in Žižekian parlance—products of "downward synthesis" (or the "Christian sublime") which enables a glimpse into the Real itself precisely by way of the minimal, radical representation of the unrepresentable Real or the Lived.

> Christ was the "son of a man," a ragged, miserable creature cruci-
> fied between two common brigands; and it is against the back-
> ground of this utterly wretched character of his earthly appearance
> that his divine essence shines through all the more powerfully. In
> the late Victorian age, the same mechanism was responsible for
> the ideological impact of the tragic figure of the "elephant-man,"
> as the subtitle of one of the books about him suggests (*A Study
> in Human Dignity*): it was the very monstrous and nauseating
> distortion of his body which rendered visible the simple dignity

---

πρὶν νῦν τὰ πλείον᾽ ἱστορεῖν, ἐκ τῆσδ᾽ ἕδρας
ἔξελθ᾽· ἔχεις γὰρ χῶρον οὐχ ἁγνὸν πατεῖν.
Οἰδίπους
τίς δ᾽ ἔσθ᾽ ὁ χῶρος; τοῦ θεῶν νομίζεται;
Ξένος
ἄθικτος οὐδ᾽ οἰκητός· αἱ γὰρ ἔμφοβοι
θεαί σφ᾽ ἔχουσι, Γῆς τε καὶ Σκότου κόραι.
Οἰδίπους
τίνων τὸ σεμνὸν ὄνομ᾽ ἂν εὐξαίμην κλύων;
Ξένος
τὰς πάνθ᾽ ὁρώσας Εὐμενίδας ὅ γ᾽ ἐνθάδ᾽ ἂν
εἴποι λεώς νιν· ἄλλα δ᾽ ἀλλαχοῦ καλά.
Οἰδίπους
ἀλλ᾽ ἵλεῳ μὲν τὸν ἱκέτην δεξαίατο·
ὡς οὐχ ἕδρας γῆς τῆσδ᾽ ἂν ἐξέλθοιμ᾽ ἔτι. (Σοφοκλῆς, *Οἰδίπους ἐπὶ Κολωνῷ*, 36–45)
Sophocles, *Oedipus at Colonus*, trans. F. Storr (Cambridge: Harvard University Press, 1912).

of his inner spiritual life. . . . Therein consists the "Christian Sublime": in this wretched "little piece of the real" lies the necessary
counterpart (form of appearance) of pure spirituality.[20]

In spite of the impossibility of access to the Real in its immediacy, symbolization (or in Laruelle's language: Thought) unstoppably takes place and
its sense is to incessantly strive to mediate the Real. Thought or Language
is touched by the Real—or rather, touches upon the Real—precisely when
a concept is radical, when it is minimal, descriptive of the Real and conditioned by its syntax.[21] The "tragic sublime," whose paradigmatic figures
are both Oedipus and Christ, is a radical one, residing on a minimum of
transcendental and correlating with the Real that suffering is.

The apotheosis (the event of his heroization) of the "greatest sinner of
them all," Oedipus, has remained one of the greatest enigmas for the modern—and Christian—interpreters of the Greek tragedy. Sophocles does not
make a slightest attempt to explain this transformation. As if this was something which needed no interpretation for his contemporaries, for those who
had the competence of direct practitioners of the cultural codes of the culture
to which they belonged, that of classical Athens. Orestes had to seek from the
Erinyes (or in Latin: the Furies) absolving of the guilt and punishment (which
consisted precisely in the insufferable feeling of guilt—a state of madness)
they brought upon him after the matricide he had committed against Clytem-
nestra. Quite differently to Orestes, Oedipus is welcomed by the Erinyes—it
seems even invited by them—into their sanctuary and allowed access to its
impenetrable zone filled with secret and sacred knowledge belonging only to
them. The Erinyes are chtonic goddesses of the pre-Olympian (pre-rational,
pre-political) race of divinities. Their horrible powers have been subjected
to "political control"—by a "political contract" made between them and the
Olympians—and they have, thus, gained a new, euphemistic name, that of
Eumenides. The powers and the category of knowledge, the direct insight into
the horrible black truth of all finite and infinite existence, the Erinyes possess is denied even to the Gods of the Pantheon. Yet again, the Erinyes, who
persecute most severely—through a form of insufferable madness consisting
in relentless sense of guilt—precisely for incest and parricide, graciously embrace Oedipus's divinization. It seems that they even preside over it, and by
welcoming him into their *abaton*, they initiate him into the terrible truth of
all mortal and immortal existence, a truth, a *theoria* insufferable to all others
except themselves and their hero Oedipus.

20. Slavoj Žižek, *Tarrying with the Negative: Kant, Hegel, and the Critique of Ideology*
(Durham: Duke University Press, 1993) 50.

21. François Laruelle, *Introduction au non-marxisme* (Paris: Presses Universitaires
de France, 2000) 46–47.

From Aeschylus' *Eumenides* we know that the Erinyes are a chtonic, collective female divinity, possessing immediate insight into the truths and powers which concern the underworld or rather, the netherworld (since in Ancient Greece death is departure into nothingness, into deprivation of existence—engulfment by the Void). From the same tragedy we also find out that the Erinyes' role, prior to their "domestication" undertaken by the Olympians and presided by Athena, was to defend the Mother's primordial primacy in signification and power—in short, the Mother's right to symbolic primacy—versus the usurpation of the status of symbolic primacy perpetuated by the Father. At the trial of Orestes in Aeschylus' *Eumenides* the accusers, the Erinyes, and the defender of Orestes in this case of matricide, Appolo, debate over the right of the mother to claim parenthood, as well as over the basic worth of a mother's life and death:

> CHORUS LEADER: You plead to set him free. But think of this—
> will this man, who shed his mother's blood,
> who spilled it on the ground, return back home,
> to live in Argos in his father's house?
> Where are the public altars he can use,
> the family cleansing rites he can attend?
> Apollo. I'll speak to that, as well. Make sure you note
> how right my answer is. That word mother—
> we give it to the one who bears the child.
> However, she's no parent, just a nurse
> to that new life embedded in her.
> The parent is the one who plants the seed,
> the father. Like a stranger for a stranger,
> she preserves the growing life, unless
> god injures it. And I can offer proof
> for what I say—a man can have a child
> without a mother. Here's our witness,
> here—Athena, child of Olympian Zeus.[22]

The inauguration of the Name of the Father as the one which presides Symbolization, and the transformation of the Erinyes into Eumenides, as the pledge of this transformation of the Law, is realized by a political, democratic vote of the gods of the Pantheon and is won by just one vote more in its favor, that of Athena the daughter of Zeus born without a mother.

> ATHENA: It's now my task to give my final verdict.

---

22. Aeschylus, *Eumenides*, ed. Alan H. Sommerstein (Cambridge: Cambridge University Press, 1989) 830–47. In translation: Aeschylus, *Eumenides*, trans. Ian Johnston (Nanaimo, BC: Vancouver Island University, 2002).

And I award my ballot to Orestes.
No mother gave me birth—that's why
in everything but marriage I support
the man with all my heart, a true child
of my father Zeus. Thus, that woman's death
I won't consider more significant.
She killed her husband, guardian of their home.
If the votes are equal, Orestes wins.
Now, members of the jury, do your job.
Shake the ballots from the urns—and quickly.[23]

After losing their case in this unprecedented trial, the Erinyes have been domesticated and persuaded—by Athena's words of reason, appealing to respect toward the goddess of Persuasion[24]– to collaborate with the Olympians: the Erinyes, the children of the Night, the horrible avengers of parricide, the have been renamed into Eumenides, the gracious ones.

The Erinyes are the daimons of the naught, the void of signification, of the blinding or paralyzing gaze into the "Head of the Medusa" the encounter with the Real is (or the fullness of being the Mother represents), and the unparalleled martyr of the "Erinyan truth" is indeed Oedipus.

The Messenger (the *Angelos*) describes the apotheosis of Oedipus:

After brief space we looked again, and lo
The man was gone, evanished from our eyes;
Only the king we saw with upraised hand
Shading his eyes as from some awful sight,
That no man might endure to look upon.
A moment later, and we saw him bend
In prayer to Earth and prayer to Heaven at once.
But by what doom the stranger met his end
No man save Theseus knoweth. For there fell
No fiery bold that reft him in that hour,
Nor whirlwind from the sea, but he was taken.
It was a messenger from heaven, or else
Some gentle, painless cleaving of earth's base;
For without wailing or disease or pain
He passed away—an end most marvelous[25]

The "awful sight that no man might endure to look upon" is the sight that has blinded Oedipus. It is a sight whose witness he has become for all humanity. He is the martyr of this divine truth. Ragged, humiliated bagger

23. Ibid., 934–44.
24. Ibid., 1101.
25. Sophocles, *Oedipus at Colonus*, lines 1873–87.

once a king, Oedipus—just like Christ—that mockery of a kinghood, has become the broken figure of humanity," one which in its sheer suffering visible in the fallen body and soul can serve the basis for universal humanity.

3. Solidarity of the Bodies in Pain

The vision of Humanity in its Cyborgian aspect, the awareness of the presence of technology and the role it plays in what is construed and understood as Human today, poignantly exposes our animal physicality in its vulnerability and helplessness. Subjectivity is always already mediation, i.e., language; and technology is a linguistic product. The Technology/Body dichotomy radicalizes—or rather renders visible in its radicality—the hierarchy between the two terms. The body is constantly disciplined, reduced to a material with which and upon which technology works. This implies that technology or discourse (our linguistic "Self") is what exhausts the meaning of the term Humanity, it is what re-presents Humanity: the sovereign right to act upon the bodies, the organisms, to act upon the animal in a masterful, domineering, subjugating fashion. The primacy of culture over the body works like any cultural supremacy—it is a form of colonization. In *Primate Visions*, Donna Haraway writes of science's orientalization of the animal.

> Simian orientalism means that western primatology has been about the construction of the self from the raw material of the other, the appropriation of nature in the production of culture, the ripening of the human from the soil of the animal, the clarity of white from the obscurity of color, the issue of man from the body of woman, the elaboration of gender from the resource of sex, the emergence of mind by the activation of body. To effect these transformative operations, simian "orientalist" discourse must first construct the terms: animal, nature, body, primitive, female.[26]

Scientific discourse is highly political, and it exercises brutal domination, humiliation, reduction of the animal or of the body—of the Organic— to mere material of no value in itself: the value is always added through scientific labor. It is either the body's or the animal's function in "Nature" as a scientific representation—a concept—or its use in Technology that adds value, that which makes it valuable, i.e., which makes sense out of the senseless bodies or makes them worth protecting. Linguistic competence brings

---

26. Donna Haraway, *Primate Visions: Gender, Race and Nature in the World of Modern Science* (New York: Routledge, 1989) 11.

forth the indispensable minimum—or the identity in the last instance—of a possibility to revolt against the subjugation, to demand recognition and aspire for emancipation is always already a discursive act. The animal, both human and non-human, is ontologically deprived of the potentiality of recognition and of achieving its own liberation. The body or the animal can produce a sheer gesture, pure act of revolt—it can produce a speechless revolution, brutal and bodily. And it will exhaust itself in that brutal bodily revolt, without bringing the necessary recognition.

Making a parallel between orientalism and "simian orientalism," Haraway quotes Marx when he writes about the people of the Orient: "They cannot represent themselves; they must be represented."[27] Indeed, the human and the nonhuman animal cannot represent themselves and they must be represented. Is it possible to re-present the animal or the body in fidelity to its animality and physicality, in fidelity to the Real and the Lived? François Laruelle's non-philosophical theory, the thinking in terms of the Real and by means of radical concepts provides an epistemological stance which makes the Thought in fidelity to the Animal-Body possible.

Concurring with François Laruelle, I will argue that Thought cannot reflect the Real but rather describe it.[28] If we take the Real to be a Symptom, an Occurrence, an Event, a sheer experience, we are, claiming, together with Lacan that the Real is Trauma, i.e., that the Real is always already the Tuché painfully interrupting the Automaton of pleasure.[29] Thus, what can be *described* is a set of symptoms—always already actualized as sheer experience, taking place in the form of trauma—and their interrelations. Also when producing pleasure, the sheer experience or the sheer Evental introduces—or rather introduces itself as—Trauma. It thrusts into the Automaton of Signification, it brings destabilization into the Signifying Chain—it produces Uncertainty.

Thinking in fidelity to the Body is theorizing against the epistemic backdrop that consists of correlating in the last instance with the instances of trauma that a body undergoes. This implies that legitimization of knowledge is sought from the reality of sheer experience. Yet again, reality is cognitively mediated. It is described by means of Language: it can never be directly made present in—or reflected into and by—Thought without a remainder. The description is carried out in terms of transcendental minimum, by means of radical concepts. Radicality consists in the transcendental

27. Ibid., 144.

28. François Laruelle, *Philosophie et non-philosophie* (Brussels: Pierre Mardaga, 1989) 50; Laruelle, *Introduction au non-marxisme*, 47.

29. Lacan, *SXI*, 54–55.

impoverishment of the concepts and their tendency to descriptively "follow the syntax of the Real."

The traumatic node, the incursion of the Real into the Signifying Chain, the taking place of sheer experience, the opening up of the void of Event devoid of Language serves as the symptom of reality—of the fact that a discourse re-presents the *Lived*. Politics is about re-presenting subject-positions that are assumed to be "authentic," i.e., coupled by an experience. In other words, any political representation claims to represent not only identities and ideas but also the experience and the lived (the "sufferings") behind the identity in order to justify an advocated political idea. Moreover, any political project assumes to be corroborated by "the truth" about the human experience, and to be legitimized by it.

Just as in psychoanalysis, also in political analysis the Symptom of the Real is the proof or the signal that a certain claim is *true* (relevant, legitimate and correctly re-presenting the interests of an identity). Hence, a symptomatic map of occurrences of the Real, a cartography of suffering is an epistemic necessity: it enables the Political Subject to circumvent arbitrareity of her/his claims that the political option s/he advocates re-presents the *life's* needs of a social group or a society. Any political discourse claims to know and address "what people go through": all political discourse resorts to the instance of the *lived*, of the experienced and the suffered as the ultimate instance of legitimization of its fundamental claims.

Apart from being a Symptom (of the Real), apart from being an instance beyond the Political (even though ultimately of highest relevance for it), Pain can be "cloned" (Laruelle) into a "radical concept," into a transcendental minimum that is a political term (Laruelle). The Real operates according to its own syntax which cannot be reflected in totality by the Language into a transcendental construct, ideational product, into a "truth" or a discourse. Yet a concept can be cloned from the Real, argues François Laruelle. A concept which correlates with the Real, which is determined in the last instance by the syntax of the Real rather than by the Transcendental (a doctrine, a system of ideas, a theory), a concept which is "affected by immanence" is one "cloned" from the Real.[30] According to Laruelle's non-philosophical terminology, the concept cloned from the Real is termed a radical concept.

Pain is one of the instances of the Real *par excellence*: it is a sheer taking-place or a pure experience, utter event regardless of whether one pertaining to the body or to the soul. Pain is by definition a pre-linguistic instance even when inflicted by a linguistic occurrence such as an injurious

30. Laruelle, *Introduction au non-marxisme*, 47.

speech act.[31] The experience of pain is sheer bodily passivity, subjection to Trauma: in its last instance, it is but that which is suffered and always already via the body. Pain is a term that is "cloned" from the Real both in its colloquial as well as in its theoretical use: it is transcendentally minimal and descriptive, referring to the memory of an experienced pain as the ultimate instance of legitimization of its meaning. Itis a term that is always already invoked in any political discourse as an instance of ultimate legitimization.

However, in the context of "Philosophy" such transcendentally impoverished or rudimentary notion does not hold the status of a politically meaningful term. In Laruelle's terminology "philosophy" is virtually all thought which does not rely on the co-relation with the Real as its ultimate instance of legitimization but rather on its auto-legitimizing discursive laws, on its auto-reflexive wishful thinking; or simply, that is the product of "auto-reflection," of "mirroring" of Thought into Thought, of Thought's "auto-fetishization."[32] In Laruellian vain, we could say that we can subsume under the notion of "philosophy" all and any political theory of today.

According to Laruelle, this is also valid of the past political thought as well, since all political theory, science, ideology and utopia has always already been a "philosophy," a speculation pretending to re-present the real/ity. The Real is always already substituted by an idea of it, a concept, an "essence," a "transcendental"—duplication of thought is created whereby Thought thinks Thought. Also when the Real is declared to be unthinkable, un-re-presentable, when it is assigned the status of that which is beyond thought as it has been done in the era of the so-called postmodernism, the situation changes only in some peripheral way: there is no longer pretension to re-present the Real, but the Thought continues to duplicate itself, Thought thinks Thought. Autofetishization of Thought continues in an absolute form.

"Pain" or "suffering" are terms which are "affected by immanence,"[33] that is, they work as direct invocation of (the memory of) an experience (of pain or suffering). Identification with the pain or the suffering itself of the Other can serve a basis of political solidarity, one that is far more inclusive than the discursive category of "humanity." In *Precarious Life*, Judith Butler argues that "humanity" is constituted through recognition which is a purely linguistic act and that in order to maximally expand the category of

31. Judith Butler, *Psychic Life of Power: Theories in Subjection* (Stanford: Stanford University Press, 1997).

32. Laruelle, *Philosophie et non-philosophie*, 17.

33. Laruelle, *Introduction au non-marxisme*, 47.

"humanity" vulnerability should be postulated as its precondition.[34] In order to radicalize this position with which I concur I will argue that solidarity with (a body) suffering (in) pain beyond and regardless of the "procedure" of recognition as human can serve the basis of political solidarity endowed with a great force for political mobilization. The acts of recognition and interpellation are product of humanist rationalism that obstructs, contains, frustrates the life-force of the radical sense of solidarity and the urge toward action a solidarity with (a body in) pain can instill.

4. The Political Action of Solidarity in Suffering

Overcoming the hierarchy between "Body" and "Soul," Nature and Culture, Biology and Technology can bring about radical sense of solidarity, unconditioned by processes of valorization (recognition). Yet it inevitably issues into action that is product of the Language, i.e., an action that is political. Moreover it originates from an instance that is heterogeneous—one that is sheer experience only *in the last instance,* yet, at the same time, unavoidably mediated by language. That purely experiential and virtually physical action of co-suffering immediately translates itself into the linguistic re-action of "identifying with the other." "Identification with"—the animal state of co-suffering with the other body—becomes signified and can therefore undergo a process of sublimation and receive political significance. Thus, "identifying with" suffering becomes "solidarity with" the suffering of the others. Out of the "Void" or out of the "Event," a process of "truth-generation" commences.[35] It is the "truth" of the necessity for solidarity, of a sense of community, of revolt against violence (in all its forms, primarily repression and affliction of pain) and of elevating this sense of solidarity into an ideal, into a utopia, that will create and participate in a political world view and set of beliefs.

Solidarity-with-the-suffering (bodies) is a radical political stance not only because the term of "suffering" or of "pain" is a radical concept in the Laruellian sense of the word, but also because it motivates action which is radical itself, that is, one which is almost pre-linguistic. In Spinozian words, it is the political action toward the very rudimentary, primitive or radical goal of "increasing power of activity" or "presence of life" versus suffering of pain as "diminishing power of activity." The suffering or the diminishing of power of activity in others is made present in our own mind and body through "imagination," argues Spinoza, and in that way we "suffer-with"—we

34. Butler, *Precarious Life,* 43.

35. Alain Badiou, *Being and Event,* trans. Oliver Feltham (London: Continuum, 2005) 173ff.

experience pain.[36] Adopting these Spinozian premises, we can infer that re-
volting against pain in the others, against the diminishing of the presence of
Life experienced by others is egotistically motivated. According to a different Spinozian logic of inference, however, based on the presupposition that
every living being participates in the Being, in Life or Nature (that is God),
and is, hence, constitutively interrelated with the others, with everything
that lives, we can conclude that one revolts in the name of Life itself rather
than in the name of her/his finite existence.

Continuing in this Spinozian vain , we can say that solidarity with
the others and revolt against the pain brought upon them stems from two
simultaneous and at first glance contradicting sources: from the "egotistic"
stance of self-preservation as well as from the "altruistic" sense of being affected by the pain that the others suffer in a way which makes the concern
for our finite being irrelevant (vis-à-vis the experience of unacceptability of
the "diminishing power of activity" of Life itself).

Our existence is conditioned by the Others, by their recognition regardless of whether linguistic or merely bodily (by way of touch, care for
our physical survival). Judith Butler shows how this inter-conditioning, this
dynamic of mutual conditioning between the Individual Self and the Other,
originates from the sense and the fact of our bodily vulnerability.

> The body implies mortality, vulnerability, agency: the skin and
> the flesh expose us to the gaze of the others, but also to touch,
> and to violence, and bodies put us at risk of becoming the
> agency and instrument of all these as well. Although we struggle
> over our own bodies, the very bodies for which we struggle are
> not quite ever only our own. The body has its invariably public
> dimension. Constituted as a social phenomenon in the public
> sphere, my body is and is not mine. Given over from the start to
> the world of others, it bears their imprint, is formed within the
> crucible of social life; only later, and with some uncertainty, do I
> lay claim to my body as my own, if, in fact, I ever do.[37]

We are constituted by the act of recognition by the Other which is pre-
linguistic since our status of vulnerably exposed bodies is a state that always
already precedes the constitution or the assertion of the Subject.[38]

Nevertheless, the sense of being exposed to potential violence, the
sense of physical vulnerability, that very "uncertainty" of whether we can

36. Benedict de Spinoza, *The Ethics*, trans. R. H. M. Elwes (Project Gutenberg, 2003), EIII, 30p, http://www.gutenberg.org/etext/3800.

37. Butler, *Precarious Life*, 26.

38. Ibid., 28.

claim our own body is what brings us back to ourselves, reduces us to the Real of our urge for survival, to the experience of a sheer sense of necessity to protect ourselves against the threat of physical annihilation or affliction by pain. And in this radical survivalist mode we sense our constitutive dependence on others—on the Other's touch that has enabled us to stay in life. I mourn the loss of the other because by losing him I lose a constitutive part of myself, I lose myself.

> we can say that grief contains the possibility of apprehending a mode of dispossession that is fundamental to who I am. This possibility does not dispute the fact of my autonomy, but it does qualify that claim through recourse to the fundamental sociality of embodied life, the ways in which we are, from the start and by virtue of being a bodily being, already given over, beyond ourselves, implicated in lives that are not our own.[39]

We are fundamentally always already given over to the others, constitutively always already beyond ourselves. Identifying with the sheer suffering of the others, with the bodies in pain always already "beyond themselves," always already exposed to threat of violence is what enables solidarity beyond what is recognized or recognizable as "human." The identification with the experience of suffering itself (of a body stripped of the masterful Subject) awakens the infantile sense of revolt against the betrayal of trust in the touch of the Other (Body) that our "pre-individual" Self desires endlessly. Our "pre-individual Self" aspires to instill certainty of (our own) survival in an absolute way. Putting it in Spinozian-Deleuzian words, our desire that Life's power of activity infinitely increases is infinite.[40] Precisely because of the infinity of this desire our pre-individual self demands that the non-violence of the Other's touch is universally guarantied, that it is guaranteed in an absolute way and proven infinitely certain.

The human animal is convoked to become "immortal" at the moment when it establishes a relation of fidelity to a truth, claims Badiou in his *Ethics*.[41] The "subject" is co-constituted simultaneously with the process of a generation of a truth about an event which has already destabilized the world as we knew it. The "subject" is the product of the process of truth generation and

39. Ibid.

40. Gilles Deleuze, *Expressionism in Philosophy: Spinoza*, trans. Martin Joughin (New York: Zone, 1990).

41. Alain Badiou, *Ethics: An Essay on the Understanding of Evil*, trans. Peter Hallward (New York: Verso, 2001) 40.

is sustained by its fidelity to the truth that constitutes it, explains Badiou.[42] And this process constitutes the human animal as "immortal."

> Man is to be identified by his affirmative thought, by the singular truths of which he is capable, by the Immortal which makes of him the most resilient [résistant] and most paradoxical of animals.[43]

The process of transformation from a mortal to an immortal animal—an animal that participates in immortality—as part of the process of truth generation is explained via Spinoza. Adopting Spinoza's definition of human essence as "perseverance in being," Badiou claims that whereas the mortal human animal perseveres in mere conservation of life, the immortal animal the subject of truth has become perseveres in *fidelity to fidelity*.[44] It is about "perseverance in being of what he is," about perseverance in fidelity to a truth by way of which he participates in eternity.[45] Fidelity to a truth inscribes the human animal in an instant of eternity, claims Badiou. And it is explained in the following way:

> The "some-one" thus caught up in what attests that he belongs to the truth-process as one of its foundation-points is simultaneously *himself*, nothing other than himself, a multiple singularity recognizable among all others, and *in excess of himself*, because the uncertain course [*tracé aléatoire*] of fidelity *passes through him*, transfixes his singular body and inscribes him, from within time, in an instant of eternity.[46]

The infinity of desire as the essence of the human animal according to Spinoza and the immortality as that which defines the human animal of truth according to Badiou are the instances that enable transcendence of the confines of our finite selves and render solidarity possible.

The pure experience of *infinite* desire that the non-threatening nature of the Other's touch is *infinitely* guaranteed is always already inevitably translated into language and checked by "Reason." The purely experiential (the Event) is necessarily mediated, transposed via and into language. Thinking in terms of radical concepts or in terms that correlate with the Real (Laruelle) enables fidelity to the sheer, pre-linguistic experiential and suspends the dictate of the Transcendental (any discursive/political "Cosmology"). Vulnerability as the precondition of human solidarity is one of

42. Ibid., 44–48.
43. Ibid., 16.
44. Ibid., 47.
45. Ibid., 45.
46. Ibid.

those radical concepts that succumb to the authority of the Real rather than to a Hegemony of Ideas as the instance of legitimization of its political relevance. It is a concept producing thought-force (Laruelle), i.e., political idea that almost immediately translates itself into action which is pure event and the "truth-generation" (the production of the Transcendental) takes place only as secondary to it.

Fidelity to the Real of suffering cannot be reflected into the Language without a remainder, as the Real cannot be mirrored by the "World" in Laruellian sense of the word, i.e., by that Web of representations, a universe (the only possible universe for us) which is of purely linguistic origin.[47] The experience is inevitably mediated by language. Nonetheless the World of Discourse, i.e., Lacan's (and the Aristotelian) *Automaton*, is inevitably rendered porous by the cracks produced by incidental thrusts of the *Tuché* (the Incident, a sheer taking place, the Event or the Real) into the *Automaton* of the signifying chain.[48] The interventions or invasions of the Real into the Language, the radical destabilization they produce are the occasions for correlating with the Real. The Real's unpredictability or rather the unpredictable changes that the Thought's correlating with it (the Real) may produce on the level of the Discursive can be the points of origin of a potentially revolutionary stance. Laruelle, Lacan and Badiou agree on one thing—that the Real is "impossible in its immediacy"; nonetheless they also seem to say that the effect of the Real is the source of radical symbolic restructurings (Lacan), linguistic re-inventions, i.e., production of "radical concepts" (Laruelle) or, put in Badiou's terms, of the "generation of new truths."

> the Real happens to us (we encounter it) *as impossible*, as "the impossible thing" that turns our symbolic universe upside down and leads to the reconfiguration of this universe.[49]

Evocation of an experience of pain, in a process of identification with the Other's suffering—rather than identification with the value of his/her life as "human"—can be the origin of solidarity transcending limitations of recognition of a "love and loss worth mourning."[50] Dwelling in the purely "evental" or the Real is impossible: we live in the World-of-Language; correlating with the "impossible Real" of suffering, undergoing the experience

---

47. Laruelle, *Philosophie et non-philosophie*.

48. Lacan, *SXI*, 54–55.

49. Alenka Zupančič, *The Ethics of the Real: Kant and Lacan (Wo Es War)* (London: Verso, 2000) 234.

50. Judith Butler, *Undoing Gender* (London: Routledge) 27; Butler, *Precarious Life*, 36.

of co-suffering, having the sense of solidarity in pain can lead to radical "reconfiguration of this universe."[51]

Solidarity will always take place in this inescapable World of the Word, and its agency is inescapably the Subject. And it will always be called upon in the name of a certain political (or ethical) truth. And this World of the Word, this "transcendental universe" is not an "illusion," not a "mirage" compared to the purely experiential or—the Real. On the contrary, in the last instance, it is always already "affected by the Real" and its purpose is to enable us to deal with the Trauma the Real is. And the modes of "dealing" with the Trauma, the truths of the Real (of suffering) are not arbitrary—they are produced in fidelity to the experienced and incessantly strive to mediate it (as truthfully as possible). The question of the "accuracy" of the mediation is a different one that we will leave aside since it is not an object of this investigation.

There is an uninterrupted continuity in the process of the Real's self-translation into the Language, or rather in the automatism of the auto-generated and inescapable course of mediation of the Real into/by the Language. The Real and the Transcendental, the suffered experience and the political truth we attempt to generate of it interchange incessantly forming an endless Moebius strip.

Politically correlating with the Real (of suffering) is about suspending the hierarchy between the "Transcendental" (the Language) and the purely experiential (the Real), about abolishing the supremacy of "Soul" or "Mind" over the "Body." Let us reaffirm that the purely experiential, the "evental" or the Real does not come down to the "bodily": rather, it can be located beyond the Body/Soul dichotomy. Correlating with the Real of the Suffering Body serves the transcendence of this asymmetrical dichotomy and enables solidarity beyond the procedure of recognition of what counts as human.[52]

The body is the location-in-the-last-instance of the suffering itself. (And I use the term "body" in its radically descriptive sense—in accordance with the methodological prerequisites of the non-standard philosophy—not as a philosophical category.) Bodily suffering is suffering at its most radical precisely because of the Body's helplessness, its exposedness to touch and to violence when devoid of that instance of mastering (of both the Linguistic and the Physical) called the Subject. And this primal sense of exposure, sense of primordial helplessness of the body is an experience that can be recognized by any-body, possibly even as "the precondition of humanity" without the procedure of valorization of what counts as *a human being*, a

51. Zupančič, *Ethics of the Real*, 234.
52. Butler, *Undoing Gender*; Butler, *Precarious Life*.

"human life worth living" (and mourning). Identification with the instance of suffering experienced by the Other that takes place beyond the procedure of recognition which assigns it the status of "human" (which is a category of exclusivity) can serve the basis of solidarity stripped of any dialectics of hierarchy enabling inclusion uninhibited by cultural and other forms of identitary division.

7

There Is Something of One (God)

Lacan and Political Theology

KENNETH REINHARD

THE QUESTION OF THE relationship of singularity and multiplicity is originary in Western philosophy, politics, and religion. In philosophy, the question of the primacy of the "one" or the "multiple" can be traced to the opposition between Parmenides and Heraclitus; in politics, to Plato and Aristotle; and in religion, to the monotheistic break with precursor and syncretic polytheistic and animistic religions. Is reality one or many? Is the republic a differentiated unicity or a totalized multiplicity? And is God a radical principle of singularity refracted into various names, aspects, and attributes, or a signifier that encompasses, fuses, and conceals the multiple fractures in our natural and supernatural knowledge? Alain Badiou has argued that this question of the one or the many is axiomatic; finally we can and must simply decide where we stand concerning the One.

> We find ourselves on the brink of a decision, a decision to break with the arcana of the one and the multiple in which philosophy is born and buried, phoenix of its own sophistic consumption. This decision can take no other form than the following: the one *is not*. It is not a question, however, of abandoning the principle Lacan assigned to the symbolic; that *there is* Oneness [il y a *de l'Un*]. Everything turns on mastering the gap between the presupposition (that must be rejected) of a being of the one and the thesis of its "there is." . . . What has to be declared is that the one,

which is not, solely exists as *operation*. In other words, there is
no one, only the count-as-one. (BE: 23–24 / EE: 31–32)

For Badiou, the possibility of the emergence of an event, something radically transformative, depends upon the decision that *the one is not*. If being were fundamentally unified, then events would only be modifications of what is, and the entropic forces of ontology would always revert to some original or final condition of stasis. Hence to decide that the one *is not* is to remain open to the chance of the new. Nevertheless, Badiou distinguishes between the "being" of the one and the "something of one," which he perhaps too casually associates here with Lacan's notion of the symbolic order. As much as the decision Badiou makes against the One is axiomatic, it does not exclude and even perhaps requires this "something of One."

Badiou is referring to Lacan's lengthy discussions of the phrase *Y a de l'Un* and its variations in his Seminars 19 (. . . *Ou pire*) and 20 (*Encore*). Badiou suggests that for Lacan the One is the signifier of the symbolic order with only *operational* value, as a procedure for the anchoring and articulation of a discursive system: the one is a *verb*, not a noun, an act not an ontology. For both Lacan and Badiou, Plato's *Parmenides* is a primary locus for the question of the One. Moreover, for both Lacan and Badiou, the One ultimately takes on *political* valence, as key to the problematics of representation and the discursive conditions of collectivity. However, unlike Badiou, Lacan's exploration of the question of One also passes through theology—through what I am calling "something of one *God*"—and I want to argue that it is only by bringing the One into explicit relationship with those monotheistic issues that we can fully understand its implications for analytic discourse and political life. Lacan's thinking on the "something of One" takes a necessary swerve back through a theological problematic, and in the process articulates the terms of a *political theology*, an essential conjunction of political and religious understandings of sovereignty, subjectivity, and collectivity.

In this talk I am developing issues I raised in recent work, where I argued that psychoanalysis can help us retrieve and rearticulate a *political theology of the neighbor*, one that would be supplementary to the political theology of sovereignty.[1] The fundamental gesture of political theology is the attribution of divine features to the person or function of the sovereign.[2]

1. See "Towards a Political Theology of the Neighbor," in *The Neighbor: Three Inquiries in Political Theology*, by Slavoj Žižek, Eric Santner, and Kenneth Reinhard (Chicago: University of Chicago Press, 2006).

2. In the "Afterword" to Jacob Taubes' *The Political Theology of Paul*, Wolf-Daniel Hartwich, Aleida Assmann, and Jan Assmann distinguish three basic thematics that orient political theology: "representation," where the earthly sovereign is considered

The key link between God and King in Carl Schmitt's account is that each has the ability to declare an exception to the rule of law. Just as God may suspend the laws of nature through a miracle, so the sovereign may declare a "state of emergency" which suspends the laws of the land. I suggested that this logic of the sovereign exception is also at work in Freud's extension of Darwin's notion of the Primal Horde. I argue that this Freudian mythical structure is isomorphic with the account of man in Lacan's formulas of sexuation from the 1970s:

Man		Woman		
$\exists x$	$\overline{\Phi x}$	$\overline{\exists x}$	$\overline{\Phi x}$	Existential
$\forall x$	Φx	$\overline{\forall x}$	Φx	Universal

Diagram 1

Briefly, to be a man is to be subject to two contradictory functions, one universal and the other existential. In the bottom left corner of the diagram, Lacan's logical symbols can be read as "all men are subject to the phallic function"—that is, the enjoyment available to all men is strictly conditioned by castration, submission to the authority of the phallus as signifier. In the second formula, just above it, we find an existential exception of this law: "there is a man who is *not* subject to the phallus." This is the function of the obscene father of the Primal Horde who claims all enjoymmen as his alone, and is thus both the agent of the man's castration and exempt from its cut. Thus in Lacan's logical reformulation of Freud, men are constituted by a universal rule (of castration, symbolic substitution) that has *one* crucial exception, the mythical Father who is imagined to transcend all limitation. Men submit to the conditions of the phallic signifier and accept the pittance of *jouissance* that it allows them only insofar as they posit a Great Father who enjoys in their stead. So like Schmitt's political theology, Lacan and Freud's account of the Father of the Primal Horde produces a "masculine" model of collectivity in which membership is a function of a topologically ambiguous point, both inside and outside the "horde" it constellates.[3] And

---

to be acting as God's representative; "dual-sovereignty," where earthly and divine authority are understood as parallel but strictly distinguished elements; and "theocracy," where political sovereignty is presented as the direct institutional embodiment of divine sovereignty. They describe Schmitt's account of political theology as a version of the "representational" theory, insofar as it argues that political orders cannot be legitimized on the basis of any immanent categories, but must have recourse to divine categories such as God's will (138–39).

3 Jacques-Alain Miller draws connections between Lacan and Schmitt in his recent

the ultimate function of this "border concept" for Schmitt is precisely to maintain or re-establish the division between inside and outside, friend and enemy, which, he argues, is the essential political opposition.

The key difference between Schmitt and Lacan begins to emerge at this point, insofar as for psychoanalysis there is necessarily another term, an excessive quantum of enjoyment first imagined as possessed by the Father of the Primal Horde. If we use the first of Lacan's four discourses, the Discourse of the Master, we can map the relationship between these terms:

sovereign	S_1	$\rightarrow$	S_2	symbolic field (nation)
	---		---	
subject	$\$$	//	a	*plus de jouir*, surplus value

Diagram 2

Insofar as it includes a non-discursive element, the *objet a*, the fragment of enjoyment left over from symbolization, Lacan's theory of political discourse is irreducible to Schmitt's. Lacan identifies the *plus de jouir* with Marx's notion of surplus value—and it is indeed its excessive role that makes political-economic transformation possible. But if the heterogeneity of the *objet a* allows for the possibility of discursive change, it most commonly remains enmeshed in the chains of fantasy, establishing an ideological foundation for the discourse of mastery or sovereignty. How can the *plus de jouir* revolutionize the master signifier of political theology? What are its implications for Lacan's *retheologization* of the "something of One"? In order to make sense of this, we need to consider Lacan's logic of feminine sexuation, and the other possibility of political theology that it suggests (see Diagram 2, right side).

In purely logical terms, men and women are almost identical: both involve an inclusive condition of membership in the world (castration), as well as an exception to that condition. For the woman, castration is articulated as a double negative: "there is no subject who is not a function of the phallus." It is as if the consolation offered to the man for his symbolic castration in the belief that somewhere there is a man who *really* enjoys is explicitly ruled out for a woman: her existential condition is that there is *no exception* to the law of the phallus. Nevertheless, Lacan posits *an exception to that lack of*

---

book, *Le Neveu de Lacan*: "If someone had the insight to perceive what of theology has passed into psychoanalysis . . . it's Lacan. Lacan is the Carl Schmitt of psychoanalysis" (263). Miller argues that Lacan's "psychoanalytic theology" is parallel to Schmitt's political theology, insofar as both emphasize the constitutive function of the exception over the normative function of the rule. See Jacques-Alain Miller, "Sur Carl Schmitt," in *Le Neveu de Lacan*, (Paris: Verdier, 2003).

exception, in the bottom formula of feminine sexuation: "not-all woman is subject to the phallic function." And the function of the "not-all" opens up a radically different mode of part/whole relations and political theology: if the man is an "individual" in the sense that he is an exemplary member of the set of all men constituted in relationship to the transcendental figure of the Father, a woman is *not* determined in symmetrical fashion as a member of the set of all women—which, according to Lacan, does not exist. Each woman is a singularity, part of the open set of women which constitutes an *infinity* rather than a totality; there is no border between inside and outside in the set of all women, or the social group determined according to a feminine structure. There is no transcendental Mother that individual women are versions of and who unifies them as a closed set. The exception has taken the place of the rule, in the sense that a woman is a member of a set that has no universal characteristics or predicates.[4]

This fundamental incommensurability between the ways in which individual men and women relate to the larger groups of which they are a part is one explanation of what Lacan calls the non-existence of the sexual relationship: there is no common basis for an intersubjective relationship between men and women, and all we can do is to compensate for this fundemental trauma, in one mode or another of *love*. On the one hand, love can be the romantic fantasy of fusion, of two-becoming-one, which is merely to *deny* the impossibility of the sexual relationship, to fight off this unbearable trauma with the illusion of love as a dual unity. On the other hand, Lacan hints that there may be another mode of love that is not illusory, and Badiou develops this notion of a love that itself *produces* sexual difference, and difference as such—a love in which one becomes *two*.

Just as love makes up for the lack of a sexual relationship in two different ways, so there are *two modes of love* that underwrite the topology of political theology, one based on the logical formulas of the man, the other based on those of women. Despite their divergences on the significance and weight of divine law, Judaism and Christianity agree about the primacy of two modes of love—of God and of the neighbor. Mankind is commanded to love God "with all your heart and with all your soul and with all your might" (Deut 6:5), and this love, I argue, is essential to the legitimization of divine sovereignty, and its transference onto the political realm. If the

---

4. This corresponds to what Badiou calls, following the work of the mathematician Paul Cohen, a generic set. We might also suggest that if the set of all men is like that of all whole numbers, a *virtual* infinity, where hypothetically an infinite number of new men may enter into that set, each time creating a new whole, the set of all women (or, not-all women) is an *actual* infinity . . . As the set of all whole numbers ($o\aleph$) vs. the set of all the points on a line ($1\aleph$).

Schmittian political theology involves an exceptional model of sovereignty that I link with the structuration of male sexuality, and in turn the injunction to love God, we might propose that another political theology can be oriented by the other great commandment in Judaism and Christianity, to love the neighbor as yourself (and which I argue is correlative with Lacan's account of the sexuation of women.) My larger argument is that neighbor-love constitutes *the other side* of political theology, both decompleting and supplementary to the political theology of the sovereign, and that the link between it and the commandment to love God must be restored in political-theological thinking.

In his seminars of 1971–72, Lacan suggested that the non-relationship of man and woman is determined by the function of what he calls "at-least-one" (*au-moins-un*), which he contracts into *hommoinzin*, to signal its fundamental relationship with male sexuality and imaginary phallic enjoyment (see Diagram 3): an hysterical woman's non-relationship to a man cannot be organized directly by the phallus, since "it is not sure that he even has one," hence "her whole policy will be turned towards what I call having *at least one* of them" (*SXVIII*, 5/19/1971). The impossibility of inscribing the sexual relationship is, in this formulation, a function of an imaginary One, which the man struggles to support, and which the woman both doubts and demands. This is the classical One of Greek mathematics, the principle of unit and *unity*, from which all the other numbers proceed.[5] In his seminar of the following year, Lacan will connect the "at least one" with the imaginary position of the primal father: *there is "au moins un," at least one* man who is *not* subject to the phallus.[6] The One, then, for Lacan first signifies the Primal Father's obstruction of the relationship between the sexes, as a kind of reduction of the phallus to an even purer signifier, a single digit, or what Lacan writes in his theory of the discourses as $S1$. This One constitues the ontological support or alibi for the wholeness of the community of men, Lacan indicates, just as the hysteric props up the paternal phallus. But just as the hysteric's support of the father's desire involves holding it *open*, unfulfilled, and dependent on something external to itself, so the One not only constitutes the sovereign function that ordinates the totality of men, but also reveals the contingency of that support, the ever present possibility of its withdrawal, and the social antagonism that is its symptom.

5. See Alain Badiou, *Number and Numbers*, for a discussion of the history of numericity.

6. Lacan here describes the function of this One as to "command": "the one who commands, this is what I first tried to put forward for you this year under the title of *Yad'lun.* . . . What commands is the *One*, the *One* makes Being. . . . The *One* makes being as the hysteric makes the man" (*SXIX*, 6/21/72).

If the "at least one" in this sense is the *first* signifier, the One as the *source* of all other numbers—as in Euclid's argument that "a number is a multitude composed of *unities*"[7]—then the formula of the woman, "*there is no x* that is not a function of the phallus," can be taken as the corresponding void, the zero that is the other side of the One. This is the aspect of women that faces the phallus, whereby she defines her relationship to it as one of lack:

$$\exists x \quad \overline{\Phi x} \qquad\qquad \overline{\exists x} \quad \overline{\Phi x}$$

$$(1) \qquad\qquad\qquad (0)$$

Diagram 3

Lacan begins his discussion of the One with Frege's theory of natural numbers, where he defines zero as the concept *being non-self-identical*, the purely conceptual origin of the actual number 1, and all other numbers. The natural numbers are derived *ex nihilo*, so to speak, in the movement from zero to one, from nothing to something. Badiou criticizes Frege's attempt to logically derive the reality of numbers via this concept of zero as circular, and finally as an ontological argument that passes itself off as a logical one. And both Lacan and Badiou find in Cantor's set theory a stronger attempt to define the relation of zero and one: if we regard zero as the empty set {ø}, then we can derive the one from it, as the number of its *parts*. The one, in this sense, is the minimal inscription of the zero, the fact that the empty set, though void, is *not nothing*, but indeed is already "something of one." Lacan returns to the *Parmenides*, which he regards as "the first foundation . . . for a properly analytic discourse" (*SXIX*, 4/19/1972), and the source of the imbrication of zero and one. In the *Parmenides*, Lacan finds traces of the Fregian idea that the One is not a fundamental ground, but something that *arises*, with plural "someness" rather than self-identical singularity.[8] Lacan argues

7. Quoted by Badiou in *Number and Numbers*, trans. Robin Mackay (Cambridge: Polity) 216.

8. Moreover, Lacan argues that the key concept Plato develops from Parmenides is that what links all theories of fundamental reality or atoms, whether water, fire, air, or earth, is that the elemental oneness they assume is *sayable*, a function of linguistic articulation. It is because Parmenides himself was primarily a "poet" rather than physicist, mathematician, or philosopher that he is able to understand the paradoxes of the one, in both its realist and nominalist functions. In the last lines of his fragments, Parmenides writes, "Thus, according to men's opinions, did things come into being, and thus they are now. In time (they think) they will grow up and pass away. To each of these things men have assigned a fixed name" (XIX).

If, as Lacan suggests, Parmenides is the poet of the One, where the One is what allows something to emerge into existence, then Plato is his disciple, advancing on the path set out by Parmenides by showing that the linguistic articulation of reality brings

that a notion of the One that can be traced to the *Parmenides* already anticipates the transformations in logic that will be necessary for psychoanalysis.
For Aristotle, Lacan's formulas of sexuation would be simply incoherent:
to say that "all x are y" and "there is an x which is not y" is a contradiction,
period. Aristotle's logic of the excluded middle is meant to describe a reality
that takes for granted the individuality of the objects that constitute it and
the subordination of parts to the whole, and much of mathematics develops
with what we could call a "realist" notion of the numerical entity, just as psychology develops in modernity as the science of the human individual. But,
according to Lacan, with the innovations of Dedekind and Cantor, among
others, the notion of the One shifts from the sign that counts the singularity
of an element of reality (one man, one woman, one apple, one God) to the
One as *real*, as the other side of the void, rather than the plenitude of its
antithesis, as was already claimed in the *Parmenides*.

We can understand this as the move from the "classical" political
theology described by the man's formula of sexuation, where the existential quantifier "there is" points to the singularity of a primal father-God,
to another political theology, based on the "not all" of the woman—which
suggests another mode of the One.[9] In *Ou Pire* Lacan says, "If between the
individual and what is involved in what I will call the *real One* . . . is it not
tangible to you . . . that I speak about the *One* as a Real, of a Real that moreover may have nothing to do with any reality? I am calling reality what is
reality, namely, for example, your own existence, your mode of sustaining,
which is assuredly material, and first of all because it is corporal. But it is
a matter of knowing what you are speaking about when you say: *Yad'lun*"
(*SXIX*, 4/19/72). The primal father exists for a man as "something of one"
that ties him to the totality of men; this is the fantasmatic reality in which
participation in a community of similar subjects is based on the existence of
a singular exception that *proves* the rule. The community of men is merely
potentially infinite; like the set of natural whole numbers, there is always
room for another man, each one in turn subordinated to the fantasy of the
primal father. But with the emergence of theories of *actual*—or we might

---

with it a problem, a *gap* between the word and the thing. Lacan argues that Plato's
theory of the Forms was his attempt to *get beyond* that disjunction, to resuture symbol
and real, precisely at the point of mathematics. But Plato's *Parmenides* will be the main
focus of Lacan's philosophical approach to the "something of One," and there the question of the Forms will be seriously threatened by the developing line of reasoning. See
Mladen Dolar's superb essay on this topic, "In Parmenidem Parvi Comentarii."

9. See François Regnault's book *Dieu est inconscient* (Paris: Navarin 1985) for
a powerful account of the function of God in Lacan's thinking. Regnault argues that
Lacan's formulas of sexuation of man and woman imply Pascal's "two Gods"—the God
of the philosophers (man) and the God of Abraham, Isaac, and Jacob (woman).

say *real*—infinity and the development of set theory, everything changes. Now, the "something of One" begins with the void, the empty set, and in Lacan's thinking it is now located on the side of the woman, in the not-all. The not-all is the sign of *actual infinity* for Lacan: rather than positing the existence of an element that would escape the universal law of castration, the not-all *decompletes the closure* assumed by the universal quantifier, without recourse to a fantasy supported by an exception. The not-all, we might say, is the *void* in the universal set of women, which acts as the something-of-one without the assumption of individuality. The "something of One" understood in set theoretical terms, then, includes the void, and, in Lacanian terms, is attached to the real. It is not a notion of self-identity, but one of difference as such. And Lacan insists that this is the point of Plato's *Parmenides*: "This is why . . . it is inadequate in the Platonic dialogue to make participation of anything whatsoever existent in the order of the similar (*semblable*). Without the breakthrough by which the *One* is first constituted, the notion of the similar could not appear in any way" (*SXIX*, 4/19/72). Lacan's argument is that rather than understanding the relationship of the realm of mimetic reality (or "similarity") as itself *similar* to and "participating in" the realm of forms, *eidos*, absolute truth and goodness of being, as a kind of continuum of decreasing reality, as the Neo-Platonic philosophers saw it, the *Parmenides* suggests a *discontinuity* between the realm of the forms and that of mimesis. The similar, the world of representations, of "reality," *depends upon the singularity of the One*, which is not to say that it "emanates" from it. The One is the originary *cut* that allows for relationships of similarity and difference, participation or non-participation in the forms, but does not itself generate those similarities.

The principle of similarity that is generated in the Master's Discourse by the radical singularity of the "something of One" of the Primal Father-God—the similarity that defines the group of "all men"—is politically problematic, according to Lacan; ultimately the solidarity of the group it produces is based on *racism*. In the final words of Seminar 19, . . . *Ou pire*, Lacan raises the spectre of the band of brothers constituted by such a political theology:

> What is it that binds us to the one who, with us, embarks in the position that is called that of the patient? Does it not seem to you, if we marry to this locus the term brother which is on every wall, Liberty, Equality, Fraternity, I ask you, at the cultural point that we are at, of whom are we brothers? Whom are we brothers of in every discourse except the analytic discourse? Is the boss the brother of the proleterian? . . . We are brothers of our patients insofar as, like him, we are the sons of discourse. . . . our *brother transfigured*,

this is what is born from analytic incantation and this is what binds us to the one that we wrongly call our patient. . . . I did not speak to you . . . about the father because I think that enough has been said to you already about him . . . to show you that it is around the one who unites, the one who says no! that there can be founded . . . everything universal. And when we return to the root of the body, if we revalorize the word brother, he is going to enter under full sail at the level of good feelings. Since I must not all the same allow you to look at the future through rose colored glasses, you should know that what is arising, what one has not yet seen to its final consequences, and which for its part is rooted in the body, in the fraternity of the body, is racism, about which you have yet to hear the last word.

In these final words of his seminar of 1971–1972, Lacan warns us against too quickly assuming that the motto of the revolution and the principle of "brotherhood" can free us from the regime of the father. If the Primal Father is the *père* who enslaves his sons and makes their lives bitter, enjoying all the surplus fruits of their labor, the band of brothers that rise up against him in the name of "liberty, equality, and fraternity" is *le pire*, as in the title Lacan gave this seminar: the *worse*, the mob that operates as an amalgam of bodies, with no point of external ordination, no principle of sovereignty. In order to avoid the violence, the racism and terror that this "fraternity of the body" would unleash, it is not enough to depose the father, the brother too must be "transfigured," and this requires a radical discursive shift, and a supplementary political theology of the *neighbor*.

In his seminar of the next year, *Encore*, Lacan elaborates the meaning of the impossibility of the sexual relationship and the nature of feminine sexuality, establishing key elements for such a political theology. These are complicated issues, and there has of course been a great deal of discussion of them, which I will not try to reherse for you today. But I do want to make a few points about Lacan's argument here that are most germane for the question of the role of the One in political theology. My claim is that in Seminar 20 Lacan needed to return to the *religious* account of the One, as a supplement to the Parmenidean and Platonic accounts, in order to explain its role in sexuation and the possibility of shifting discourses. Lacan's account of sexuation in *Encore* requires something that is not available in mathematics: a logic of universal and particular that is not founded on the classical rule of the excluded middle, hence that can tolerate the conjunction of an absolute rule *and* its singular exception (as is the case in what is called Intuitionist logic), but does not bracket or even deny the actuality of infinity, as Intuitionist logic is forced to do. Alain Badiou has argued that

Lacan fails to bring these elements together, and only posits an "inaccessible infinity," one that exists from the perspective of the finite as a function, an idea, a point, with no real existence. It has often been remarked that it is no accident that Cantor uses the Hebrew letter aleph (א) to signify the modalities of infinity, since it is the first letter of the Hebrew alephbet as well as of the Kabbalistic notion of *ain sof*, literally, "without end," which signifies the material infinity of God prior to creation. Cantor understood his concept of the transfinite numbers as "inspired," a divine revelation which would contribute to the philosophical development of Christianity—perhaps, we might suggest, by bringing to it the Jewish notion of infinity.[10] Cantor's project can be understood thus as the attempt to *de-secularize infinity*, that is, neither to theologize a secular concept nor to secularize a theological one, but to show the precise overlap of mathematics and theology at the point of real infinity, a conjunction that can only be perceived by abandoning the historicist assumption that knowledge requires progressive secularization.[11] Like Cantor, Lacan returns to theology in order to find there an instance of *real infinity*, as a supplement to the only limited or hypothetical infinity that is all that Intuitionist logic offers.

In *Encore*, Lacan argues that the impossibility of the sexual relationship can be understood in terms of the *love of God* that stands between men

10. Cantor writes in a letter to a Dominican priest, "*From me, Christian philosophy will be offered for the first time the true theory of the infinite.*" Cited by Bruce A. Hedman in "Cantor's Concept of Infinity: Implications of Infinity for Contingency," *Perspectives on Science and Christian Faith* 46 (1993) 8–16, http://www.asa3.org/asa/PSCF/1993/PSCF3-93Hedman.html. Hedman cites as his source a letter dated February 15, 1896, from Cantor to Esser. In Herbert Meschkowski, "Aus den Briefbüchern Georg Cantors," *Archive for History of Exact Sciences* 2 (1965) 503–19.

11. In his essay "Sujet et Infini," Alain Badiou points out that Lacan's thinking on feminine *jouissance* in the seminars around *Encore* seems to oscillate between the contradictory assumptions of an actual infinity (in line with the claims of Set Theory) and its denial (as asserted by Intuitionist logic). It is only by means of Intuitionist, non-classical logic that Lacan can understand the not-all as neither contained in the phallic function nor as its negation; this leads Badiou to argue that the infinite for Lacan is merely posited as *inaccessible*, and is no more than a modality of the finite: "The infinite does not authorize the determination of an existence by negation. The infinte is only a function of inaccessibility. . . . Lacan does not need for his purposes the *existence* of an infinite set. It is enough for him that there is an inaccessible point *for the finite*. . . . This explains well enough why feminine *jouissance* ultimately has the structure of a fiction: the fiction of inaccessibility. From there comes the organic link between that *jouissance* and God" (*Conditions* [Paris: Éditions du Seuil, 1992] 295). Finally, for Badiou, Lacan's logic of sexuation remains classical, pre-Cantorian, without an account of the actual infinite, and this *failure*, Badiou suggests, is what forces Lacan to have recourse to a theological language in which the infinity is merely claimed. For Badiou, of course, the axiom of infinity is crucial, and Cantor's contribution is precisely to "laicize the infinite" from its religious meanings (302).

and women, blocking their intersubjective conjunction. Apparently it was Althusser who first suggested to Lacan that his account of the impediment to the sexual relationship looked a lot like God:

> Well-intentioned people—who are far worse than ill-intentioned ones—were surprised when they heard that I situated a certain Other between man and woman that certainly seemed like the good old God of time immemorial. . . . Materialism believes that it is obliged to be on guard against this God, who as I said, dominated the whole debate regarding love in philosophy. . . . It seems clear to me that the Other—put forward at the time of "The Instance of the Letter" as the locus of speech—was a way, I can't say of laicizing, but of exorcising the good old God. After all, there were even people who complimented me for having been able to posit in one of my last seminars that God doesn't exist. Obviously they hear—they hear, but alas, they understand, and what they understand is a bit precipitate. So today, I am instead going to show you in what sense the good old God exists. . . . This Other—assuming there is but *one* all alone—must have some relationship with what appears of the other sex. (*SXX*, 68–69)

Why does Lacan have recourse to the God of monotheism in this seminar? In what sense is a notion of "something of one God" a necessary supplement to the mathematical and philosophical accounts of the One that had dominated his previous year's seminar? First of all, monotheism is crucial for Lacan's understanding of the impossibility of the sexual relationship in its largest, cosmological terms. The polytheistic world was based on the assumption of a sexual relationship between heavens and earth; there is an intrinsic harmony and reciprocity between the worlds of God and humans, the one is a specular projection of the other; together they form an ideal couple. Moreover, the Neo-Platonic influences on Christianity restored some of these aspects, in the notion of the "emanations" that linked the divine and earthly realms. According to Lacan, the radical break with this imaginary cosmology was introduced by the single stroke of Judaism: the Jewish God is *not like* the human beings he created, even if they are made in his image, he is fundamentally a point of *incomparability*. And if there is *no continuity* between God and human beings, no ontological or epistemological common ground for relationship, only love can make up for the lack of a relationship:

> Aristotle's whole concern was . . . to conceive of being as that by which beings with less being participate in the highest of beings.

> And Saint Thomas succeeded in reintroducing that into the Christian tradition. . . . But do people realize that everything in the Jewish tradition goes against that? The dividing line there does not run from the most perfect to the least perfect. The least perfect there is quite simply what it is, namely radically imperfect. (*SXX*, 99)

The singularity of God, and the commandment above all to *love* God, is what separates man and woman, or any subjects who choose to enter into those positions, preventing any imaginary account of their intersubjective or "mystical" union. Lacan locates the God of monotheism at the place of the signifier of the lack in the Other, on the woman's side of the formulas of sexuation: S(Ⱥ)—the place of woman's supplementary *jouissance*. Lacan writes, "Why not interpret one face of the Other, the God face, as based on feminine jouissance? . . . And as that is also where the father function is inscribed, insofar as castration is related to the father function, we see that that doesn't make two Gods, but that it doesn't make just one either" (*SXX*, 77). Lacan suggests that the supplementary jouissance of a woman instantiates a supplementary function of the Other: this is something additional to or subtracted from the function of the Father of the Primal Horde, the unbarred Other whose singularity suspended the community of men in his thrall. This is the Other now as decompleted, no longer simply One in quite the same way, and by no means Two—but perhaps *something of One*, some element of oneness: not the signifier of primal repression, but *the signifier that holds open the lack in the Other*, the signifier of the hysteric, pointing out the master's *inability* to transgress his own law—pointing not at the obscenity but the impotence of the father.

Lacan writes in *Encore*, "The aim of my teaching . . . is to dissociate *a* and A by reducing the first to what is related to the imaginary and the other to what is related to the symbolic. It is indubitable that the symbolic is the basis of what was made into God. It is certain that the imaginary is based on the reflection of one semblable in another. And yet, *a* has lent itself to be confused with S(Ⱥ). . . . It is here that a scission or detachment remains to be effectuated" (*SXX*, 83). This confusion of the *objet a* and the signifier of the lack in the Other involves the holophrasis of the Other, the *filling up* or masking of the lack in the Other that the woman would insist upon. This is to grant fantasmatic reality to the Other, to remain in the thrall of the God who would hold up the promise that someday our desires will be fulfilled, our impossible jouissance realized, the God who as exception to the rule of castration still holds open the promise of wholeness. To allow the *objet a* to fall from its position in this fantasy requires a fundamental *shift in discourse*, a traversal of fantasy: we can no longer see ourselves in specular relationship to our brothers, our imaginary doubles; we need to take the risk, following the direction of the woman's jouissance, of *separating* from our imaginary and symbolic supports in the Master's Discourse. Lacan writes,

> Marx and Lenin, Freud and Lacan are not coupled in being. It is via the letter they found in the Other that, as beings of knowledge, the proceed two by two, in a supposed Other. What is new about their knowledge is that it doesn't presume the Other knows anything about it. . . . One can no longer hate God if he himself knows nothing. . . . When one could hate him, one could believe he loved us, since he didn't hate us in return. . . . The misfortune of Christ is explained to us by the idea of saving men. I find, rather, that the idea was to save God by giving a little presence and actuality back to that hatred of God. . . . That is why I say that the imputation of the unconscious is an incredible act of charity. (*SXX*, 97–98)[12]

The God who is unconscious, signified by the woman's *jouissance* of an Other that is incomplete, is the first step towards a new political theological orientation. The God whom Jesus supports is *lacking something*; indeed, he is the very embodiment of the tension in the something of One God.

The political theology implicit in Lacan's discourses already goes beyond that of Schmitt, insofar as it not only accounts for the topology of exception, which in Lacan's terms is articulated on the symbolic level as the function of S_1, but also indicates the correlative function of enjoyment, the *plus de jouir* or surplus value. The Lacanian political theology of the sovereign, thus, is constellated around two primary terms: the signifier of the primal father, the exception to the rule he ordains, *and* the surplus enjoyment that is the product of his rule, and which organizes the fantasy of the male subject, captivates him in the spectacle of the Other's *jouissance*:

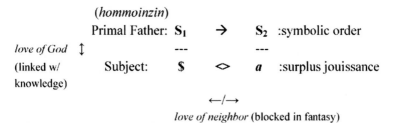

Diagram 4: Political Theology of the Sovereign

12. On this passage cf. Badiou, *Theoretical Writings*, ed. and trans. Ray Brassier and Alberto Toscano (New York: Continuum, 2004) 132.

The political theology of the sovereign, in its Lacanian articulation onto the Master's Discourse, is based on the primacy of the master signifier, and its support in the treasury of signifiers of the symbolic order (of knowledge, faith, the Church, the State, etc.). The rule of this signifier is propped up by the unconscious fantasy of an object of enjoyment; this is the level at which the love of the neighbor lies dormant, as the blocked fantasmatic relationship of a subject and an object.

For Lacan, however, there is *another* One, beyond the "existential one" of the primal father incarnated in the Master's Discourse, and the goal of analysis is to *shift discourses*, hence to *shift political theologies*, from one based on the Master and the masculine formulas of sexuation (and correlative with love of God) to one based on the Analyst and the feminine formulas of sexuation (productive of love of the neighbor):

$$
\begin{array}{llll}
\textit{love of neighbor} & \text{(traversed fantasy; I am my neighbor)} \\
\leftrightarrow \\
\\
\text{self:} \quad a \quad \rightarrow \quad \mathrm{S} \quad \text{:neighbor} \\
\qquad \text{---} \qquad \text{---} \qquad \updownarrow \ \textit{love of God} \\
\text{lalangue:} \quad \mathrm{S_2} \quad /\!/ \quad \mathrm{S_1} \quad \textit{Yad'lun} \quad \text{(God/knowledge link broken)}
\end{array}
$$

Diagram 5: Political Theology of the Neighbor

The political theology of the neighbor does not eliminate the relationship to a transcendental, divine signifier, but transforms it. Now, a new master signifier, a new something of One, is the *product* rather than the agent of the discourse. This *Yad'lun* could also be represented by the signifier of the lack in the Other [$S(\bar{A})$], but what is key is that it is no longer that which sutures the subject into the symbolic order—now S_1 and S_2 are disconnected; now the "subject" of the love of God is not the self, but *the neighbor*.[13] The love of

13. This shift from the Master's discourse, and the political theology of the sovereign, to the Analytic discourse, and the political theology of the neighbor, involves a transformation of the very notion of *the world* constituted by a discourse: "For quite some time it seemed natural for a world to be constituted whose correlate, beyond it, was being itself, being taken as eternal. This world conceived as the whole (*tout*), with what this word implies by way of limitation, regardless of the openness we grant it, remains a conception—a serendipitous word here—a view, gaze, or imaginary hold. And from that results the following, which remains strange, that someone—a part of this world—is at the outset assumed to be able to take cognizance of it. This One finds itself therein in a state that we can call existence, for how could it be the basis of the 'taking cognizance' if it did not exist? Therein has always lain the impasse, the vacillation resulting from the cosmology that consists in the belief in a world. On the contrary, isn't there something in analytic discourse that can introduce us to the following: that every subsistence or persistence of the world as such must be abandoned?" (*Encore*, E: 43/ F: 43).

God that functions here as the structure of sovereignty is the result of love of the neighbor, not its guarantor. And most importantly, the subject has traversed the fantasy of neighbor love: now the subject has come into the position of the *plus de jouir*, now the subject *is* its neighbor. The traversed fantasy, moreover, is no longer below the bar, repressed and unconscious, but is now explicit, open, enacted. And the truth of the discourse? Now it is not a symbolic order constructed around a stabilizing primary signifier, but signifiers freed from ordination and subordination—*insubordinate* signifiers, we might say, or what Lacan calls "lalangue." Another model, however, might lie in one Jewish understanding of the status of the law after the Messiah comes: just as Jesus said, it won't be abolished nor sublated, but left present in all its signifyingness, but no longer binding. Or to follow Benjamin and Kafka, the law, and sovereignty itself will remain just as it was—except for a "slight adjustment" . . .

The world constituted between the Master's and University discourses is conceived as a "whole," as unified, eternal, and closed. Here, the One (♦) is fully sutured to the All (©), and the fullness of being is guaranteed by its reciprocal relation with the imagined totality of meaning, or knowledge. To "believe in a world" then implies the assumption of a "sexual relationship" between being and meaning, matter and spirit, humanity and God. This reciprocity of meaning and being in the Master's discourse derives from the conventional functioning of philosophical language: "Language—the language forged by philosophical discourse—is such that, as you can see, I cannot but constantly slip back into this world, into this presupposition of a substance that is permeated with the function of being" (44). The shift into the Analytic discourse, or the political theology of the neighbor, requires the "abadonement" of such a notion of the world, and the "breaking up" or "shattering" of the petrified linkage of ♦ and © in philosophy for the sake of the release of language as *lalangue*: "Our recourse, in *lalangue*, is to that which shatters it. Hence nothing seems to better constitute the horizon of analytic discourse than the use made of the letter by mathematics." The variables or "mathemes" that constitute the basic elements of mathematics are pure signifiers, absolutely empty; conventionally, however, they are put into the service of both being and meaning. If the subject of the Master's discourse is granted being by language, the subject of the Analytic discourse finds its "para-being" in *lalangue*: "Isn't it thus true that language imposes being upon us, and obliges us, as such, to admit that we never have anything by way of being? What we must get used to is substituting the 'para-being' (*par-être*)—the being '*para*,' being beside—for the being that would take flight" (44). If the discourse of the Master establishes the being/meaning relationship that creates the world as *whole*, the discourse of the Analyst involves a truth that is not-all, and a being that is *para-being*, or being *besides itself*, being *besides* or *next to* rather than being *there*.

8

Woman and the Number of God

LORENZO CHIESA

ACCORDING TO A WELL-ESTABLISHED or even hegemonic interpretation, which gained considerable consensus during the 1980s and 1990s in the context of numerous debates concerning the relationship between feminism and psychoanalysis, the role of the divine in the late Lacan should be closely associated, if not identified, with that of feminine *jouissance*.[1] The main aim of this essay is to challenge this reading and explain why, in Seminar XX, Lacan rather claims that feminine *jouissance* lies at the basis of *one* of the faces of God—as "one face of the Other."[2] Certainly, the crucial sixth lesson of this Seminar, significantly titled by Jacques-Alain Miller "Dieu et la jouissance de la femme," advances for the first time in a clear way the hypothesis of an enjoyment that is "beyond the phallus"[3]—this "beyond" will have itself to be examined closely, following Lacan's repeated warning that the "supplementary" or "additional" (*supplémentaire*) function, the "*en plus*," it entails

1. See, for instance, J. Rose, "Introduction—II," in *Feminine Sexuality: Jacques Lacan and the école freudienne*, ed. J. Mitchell and J. Rose (New York: Norton, 1982) 50–57. Mitchell's and Rose's introductions to Lacan's and his school's writings on feminine sexuality remain, however, among the best available in English to date. Of particular interest is Rose's critique of Irigaray's feminist appropriation of Lacan, the fact that the latter's "refusal of the phallic term brings with it an attempt to reconstitute a form of [feminine] subjectivity free of division . . . a concept of the feminine as pre-given," which ultimately identifies the maternal body with "an unmediated and unproblematic relation to origin" (54–57).

2. Jacques Lacan, *The Seminar of Jacques Lacan, Book XX* (New York: Norton, 1999) 77.

3. Ibid., 74.

should by no means be located in a transcendence[4]—and articulates it with reference to the experience of female Christian mystics such as Hadewijch from Antwerp and St. Theresa (whose statue by Bernini famously appears on the front cover of Seminar XX). However, not only does Lacan specify that mysticism can also at times embrace phallic *jouissance*—he makes, in passing, without giving any more detail, the example of Angelus Silesius[5]— just as, conversely, feminine mystical *jouissance* can equally be felt by male mystics (such as John of the Cross[6]), but most importantly, only a few lines after maintaining that *the* divine face of the Other is supported by feminine *jouissance*, he also somehow contradictorily concludes that while the connection between sexual difference and the divine "doesn't make two God . . . it doesn't make just one either" (*ça ne fait pas deux Dieu . . . ça ne fait pas non plus un seul*).[7]

It is my intention to unravel this decisive and underestimated formula, which will inevitably also lead me to an investigation of the role of number in Seminar XX, as well as of the closely related notion of love.

Jouissance Étrange and Jouissance Être-Ange

In the opening of Seminar XX, Lacan introduces *jouissance* in a dense but enlightening lesson. If psychoanalytic discourse—and its novel determination of the status of all other discourses—starts off from the empirical acknowledgment that human sexuality is inextricably entwined with the absence of the sexual relationship, or, more precisely, that, insofar as it is impossible to enunciate this relationship as One, it can only be supposed, then the presupposition of a "*jouissance* of the body as such" (i.e., of the body as One)—which Lacan identifies with being—must be referred to the asexual (*asexué*) body.[8] Psychoanalysis seems to accept, at least provisionally, the logical necessity of this conclusion but rejects *in toto* its reality; in doing so, it breaks with any (Aristotelian) philosophical discourse on being and substance,[9] in order to focus, in its theory and practice, exclusively on the *sexual jouissance* involved in a (barred) relationship—between sexed human beings as beings of language—that does not make One.

4. See ibid., 74, 77.
5. See ibid., 76.
6. See ibid.
7. Ibid., 77.
8. Ibid., 6–9.
9. See ibid., 11.

The impossibility to establish the sexual relationship as One follows from the fact that, although there are two sexes, *sexual jouissance* can only be mediated symbolically—for both men and women—by the phallic organ and the signifier which is derived from it. As Lacan has it, "woman's sex does not say anything" to man, or better, for him, "nothing distinguishes wom an as a sexed being, but sex," the phallic bodily enjoyment he obtains from her during intercourse.[10] The specification that sex—bluntly put, in the sense of "having sex"—ultimately differentiates woman as a sexed being while her biological sexual characteristics do not (either because, as in the case of the primary characteristics, like the vagina, they are not as such symbolizable, or, as in the case of the secondary, like the breast, they are symbolizable only phallically, and thus reduce woman to the role of mother) is here of crucial importance. Lacan's argument is not that woman is less sexed than man—or even, beneath the symbolic dominance of the phallus, potentially asexed—as a precipitous reading of these pages could suggest ("nothing distinguishes woman as a sexed being"), but rather that, given the asymmetry of the phallic signifier, her sexuation, and following this her *jouissance*, is "strange" (*étrange*).[11] *L'étrange* must by all means not be confused with *l'être ange*, "being-an-angel," although the two terms are homophonous.[12] The latter in fact points to an asexual *jouissance* which Lacan denounces to begin with as the structural illusion originating from the being-One of a chimerical body, or we may add, from the ultimate fantasy of male totalization.

Unsurprisingly, in the same context, Lacan also states that *jouissance* insofar as it is sexual can only be phallic, for both men and women: "Analytic experience attests precisely that everything revolves around phallic *jouissance*." Having said this, at the same time, "woman is defined by a position that I have indicated as 'not-whole' [*pas tout*] with respect to phallic *jouissance*."[13] So, if on the one hand, as we have just seen, the sex of woman says something to man only through the intermediation of his *jouissance* of her body, on the other, since she is not entirely contained within phallic *jouissance*, the latter will also be "the obstacle owing to which man does not come to enjoy woman's body": what he enjoys is rather the "*jouissance* of the organ."[14] In other words, to the extent that *jouissance* is sexual, and hence phallic, it is marked for man by a hole; man never relates to Woman as such, which is why Lacan bars the determinate article, the "*la*," of "*la femme*."

10. Ibid., 7 (translation modified).
11. Ibid., 8.
12. Ibid.
13. Ibid., 7.
14. Ibid.

Moving from this premise, it is now a question of seeing how this fault (*faille*) or gap (*béance*) within *jouissance* may be accomplished, or alternatively avoided, as such by woman.[15] In the first lesson of Seminar XX, Lacan seems to provide two answers: it can either be realized as a *phallic jouissance* that is *étrange* in comparison with that of man, in the sense that it deals with the non-totalizability of *jouissance* (with its structural being deficient, or "in default") differently from male *jouissance*, or it can be evaded to attempt to achieve the totalization of *jouissance* by positing precisely what is lacking as the enjoyment of an asexual *être ange*, taking the impasse of phallic *jouissance* as an alibi for a mythical—and ultimately male oriented—de-sexualization. Note that up to this point Lacan has not yet invoked what, in later lessons, he will call "Other *jouissance*," a feminine *jouissance* that is neither phallic (it famously lies beyond the phallus, and consequently cannot be considered as sexual) nor angelical (and thus totalized) but, as we shall analyze shortly, mystical. By way of anticipation, it can therefore be advanced that Seminar XX is concerned with four different kinds of *jouissance*: *a*) masculine phallic *jouissance*, which in attempting to totalise enjoyment ends up uncovering its very non-totalizability; *b*) feminine phallic *jouissance*, or *jouissance étrange*, which is the non-totalization *inherent to* and mutually dependent on the thwarted process of totalising enjoyment; *c*) asexual and mythical *jouissance être ange*, which is the totalized fantasy of male phallic *jouissance* (often applied to woman or adopted by her, as we shall see); *d*) asexual but really existing feminine *jouissance stricto sensu*, which is a mystical supplement (or *en plus*) of phallic *jouissance*. In order to refrain from locating it in a transcendent place, we could also call it "*non*-totalizability as such"; feminine *jouissance stricto sensu* is, for Lacan, beyond the phallus (and its inherent non-totalization) but this beyond is incomprehensible without the phallus.

Let us now dwell on phallic female *jouissance*, the *jouissance étrange*. As Lacan has it in a later lesson of Seminar XX, woman phallically "possesses" man just as much as man "possesses" woman; she is far from being indifferent to the phallus (i.e., in common parlance, to "her man"). Or, more accurately, "it is not because she is not-wholly in the phallic function that she is not there at all"; being not-whole in it involves, rather than excludes, being "*not* not at all there," to the extent of being "in full" (*à plein*) in it where sexual *jouissance* is concerned (in other words, as I have already remarked, woman—her *pas-toute*—is not less sexed, i.e., phallically engaged, than man).[16] What is then so "strange" about feminine phallic *jouissance*?

15. Ibid., 8.
16. Ibid., 73–74.

In a few words, woman approaches, and preserves, the phallus in her own way; she complies with the "requirement of the One" (*l'exigence de l'Un*), which is inseparable from phallic *jouissance*, by replacing the "One of universal fusion" that underlies masculine phallic *jouissance* with a singular "one by one" (*une par une*).[17] For women, the other sex as masculine is phallically the one that takes them one by one. Lacan makes two examples to explain this. The first is topological—and for this reason, at least in his intentions, should be regarded as more than an analogy, since, as he reminds us, his teaching equates topology with structure. The *pas-toute* of woman means that the phallic space is not homogeneous. However, the very fissure that characterizes it as such could be regarded as "compact," or somehow countable, despite being constituted by an infinite number of sets that are themselves infinite. More precisely, although the phallic field is covered by open sets (i.e., by an infinity of non-totalizable, i.e., singularly infinite, women), the set of these open sets can eventually be conceived as "a sub-superimposition [*sous-recouvrement*] of open spaces that constitutes a finitude."[18] While the operation in question does not make the open spaces strictly speaking countable—since they remain after all infinite—it nevertheless makes it possible to consider them as elements constituting a finite series. That is to say, they are as such uncountable but can nevertheless be counted one by one.

Leaving aside any consideration on whether Lacan's use of topology or set theory can been regarded as technically correct, the point he puts forward concerning the heterogeneity—or asymmetry—of sexual difference as a symbolic field is extremely clear. To put it simply, woman is, at the same time, infinite and finite, uncountable and countable, or better, she becomes countable and able to count precisely insofar as she exposes the non-totalization of the count. According to Lacan, the myth of Don Juan depicts this perfectly: he has women one by one; as long as he knows their names, he can list them and hence count them. Yet, if, at a given point in time, he has possessed, say, one thousand and three women, this cannot be seen as a closed/totalized set but only as the one thousand and third time—and obviously not the last—he counts again woman as one. This different form of counting, which inherently hinders even the semblance of successful totalization—the series is never believed to be *a* set, or even a progression towards a closed set, while its elements are monotonously counted as always the same undifferentiated element—explains why—and this has not been emphasized enough by critics—Lacan unexpectedly calls Don Juan a

17. Ibid., 10.
18. Ibid. (translation modified).

"*feminine* myth"; the one-by-one as opposed to the attempted One of masculine phallic totalization is a feminine—but nonetheless phallic—counting
that shows "what the other sex, the masculine sex, is for women."[19]

We now need to take a step back and ask ourselves: Why does phallic
jouissance—as the only possible sexual *jouissance*—underlie the "requirement of the One"—or its "one-by-one" feminine variation—in the first
place? Lacan explains this by and large underrated, yet fundamental, issue
right at the beginning of the first lesson of Seminar XX. Phallic *jouissance*
depends on love as "the desire to be One"; *jouissance* is not a "sign of love,"
but it remains nevertheless "secondary," i.e., epiphenomenal, with respect to
it.[20] The body of man and woman as beings of language is certainly sexed
symbolically (in an asymmetrical way), but the sexual *jouissance* of the body
of the Other "remains a question, because the answer it may constitute is
not necessary. We can take this further still: it is not a sufficient answer
either, because love demands *love*. It never stops demanding it. It demands
it . . . *again* [*encore*]."[21] Thus, against doxastic readings of the title of Seminar
XX, "*encore*" does not primarily refer to the "I want more!" of phallic *jouissance*, or to the feminine/mystical *jouissance* beyond the phallus, but to love.
The following argument should by now be adamant: human sexuality issues
from the primacy of the "there is no sexual relationship," from an impossibility, and *jouissance* should consequently be seen, first and foremost, as
a "negative instance," which as such, "serves no purpose/is worth nothing"
(*ne sert à rien*).[22] That is to say, it is the demand of love as a—thwarted, "impotent," Lacan specifies[23]—desire to be One that eventually sustains human
sexuality—and thus, indirectly, reproduction and the preservation of the
species—as based on a non-relationship, or better, a relationship that is not

19. Ibid. Renata Salecl fails to make this point when she reduces the feminine myth
of Don Juan as discussed by Lacan to a fantasy that "proves that there is at least one man
who has it from the outset, who always has it and cannot lose it. . . . Since women often
are concerned that a man may completely lose himself when he is with another woman,
the fantasy of Don Juan reassures women that there is at least one man who never loses
himself in a relationship" ("Love Anxieties," in *Reading Seminar XX* , ed. S. Barnard and
B. Fink [Albany: State University of New York Press, 2002] 96).

In other words, Salecl identifies Don Juan with the primal Father of the horde as
seen by women (rather than by his sons), that is, she associates him with the exception to the logic of castration, and to the hole of *jouissance*, which sustains the phallic
function. This reading mistakenly confines the singularising count of the one-by-one
(the feminine phallic function) within the count of the One of universal fusion (the
masculine phallic function).

20. Lacan, *SXX*, 5–6.

21. Ibid., 4 (my emphasis).

22. Ibid., 3.

23. Ibid., 6.

One, between the sexes (in other words, we eventually even manage "to give a shadow of life to the feeling known as love. This is necessary, really necessary; it is necessary that this goes on [ça dure encore]. It is necessary that, with the help of this feeling, this leads, in the end . . . to the reproduction of bodies").[24] To put it very bluntly, as beings of language, we do not primarily *make* love because sex is "fun." Rather, we (strive to) *have* sex because we love, whatever our polymorphously perverse motivations for sleeping with the other may be. *Jouissance* is nothing else than a by-product of the impossibility of the One desired by love.

Here, we should pay particular attention to the fact that Lacan obliges us to rethink thoroughly the opposition between love and desire—on which he had insisted throughout his earlier Seminars—in the more general terms of an interaction, if not of a non-eliminable presence of desire within love. Love can well be, as a passion, as the desire to *be One*, the "ignorance of desire," yet this does not in the least involve a weakening of the *desire* to be One.[25] Lacan's question "Is love about making one?"—which at first sight seems to be redundant in a context that defines love as the desire to be One—cannot simply be answered affirmatively:[26] love as the *desire* to be One always goes together with the "again!" of the demand of love, hence it would be misleading to identify it with a final "making one" (*fair un*). Love does not make one; love desires to be One. In other words, the capitalized One at stake in love—as *desire* to be One—does not lead us back to what is allegedly the most primordial, the "earliest of confusions"; it rather puts on evidence the fissure of the One (the One of the enunciation "*Y a d' l'Un,*" "There's such a thing as One") as consubstantial with the "essence of the signifier," a differential gap that alone allows us to propose a discourse on *jouissance* and being.[27] If Lacan concludes the first lesson of Seminar XX by returning to the irreconcilability of "being absolute" with "being sexed," this is not just a reminder of the fact that angelical *jouissance*, the supposed being-One without fissure of a totalized body, would necessarily be asexual, but that we can finally think the being of God, a *non*-angelical One *with* a fissure, an *absolute with a gap*—a being about which we are obviously in a position to enunciate something (as theology proves), and which, as we shall see, implicitly upholds all of our enunciations—only in relation to sexual *jouissance* and its non-phallic feminine supplement.

24. Ibid., 46 (translation modified).
25. Ibid., 4.
26. Ibid., 5.
27. Ibid.

From *l'autre Satisfaction* to *l'Autre Jouissance*

It would not be exaggerated to suggest that, in Seminar XX, Lacan goes as far as positioning love and desire on the side of the satisfaction of needs, as opposed to—albeit inseparable from—what he names the "other satisfaction" of—the uselessness of—phallic (masculine and feminine) *jouissance*. This topic is extensively covered in the fifth lesson. The sixth lesson then introduces feminine *jouissance* as "beyond the phallus." Contrary to what has been wrongly proposed by several critics, Lacan's efforts are here overall aimed at distinguishing *l'autre satisfaction*, i.e., phallic (masculine and feminine) *jouissance*, from *l'Autre jouissance* (or, as it is most often referred to, *la jouissance de l'Autre*[28]), i.e., an exclusively feminine non-phallic *jouissance*, it is now a matter of investigating how the discussion of precisely these two notions paves the way to his conclusion that while this differentiation "doesn't make two God . . . it doesn't make just one either"—a topic that I shall analyze in detail in the third and final section of this article.

The fifth lesson of Seminar XX revolves around the contrast between the satisfaction of needs and "another satisfaction." More specifically, against any naturalist-reductivist reading, the satisfaction of needs in the human being can only be grasped indirectly as what is lacking to/does not fulfil (*fait défaut*) this other satisfaction, which "supports itself from language" and can be defined as "*jouissance*."[29] This specification thus entails an elaboration on the previous assumption according to which *jouissance* is epiphenomenal with regard to love-desire and their indirect fulfilment of the sexual biological function; to put it simply, *a*) love-desire makes reproduction possible, and *b*) *jouissance* is a by-product of their interaction with, if not replacement of (sexual) need, yet, nevertheless, *c*) (sexual) need

---

28. See, for instance, ibid., 4, 24, 83. Bruce Fink seems to be taking for granted the equation between "another satisfaction" and "Other jouissance" as a peculiarly feminine form of enjoyment. As he promptly acknowledges, this leads him to an impasse, since the former is defined by Lacan as a "satisfaction of speech," while the latter is seen as unspeakable: "He even says at one point in the seminar that it [Other jouissance] is 'the satisfaction of speech.' How that is compatible with the notion that it is an *ineffable* experience where the bar between signifier and signified does not function, I do not profess to know." Shortly after, he opts to attribute this apparent contradiction to Lacan's own inconsistent arguments: "We need not assume that there is some sort of complete unity or consistency to his work, for he adds to and changes things as he goes along" (Fink, "Knowledge and Jouissance," in *Reading Seminar XX*, 40). The reading I propose, whereby the "other satisfaction" amounts to phallic *jouissance* as different from Other/feminine/non-phallic *jouissance*, shows that Lacan is far from contradicting himself.

29. See *SXX*, 51 (translation modified).

as such, its "non-other" satisfaction (i.e., satisfaction *tout court*), can only be approached in a roundabout way by means of the other—unsatisfied—satisfaction of *jouissance*.[30]

Moving from this interweaving of need, love-desire, and *jouissance*, how should we decipher Lacan's crucial claim that other satisfaction "supports itself from language"? In a few words, this simply means that *jouissance* does not precede the institution of human reality as a linguistic reality.[31] Or, at least, that any special discourse about an alleged pre-discursive reality, and an associated *jouissance* which would not be deficient, is necessarily mythical for the reason that being a "man" or a "woman" (as much as being a "child") does not per se denote anything like a pre-discursive reality; that "men, women, and children are but signifiers. . . . A woman seeks out a man qua signifier. A man seeks out a woman qua . . . that which can only be situated through discourse."[32] More generally, there is no such thing as a "human species" at the level of pre-discursive reality; the species—and its sexual *jouissance*—is only made possible "thanks to a certain number of conventions, prohibitions, and inhibitions that are the effect of language."[33] From this perspective, *jouissance*, love, and desire all equally follow from *homo sapiens'* rupture with the immanence of animal need; this predicament is scientifically accountable in terms of the premature birth that characterizes the speaking being, which is itself responsible for a prematuration of sexuality that goes together with (sexual) neoteny, the retention of infantile traits in adult individuals—a series of intricate points Lacan reiterates in passing even in the very lesson of Seminar XX that we are scrutinizing, thus admitting that his treatment of *jouissance* still depends on the biological theses he discussed at length in his early Seminars of the 1950s.[34]

Having said this, the very fact that *jouissance* only sustains itself from language, that is, from the absence of the sexual relationship that determines human *sexuality* (in this context, Lacan even evokes the polysemy of the English verb "to fuck" as referring to both copulation and something that does not work[35]), entails necessarily the supposition of a mythical substance

30. In this light, it is not a coincidence that the last sentence of the fourth lesson announces that the main theme of the fifth concerns the point "where love and sexual jouissance meet up." Ibid., 50.

31. See ibid., 55.

32. Ibid., 33.

33. Ibid.

34. "In the end, if this jouissance comes to someone who speaks, and not by accident, it is because he is a premature child." Ibid., 61. (translation modified).

35. See ibid., 32. "Human sexuality is 'sexual' (and not simply 'reproductive') precisely insofar as the unification at stake, the tying of all the drives to one single Purpose,

that enjoys itself absolutely. If, on the one hand, there is "*jouissance* of a body" (*jouir d'un corps*)—in the subjective and objective sense allowed by the ambiguity of the genitive—only insofar as this very body is symbolized—or, which is the same, insofar as the "signifier is the cause of *jouissance*"[36]—on the other hand, as we have already observed at the beginning of this essay, psychoanalysis posits itself as a discourse about the foundation of discourse as such on an inevitable supposing of substance. Throughout the first half of Seminar XX, Lacan also attempts to move beyond this oscillation by introducing a new form of substance, a *substance jouissante*, through which both the myth of absolute *jouissance* and the *jouissance* of the symbolized body could dialectically be thought anew by psychoanalytic discourse. He contends that a theory of *substance jouissante* would permit psychoanalysis to overcome the Cartesian dichotomy between extended and thinking substance, body and language, without refuting it. While with respect to substance *qua* really existing body, *jouissance* can only be enjoyed *in part*, given that there is no sexual relationship as One—"One can only enjoy a part of the Other's body, for the simple reason that one has never seen a body completely wrap itself around the Other's body, to the point of surrounding and phagocytizing it. . . . We must confine ourselves to simply giving it a little squeeze, like that, taking a forearm or anything else—ouch!"[37]—with regard to substance *qua* language, there is a logical necessity to posit absolute *jouissance*. But, as Lacan has it in a later lesson of Seminar XX, necessity goes here together with impossibility, or better, that which is necessary in logic *qua* the founding exception to the rule is impossible in reality.[38] We thus have to conceive of one mythical man, the Father (of the horde), for whom the phallic function that decrees the partiality of *jouissance*—that is, the fact that there is no sexual relationship, or, which is the same, that human sexuality equates with the absence of the sexual relationship as One—is not valid. To put it differently, we have to *think* of a non-existing self-enjoying absolute substance that embodies "the correlate of the *fact* that there's no such thing as a sexual relationship":[39] Lacan calls Him "the substantial as-

---

never really works, but allows for different partial drives to continue their circular, self-perpetuating activity" (A. Zupančič, *Why Psychoanalysis? Three Interventions* [Uppsala, Sweden: NSU Press, 2008] 17).

36. *SXX*, 24. This causality of the signifier with respect to *jouissance* should be carefully compared and contrasted with Lacan's well-known formula for which the object *a*—that which both prevents the totalization of the Symbolic and consents to its suture, its making-one as not-One—is the cause of desire.

37. Ibid., 23.

38. See ibid., 59.

39. Ibid. (my emphasis).

pect of the phallic function" (*le substantiel de la function phallique*) and then proceeds to formalize it as $x–Fx (there is an x, the Father, for which Fx, the phallic function, is negated) in his so-called formulas of sexuation.[40]

I believe that it is only through such an embryonic theory of *substance jouissance* that we can reconcile Lacan's apparently contradictory claims for which, on the one hand, as examined above, "psychoanalytic discourse . . . is lent support . . . by the fact that it *never resorts to any substance*, never refers to any being"[41]—as One existing body, we should add—yet, on the other, "*the substance of the body*, on the condition that it is defined only as that which [really] enjoys itself," that is, on condition that the enjoying body is not One, "*is precisely what psychoanalytic experience assumes*"[42] (note how the far from coincidental shift in these two passages from psychoanalysis as a "discourse" to psychoanalysis as an "experience," from theory to practice, or, more to the point, from a language finally centered on the factuality of the *body* to that same body as nonetheless profoundly *affected* by language, complicates my argument while also reinforcing it). This said, I would also suggest that the very reading I am advancing is a palpable instantiation of the fact that, as Lacan himself acknowledges, to speak about *jouissance* puts more than ever "this *the Other*" (*ce* l'Autre), i.e., the Symbolic as such—as *the Symbolic*—into question.[43] In brief, it is precisely an enquiry into substance from the standpoint of enjoyment that indicates how the really existing Other as not-One can ultimately be thought only against the background of an absolute One ("As long as somebody will say something, the God hypothesis will persist"[44]) and, vice versa, how any cogitation about the symbolic whole (as epitomized by "*Y a d' l'Un*") goes hand in hand with the non-totalizability of linguistic reality.

Before returning to this decisive issue in the next section, I intend now to focus on feminine *jouissance* as a different way of putting the consistency of the Other into question: instead of challenging it by means of language, that is, by uncovering the logical inextricability of the One and the not-One in the symbolic order, as phallic *jouissance* does, feminine *jouissance* rather indicates that this order is as such not entirely sayable. While the "other satisfaction" of phallic *jouissance* ultimately amounts always to a *jouissance* of speech,[45] in the sense that, as we have seen, it supports itself from

40. Ibid., 59, 78ff.

41. Ibid., 11.

42. Ibid., 23 (my italics; translation modified).

43. See ibid., 38 (translation modified).

44. Ibid., 45 (translation modified).

45. See ibid., 64.

language and can even be regarded as a (always deficient) satisfaction of the "blah-blah,"[46] all that women can say about their *jouissance* beyond the phallus—as exemplified by the "sporadic" writings of mystics—is that "they feel it [*ils l'éprouvent*], but know nothing about it."[47] This repeated reference to speech clearly confirms that Lacan distinguishes *l'autre satisfaction* from *l'Autre jouissance*; to sum up, we could suggest that not only is there a satisfaction that is other with respect to the satisfaction of needs, but that this very "other satisfaction," phallic *jouissance*, has its Other. In spite of a general tendency among Lacanians to write this other otherness with a capital O, we should resist the temptation to turn it into a transcendent entity. The "supplementary" nature of unspeakable feminine *jouissance* should rather be understood as that which, in "escaping" symbolization, depends on it *qua* its inherent impasse, as the *not-all of* symbolization:[48] conversely, woman's "beyond the phallus" or "*en plus*"—"Be careful with this 'more'—beware of taking it too far too quickly," Lacan warns us[49]—that is, her being not entirely contained within the phallic function, should be considered as a precondition for the Symbolic as such, since the latter is not-One, and can propose itself as a One only on this basis.

The best way to understand the non-transcendence of feminine *jouissance* with regard to the Symbolic is by analysing closely its relation with sexual difference. As I have anticipated, Lacan has no hesitation in stating that *jouissance* insofar as it is sexual is phallic.[50] If feminine *jouissance* lies "beyond the phallus," it inevitably follows that it must be seen as non-sexual. Yet, at the same time, this does not entail that it is asexual *sensu stricto*. Rather, *feminine* jouissance *is non-sexual within the sexual relationship (that is not One)*. Feminine *jouissance* derives from woman's "being the Other, in the most radical sense, *in the sexual relationship*," Lacan says: "woman is that which has a relationship to *that* Other."[51] In other words, feminine *jouissance* is the consequence of woman's unique direct relation with the Other as barred, as not-One, or better with the barred Other as it can only

46. Ibid., 56. At this point, Lacan goes as far as explicitly associating this satisfaction with Freud's pleasure principle. That is, here, the supposed satisfaction of needs is directly equated with "other satisfaction"; in the case of the human animal, the former can only be mediated by language and its logorrheic *jouissance*.

47. Ibid., 76 (translation modified). Note that throughout this passage Lacan uses the masculine, or mixed, personal pronoun *ils*, not the feminine *elles*, which confirms that "woman" (and her specific mystical *jouissance*) is not limited to biological females.

48. See ibid., 24, 33.

49. Ibid., 74.

50. "Jouissance, qua sexual, is phallic." Ibid., 9.

51. Ibid., 81 (my italics).

be *marked by the signifier*—"Woman has a relation to the signifier of that Other, insofar as, qua Other, it can but remain forever Other. I can only assume here that you will recall my statement that there is no Other of the Other. The Other, that is, the locus in which everything that can be articulated on the basis of the signifier comes to be inscribed, is, in its foundation, the Other in the most radical sense. That is why the signifier . . . marks the Other as barred: S(Ⱥ)."[52] Woman's relation with the "most radical" Other when she experiences feminine *jouissance* is thus far from coinciding with any attainment of the unity of an alleged pure Real/substance, that is, with the mythical end of sexual difference—and of the symbolic order along with it—which is instead evoked by the image of the *être-ange qua* the purely asexual enjoyment of the body as One, fictitiously situated outside of the Other (or before/after it).

L'être-ange must therefore be opposed to both phallic *and* non-phallic feminine *jouissance*, both the *jouissance étrange* through which woman relates to the male sex by being taken/counted "one by one" and the silent "impulses of fervour and passion [*jaculations*]"[53] experienced by the female mystics, which men cannot relate to. Furthermore, not only is the mystic's expressing "the God face" of the Other—an expression we still need to unravel fully—not enough to make her an angel, but the angel can only be obliquely materialized in linguistic reality in the far less edifying body of the hysteric. Lacan advances this point concisely but effectively when he claims that hysteria aims at the "outsidesex [*horsexe*]," and for this reason stands for a "playing the part of/pretending to be the man [*faire l'homme*]"; to put it differently, the hysteric is a "*hommosexual* [*hommosexuelle*]"—a "man-sexual" rather than a homosexual—in the sense that she attempts to embody the epitome of the male-phallic fantasy of overcoming sexual difference in an asexual being as being One.[54]

---

52. Ibid.

53. Ibid., 76 (translation modified).

54. Ibid., 85 (translation modified). Édith De Cock speaks of a "*hors sexe*" in relation to feminine *jouissance*. This is confusing in light of Lacan's restricted application of the term in question to hysteria. It also completely misses our explanation of the difference between feminine *jouissance*'s *non*-sexuality *within* the sexual relationship as opposed to the angelic mirage of *a*sexuality that enchants the hysteric. Furthermore, De Cock states that other *jouissance* "touches in equal measure man and woman, and can be located on both sides" of the graph of sexuation: this is a clear misunderstanding of Lacan's argument, which rather advances that both biological females and males can symbolize themselves as "woman" (i.e., on the right-hand side of the graph) and, consequently, experience feminine *jouissance*. É. De Cock, "Encore (1972–1973)," in *Lacaniana: Les seminaries de Jacques Lacan*, ed. M. Safouan (Fayard: Paris, 2005) 307.

How should we then understand more precisely the *non*-sexual *relating* of feminine/mystical *jouissance* to the concreteness of human sexuality—characterized as it is by the absence of the sexual relation and the hegemony of the phallic function? Lacan answers this question in passing when he criticizes the medical notion of frigidity as well as the contiguous distinction—endorsed, in the wake of Freud, by many psychoanalysts, especially women—between clitoral and vaginal *jouissance* (whereby one of the two, depending on the theory, could be deemed as a physiological condition, an orgasm, that would be at least in part independent from the phallic organ, or one of its surrogates, and intercourse). These issues are badly posed, Lacan contends, since what is at stake in feminine *jouissance* as such has nothing to do with sex, with "matters of cum [*affaire de foutre*]":[55] if, as he suggests, woman experiences feminine *jouissance* without being able to talk about it, then "frigidity" could represent nothing else than man's complete incapacity to grasp this feeling—i.e., his reduction of a *jouissance* that is not sexual to an absence of *jouissance* tout-court.[56] Similarly, the distinction between clitoral and vaginal *jouissance* would remain after all internal to sexual, i.e., phallic *jouissance*, and therefore render the endeavour to establish which is more "feminine" meaningless.[57] We could also formulate this by resuming the difference between "other satisfaction"—as phallic *jouissance*—and "*jouissance* of the Other"—as

55. Lacan, *SXX*, 77. "The Other jouissance advanced by Lacan in his seminar *Encore* [is] unrelated to what is sexual. . . . It is not a boudoir story [*affaire de lit*]; it is not Charcot's 'There is always something sexual'; it is not the 'G' point" (J.-P. Lucchelli, *Le malentendu des sexes* [Rennes: Presses Universitaires de Rennes, 2011] 121).

56. "If she simply experienced it and knew nothing about it, that would allow us to cast myriad doubts on this notorious frigidity" (Lacan, *SXX*, 75). Lacan does not specify whether the "frigid" woman is to be fully identified with the mystic *as seen by man* (one possible interpretation), or whether the fact that a mystic after all *speaks/writes* about—i.e., formalizes, like Lacan does with his schemas about the barred Other . . . —her knowing nothing about feminine *jouissance* should induce us to consider the "frigid" per se as a failed mystic—a woman who, while reducing to zero her participation in the phallic function, also fully preserves its empty form to the detriment of her *pas-toute*. Lacan also fails to articulate the link between the frigid and the hysteric, as well as to elucidate whether it is possible for a mystic to normally partake of the phallic function—the answer should be "yes" given that, as we have seen, the *pas-toute* is supplementary, i.e., it does not as such involve a diminishing of woman's phallic sexuation.

57. On this point, see also J. Rose, "Introduction—II," 44. The "degree" of femininity could, however, hypothetically be calculated within the domain of the phallus on the basis of the difference between *feminine* phallic *jouissance*, the "one-by-one," and woman's own adoption of *masculine* phallic *jouissance*, the latter being a possibility Lacan seems to contemplate, as I shall discuss shortly, in certain passages of Seminar XX with regard to the (phallic) mother and her incestuous *jouissance*.

feminine *jouissance* beyond the phallus—that we have discussed at length earlier: bluntly put, Lacan seems to be implying that the feminine *jouissance* beyond the phallus is not a satisfaction, at least to the extent that satisfaction is always regarded as ultimately having a sexual origin. Alternatively, we could speak of a "non-sexual satisfaction," which is possibly the reason why Seminar XX refers to it in terms of a "*jaculation*"—as opposed to an "ejaculation"—a passionate impulse that evokes the idea of throwing something with an initial upward direction.

Much of what we have been discussing so far can be recapitulated by means of the so-called formulas of sexuation, which Lacan introduces at the beginning of the seventh lesson of Seminar XX. If we focus on the graph (see below), we can see that woman—as schematized in the right half—is first and foremost passively implicated in masculine sexuality—i.e., the left half—by means of the phallic male function as *a*, the object *a*, in the relation $ (barred subject) → *a*, which is to say that she stands as the object cause of man's desire in fantasy. Lacan already observed earlier in the Seminar that, from the perspective of one side of sexual identification, the male side, the object *a* is that which "is put in the place of what cannot be glimpsed of the Other"[58]—here, it is important to remember that, as Lacan already specified in the first lesson, man never relates to the Other/Woman as such (the fact that jouissance, qua sexual, is phallic ultimately means that "it is not related to the Other as such"[59]). More precisely, "it is inasmuch as object *a* plays the role somewhere—from a point of departure, a single one, the male one—of that which takes the place of the missing partner, that what we are used to seeing emerge in the place of the real, namely, fantasy, is constituted."[60] In other words, fantasy is a masculine phallic way—or, even more generally, man's only way—to relate to woman sexually; it is a replacement for the fact that, in the case of human beings as beings of language, the sexual relationship does not exist as One. In this sense, fantasy emerges at the place of the missing partner as real, i.e., as the not-all of the symbolic order, and makes one of it. Fantasy articulates the non-correlation of subject and object in the case of *homo sapiens*, it adjusts the otherwise defective desire of the former for the latter. In other words, the object can be such only as object of desire in fantasy, where it supports the male subject as vanishing, as a non-totalizable sexed existence alienated in language.

58. Lacan, *SXX*, 63.
59. Ibid., 9.
60. Ibid., 63.

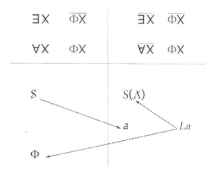

Can *woman* ever enter phallic sexuality *qua the fantasy* $ ◊ a by taking up an *active* role in it? Although Lacan seems to categorically exclude this option when he maintains that "for ~~Woman~~, something other than object *a* is at stake in what comes to make up for [*suppléer*] the sexual relationship that does not exist"[61]—a point that is clearly reinforced by the graph of sexuation: $ lies exclusively on the masculine side, while *a* lies exclusively on the feminine side *qua object* of $[62]—there is, however, a passage in the third lesson of Seminar XX which deeply problematizes this assumption. In it, Lacan speaks of the mother and unequivocally claims that "woman's *jouissance* is based on a supplementation for this not-whole [*une suppléance de ce pas-toute*]"—note that he uses the same verb/noun he used in the previous quote—inasmuch as "she finds the cork for this *jouissance* [based on the fact] that she is not-whole . . . in the *a* constituted by her child."[63] While the latter argument about woman *qua the phallic mother* is a consolidated hypothesis that Lacan had formulated already in the 1950s, especially in Seminar IV, it directly contradicts the former passage: here woman (*qua mother*) clearly *does* make up for (*suppléer*) the sexual relationship that does not exist with *nothing else than her child as object a*. A possible way out of this impasse may consist in taking literally Lacan's other pronouncement, also found in the third lesson, according to which "woman serves a function in the sexual relationship only *qua* mother."[64] This should not only be read from man's perspective—i.e., male phallic sexuality as the fantasy $ ◊ a ultimately revolves around an attempted reduction of Woman to object *a*, i.e., to a (castrated and unconscious) resumption in everyday adult sexual

---

61. Ibid., 63.

62. The unidirectionality of the arrow in $ ◊ a should, however, be complicated insofar as *a* is, for Lacan, the object-*cause* of desire.

63. Lacan, *SXX*, 35.

64. Ibid.

life of the Oedipal dialectics between child, mother, and the phallus[65]—but also from that of woman's own subjectivity. Does this mean that woman as mother occupies the position of $ whenever she relates to her child as object *a*? Would this statement not inevitably lead us to conclude that either woman as mother is, in the sense of sexuation (which is symbolical, not biological), a "man," or that, against the graph of sexuation, $ (the subject alienated by language who partly separates himself from this alienation, and thus relates himself to his object, only thanks to phallic sexuality *qua* fantasy) is not a prerogative of man?

I think that we can solve these tensions and paradoxes only if we admit that Lacan should have added to his graph the function *La* barred→*a*, that of woman *qua* mother. *Mutatis mutandis*, i.e., against the background of the premise that, unlike man, woman is not entirely contained by the phallic function—which is what is depicted by the function *La* barred→S(Ⱥ)—*La* barred could even be conceived as a *feminine* $, one that in the case of the mother relates to an *a*. That is to say, once more, that woman is herself as alienated and sexed in and by language as man; we have seen how her being beyond the phallus is para-linguistic and para-sexual. In addition to this, the function of woman as phallic mother implies a redoubling of *a*, which should now also be located on the male side, or, in the case of the pure function of the incestuous Mother, on the vertical line dividing the sexes. In the latter case, we would thus obtain the function $→*a*←*La* barred, a perfect depiction of the mythical attainment of the symbiotic relation that mother and child attempt to construct before the resolution of the Oedipus complex, that is, before castration. Let us not forget that, for Lacan, woman *qua* phallic mother *does* indeed endeavour to overcome sexual difference incestuously, that is, to put an end to it by assimilating/phagocytising her child.[66] As a consequence, the statement "woman serves a function in the sexual relationship only *qua* mother," which in Seminar XX Lacan seems to understand primarily in the sense of "*from man's perspective*, woman serves a function in the sexual relationship only *qua* mother"—i.e., to put it bluntly, in their post-Oedipal, "mature" relationships with women, all men tend

65. That is to say, insofar as the male $ objectifies himself imaginarily in the void of the woman/other, i.e., achieves identification only by seeing himself as that which sutures woman's desire—the *real* object-*cause* of desire—he unconsciously repeats in the fantasy his offering of himself as imaginary phallus to the mother.

66. This is possibly the reason why Lacan does not add the function of woman *qua* Mother to the graph of sexuation, since it would simply involve the dissolution of sexual difference, the overcoming of the vertical line dividing the sexes. Having said this, given that the incestuous Mother is an idealized tendency rather than a reality, a redoubling of *a* on the male side of the graph could have rendered her really existing version (the phallic mother) as a function *inherent* to sexual difference.

to re-create the relationship with the mother[67]—conceals another, more troubling, statement: "As soon as, *from woman's perspective*, woman serves a function in the sexual relationship only *qua* Mother, sexual difference, and the symbolic order with it, are at risk."

At this stage we are in a position to shed some further light on the intricate claim that "woman's *jouissance* is based on a supplementation for this not-whole [*une suppléance de ce pas-toute*]" inasmuch as "she finds the cork for this *jouissance* [based on the fact] that she is not-whole . . . in the *a* constituted by her child." What still remains to be explained is why that which works as a supplementation (*suppléance*)—or replacement, substitute, stand-in—for a non-totalization is presented in terms of a cork (*bouchon*), whose primary use is to refrain something excessive from overflowing (as Fink notices, *bouchon* could also be rendered as "stopper"). I believe that Lacan is here trying to think the *supplémentaire*, that is, "additional," function of feminine *jouissance* (its "beyond," or "extra"—*en plus*—element) together with the *suppléance*, that is the supplementation (which makes up for a deficiency)—itself a *jouissance*—provided by the child/object *a* as a "cork." On closer inspection, in the sentence in question, he is clearly using the term *jouissance* in two different ways: feminine *jouissance*, the *jouissance* of the not-all as such, is corked—that is to say, contained—by means of a child *qua* the object *a*, which, as a supplementation to the negatively additional character of feminine *jouissance*, produces itself a form of phallic *jouissance*. The maternal function *La* barred→*a* comes in the place of the mystical function *La* barred→S(Å), but if the latter is completely foreclosed by the former, this leads to the disappearance of woman's very presence in the phallic function (*La* barred→Φ) *qua* woman—and not simply *qua* the phantasmatic object *a* of masculine desire—as well as eventually to the disappearance of sexual difference (and the human species) as such. In other words, *La* barred, that is, the fact that there is no universal category for woman, no *The* woman; *La* barred→S(Å), that is, her privileged relation to the non-totalizability of the symbolic order, which is precisely that which prevents us from obtaining a universal category for woman; and *La* barred→Φ, that is, woman's own non-masculine way of relating to the phallic function as a non-universal category, are all mutually dependent and could not be obtained in isolation. The maternal function destabilizes or even suspends this balance; at its purest, it is that which would turn *La* barred into *La*, transform woman into an angelical Mother only after she has incestuously assimilated her child. To move from St. Theresa's jaculations to the Assumption of Mary who sits on

---

67. "Analytic discourse . . . brings into play the fact that woman will never be taken up except *quoad matrem*." Lacan, *SXX*, 35.

the Throne together with the Child Jesus one must pass through the devouring mother (by now sexually undifferentiated, like Goya's Saturn as pictured on the front cover of Seminar IV); or, which is the same, to move from *La* barred→S($\cancel{A}$) to *La* one must pass through *La* barred + *a*.

God: Between Feminine *Jouissance* and Love

Let us now consider in more depth Lacan's suggestion that "for Woman, something other than object *a* is at stake in what comes to make up for [*suppléer*] the *sexual* relationship that does not exist." We should now be able to grasp that this is nothing else than the *feminine phallic* function, depicted as *La* barred→Φ in the graph. We have already encountered it in the guise of the "one-by-one" by means of which woman indirectly symbolizes the male sex as a Don Juan. Just as man does not relate sexually—i.e., phallically—to the feminine Other as such, that is to say, there is no $ -La barred function but rather the phantasmatic function $→a, so woman does not relate sexually— i.e., phallically—to the masculine Other as such, that is to say, there is no *La* barred→$ function but rather the *La* barred→Φ function. In other words, just as, for man, woman is only an object-cause of desire, so, for woman, man is exclusively a symbolic phallus. Woman symbolizes man as a Φ that can turn her, *La* barred, into *a singular woman*, a non-capitalized *la*, only within an infinite, non-totalizable series of women—a within that therefore remains a *without*, or, to use one of Seminar XX's most recurrent puns, an existence that *ex*-sists. Most importantly, the *La* barred→Φ function—i.e., "for Woman, something other than object *a* is at stake in what comes to make up for [*suppléer*] the sexual relationship that does not exist"—does not in the end contradict Lacan's other claim that "woman serves a function in the sexual relationship only *qua* mother." The two statements are compatible precisely because human sexuality is based on a sexual relationship that is not-One, that is, on the non-coincidence between Φ and *a* as sexual objects: while, *for woman*, Φ is that which makes up for the sexual relationship (that does not exist), at the same time, within the same relationship as not-One, *for man*, "woman serves a function in the sexual relationship only *qua* mother" (as lost object). For what we know, Don Juan might well have been after his mother; his seducing women, allowing them to *make themselves* be counted one by one, outside of any universal category of Woman, that is to say, as singularities, could easily have been sustained by the phantasmatic function $→a, the thwarted desire for "the One of universal fusion."[68]

68. Or also, woman symbolizes man only indirectly, that is, by means of his inability of having (Woman through) all women at once. On the other hand, if we read

Having said this, as I have anticipated, if woman does not relate sexually—i.e., phallically—to the masculine Other as such, she nevertheless enjoys a privileged non-sexual relation with what Lacan calls the "most radical" Other, the Other as barred, as not-One, or better, with the barred Other insofar as it can be preserved in its non-totalizability only through the mark of the signifier (in other words, it is only by means of *propositions* such as "there is no Other of the Other," no metalanguage, that we avoid to turn the in-itself of the not-One into the alleged oneness of this very not-One). Lacan formalizes this relation as *La* barred→S($\bar{A}$) and argues that it is the function of an unspeakable *jouissance* that is specifically feminine, which, due to its openness towards the radical otherness of the barred Other, makes woman have "more of a relationship to God than anything that has been said in speculation" about him.[69] More specifically, in experiencing God *qua* the non-totalizability of the symbolic order, feminine *jouissance* approaches him in a way that is contrary to any theology that, following Aristotle's notion of the unmovable mover, or ultimate sphere, has identified the divine with a "supreme Being," a One who fully enjoys himself.

It should be clear by now that Lacan's main presupposition here is that God is nothing else than a name for the paradoxical status of the symbolic order, of language as such—"It is indubitable that the symbolic is the basis of what was made into God"[70]—suspended as it is between its making One and its being not-One, its producing the semblance of unity and this very production's reliance on the maintenance of a non-totality. To put it bluntly, God is nothing but saying: "The Other . . . is the only place . . . that we can give to the term 'divine being,' God, to call him by his name. God [*Dieu*] is the locus where, if you will allow me this wordplay, the *dieu*—the sayer [*dieur*]—the saying [*dire*], is produced. With a trifling change, the saying constitutes God. And as long as somebody will say something, the God hypothesis will persist."[71]

We should not lose sight of the fact that this impasse of the Symbolic as such—which is, at the same time, responsible for making it work—is precisely what human sexuality *qua* the absence of the sexual relationship amounts to. If woman existed as *La*, if she were not not-whole, i.e.,

---

the formula "woman serves a function in the sexual relationship only *qua* mother" as "*for woman*, woman serves a function in the sexual relationship only *qua* mother," the contradiction may be overcome only by admitting that this formulation is inherently paradoxical, since the function of the mother ultimately amounts to an attempt to transcend the sexual relationship by deactivating sexual difference.

69. Lacan, *SXX*, 83 (translation modified).

70. Ibid.

71. Ibid., 45 (translation modified).

universalizable, then her *jouissance* would correspond to that of the supreme Being theorized by theology. But there is no such thing as Woman,
no *être ange*. Woman ex-sists as *La* barred, as a *jouissance* that is mystical, not mythical, while it is man's desire to be One that attributes angelical
features to her. In this sense, although there is indeed a close connection
between feminine non-sexual *jouissance* as a privileged relation to God *qua*
the non-totalizability of the symbolic order and the angelical being that the
phallic fantasy (including hysteria) projects on its unsayability and lack of
knowledge, psychoanalysis should by all means keep them separate. Lacan
spells this out very clearly when, in the same context, he claims that "the
aim of my teaching . . . is to dissociate *a* and A by reducing the first to what
is related to the imaginary," that is, to the phallic fantasy as $\$\rightarrow a$, "and the
other to what is related to the symbolic,"[72] that is, ultimately, to the Other
as irreducibly barred—which should be rendered as $S(\bar{A})$, as $\bar{A}$ *qua* marked
by the signifier, rather than just as $\bar{A}$, in order to prevent any relapse into
another form of mythical/metaphysical discourse, that of the totalisation
of non-totalizability, of the idealistic hypostatisation of the not-One of language into *a* real not-One.[73] In other words, God *qua* the symbolic order
tout-court is, so to speak, more on the side of the barred Other, but, Lacan
adds, he is also inevitably "confused" with object *a*,[74] that is, with that which
makes one of the Other. Here we obtain a straightforward understanding
of why sexual difference "doesn't make two God," yet "it doesn't make just
one either": there is a necessary splitting between God as object *a*, the male
phallic One which tends towards universal fusion with the angelical Mother,
and God as $S(\bar{A})$, the non-phallic feminine *jouissance* of the mystic as the
most concrete instantiation of the not-One. God can be seen, *at the same
time*, as both *the* One and the *not*-One, or rather, as their inextricability:
this duplicity does not make two but neither is it reducible to just one. (Note
moreover that Lacan speaks of "two God" [*deux Dieu*] in the *singular*; this
should remind us that his theo-logical speculation is not to be associated

72. Ibid., 83.

73. In this regard, in an earlier lesson, Lacan is even more adamant: "I wasn't making a strict use of the letter when I said that the locus of the Other was symbolised by
the letter A. On the contrary, I marked it by redoubling it with the S that means signifier
here, signifier of A insofar as the latter is barred: S ($\bar{A}$). I thereby added a dimension to
A's locus, showing that qua locus it does not hold up, that there is a fault, hole, or loss
therein. Object *a* comes to function with respect to that loss. That is something which is
quite essential to the function of language" (ibid., 28). The idealistic drift Lacan is strug-
gling to avoid is precisely that which can be imputed to Quentin Meillassoux's notion of
the "necessity of contingency." I have developed this in L. Chiesa, "Hyperstructuralism's
Necessity of Contingency," *S* 3 (2010) 159–77.

74. See Lacan, *SXX*, 83.

with any attempt to resume a polytheist notion of the divine based on the cosmological complementarity of the opposition between a masculine God and a feminine Goddess. What is rather a stake for him is the way in which sexual difference obliges us to rethink, in a properly dialectical fashion, the one and only God of monotheism as continuously moving from one God to two God, and back.)

The oscillation of God—i.e., of the symbolic order as such—between *the* One and the *not*-One is echoed within the One pole itself, the totalising/imaginary side of God, that of phallic *jouissance*, which Lacan strictly associates with love. As we have already discussed, love is the frustrated *desire* to be One, which repeatedly issues into a not-One, and, at the same time and through the same movement, the desire to be *One*. The latter is as such impossible insofar as human sexuality corresponds to the absence of the sexual relationship, that is, of the relationship between two Ones ("Love is impotent, though mutual, because it is not aware that it is but the desire to be One, which leads us to the impossibility of establishing the relationship between 'them-two' [*la relation d'eux*]. The relationship between them-two what?—Them-two sexes [*deux sexes*]";[75] or also: "the Other [subject] cannot in any way be taken as a One"[76]). We are then left with what Lacan calls the "duet" (*duo*) of sexual intercourse, the not-two of the epithalamion, and its related phallic *jouissance*.[77] As we have already explained, at least on the male pole of sexual identification, this *jouissance* enjoys nothing else than the object *a*, that is to say, the object that, thanks to the fantasy $\$ \rightarrow a$, puts itself in the place of what cannot be glimpsed of the Other. For this reason, insofar as *a* takes the place of the real missing partner, or rather accompanies her absence, human sexuality—along with the possibility of reproduction it entails—is always necessarily a perverse *ménage à trois* with God, Lacan adds.[78] While in his early discussions of fantasy in the 1950s he had associated phallic *jouissance* with perversion as a non-normative, deviant form of sexuation, in Seminar XX he goes as far as arguing that "the act of love" *tout-court*—the brutally physical act of love-making dictated by the *desire* to be One as distinguishable from "*making* love," i.e., *creating* love out of the delusional desire to be *One* (which would be instantiated, for instance, in poetry)—"is the male's polymorphous perversion."[79] In other words, not

---

75. Ibid., 6.

76. Ibid., 49.

77. Ibid., 57.

78. See ibid., 70.

79. Ibid., 72. To cut a long story short, for Lacan, lovemaking *qua* perversion is the male universal *in actu*, the only possible universal qua immanent life of the species . . .

only is God imaginarily embodied in love in the object *a* so that we ourselves can make One as isolated subjects—in this sense Lacan can claim that "love never makes anyone go beyond oneself [*l'amour ne fait jamais sortir quiconque de soi-même*],"[80] and the very myth of the fusional One with the angelical Mother in the end depends on "the mirage of the One you believe yourself to be"[81]—but, following closely his clinical notion of perversion (for which the desire of the pervert is fully aligned with the desire of the Other), this reduction of S($\cancel{A}$) to object *a* ultimately also amounts to a direct enjoying *for* the Other/God, for the unity and consistency of its meaning.[82]

To sum up, as Lacan himself concludes, male phallic *jouissance*—that of sexual intercourse—is therefore eminently masturbatory and idiotic.[83] Although this is not explicitly spelled out in Seminar XX, we need to bear in mind the etymology of the latter term, which derives from the Greek *idios*, that is, "private," "one's own." Seminar XX abounds with reference to idiocy and stupidity (*bêtise*) (*bêtise* in French is strictly associated with *bête*, beast: this perfectly encapsulates the masculine attempt to return to the solipsistic closure of the animal environment[84]). Furthermore, not only is phallic *jouissance* presented as idiotic, but so are, unsurprisingly given what we have just said, God—one of his faces—and love. In a passage from the fourth lesson which we have already scrutinized from a slightly different angle, right after having admitted that "it is impossible to say anything without immediately making Him subsist in the form of the Other," Lacan proceeds to diametrically oppose the discourse of history to psychoanalytic practice: if the former is entirely aimed at "making us believe that it has some sort of meaning," the latter is, on the contrary, focused on the stupidities told by the patient, which should be regarded as "effects of saying," inseparable from language as such; these effects that "agitate, stir things up, and bother speaking beings" are eventually useful, in that they lead people to "accommodating themselves . . . managing all the same," and eventually reproduce, by "giving a shadow of life to the feeling called love."[85] To put it briefly, God (as a non-barred Other) is automatically evoked whenever we say something; for this very reason, saying as such necessarily involves saying something—more or less—stupid (since the Other is actually barred);

80. Ibid., 47.

81. Ibid.

82. Thus, when religions preach to love God, what they really mean is that "by loving God, we love ourselves, and by first loving ourselves . . . we pay the appropriate homage to God." Ibid., 70–71.

83. See ibid., 81.

84. *Bêtise* was until recently rendered in French as *besterie*, being a beast.

85. Ibid., 45–46.

yet it is only stupidity, rather than the attempt to formulate a meaningful discourse, which upholds our love stories—as a stand-in for the absence of the sexual relationship—and thus the species as a whole.

The connection between God and stupidity is also the theme of a particularly intriguing, and complicated, part of the second lesson. In this context, Lacan recovers in the "collectivisation of the signifier"—or better, in confusing the semblance of linguistic totalization, which speech inevitably presupposes, with the in-itself of a unity—the fundamental stupidity of logics, and links it with the figure of God as the "supreme signifier," *the* One, the utmost Being of Aristotelian origins who fully enjoys himself. He then adds that this stupidity is openly witnessed by the smiling angels as often portrayed in ecclesiastical paintings and frescos: "If an angel has such a stupid smile, that is because it is up to its ears in the supreme signifier."[86]

This remark gives us an excellent opportunity to stress once again the distance that separates *l'être ange* from *l'être étrange*. For Lacan, woman is certainly not an idiot. Given the textual evidence, those critics who support the equation between femininity and the angelical being would also need to account for the equation between femininity and stupidity. Far from being reducible to the angel fantasized by man, woman's strangeness precisely amounts to her *being not-all within the phallic function*. What is "strange" here is the inextricability of her phallic function, *La* barred→Φ, from her having a privileged relation with the fact that there is no Other of the Other, that is, *La* barred→S(Ⱥ). In other words, her opening towards the God of non-totalizability, towards the Other as a One that is ultimately a not-One, is only possible because of the co-dependence of *La* barred→S(Ⱥ) with *La* barred→Φ. Woman's *specifically* feminine *jouissance* is only possible because of her feminine *phallic jouissance*, and vice versa. The short passage from the sixth lesson of Seminar XX that seems to associate the feminine *jouissance* of the mystic with woman's strangeness—and which commentators often quote out of context[87]—should itself be read according to these lines. Mystics are by no means angels.[88] Mystical

86. Ibid., 20.

87. See, for example, S. Barnard, "Tongues of Angels: Feminine Structure and Other Jouissance," in *Reading Seminar XX*, 179. Barnard goes as far as speaking of "the strange being of the angel." Her rhapsodic reading of Seminar XX, which uncovers improbable pseudo-concepts such as the "*(m)Other-placenta-subject-to-be*" and the "opaque textual surface of the spider web" (ibid., 182–83) in relation to feminine *jouissance*, epitomizes those that this article aims at contrasting.

88. Bernini's statue of an ecstatic Saint Theresa being pierced by an angel that figures on the cover of Seminar XX can therefore be highly misleading. Jacqueline Rose insightfully notices that it makes Lacan's own question, "And what is her *jouissance*, her *coming* from? [*Et de quoi jouit-elle?*]" (Lacan, SXX, 76, Rose's translation) redundant (see J. Rose, "Introduction—II," 52).

women who are *not-all* in the phallic function are nevertheless still *à plein* in it; to put it bluntly, although mystics put into practice their not-all *more* than other phallic women, they are *not* for this reason *less* phallic than them, since, as we have repeatedly pointed out, feminine non-phallic *jouissance* is additional (by means of subtraction). In principle, St. Theresa's non-sexual jaculation does not in the least exclude her from experiencing sexual enjoyment when she makes herself be counted as a singular, non-universalizable woman, by a womaniser like Don Juan.

What I think Lacan fails to unravel when he confronts the inseparability of the feminine "*not-all* in the phallic function" from the "not-all *in* the phallic function" (and vice versa) is the *different* degrees at which *all* women (who are not symbolically men) can "activate," so to speak, the *en plus*/extra component of the *pas-toute*. Not only a libertine and a mystic can coexist in the same woman, but a mundane courtesan entirely caught up in the perverse intrigues of her king could well become as mystical as a frigid saint without ever leaving his palace or renouncing her sexual practices. Conversely, this matches the fact that woman's remaining nonetheless "fully" in the phallic function entails very dissimilar ways of concretely relating to the phallus and the organ it symbolizes: if, on the one hand, the hysteric is so phallic that, as Lacan has it, she would like to be a man to the extent of embodying his basic fantasy, on the other, it is highly unlikely that she will ever sleep with Don Juan after actively seducing him . . .

Another contiguous issue that remains unexplored by Lacan concerns the exact status of *feminine phallic jouissance*. Besides the numerical consideration according to which the latter gives rise to a notion of the one as singular that differs from the male One of fusion, how does woman enjoy *phallically*? Is she also involved in a *love* triangle with God? My tentative answer is affirmative, but only on condition of adding that her *ménage a trois* cannot take the shape of the fantasy $\$ \rightarrow a$ (as we have seen, it is only woman *qua* mother who attempts to realise the male phallic fantasy, to pass from the desire to be One to directly being One by using her child as a phagocyted appendix). By way of an approximation, I would suggest that woman's love relation to the other sex—and to God as an Other that is, in this case, a One—must still be conceived through the function *La* barred$\rightarrow \Phi$ or, better, through a desire to be *one* only within a one-by-one series; having said this, we also need to specify that, from the stance of love and the different angle it takes on the paradigm of singularity, this function now turns into a "want[ing] to be recognized by [man] as his one and only"—as Lacan proposes in a text written in the same year he delivered Seminar XX.[89] Such

---

89. J. Lacan, "L'Étourdit," in *Autres écrits* (Éditions de Seuil: Paris, 2001) 464.

a request for exclusivity obviously still presupposes, as its reverse side, the open sets of all other women—out of which *a* woman emerges as a singular ex-sistence to be loved.[90]

This matter, which Lacan does not explicitly tackle, and which I can only outline here, would eventually even oblige us to rethink the number of God. While God is neither "two God"—since A *equals* Å—nor "just one"—since A is A *and* Å—he is clearly, for this very reason, also One in two codependent but utterly different ways, masculine and feminine. We should probably invoke here the number three, which is, for Lacan—since his early seminars—the irreconcilable number of the symbolic, to be understood as the result of the non-complementarity between not-One, not-two, and two-Ones. God is *a*, S(Å), but also Φ; that is to say, he is the *object* of masculine phallic *jouissance* (fantasized through the angel, fleetingly realized by the Mother, and negatively embodied by the hysteric), the *hole* of feminine non-phallic *jouissance*, as well as the *symbol* of feminine phallic *jouissance* (woman only has a relation with Φ as the symbol of the *differentiality* of the symbolic as such, with a *One* that is a one and a not-One[91]). The apparent two of God, his being A and Å at the same time, is itself split by the fact that, from the stance of Å, that of woman, God is also an other A. God is a one that is not-One and a not-two that is not *a* two-Ones.

90. It is possibly at this dimension that cliché expressions such as "you make me feel so special" hint.

91. In this sense, Geneviève Morel can rightly remark that "woman can only recognize the *virility* of her partner by marking it with symbolic castration." G. Morel, "Feminine Conditions of Jouissance," in *Reading Seminar XX*, 80 (my italics).

9

Secular Theology
as Language of Rebellion

Noëlle Vahanian

The universe with all its galaxies, its suns and planets, cold or hot, nearby and light years away, evokes at times that oceanic feeling that Romain Rolland mentioned to Freud as the source of religious sentiments. If Freud, by his own admission, couldn't conjure up that oceanic feeling, I must admit that the feeling for me is rather uncanny. That is, if that feeling might correspond for some to the yoking of the atman with the Brahman, to an "indissoluble bond, of being one with the external world," and for Freud then, if it must be genetically explained away as the survival of the feeling of limitlessness that is the mark of primary narcissism, it is for me both mystical and suicidal: a nearly complete obliteration of my existential becoming in and of language here and now and a rapture—a robbing of life to return to nowhere and to oblivion.[1]

The exteroceptive self, nothing at its core and constituted by its reflections, in its unfocused and confounding gaze into the unbearable vastness of the universe catches a glimpse of a really tiny speck—like a minuscule impurity on a camera lens—but enough to interrupt and ruin a cosmic immersion and forcing instead a self-conscious filmic view where the self strangely recognizes itself in what it does not see—a bodily mirror image—because of that scratch on the surface that betrays the eye of an other's gaze calling the self to itself, the eye of an other who might be the self whose imaginary contours flicker ever so dimly, the eye of an other who, like a blind spot, marks a gaping hole

1. Sigmund Freud, *Civilization and Its Discontents*, trans., James Strachey (New York: Norton, 1989) 12.

192

in the narcissistic imaginary self. *The vastness beyond the horizon, that which drowns me in an ocean when I am standing on firm land, is that gaping hole in me that engulfs me—inside or outside, I see myself, a film, a membrane, a betwixt and between, a mirage appearing at the confluence of the two infinites: I am as small as the universe is large.*

~

Introduction

My thesis, in the abstract, is fairly straightforward and not novel. After all, one has only to go back to the Gospels to find Jesus preaching a praxis of rebellion against an established order. At the same time, a secular theology of language is, according to what most ordinarily passes for theology, an oxymoron. First, as a theology of the Death of God, it is without a Supreme Being: it is lacking in Truth. Second, as a theology of the postmodern linguistic turn, it belongs to and is of the order of a constructed reality: it cannot transcend this established world-order against which it is nevertheless rebelling. Thus, the aim of this essay will be to articulate in what rebellion may consist given the impassability of the Death of God and the linguistic turn: there is no way out, only a better way in. The "way in" will be understood as the *relationship* of a subject to her accession to the Symbolic order.

In the first part of the essay, the focus will be on the "way in" as the way of the triumph of religion, in a generative interpretation of Jacques Lacan's remarks in his *Triomphe de la religion*. I will begin with an analysis of Lacan's own prophetic declarations on the future of religion, declarations that, in the work in question, appear to be at odds with Freud. I will surmise, however, that this triumph of religion, true religion as it may be, is still a religious illusion in its necessitating a total conversion without remainder to, and a passive or an unconditional acceptance of the symbolic order. To the contrary, I want to suggest that such a true religion, as Lacan might say, is precisely what a secular theology of language cannot follow in the light of the force (or the faith) that animates it, a force that I conceive as the "rebellious desire to no end."

In the remainder of the essay, I will focus on this notion of rebellion by painting an imaginative picture of this subversive force, where it will appear against the Lacanian backdrop of accession to the symbolic order as a counter to its passive acceptance, as an active way to engage it, as a theological way into this world-for-us rather than out and elsewhere beyond. Three heuristic scenarios will cast this "rebellious desire to no end" situated at the entry point of linguistic reality as, in order of appearance, the power of neurotic dissent, the power of masochistic perversion, and the power of paranoiac doubt.

Let me begin here, however, with some preliminary remarks first, to briefly and probably ever so clumsily convey my understanding of a secular theology of language, and second, to offer a context for these loose notions—"subjectivity under erasure" and "rebellious no"—by claiming their kinship with Julia Kristeva's conceptions of a "subject in process/on trial" and of "rejection."

It is in being secular that a theology of language, after the Death of God and the postmodern linguistic turn, does not deny God. God, here, is first and foremost a word, and it is all the more the Word for lacking a referent, for its ontological emptiness. God as precisely the Word marks the genesis of linguistic reality, entry into speech. The Word made flesh is the incarnation of language and speech, of a social order conceived and conveyed linguistically, embodied in our social practices, all the way down to the social practice of the self. God, in this way, is the Word that bears witness to the phenomenal dimension specific to the human condition. In this view, the Word is made flesh as the Real is barred from the Symbolic.

Thus, if after Lacan one might come to accept that desire as lack grounds and founds a socially and linguistically constituted subjectivity, secular theology, therefore, becomes a theology of language centered on an Other that it knows is an illusion—illusion of the real or illusion of the imaginary—and destined to desire to no end. It is a theology where the personal relationship between God and man in Christ—the word incarnate—becomes an intra-subjective process in an inter-subjective tongue yielding a subjectivity under erasure. Most importantly however, Secular theology, in spite of lacking in Truth, has little to do with religion as a mass delusion to help ease the sorrows of finitude and swallow the discontents of civilization. It is, to the contrary, a rebellious desire to see that there is nothing to see. Concretely, desiring to no end becomes a subversive force, a "rebellious no" to a big Other whose norms, language, and ideals are ready-made forms, masks, and idols.

In this way, it might be helpful to think of theological discourse as akin to how Julia Kristeva speaks of art, or poetry (or schizophrenic language), most notably in her *Revolution in Poetic Language*, which, coincidentally, was originally published the same year that Jacques Lacan professed the triumph of the Roman religion in Rome.[2] Kristeva's materialist philoso-

---

2. Julia Kristeva, *Revolution in Poetic Language*, trans. Margaret Waller (New York: Columbia University Press, 1984). Originally published in French by Éditions du Seuil, 1974.

phy of language underscores *text* as a material production whose process depends on the generation of a subject "in process/on trial," a subject on the threshold betwixt and between, on the one hand, the semiotic process of ordering of the drives within a biological and social environment and, on the other, the symbolic process centered on a subject of enunciation, or an "I." According to Kristeva, unlike negation (saying "No") which presupposes acceptance of or accession to the symbolic and which is therefore conditional on a posited, unitary subject, "rejection" or "negativity" is this pre-verbal drive-force spearheading the signifying process as it generates the subject. Rejection, unlike negation, is a basic biological operation of scission whereby an object is posited as both real in its separation from the body and as a signifiable in its absence, as this body is "caught within the network of nature and society."[3] Kristeva therefore points out Freud's own recognition of the drive of rejection in the infant's "fort-da" game. The latter might be seen as an illustration of rejection as the "dialectical notion specific to the signifying process, on the crossroads between the biological and the social order on the one hand, and the thetic and signifying phase of the social order on the other."[4] That is, with respect to "the thetic and signifying phase," it is because he has thrown the toy out of his crib, posited the object "as real in its separation from the body," that the infant can utter "O-O-O," as in *Vort,* to signify its absence. But, with respect to "the biological and social order," it is because the infant has renounced the instinctual satisfaction of an ever present mother that he finds satisfaction in being able to signify his toy's absence through his "O-O-O-O."

Without rejection, therefore, there is no signifying process, but when rejection is normalized, as for instance, when there is an intellectual acceptance of repression—civilization is the necessary price to pay for security—it loses its dynamism and ready-made words, masks, and idols lock up the subject in the straitjacket of "unitary and technocratic visions," to borrow Kristeva's own words. This explains why even though the emergence of poetry is, according to Kristeva, "the expenditure of the thesis of establishing the socio-symbolic order and . . . the bringing into play of the vehemence of drives through the positing of language," over time what appears as transgressive is often assimilated into the symbolic order, and loses its initial function: even poetry becomes a "fetishization," and as such yet another mark of the intellectual acceptance of repression.[5] Still, Kristeva, in speaking of the "struggle of

3. Ibid., 122.
4. Ibid., 124.
5. Ibid., 83.

poetry against fetishism" characteristic of nineteenth-century poetry and the twentieth-century literature it heralded, explains that

> Recovering the subject's vehemence required a descent into the most archaic stage of his positing, one contemporaneous with the positing of social order; it required a descent into the structural positing of the thetic in language so that violence, surging up through the phonetic, syntactic, and logical orders, could reach the symbolic order and the technocratic ideologies that had been built over this violence to ignore or repress it. To penetrate the era, poetry had to disturb the logic that dominated the social order and do so through that logic itself, by assuming and unraveling its positions, its syntheses, and hence the ideologies it controls.[6]

While it is not within the purview of this work to demonstrate the theological dimension of Kristeva's materialist conception of rejection, in claiming a kinship with both her concepts and her project, I am assuming their theological potential. In what follows then, one can think of the "rebellious desire to no end" of a secular theology of language as a subversive force making palpable the movement of rejection that posits the real in order to give it over to the symbolic. This "rebellious no" is, therefore, not merely an oppositional force or a nay-saying stance, it voices the expenditure of drives exceeding the order of the symbolic so as to give this order flesh again. In this essay in particular, I will try to subvert the logic that explains the disorders of neurosis, paranoia, and perversion in terms of failed or incomplete accession to the symbolic order. My aim is not to celebrate madness; this would only be to give way to the logic dominating the social order. My aim is to read these disorders both for the rebellious power or force they manifest and as heuristics for rethinking, re-energizing, and re-vitalizing accession to the symbolic order so as to open this order up to its own madness.

Part I. The Triumph of the Religious Illusion

Secular theology after Lacan is not a theology, according to Lacan. In the same way that Lacan operated a "return to Freud" by way of which he refused to conflate the Freudian text with some basic tenets of Freudian psychology to be swallowed whole and recited like a mantra, theology after Lacan does not swallow whole Lacan's declaration, notably at a 1974 press conference in Rome, concerning the truth of the Roman religion: "La vrai religion, c'est la romaine.... Il y a *une* vrai religion, c'est la religion chrétienne" (The

---

6. Ibid., 82 and 83.

true religion, it's the Roman. . . . There is one true religion, it's the Christian religion).[7] Lacan's position concerning religion appears so vastly at odds with that of Freud, for whom religion's mechanism as wish-fulfillment meant it was an illusion, and its hold on so many, both a moral instrument of control serving the aims of civilization and, not unparadoxically, an infantilizing force slowing down its progress. For Lacan, the symptom of an encounter with an impossible real—like a childish feeling of helplessness—is not the religious mass delusion concerning an omnipotent God, the Father, granting its deepest wish for everlasting protection to the child. Instead, psychoanalysis is the symptom: "la psychanalyse est un symptôme. . . . Elle fait nettement partie de ce malaise de la civilisation dont Freud a parlé" (Psychoanalysis is a symptom; it clearly belongs to the discontent of civilization of which Freud spoke).[8]

This is a symptom particular to a historical period marked by the ascendency of scientific discourse.[9] But this discourse walls the subject in, objectifies her to the point of alienating her by robbing her life of its discrete meaning. What this implies specifically, as Philippe Julien reminds us in his *Pour lire Jacques Lacan*, is that the subject of psychoanalysis is thus the subject of science—a Cartesian subject. In shorthand: no Cartesian subject, no Freudian Unconscious.[10] That is, when God is dead, nothing is permitted—the superego is born.[11] Or in other words, the discontent of civilization—Foucault makes a similar case concerning the internment of unreason in his *Madness and Civilization*—corresponds to the historical advent of a rational subject as the subject of scientific discourse. The abnormal subject is first immoral, because she is like a child who needs to be grown up, then she is neurotic, because of an incomplete resolution of the Oedipal complex, now she needs to understand that her *objet petit a*—unattainable object of desire—is an effect, necessary counterpart, of her accession to symbolic castration. The constant, from the seventeenth century on, is the descendent of the Cartesian subject, for as Lacan says, "le sujet sur quoi nous opérons en psychanalyse ne peut être que le sujet de la science" (The subject we deal with in psychoanalysis can only be the subject of science).[12] The charac-

7. Jacques Lacan, *Le triomphe de la religion précédé de Discours aux catholiques* (Paris: Éditions du Seuil, 2005) 81. My translation.

8. Ibid. My translation.

9. Ibid., 80–81.

10. Philippe Julien, *Pour lire Jacques Lacan* (Paris: Points, 1990) 135.

11. Lacan, *Le triomphe de la religion*, 36.

12. Jacques Lacan, *Écrits* (Paris: Éditions du Seuil, 1966) 259. Cited in Julien, *Pour lire Jacques Lacan*, 135. Translation from Philippe Julien's *Jacques Lacan's Return to Freud: The Real, the Symbolic, and the Imaginary*, trans. Devra Beck Simiu (New York: New York University Press, 1995) 108.

teristic *malaise* of this subject is its alienation in language, the point where language no longer speaks, where language and speech come apart because this rational subject is split from its embodied ground.

Perhaps we could risk the position that, for Lacan, psychoanalysis is the symptom of the unconscious, an unconscious itself the symptom of a particular historical subject—an alienated subject? This is why he claims that the symptom is—though not the real in itself—what is most real, but that it will likely be supplanted by a surplus of religious meaning—allow me to paraphrase and loosely translate from his *Triomphe de la religion*: religious meanings will be secreted; humanity will be healed of psychoanalysis, because this symptom, drowned in religious meaning, will eventually be repressed; thus, religion is made to heal, that is, it is made so that people won't notice what is wrong.[13]

So, Lacan explains, psychoanalysis will have given us a just measure of the *parlêtre*, of the one whose being is to speak, and when in the beginning was the Word and the Word was made flesh, this is the beginning of what goes wrong. "C'est quand le Verbe s'incarne que ça commence à aller vachement mal. Il [l'être charnel] n'est plus du tout heureux" (It's when the Word becomes flesh that things start to go really badly. He's [the carnal being] not happy at all anymore).[14] Or, what ravishes him, ravages him.[15] But psychoanalysis does not have the power of religion to give meaning to everything, including the human being. The more science uncovers the real, shoves it into our lives, the more religion will take hold of us.[16]

Religion, *true* religion or the Roman religion for Lacan, makes meanings that seduce or thrill us. These may be illusory insofar as they cover up what is wrong, the real, but that is precisely why they are not the symptom of this real, and instead its cure. Like the pharmakon, perhaps, the poison is the remedy. Religion has the power to "heal," and nothing is less in vogue these days than the notion of "faith-based therapy." To wit, the benefits of religion and spirituality for our well-being have recently become the subject not only of scientific research articles, but also of research institutes, government funded research grants, popular self-help books, and magazine cover stories. A quick survey of both lay and scholarly literature on this topic reveals that this benefit is often cited as an established fact, demonstrated through scientific research—though precise sources are not always cited.

---

13. Lacan, *Le triomphe de la religion précédé de Discours aux catholiques*, 81–82, 87.

14. Ibid., 90. My translation.

15. Ibid., 91. Lacan says that his patients come back to him for years, because the Word ravishes them, "les fais jouir . . . Ils jubilant."

16. Ibid., 78–79.

Here are some examples. If Claudia Kalb's November 2003 *Newsweek* article, titled "Can Religion Improve Health? While the Debate Rages in Journals and Med Schools, More Americans Ask for Doctors' Prayers," offered a more nuanced perspective from the scientific community on integrating religion within the medical field, in the short July 2008 *Newsweek* piece "Working Out With Jesus," on the Gospel fitness trend in mainly minority communities to combine aerobic workout with spiritual redemption, Sarah Ball unambiguously asserts that "studies show a correlation between prayer and good mental health."[17] Even more recently, CNN's *Belief Blog* of November 10th, 2011, featured a post by Gabe LaMonica concerning a "new study" linking regular religious attendance to "a more optimistic, less depressed, and less cynical outlook on life."[18] As noted by Thomas G. Plante, the Santa Clara Professor of Psychology whose work as a screener for Catholic seminaries and research interests on the psychological benefits of religion and spirituality have earned him some media coverage in the past few years, if psychology's efforts to establish itself as a science during the better part of the twentieth century means that it "tended to shy away from all things religious or spiritual," in recent years, psychology has "embraced spirituality and religion more."[19] To that effect, David Bjerklie's February 2009 short piece in *Time* magazine, "Keeping (or Finding) the Faith," mentions the 2006 University of Pennsylvania Center for Spirituality and the Mind, where researchers can examine MRIs of the brain that prays, and the self-help guide to the health benefits of spirituality titled *How God Changes Your Brain*, coauthored by Andrew Newberg (the center's director) and Mark Robert Waldman.[20] But there is also—and this is far from a complete enumeration—Duke University's Center for Spirituality, Theology, and Health, founded in 1998. Its current director, Harold G. Koenig, considered "an expert" in the field of religion and health, has testified before the U.S Senate and the House of Representatives on the effects of religious practice on health. In short, religious practice is seen more and more as part of a regular health regimen, on a par with your exercise routine, a well-balanced

17. Claudia Kalb, "Can Religion Improve Health?" *Newsweek*, November 10, 2003, 44–50, 53–54, 56; Sarah Ball, "Working Out With Jesus," *Newsweek*, July 28, 2008.

18. "Study Links Regular Religious Service Attendance, Outlook on Life," http://religion.blogs.cnn.com/2011/11/10/study-links-regular-religious-service-attendance-outlook-on-life/.

19. Thomas G. Plante, "Integrating Spirituality and Psychotherapy: Ethical Issues and Principles to Consider," *Journal of Clinical Psychology* 63.9 (2007) 892.

20. David Bjerklie, "Finding (or Keeping) the Faith," *Time*, February 12, 2009; Andrew Newberg and Mark Waldman, *How God Changes Your Brain: Breakthrough Findings from a Leading Neuroscientist* (New York: Ballantine, 2010).

diet, antioxidant-rich vitamin-enhanced water, and fish oil supplements. Religion makes meanings that not only seduce and thrill, they also alter the brain of the sensible subject of science to render him insensible to—they cover up—what is wrong.

Part II. The Left Behind

Nevertheless, the triumph of religion, à la Lacan, still risks a return of the repressed in the guise of unbelief or even disbelief. The incredible is sometimes too good to be true, so that the left behind can't stomach the cure and want to feel the pain of the Word made flesh. They are the crucibles of the real. It is for them that a theology of language is relevant—a theology after Lacan.

If there is meaning to be had for such a theology of language, it is neither thanks to the powerful deflection of a religious illusion nor to the veiling of what is wrong, but instead, it is in the revolutionary power of a disillusioned subject harnessing a desire to no end. This power is the agency of the subject who is not one—its agency as a non-subject or a becoming fluid is its recalcitrance to subjectivity.

Neurosis, perversion, or paranoia can serve as heuristic devices for schematizing this recalcitrance's operative. While psychoanalysis has explained these disorders as symptomatic of abnormal or incomplete or not wholly successful or failed accession to the symbolic order, a theology of language views them respectively as 1) the power of dissent, 2) the power of perversion, and 3) the power of doubt and suspicion.

In the first case, neurosis, the big Other's castrating agency is not swallowed whole. The dissident subject initially refuses, not however most importantly for us, the authority of the Name of the Father. What is crucial, though, is what comes as a result of this not altogether smooth-sailing accession to symbolic castration, namely, the subject's refusal or resentment to grant legitimacy to the big Other or the symbolic order *even as this subject would have traversed the fantasy* as it were, that is, even as it would have recognized its own implication in the power it grants this big Other. This pseudo-neurotic (who has traversed the fantasy) desires to no end, freed from the ensnaring fantasy of an object cause of desire, the fantasy of an object that can be possessed and is possessed by some Other and that could answer her primordial desire once and for all. But, what she retains of the neurotic posture is her resentment as a rebellious force. What she rebels against is thus not so much a big Other to which she did not agree, what she rebels against is the *rule of Nobody (not of a They, but of just anybody)*. For accession to symbolic castration means tacit agreement with the privileged status of the descendent of the Cartesian subject of science: the consumer, the patient, etc. One has to be willing to risk testing the limits of normalcy and citizenry or else these limits shrink. Just as our industrial agricultural practices have led to higher caloric but less diversified and nutrient-rich diets—the fruit or vegetable variety that travels long distances the best, that has the longest yield, and that is the most pest and disease resistant is always favored over others—so, too, our schools and our social and medical practices, our languages, reinforce a type of human, a *parlêtre* without an unconscious—however oxymoronic that is: the Normal human is symptom free, and he can only be symptom free if he's oblivious, insensitive, deaf to what is wrong. Perhaps this is a *parle-sans-être*. The point is to rebel against becoming such a blemish-free subject.

To rebel is to want to desire to no end so as not to be the victim of an impossible desire whose manifestations through anxiety, depression, or compulsions, for instance, fall under medical conditions. However, since the term *neurosis* is no longer used as a diagnostic category in the Diagnostic and Statistical Manual of Mental Disorders, its falling out of grace makes it an interesting candidate for co-option and rehabilitation. The post-neurotic *wants* to find it difficult to live in an environment that requires its adaptability, docility, flexibility, and malleability.

Let's make clear, however, that mental illness is neither the necessary point of departure nor the desideratum for a theology of language. The post-neurotic is not intent on feeling maladjusted in society or uncomfortable in her skin, her aim is to make life significant, not alone in her bubble, but in a world with others for whom life is not a prescription to perform like the Jones. A mimetic desire, a desire of the Other, is most obviously, lack—a chasing after an unwanted object, and for that reason, a chasing after some impossible Thing never to be possessed. Like chasing after speed only to find oneself riding on a commercial jet engine airplane cruising at an average speed of five hundred miles per hour, a mimetic desire of the Other underwhelms and deflates. The will to desire to no end is different. The will to desire to no end, like the thrill your dog feels for the wind flapping its ears and the smells hitting its snout from the car's passenger rolled-down window, is borne with resistance, friction, and force. In this case, the movement of resistance works opposite that of repression. What do you want? I know that I want a fiction: a something that I cannot have, but I want this fiction as such a fiction rather than as a make-believe illusion—which it would be if I did not know what I wanted, that it was a fiction. Thus every iteration of the desire to no end speaks for a fiction, engages in the fiction, and in fact, makes the fiction a fiction.

The second heuristic case is that which seeks hold of the power of perversion. In this case, the big Other's reprimand and severity, its incisive cutting, is a manipulation by the becoming subject to disavow "as if" to serve its own deepest desire. The masochistic desire to suffer the Law of the Father hides not so much the guilt of an untamed wish, but the fulfillment of this wish. It is a transgression of the Law insofar as it is a perversion of the Law. At the same time, it appears as an affirmation of the Law, if not as a condition of its fulfillment.

Take the case of feminine masochism as interpreted by Žižek in "Are We Allowed to Enjoy Daphnée du Maurier." The perversion in question is not that of the masochistic fantasy wherein the woman finds pleasure in her subjection to male violence, rather, it is in the paradox that the staging of such "a masochist scenario is the first act of liberation: by means of it, the servant's masochistic libidinal attachment to his master is brought into the light of day, and the servant thus achieves a minimal distance towards it."[21] As opposed to interpreting feminine masochism as evidence of internalized patriarchal values (an affirmation of the Law), the veil of fantasy puts these values in their place—at the level of make-believe—insofar as staging the epitome of patriarchal oppression is in effect a way of de-legitimizing or transcending the real of patriarchy (in sum, the condition of the Law's fulfillment is its fictionalization—its disavowal). That is to say, it is not enough to acknowledge patriarchal oppression and to consciously reject it. This realization and condemnation would amount to a bourgeois realizing that a commodity has no special magical powers and that money is just a tool meant to facilitate and orchestrate the social exchange of goods and services: his very "participation in social exchange" would attest to the contrary, namely to the hold—as though endowed with magical powers— commodities have on him.[22] Similarly then, to condemn the patriarchal configuration of the sexual fantasy is to avow that patriarchal reality—that it has a real haunting hold. It is another iteration of the paradox of the atheist who professes the death of God, but has internalized all the prohibitions, such that if God is dead, then nothing is permitted, or following Žižek who repeats Lacan's formulation, "God is unconscious."[23]

One of Žižek's illustrations of this paradox harks back to Kierkegaard's *Sickness Unto Death* on the declensions of despair as forms of original sin. Whether this despair is authentic or not and whether or not one recognizes

21. Slavoj Žižek, "Are We Allowed to Enjoy Daphnée du Maurier?" *Lacan.com* (2005), http://www.lacan.com/zizdaphmaur.htm.

22. Slavoj Žižek, *How to Read Lacan* (New York: Norton, 2007) 94.

23. Ibid.

one's despair, this sickness of existence is intractable, for the true Christian cannot despair—he is eternal and one with God. Similarly to one of those declensions of despair, Žižek mentions someone who might identify as a Christian while failing to endorse his "interpellated symbolic identity"—in his heart, he does not believe that with which he nevertheless identifies. This Christian in name only will, therefore, feel the "superego pressure of guilt," for not being a true Christian.[24] But could he ever, could anyone ever, profess to be what they feel they are in their heart? Is this divided self not the kernel of the Kierkegaardian sickness, of existential despair? Žižek's Lacanian version of the Kierkegaardian sickness suggests that this superego pressure of guilt for not being a true Christian depends on a deeper betrayal, a betrayal "that pertains to the act of interpellation *as such*," the act whereby symbolic identification meshes with the Ego-Ideal, with internalized norms and ideals.[25] The divided self is the result of this betrayal. That is, one can only fail to be a Christian if, to borrow from William James, Christianity as a hypothesis is a "living option" that "makes some appeal, however small, to your belief."[26] When Christianity "appeals," this means, in Žižek's terms, that one has found "a way of 'giving up on one's desires,'" through symbolic identification with the Ego-Ideal.[27] It is this betrayal of the law of desire with a (Christian) Ego-Ideal that is the core of (Christian) existential despair.

If for Kierkegaard, we might say that the true Christian would not have to give up on her desires in order to be with God—she would not be a divided self—for Žižek, then, and going back to the previous point concerning Lacan's formulation, "God is unconscious," the true atheist is only a hedonist out of guilt for this initial betrayal of the law of desire by his symbolic identification with the (atheistic) Ego-Ideal. All prohibitions—even the prohibition against prohibitions of the permissive society—depend on this original betrayal of desire and they all depend on this internal injunction to maintain satisfactory identify with this Ego-Ideal. In this sense, "God is unconscious." But what is more, the atheistic Ego-Ideal of the permissive society as the inverse of the Christian Ego-Ideal therefore entails the necessary repression of prohibitions themselves, such that "the unconscious is the site of prohibitions."[28] Thus, the atheist's freedom means that "unconsciously,

24. Slavoj Žižek, *For They Know Not What They Do: Enjoyment as a Political Factor* (New York: Verso, 2002) lxx–lxxi.

25. Ibid., lxxi.

26. William James, "The Will to Believe," in *Writings, 1878–1899* (New York: Library of America, 1992) 458.

27. Žižek, *For They Know Not What They Do*, lxxi.

28. Žižek, *How to Read Lacan*, 92.

he continues to believe in God."[29] But thus also, according to this logic, "permitted *jouissance* necessarily turns into obligatory *jouissance*"—which obligation makes it more and more difficult to simply enjoy anything at all at the same time as it leads to a "striving toward excessive enjoyment."[30]

We can think of two intertwining ways, then, in which it is possible to understand that "nothing is permitted." First, since everything is obligatory, this is a supreme injunction to enjoy everything, oneself, one's job, etc., and this injunction becomes an intolerable pursuit of a purely subjective experience of pleasure—what Žižek terms an autistic-masturbatory, "asocial" *jouissance* whose supreme case is drug addiction.[31] Second, there is also the Sartrian Existentialist sense in which when there is no God (and thus "God is unconscious"), one is responsible for oneself and for everyone else too. In the absence of an external supreme authority, prohibitions themselves become internalized and this of course redoubles their efficacy only to "sabotage your enjoyment."[32] The permissive society is paradoxically the society where individual behavior seems to be most heavily regulated (from the learned behavior of compliance to strict national security guidelines at airport security checks—knowing to expedite the removal of your shoes, belt, and extra garments, so as not to hold up the line—to learning to project the "right" body image, a constant "onscreen" "camera-ready" friendly face, etc.). The point here is that the most "transgressive" behavior or production (think of the commodification of the "shock value" of a broadcast show like *Fear Factor*, for instance) is only the flip side of a God who is unconscious, of a conscious injunction to reject God and His patriarchal archive.

This is why to the contrary of suggesting an internalization of patriarchal values, the externalization of the most intimate desires in the acting out and staging of the feminine masochistic fantasy renders to fiction what is a fiction, it is a "form of disavowal," "an 'as if' which suspends reality."[33] For, I think that even if this perversion could be seen as just another "transgressive" performance which would thus make this perversion a modality or declension of ideology (the flip-side of repressed prohibitions), its power is in the distanciation it produces. This distanciation is a rebellious force. It is the theatrical ploy of the child who makes up and changes the rules of a game as he goes along while acting as though the rules were established laws agreed

29. Ibid., 91.

30. Slavoj Žižek, *The Parallax View* (Cambridge: MIT Press, 2006) 310.

31. Ibid., 311.

32. Žižek, *How to Read Lacan*, 92.

33. Slavoj Žižek, *The Žižek Reader*, ed. Elizabeth Wright and Edmond Wright (Malden, MA: Blackwell, 1999) 153.

to by all participants from time immemorial, who pretends that he is not the same one who participates and who directs his play: "Now, I am going to hide behind the curtain. Pretend you didn't know. Now say 'Oh! Where's Charlie?' Now, don't find me yet!" This is also the life force exhibited in the movie *Life Is Beautiful*, in which a father hopes to help his son survive the atrocities of life in a concentration camp by presenting, framing, veiling the struggle for survival as a child's game to pass the time. While one can readily see the salutary intention of the father, a closer look at the required logic for this ploy's effectiveness would reveal its masochistic perversity: one must pretend that the gruesome is fun—there will be pleasure in pain. It is a game, but the son must win. More than imaginative play or illusion, the ploy, if it could really work, would amount to reducing the real cruelty of camp life under the authoritarian, inhumane rule to a fiction with which life, as affirmative, active force, has little to do.[34]

There is, nevertheless, another side to the force of perversion, one which, if we were to follow these categories closely, we would align more properly with sadism than with masochism. A reading of Žižek's chapter, "The Perverse Subject of Politics: Lacan as a Reader of Mohammad Bouyeri,"[35] can help disentangle the knot of the perverse.

Mohammad Bouyeri is indeed the Dutch-Moroccan Islamist responsible for the brutal death in 2004 of the Dutch filmmaker Theo Van Gogh, for his short film *Submission*. The film, the screenplay of which was written by Ayaan Hirsi Ali, the Somali-Dutch feminist critic of Islam, highlights three verses of the Quran that appear to sanction violence against women. These verses are tattooed on a woman's body and revealed through a transparent chador. The skin that must be covered in submission reveals the sacred text that condones abuse through what is typically a seductive ploy. Bouyeri shot and stabbed Van Gogh to death. Attached to one of the two daggers he left implanted in Van Gogh's body was an open letter addressed to Hirsi Ali. It is this letter that Žižek analyzes more closely to reveal how deception, for the perverse, sadistic subject, is a double-edged sword.

That is, on one hand, the sadist's perversion is, in Lacan's words, "an inverted effect of the fantasy. It is the subject who determines himself as an object, in his encounter with the division of subjectivity."[36] On the other, the perverted subject believes that it is the others who are deceived—"the pervert displaces division onto the Other" and deceives himself into believing

---

34. *La vita è bella* (original title), directed by Roberto Benigni, 1997.

35. Žižek, *How to Read Lacan*, ch. 8.

36. Jacques Lacan, *The Four Fundamental Concepts of Psychoanalysis*, ed. Jacques-Alain Miller, trans. Alan Sheridan (New York: Norton, 1998) 185. Here cited in Žižek, *How to Read Lacan*, 105.

that he possesses the truth, that it is his responsibility to execute the will of a big Other, assert the rule of this Other's law.[37] Thus, Mohammad Bouyeri was convinced—"knew"—that Hirsi Ali should die to prove not what she believed but that she truly believed it—to be consistent with herself, if she were truly not afraid of God's judgment, she should want to die. But in this case, it is Bouyeri who wanted to make sure that Hirsi Ali's actions were consistent with her beliefs. As Žižek puts it:

> a pervert is not defined by the content of what he is doing (his weird sexual practices). Perversion, at its most fundamental, resides in the formal structure of how the pervert relates to truth and speech. The pervert claims direct access to some figure of the big Other (from God or history to the desire of his partner), so that, dispelling all the ambiguity of language, he is able to act directly as the instrument of the big Other's will.[38]

In this same chapter Žižek rhetorically asks, "What if the rule of law can only be asserted through wicked (sinful) meanings and acts? What if, in order to rule, the law has to rely on the subterranean interplay of cheatings and deceptions?"[39] In the passage cited, he is directly referring to Shakespeare's *All's Well That Ends Well,* where Count Bertram has to be duped into consummating a marriage into which he was forced by the king in order to recognize his lawful wife. Helen, the wife, makes herself pass for Diana, the woman Count Bertram would rather have married. The marriage is finally consummated and the law fulfilled.

While Helen and Diana deceive Bertram in order to assert a rule of law, we can easily recall, as Žižek also reminds us, how Arendt suggested that this mechanism was internalized by the Nazis—who were, for the most part and to begin with at least, average, normal, law-abiding citizens—to help them justify their murderous actions: in order to fulfill the law of the land—a perverted inversion of the biblical first commandment—one had to believe that the real temptation to be avoided was that of not killing, that is, unless one were animated by some fanatic intransigence, where one "knows" it is the others who are deceived. The fanatic pervert, therefore, does not see the virtue of the Shakespearian stratagem, that there is no other way to the truth but through the lies. He refuses this postmodern, linguistic condition. His fanaticism is one with his inability to enter play through a ploy. He counters playfulness with destruction. This is not civil disobedience, a breaking of the letter law for the sake of the spirit of law. This is not

37. Lacan, quoted in Žižek, *How to Read Lacan,* 110.
38. Ibid., 116.
39. Ibid., 112.

tax evasion either, a following of the letter of the law meant to break the spirit of law. But likewise, this mode of perversion, entrenched in its fanaticism and certain of its absolutes, has no need for a theology of language.

Let us look at the third heuristic device useful for a theology of language, the case of paranoia whose force is the power of suspicion and doubt. Delusion, ironically, unmasks the other delusion—the delusion of the big Other's ontological supremacy, of its realism. The becoming subjects rebels against this fetishized social order. It questions its motives, its sincerity, it puts language to the test, defying it to speak the truth.

In "Louis Armstrong: A Rhapsody on Repetition and Time," Jeffrey Robbins focuses on the 1932 short film *A Rhapsody in Black and Blue*, in which Louis Armstrong plays "the role of the lazy, shifty, ne'er-do-well husband," who, as Robbins writes,

> wants only to sit idly and to listen to his jazz records while his wife, looking the part of a mammie, beats him senseless over the head to get him to do his house chores. But as quickly as his wife leaves the room, Armstrong drifts into sleep to the sounds of his own horn blowing. The next scene cuts to Armstrong in a dream sequence emerging out of the midst of a soapsudded floor decked out in full jungle regalia where he plays his trumpet and sings for the African jungle King of "Jazzmania."[40]

Embedded in the short is one of Armstrong's famous renditions of "Shine," the song whose lyrics are in themselves a commentary on coon song and blackface racial stereotypes:

> Oh chocolate drop, that's me
> 'Cause, my hair is curly
> Just because my teeth are pearly
> Just because I always wear a smile
> Like to dress up in the latest style
> 'Cause I'm glad I'm livin'
> Take troubles all with a smile
> Just because my color shade
> Is different maybe
> That's why they call me "Shine"

As the King of "Jazzmania" bobs his head and falls asleep to Armstrong playing his famous syncopated repetition of the same High C note, the dream sequence ends and at the end of the song the lazy husband wakes

40. Jeffrey Robbins, "Louis Armstrong: A Rhapsody on Repetition and Time," in *Heaven Knows I'm Miserable Now*, ed. Michael Grimshaw (Palgrave Macmillan, forthcoming).

up to the sound of the record spinning. Robbins writes that at that point, "Armstrong is no longer playing for the pleasure of this caricature of an African king, but for himself, to himself, in a state of dreamlike wonder," and that this "is a realization of Deleuze's attempt to think difference apart from representational identity."[41] While Armstrong has been criticized for his clownish "crowd-pleasing" performances, for his willingness to play to the prejudicial stereotypes of a popular audience, Robbins is suggesting that this mask, alike the one worn by Ralph Ellison's invisible man who hides in plain sight, is transcended by the virtuosity of the music. The commentary is embedded in the film story plot, and in this way could easily appear to be co-opted by the ridiculous depictions of the black man: a lazy man dreaming a ridiculous fantasy. But whose wish does this dream answer? Who could wish to sing to a buffoonish, lazy king? Who would want to sing so lightheartedly one's heart out?

Either Armstrong's subjectivity is perfectly interpellated by this racist ideology: his symbolic identification with the racist Ego-Ideal successfully represses and deflects and sublimates the deeper betrayal of desire that makes this interpellation possible, and in this case he is truly hiding—hiding from himself included—in plain sight. As Robbins reminds us, Ellison's invisible man "confesses that he likes Armstrong 'because he's made poetry out of being invisible' . . . 'I think it must be because he's unaware that he *is* invisible.'"[42]

Or, like the word incarnate, like the repetition of Louis Armstrong's High Cs that pound through our flesh to make us feel the pulse of an invisible man under a leopard's jungle suit, the force of suspicion recalls us to faith in words—not that words are sound, but that sounds matter. The act of interpellation, this call to inhabit *unsound* norms and prejudices alike, does not amount to a capitulation of desire and a cheapening, hollowing of one's being under the guise of the forging of an identity. Instead, it creates an excess, this is the Deleuzian difference in repetition: Armstrong playing for himself and by himself—the sound of an invisible man whose invisibility is made visible by an absurd dream sequence central to a stereotypically racial plot—together with the "musical time-bending" quality of the film exemplify an eternal return "wherein the 'returning is the becoming-identical of becoming itself.'"[43]

Perhaps another way to think of the rebellious force of suspicion and doubt against the fetishized social order is in how it relates to interpassivity.

41. Ibid.

42. Ibid. Robbins quotes Ralph Ellison, *The Invisible Man* (New York: Modern Library, 1994) 7–8.

43. Ibid. Robbins quotes Gilles Deleuze, *Difference and Repetition*, trans. Paul Patton (New York: Columbia University Press, 1995) 41.

Interpassivity is the notion according to which the big Other , as the object, the fictional role, the social mask, the persona—the Word—becomes entrusted with the task of expressing our most intimate feelings and attitudes so that we can stay actively engaged in a way that makes no difference. It is how "*I am passive through the Other.*"[44] Žižek exemplifies this notion in many ways, but for instance, he calls attention to the function of the Tibetan prayer wheel, which, in turning, does the praying in the monk's stead, so that he may be free, free from his own depths, to do some other task.[45] Žižek also warns that today the greater danger to passivity is the "pseudo-activity" of people trying to "do something" to change the status quo, like the endless academic debates meant to give both the illusion of pro-action and the excuse not to do anything.[46] Of course, it is also possible to think of speech in this way, where canned words give one the satisfaction of having said something when nothing truly will have been given over to speech—like the little girl who speaks gibberish while ecstatically feeling as though she's demonstrated her expert knowledge in all things important. Thus, the important feature of interpassivity is that inasmuch as it entails the displacement onto some form of the big Other of one's intimate feelings, it enables the bracketing out of one's psychological "inner states," so that one neither need feel awkward and self-conscious nor obligated to reveal one's true self. Nevertheless, and this is the added bonus of the interpassive mode, one still feels honest or in the case of pseudo-activism, one still feels pro-active, as though "the emotions I perform through the mask (the false persona) that I adopt can in a strange way be more authentic and truthful than what I assume that I feel in myself."[47]

And yet, in the face of interpassive disengagement through pseudo-activism, Žižek states that "the first critical step is to *withdraw into passivity* and to refuse to participate."[48] The point, here, is to enact the precise opposite of interpassivity wherein "*I am active through the Other.*"[49]

Enter: heuristic paranoia. Words are leopard jungle suits, whether we feel the pseudo-activity of our own stammering speech or the mouth-piece passivity of an inherited, imposed, and unescapable language. Otherwise put, when the activity is speech or when we are talking about the Word made flesh, words are both how *I am active through the Other: how I am*

44. Žižek, *How to Read Lacan*, 26.

45. Ibid., 23.

46 Ibid., 26.

47. Ibid., 32.

48. Ibid., 27.

49. Ibid.

disengaged from these words, they don't represent me, I play a role, I don't mean what I say ("I dream of playing for the king of Jazzmania") and how I am passive through the Other: these words conveniently bar me from myself, the more I talk, the more I forget what is wrong, I still play a role, I don't say what I mean ("I dream of playing for the king of Jazzmania"). But, in the end, it is always the others who decide if a lie is lie enough to ring true.

Back to Armstrong. There is a silent cacophony that emerges from *A Rhapsody in Black and Blue*; Armstrong plays his role so well that he exposes the lie. The words are not sound, the images are unsound, but to those who are left behind and who desire to no end, the sound matters.

I know that words are empty metaphors and lies. I don't believe in them, but I speak all the more fluently, effortlessly, because I am not really speaking, I let the Nobody speak for me, do the work on my behalf. The cog in the wheel of the language game is without thought, an automaton in the service of the one whose knowledge is a pit of ignorance. I/t speaks in spite of this stratagem, that is I/ts stratagem: the subject mimics, parrots; whereas, I/t silently rests—unravels, manifests itself as the impossible real, like the encounter of an author and her work, the signifier and signified, a letter and its trace in the sand—a man and his jungle suit.

10

Making the Quarter Turn

Liberation Theology after Lacan

THOMAS LYNCH

LACAN'S FOUR DISCOURSES SCHEMATIZE the possible social functions of
language. It is the closest he comes to charting the nature of ideology.[1] His
description of the imposition and cultivation of master signifiers, as well
as the forms of resistance, operates by quarter turns. Moving through the
master, university, hysteric, and analyst's discourses, these turns show how
the subject's alienation from the master signifier generate forms of resistance which are nonetheless indebted to the master signifiers they oppose.
This dependent resistance is the focus of this essay. Using Lacan to analyze
the relationship between different discourses shows how the imposition of
a symbolic regime in the master's discourse can be simultaneously opposed
and maintained by the hysteric's. This insight is crucial in the consideration
of ideology. It is recognising this dependence that leads to a genuine revolution, one which not only changes elements of a particular social or political
situation, but changes the understanding of the situation itself.

The Lacanian critique of ideology has of course been popularized
by the work of Slavoj Žižek, who combines this critique with readings

1. Ideology is used here in the Althusserian sense of the "reproduction of the conditions of production" (see Althusser, "Ideology and Ideological State Appartuses (Notes
toward an Investigation)," in *On Ideology*, trans. Ben Brewster [London: Verson, 2008]
1). Understood in relation to Lacan's four discourses, ideology is thus not only the
material reproduction of the conditions of the means of production, but also the self-
perpetuation of any "symbolic."

of German Idealism and, amongst other things, Christianity. Žižek takes seriously the Marxist notion that all criticism begins with the criticism of religion. Rather than this criticism resulting in the rejection of Christianity, however, it ends with its sublation into a materialist theology. Given that Žižek is interested in using Lacan to sublate Christianity as part of a critique of contemporary ideology, it is striking that there are no references to liberation theology in his work. This essay seeks to address this absence by staging the Žižekian sublation of Christianity within liberation theology. The need for this transition is identified by returning to Lacan, differentiating theological tendencies using the four discourses. Lacan, and considering how the quarter turn may propel liberation theology beyond theology as it is usually understood.

It is a particularly apt moment to stage this Lacanian reading of liberation theology. Since the 1990s, liberation theology has re-examined its positions on gender, sexuality and race.[2] While these re-examinations are important, it is my contention that they leave intact an underlying theological discourse which is inclined to reinstitute forms of oppression—it is a dependent form of resistance. Liberation theology's theology remains a "no-go area."[3] The questioning of the meaning of theology amounts to undergoing a quarter turn, producing a new form of theological discourse.

An initial summary of liberation theology's self-critique and its relationship to traditional theology will provide the necessary background for analysing liberation theology in terms of Lacan's four discourses. This summary will culminate with a consideration of the work of Manuel Mejido, who draws on Habermas and Lacan to draw a distinction between the two forms of theology. Following a mapping of theological discourses, the essay concludes by considering the form of theology that emerges by making the quarter turn from within liberation theology.[4]

---

2. For examples of liberation theology's response to each of these, see Ivan Petrella, *Latin American Liberation Theology: The Next Generation* (Maryknoll, NY: Orbis, 2005).

3. Alistair Kee, *Marx and the Failure of Liberation Theology* (London: SCM, 1990) ix.

4. This essay is concerned with a specific aspect of liberation theology, namely, that which critiques the practice of theology in general and sees that critique as part of its broader push for liberation. The emphasis will thus be on the theoretical aspects of liberation theology. While these criticisms highlight theoretical shortcomings, they in no way reduce the significance of the intervention of liberation theology as a praxis that emerged from and responded to the suffering of the poor and oppressed in Latin America. In taking seriously the intervention of these liberation theologians, we are motivated to consider theoretical avenues which could inaugurate their important work.

Theology, Liberation Theology, and Self-Critique

In the 1960s, Latin American Roman Catholic liberation theology emerged as a praxis rooted in the synthesis of Marxism and Christianity. Its initial formulations primarily focused on opposing capitalism, colonialism, and racism.[5] Thought it never expanded beyond a fervent minority, liberation theology's legacy has persisted in theology's continued efforts to investigate and critique forms of oppression while simultaneously engaging in a process of self-inquiry into Christianity's own role in supporting oppressive practices. In doing so, they were also forced to confront the role of the Catholic Church in maintaining social and political hierarchies. In the process of this confrontation, liberationists began to question academic and ecclesial forms of theology. Rooting itself in the "preferential option for the poor," liberation theology sought to do theology from the perspective of those who felt excluded by those discourse.

The initial wave of liberation theologians contained a range of responses to this tension between more traditional forms of theology and liberation theology. Some counselled reform of the Catholic Church. For example, the most well-known liberation theologian, Gustavo Gutiérrez, never saw himself in opposition to the teachings of the Catholic Church. Rather than opposing the Catholic tradition, he sought to help the institution rediscover the depths of that tradition. In presenting liberation theology as a form of recapitulation, Gutierez is a prime example of the dominant position within liberation theology. For this position social liberation was part of soteriological liberation, but novel in its emphasis on the former. For liberation theology, to ignore the material liberation of the poor is to jeopardise spiritual liberation. This material liberation is rooted in charity, but extends beyond individualized acts of kindness to become a theological impetus for social change. As Gutiérrez explains,

> This point of view leads us far beyond the individualistic language of the I-Thou relationship. Charity is today a "political charity," according to the phrase of Pius XII. Indeed, to offer food or drink in our day is a political action; it means the transformation of a society structured to benefit a few who

5. For the sake of readability, unless otherwise indicated from this point onward liberation theology will be used to denote this specific variant of liberation theology. For a general survey of the history of twentieth-century Latin America liberation theologies, including the emergence of Protestant perspectives, see Christian Smith, *The Emergence of Liberation Theology: Radical Religion and Social Movement Theory* (Chicago: University of Chicago Press, 1991). For a brief, general example of the main precepts of Roman Catholic, Latin American liberation theology, see Leonardo Boff and Clodovis Boff, *Introducing Liberation Theology* (Maryknoll, NY: Orbis, 1996).

appropriate to themselves the value of the work of others. This transformation ought to be directed toward a radical change in the foundation of society, that is, the private ownership of the means of production.[6]

This rereading maintains continuity of the theological tradition while introducing the methodological shift of "the preferential option for the poor." While this phrase captures the overall orientation of liberation theology, it also summarizes the minimal shift in theological methodology necessary to move from theology to liberation theology. As Roberto Oliveros explains, if theology is defined as speaking about God, then liberation theology is defined by the recognition that "to speak of the poor is to speak of Christ."[7] Theology must emerge from the position of the poor or oppressed, lest it become mere legitimation of or excuse for unjust situations.

Liberation theology's theological and ecclesial critics, in the Congregation for the Doctrine of Faith (CDF) and academic theology, claimed that liberation theology was not a rereading within the tradition, but a new discourse that introduced something new.[8] The Vatican described liberation theology as a break with orthodoxy, especially focusing on the role of Marxism. Indeed, it was largely on the grounds of his engagement with Marxism that the Congregation for the Doctrine of Faith criticized the work of Gustavo Gutiérrez. In its *Instruction on Certain Aspects of the "Theology of Liberation"* the Congregation's rejection of Gutiérrez's theology cites Marxism as the "determining principle from which he goes on to reinterpret the Christian message."[9] For the CDF, Gutiérrez's theology was a manipulation

---

6. Gustavo Gutiérrez, *A Theology of Liberation: History, Politics, and Salvation* (London: SCM, 2001) 192.

7. Roberto Oliveros, "History of the Theology of Liberation," in *Mysterium Liberationis: Fundamental Concepts of Liberation Theology*, ed. Ignacio Ellacuría and Jon Sobrino (Maryknoll, NY: Orbis, 1993) 6.

8. For an excellent compendium of the criticism offered by the CDF as well as Catholic and Protestant theologians, see Alfred T. Hennelly, ed., *Liberation Theology: A Documentary History* (Maryknoll, NY: Orbis, 1990).

9. Congregation for the Doctrine of the Faith, "10 Observations on the Theology of Gustavo Gutiérrez," in *Liberation Theology: A Documentary History*, ed. Alfred T. Hennelly (Maryknoll, NY: Orbis, 1990) 349. This point is largely regarded as inaccurate, but it's important to recognize the extent to which this Marxism was viewed by the Vatican as disrupting the practice of theology. This is repeated in its later instruction, which cautions against "the deviations and risks of deviations" which might mislead the faithful as a result of liberation theology's "use, in an insufficiently critical manner, [of] concepts borrowed from various currents of Marxist thought." Congregation for the Doctrine of the Faith, "Instruction on Certain Aspects of the 'Theology of Liberation,'" in ibid., 394.

of Christianity which engaged in selective readings of the Bible and theo-logical tradition in order to justify class conflict and revolutionary politics.[10]

It was not just the Vatican that saw liberation theology as a break with the Catholic Church and its orthodoxy. For some liberation theologians, failed attempts to reform social and ecclesial institutions led to a more radical opposition to both. Jean Bertrand Aristide and Camilo Torres were both forced to leave the priesthood because of their political activities.[11] Shortly before his expulsion, Aristide preached on the division separating the church of the poor and the church of the ruling class: "the church that walks in truth cannot remain under the control of the church that sits at the table. The church that walks in truth cannot sit with its head bowed before that other church."[12] In his sermons Aristide pushed liberation theology beyond a mere methodological shift to a confrontation between the truth of Christianity and the dominant institutional forms of the tradition. Initially, this opposition was conceived in moral and political terms. Later, the con-frontation between the two churches provided the grounds for a challenge on theological grounds. As Aristide would later claim, "Liberation theol-ogy . . . gives way to a liberation of theology, which can also include libera-tion from theology."[13] This assertion marked an important transition—in positing a difference between itself and the traditional theology of ecclesial authorities, liberation theology opens the way to liberation from theology.

While Aristide opened the possibility for liberation theology beyond theology, his statement is a gesture within his larger political and moral objec-tions. Manuel Mejido offers a critique of theology which preserves these mor-al or political elements, but also deepens the theoretical aspects, expanding on what such a liberation theology beyond theology might be. Mejido uses Habermasian language of historical-hermeneutic and critically oriented sci-ences to describe the distinction between traditional and liberation theology.[14]

10. Congregation for the Doctrine of the Faith, "10 Observations on the Theology of Gustavo Gutiérrez."

11. On Aristide, see Amy Wilentz's foreword to Jean-Bertrand Aristide, *In the Par-ish of the Poor: Writings from Haiti*, trans. Amy Wilentz (Maryknoll, NY: Orbis, 1990), and Peter Hallward, *Damming the Flood: Haiti, Aristide, and the Politics of Containment* (London: Verso, 2007). On Torres, see Camilo Torres, *Revolutionary Priest: The Com-plete Writings & Messages of Camilo Torres*, ed. John Gerassi (London: Cape, 1971). The epigraph to this collection of his writings is his most famous statement: "I took off my cassock to be more truly a priest."

12. Aristide, *In the Parish of the Poor*, 88.

13. Peter Hallward, "'One Step at a Time': An Interview with Jean-Bertrand Aris-tide," in *Damming the Flood: Haiti, Aristide, and the Politics of Containment* (London: Verso, 2007) 318.

14. Manuel J. Mejido, "Beyond the Postmodern Condition, or the Turn to

Liberation theologians break with historically dominant theology in that they "are not satisfied with the interpretation of the meaning of transcendence" but "generate a theological knowledge that is 'interested' in its own liberation through the liberation of socio-historical misery."[15]

More specifically, traditional or historical-hermeneutical theology is concerned with defining and interpreting the transcendent. Mejido contrasts this approach with the "making of transcendence":

> the theologies of liberation generate a theological knowledge that theoretically aims to grasp the invariance that exists between the kingdom and the socio-historical conditions of misery and praxeologically aims to overcome this invariance through the making of transcendence understood as the making of "better" history. This theological knowledge has been possible only to the extent that transcendence has been grasped through the category of social labor (that is, the dialectic of praxis and poeisis, interaction and labor). Insofar as the theologies of liberation have posited social labor as the very conditions of possibility for the making of transcendence (the making of "better" history), we say they have labored under an interest in the making of liberation; that is, they have labored under an emancipatory cognitive interest.[16]

While Mejido's division of theology is a helpful example of the liberation form theology, we can identify two problematic moments. First, he too readily identifies liberation theology with critically oriented science. While liberation theology does define its task in terms of praxis, the insights of this praxis are still determined by the results of historical-hermeneutic interpretations. To some extent this determination is natural; the historical-hermeneutic form of theology is that form through which theology arrives at the point of generating its critically oriented form. Second, and relatedly, the 'making of transcendence' remains vague, especially as it relates to an inherited tradition in which the transcendence already plays an important

Psychoanalysis," in *Latin American Liberation Theology: The Next Generation*, ed. Ivan Petrella (Maryknoll, NY: Orbis, 2005) 119–46. Mejido further elaborates the notion of liberation theology as a critically oriented science in Manuel Jesus Mejido Costoya, "Theology, Crisis and Knowledge-Constitutive Interests, or Towards a Social Theoretical Interpretation of Theological Knowledge," *Social Compass* 51.3 (2004) 381–401. Note that Mejido and Mejido Costoya are the same individual.

15. Mejido Costoya, "Theology, Crisis and Knowledge-Constitutive Interests," 393–94.

16. Mejido, "Beyond the Postmodern Condition," 119–20.

role. Both of these points can be grasped more clearly by understanding liberation theology in terms of Lacan's four discourses.

Theology and the Four Discourses

In *Seminar XVII*, Lacan introduces his discourses by explaining that they "are nothing other than the signifying articulation, the apparatus whose presence, whose existing status alone dominates and governs anything that at any given moment is capable of emerging as speech."[17] The discourses of the master, university, hysteric and analyst schematize the relationships between the master signifier, knowledge, split subject and *objet petit a*, as they alternately occupy the positions of agent, other, product and truth. Understanding these configurations enables an analysis of four key social phenomena: "governing, educating, protesting and, revolutionizing."[18]

$$
\begin{array}{cc}
\mathrm{U} & \mathrm{M} \\[4pt]
\dfrac{S_2}{S_1} \to \dfrac{a}{\cancel{S}} & \dfrac{S_1}{\cancel{S}} \to \dfrac{S_2}{a} \\[12pt]
\mathrm{H} & \mathrm{A} \\[4pt]
\dfrac{\cancel{S}}{a} \to \dfrac{S_1}{S_2} & \dfrac{a}{S_2} \to \dfrac{\cancel{S}}{S_1}
\end{array}
$$

In the previous section's discussion of theology we can identify three forms of speech, each of which can be found to "lodge" itself within one of the discourses. First there is the speech of ecclesial authority, which for our purposes is the Vatican. There is no greater example of the master's discourse than a form of speech that claims infallibility. Second, what we might call the dominant practice of theology adopts the form of university discourse. In this context, "dominant practice of theology" indicates theologies that operate in accordance with the decrees of the ecclesial authorities. This mode of theology is consistent with Mejido's category of historical-hermeneutic sciences in that theology is primarily understood as the interpretation of transcendence as revealed by texts and communities. Third, liberation theology operates as the hysteric's discourse in a manner similar, but not identical, to Mejido's critically oriented science. Having made these three identifications enables a deeper understanding of the functioning of each form of theological speech and the relations between the forms.

17. Jacques Lacan, *The Seminar of Jaques Lacan, Book XVII: The Other Side of Psychoanalysis* (London: Norton, 2008) 166.

18. Ibid., 107.

The Discourse of Theological Masters

Lacan describes the master's discourse with repeated references to Hegel's master-slave dialectic.[19] The master subjugates knowledge, which Hegel locates with the slave. This subjugation is inherently incomplete, a fact noted by Lacan in his description of the top half of the discourse as "impossibility."[20] This failed subjugation generates the *objet petit a*, the surplus value/jouissance produced by the labour of the slave. This moves us to the lower half of the discourse, which contains the matheme of fantasy. The matheme's location beneath the master and his knowledge indicates the repression of fantasy. This repression offers a key insight into the functioning of ecclesial authority—it supresses fantasy.[21] The master is only aware of the top half of the equation. He (and in this context the masculine pronoun seems appropriate) is not aware of the production of jouissance and represses the truth of split subjectivity. The master's discourse is one of totality and simplicity, excluding those fragments which disrupt its smooth flow.

University Discourse
and the Dominant Mode of Theology

As stated above, the phrase "dominant mode of theology" is equivalent to Mejido's category of historical-hermeneutic science. Theology is here concerned with the interpretation of received master signifiers and aims at constructing a total knowledge. Lacan is critical of the university, which "has an extremely precise function, in effect, one that this very moment is related to the state we are in with respect to the master's discourse—namely, its elucidation."[22] As Mark Bracher explains, in the process of forming a "totalized system of knowledge/beliefs . . . we are made to produce ourselves as (alienated) subjects, $\S$, of this system."[23] The university discourse pursues the troubling gap of the *objet petit a*, convinced of the ability to eventually complete knowledge. In this pursuit it inadvertently produces the potential

19. Ibid., 79, 170–71.

20. This impossibility, along with the inability of the bottom half, is elaborated in *Seminar XVII*, but is not added to the diagram until *Seminar XX*. See Jacques Lacan, *The Seminar of Jacques Lacan, Book XX: On Feminine Sexuality, the Limits of Love and Knowledge*, new ed. (London: Norton, 2000) 16–17.

21. Mark Bracher, "On the Psychological and Social Functions of Language: Lacan's Theory of the Four Discourses," in *Lacanian Theory of Discourse: Subject, Structure and Society*, ed. Mark Bracher et al. (New York: New York University Press, 1994) 117.

22. Lacan, *Seminar XVII*, 148.

23. Bracher, "On the Psychological and Social Functions of Language," 115.

of its undoing—the $. In its effort to know more and more, to close the gap of the *objet petit a*, it eventually produces the failure that is the divided subject, but this subject still does not realise that it *is* this division.

One of the clearest examples of theology in this mode is found in the work of theologians who describe themselves as "radically orthodox." John Milbank, for example, promotes a knowledge rooted in the "harmonious order intrinsic to God's own being."[24] This order allows for differences, but only differences that occur within the harmonious order. Dissonant, negative, or antagonistic differences are condemned as nihilistic.[25] Milbank, responding to Žižek's Lacanian ontology, argues the logic of Christianity is paradoxical rather than dialectic and "there is never any contradiction, conflict, or tension."[26] Rather than a world that is "intrinsically conflictual," he reasserts a Thomistic alternative, "namely that being qua being might be an embodied plenitude, identical with the infinite realization of all actual and possible essentialities."[27] There are no divisions. Being is whole.

Academic theology in general conforms to the university discourse, though it can be difficult to differentiate between this form of theology and the discourse of the master. For instance, a recent document published by the International Theological Commission concludes that theology is able to criticize local tradition, but "criticism is not appropriate with reference to apostolic tradition itself."[28] Further, in clear submission to the authority of the master's discourse the document asserts that "theologians should always recognize the intrinsic provisionality of their endeavors and offer their work to the church as a whole for scrutiny and evaluation."[29] Because clergy are often responsible for education, the lines between the two discourses may become blurred. It should be noted, however, that there is also a theology in the mode of the university discourses that moves in the direction of the hysteric's discourse as well. Theologians censured by the Vatican would be an example of this alternate tendency.

24. John Milbank, "The Double Glory, or Paradox Versus Dialectics," in *The Monstrosity of Christ: Paradox or Dialectic?*, by Slavoj Žižek and John Milbank (Cambridge: MIT Press, 2009) 437.

25. John Milbank, *Theology and Social Theory: Beyond Secular Reason*, 2nd ed. (London: Wiley-Blackwell, 2005) 437.

26. Milbank, "Double Glory, or Paradox Versus Dialectics," 187.

27. Ibid., 131.

28. International Theological Commission, "Theology Today: Perspectives, Principles, and Criteria," *Origins: CNS Documentary Service* 41.40 (2012) 648.

29. Ibid., 651.

The Hysteric's Discourse and the Protest of Theology

The hysteric's discourse is the first to acknowledge the split of the subject. The hysteric ceaselessly carries out an interrogation of master signifiers, stemming from the "failure of the subject, $\math$, to coincide with or be satisfied by the master signifiers offered by society and embraced as the subject's ideals."[30] The hysteric is onto the master's game.

In the sections on the four discourses, Lacan makes connections to Marx. He identifies S2 in the master's discourse as the place of the proletariat. The proletariat, then, cultivates the knowledge that is the other of the master, in the process generating a surplus that Lacan identifies both as surplus *jouissance* and surplus value.[31] In the hysteric's discourse, this surplus becomes the truth of the agent, the split subject. This subject is the figure of protest, able to see that something is wrong, producing knowledge of the inadequacy of its received master signifiers, but unable to move beyond the cultivation of this knowledge.

It is here that the hysteric's discourse stalls. For Lacan, the desire of the hysteric is problematic: "What the hysteric wants . . . is a master."[32] This immediately calls to mind Lacan's "Impromptu at Vincennes" included as an appendix to *Seminar XVII*. During the discussion, Lacan says to the gathered student protesters, "the revolutionary aspiration has only a single possible outcome—of ending up as the master's discourse. This is what experience has proved. What you aspire to as revolutionaries is a master. You will get one."[33] The aspiration for a master is derived from the continued determinations of the received master signifier. For the hysteric, the master signifier is both the cause of its alienation and a point of stability. Put another way, the familiar alienation of received master signifiers is itself a comforting stability. Again Bracher puts it succinctly: "Despite its refusal to follow the master signifier . . . the hysterical subject remains in solidarity with it. This solidarity manifests itself in the wish of anxiety for security and stability, the search of meaninglessness for a meaning or identity."[34]

In this way, liberation theology is a Copernican revolution. In *Seminar XX*, Lacan explains that Copernicus' contribution was moving the pivotal point from the earth to the sun. This move is no revolution, for moving the pivotal point "involves nothing that in itself subverts what the signifier

30. Bracher, "On the Psychological and Social Functions of Language," 122.

31. Lacan, *Seminar XVII*, 21, 147.

32. Ibid., 129.

33. Ibid., 207.

34. Bracher, "On the Psychological and Social Functions of Language," 122–23.

'center' intrinsically preserves."[35] The great revolution lies with Kepler, not Copernicus. In the Keplerian revolution the earth ceases to rotate on the basis of a center—"it turns in an ellipse, and that already throws into question the function of the center."[36] In the midst of this discussion Lacan connects these contrasting revolutions to politics, informing the leftists in attendance that their world "remains perfectly spherical."[37] Similarly, the hysteric struggles to escape its Copernican function, simply moving the center without questioning the broader shape of the political situation. At the theoretical level, part of the failure of liberation theology is articulated in understanding the function of the master signifier in the hysteric's discourse. In this it is not unique as, for Lacan, all attempts at Revolution fail, in that "the idealized object or its attributes function as master signifiers around which a new (totalizing, imperialistic) system is constituted."[38]

It is essential to be clear about the implications of making this connection between liberation theology and the hysteric's discourse. Most importantly, it is not advocating a rejection of liberation theology. We are moving towards theology in the form of the analyst's discourse and Lacan informs us that the purpose of this final form is the hystericization of discourse.[39] More specifically, the hysterical moment of the analyst's discourse is the hystericization of the master's discourse, the moment when the master "loses the certainty of being equal to her signifiermediated selfhood as established in the big Other, when she begins to doubt and question whether the signifying units of the symbolic order provide a sufficient guarantee of identity."[40] As Bruce Fink notes, the hysteric hones in on the gaps in the Master's knowledge. Its motivation in doing so, is "hidden motor force, is the real."[41] The real, for Lacan, is the impossible, that which cannot be represented within the Symbolic. The hysteric thus operates from the gap introduced by the impossibility of the divided subject's full identification with the master signifier's it has received.[42]

Liberation theology understood in terms of the hysteric's discourse thus results in the following conclusions. First, it is an essential moment of

35. Lacan, *Seminar XX*, 42.

36. Ibid., 42–43.

37. Ibid., 42.

38. Bracher, "On the Psychological and Social Functions of Language," 120.

39. Lacan, *Seminar XVII*, 33.

40. Adrian Johnston, *Žižek's Ontology: A Transcendental Materialist Theory of Subjectivity* (Evanston: Northwestern University Press, 2008) 259–60.

41. Bruce Fink, *The Lacanian Subject: Between Language and Jouissance* (Princeton: Princeton University Press, 1995) 134.

42. Ibid., 131.

protesting both ecclesial authority and the forms of theology that legitimate that authority. Second, even in this questioning it remains problematically determined by the master signifiers instituted and interpreted by these other forms of discourse. Third, liberation theology thinks from the impossibilities of these discourses. That is, it emerges from the failure of split subjects to identify with master signifiers that reject these subjects' constitutive division. Finally, it opens up the possibility of something after liberation theology—a new form of theological reflection which includes the moment of liberation but moves on to occupy the analyst's discourse.

Theology and the Analyst's Discourse

To understand the implications of theology in the mode of analyst's discourse it is helpful to return to Mejido's discussion of critically oriented sciences. In our earlier consideration of his argument, we diagnosed two problematic moments: liberation theology is too readily identified with critically oriented sciences and the "making of transcendence" remains a vague concept. Understanding liberation theology in terms of the hysteric's discourse addresses the first issue. While liberation theology does provide a critique of ecclesial and academic theology, it leaves intact the broader Symbolic which supports those discourses. Liberation theology is critically oriented, but its attempts to "make transcendence" collapse back into the same master signifiers. Liberation theology on the whole exhibits both of the main elements of the hysteric's discourse. It interrogates the master signifier, while desiring to be mastered and consequently reinstating the master signifier that it has received rather than produced.

This point warrants further clarification. Asserting that liberation theology reinstates the master signifiers of ecclesial authority, is not criticising liberation theology's continued use of a particular set of terms or concepts—God, eschatology, sacrament, and so on. Rather it is to suggest, first, that these signifiers are primarily received. Second, and consequently, it is to claim that these "mean" in the same way. For example, liberation theology may, to some extent, immanentize the eschaton, but the eschaton is still deeply wed to the notion of final deliverance, resurrection of the dead and final judgment. The kingdom of God may take on new meaning in the course of human history, but it maintains its transcendent signification as well. The eschaton may signify a utopian impulse within history, but it maintains a dimension that exceeds that history as well.[43] To hold out hope

43. See, for example, João Batista Libânio, "Hope, Utopia, Resurrection," in *Mysterium Liberationis: Fundamental Concepts of Liberation Theology*, ed. Ignacio Ellacuría

for the resurrection of the dead and final judgment is still to await the arrival of the whole, of completeness.

It is helpful to remember that liberation theology as the discourse of the hysteric is not the opposite of the master of ecclesial authority, but to the elucidation of the master's discourse by dominant modes of theology (university). It remains within the same Symbolic, but pries open the gaps that the university discourse elides in its presentation of a totalizing knowledge. Liberation theology effectively problematizes the master signifiers of ecclesial authority, but remains determined by the assumptions that undergird that authority.

This schema lays out two sets of discourse, opposites of one another, which are fundamentally antithetical. The master/university dyad is mutually reinforcing. The university discourse elucidates the master signifier instituted by the master signifier. In terms of Christianity, theology has served the function of elucidating the master signifiers of ecclesial authority. Theology is to be done for and in the church. Its object is the God who is the ultimate master. This theology in the mode of the university discourse works to seal the fissures of the knowledge that occupies the place of the other—that is knowledge, as the agent of theological discourse, interrogates the remainder of the *a*, left over and repressed in the master's discourse.

Opposed to the master/university is the hysteric/analyst dyad. The hysteric realizes the divided nature of subjectivity and rails against the master signifier, but the produced knowledge remains knowledge of the master signifier. That is, the knowledge is of the master signifier rather than the remainder, the *jouissance* that is the truth of the hysteric. Liberation theology, in occupying this role, is still determined by the ecclesial discourse from which it receives its master signifier. It is only in moving beyond this, to the analyst's discourse, that we are able to replace the master signifiers that we have received with the master signifiers we have produced. This new master signifier is stripped of security and stability. "In the absence of every version of [the big Other], what remains lacks any guarantee of consistency right down to the bedrock of ontological fundaments. Strife, potential or actual, reigns supreme as a negativity permeating the layers and strata of material being."[44]

Liberation theology thus starts from a recognition of fractured reality, but it preserves the fantasy of both a past and future characterized by wholeness. This wholeness is the knowledge of the Christianity, the promise that it will one day be as it was. As Lacan points out, this idea is inherently

---

and Jon Sobrino (Maryknoll, NY: Orbis, 1993) 716–27.

44. Adrian Johnston, "Conflicted Matter: Jacques Lacan and the Challenge of Secularising Materialism," *Pli: The Warwick Journal of Philosophy* 19 (2008) 172.

political, for "the idea that knowledge can make a whole is . . . immanent to the political as such."[45] Liberation theology, in defining itself as both a theological and political movement, is limited by this fantasy. The analyst's discourse is the discourse that pushes liberation theology to the recognition that not only is reality fractured, but the real is fracture.

How then does this liberation theology after Lacan function? How does liberation move from the hysteric's discourse to the analyst's? It is clear that this move does not involve the destruction of master signifiers as such. All the discourses retain the master signifier, but change the relation between it and the subject.[46] Rather than focusing on motion of these master signifiers, we should focus on the rotation of the *object petit a*. In the master's discourse it is produced. For the hysteric it becomes the repressed truth which drives the $ to question the master signifier. When we reach the analyst's discourse, it becomes the agent, motivated by the knowledge of the analyst. At this point, we see a reversal has occurred. The bottom half of the master's discourse (the fundamental fantasy) has been inverted and now occupies the top half of the analyst's. This reversal is the traversing of fantasy.[47]

The traversing of the fantasy consists of changing the relationship of the subject to her desire. The divided subject is divided through the experience of the other's desire, described in Lacan's linguistic reformulation of the Oedipus complex. This alienation becomes the basis of the fantasy—fantasy is the way that the subject relates to the desire of the other. At the heart of fantasy is the belief in wholeness—there once was a completed enjoyment and one can find this completion again. As Adrian Johnston emphasizes, to traverse the fantasy is to crush this illusion of any form of a big Other, whether it "be conceived of as God, Nature, the analyst, or whatever."[48]

Importantly Johnston includes the analyst in his list of potential big Others. The analyst must refuse the natural tendency of the analysand to elevate the analyst to the "subject supposed to know." The analyst does not

---

45. Lacan, *Seminar XVII*, 31.

46. Bracher: It is key to note that the analyst's discourse does not escape the functioning of the master signifier; rather "its master signifiers are produced by the subject rather than imposed upon the subject from the outside" ("On the Psychological and Social Functions of Language," 124).

47. This formula ($◊a$), of course, is also the formula for perversion, as Lacan explains in "Kant with Sade." In the perverse fantasy the divided subject sees herself as identical to the desire of the Other, completely fulfilling a desire that she knows. See Jacques Lacan, "Kant with Sade," in *Écrits*, trans. Bruce Fink (London: Norton, 2006) 645–68. The difference here is that the analyst's knowledge is functioning as the truth of the discourse: the subject cannot mistake herself as the full satisfaction of the desire of a big Other that does not exist.

48. Johnston, "Conflicted Matter," 171.

hold the answer. Rather, in analysis the agent is not the analyst but the *objet petit a*. The knowledge of the analyst is the truth of the analyst's discourse, but this truth remains unstated as the divided subject comes to realise the impossible nature of her relationship to her desire. In refusing to be the agent of the analyst's discourse, the analyst helps the analysand recognize one of the truths of psychoanalysis—there is no big Other. "This impossible relationship from object *a* to divided subject is the basis for the development of transference, through which the subject will be able to encircle his object. This is one of the goals of an analysis, '*la traverse du fantasma*,' the journey through the basic fantasy."[49]

The traversing of the fantasy then is accomplished through the inverting of the master's discourse. This process occurs through the realisation that there is no big Other and the contingency of master signifiers. The questioning of the hysteric leads to the freedom of the traversed fantasy. Johnston highlights this theme in his reading of Žižek:

> Žižek's revolutionary recasting of the notion of human freedom is tied to his . . . traversing the fantasy of there being a big Other of any type whatsoever, namely, an ultimate Master-guarantor with sufficient determining authority to orchestrate an integrated and synthesized functioning of the multiple strata of being. Both the Real and the Symbolic are barred, that is, they never achieve the status of systems in which all potential bugs and loopholes are eliminated so as to prevent disruptions of natural or cultural patterns of determinism.[50]

This culminates in the establishment of a new fantasy: ". . . the divided subject assumes the place of the cause, in other words, subjectifies the traumatic cause of his or her own advent as subject, coming to be in that place where the Other's desire—a foreign, alien desire—had been."[51] This end of analysis should not be understood as a conclusion but the inauguration of a different relationship to the master signifier. What the analyst's discourse "produces is nothing other than the master's discourse, since it is S1 which comes to occupy the place of production. . . . Perhaps it's form the analyst's discourse that there can emerge another style of master signifier."[52] This new style of master signifier is one devoid of illusions of completion. The structure of fantasy persists, but the nature of fantasy is changed.

49. Paul Verhaeghe, "From Impossibility to Inability: Lacan's Theory on the Four Discourses," in *Beyond Gender: From Subject to Drive* (New York: Other Press, 2001) 31.

50. Johnston, *Žižek's Ontology*, 208.

51. Fink, *Lacanian Subject*, 62.

52. Lacan, *Seminar XVII*, 176. See also Fink, *Lacanian Subject*, 62–63.

This, then, is the task of theology in the mode of the analyst's discourse: to bring about the realisation that there is no big Other and to allow that knowledge to reconfigure the subject's relation to her desire in order to produce new master signifiers. To do so is not to "fix" the subject. Lacanian discourse does not hold out the promise of wholeness. The answer it offers is the realisation of the contingency of the master signifiers, the first step in assuming the freedom necessary for Mejido's task of the "making of transcendence" as the "making better of history." This answer is not a comfort, but brings about a new form of anxiety—the anxiety of freedom. It holds out the "utopian" moment of a possible existence "beyond neurosis."[53]

The Atheism in Christianity
and the Task of Liberation

Žižek has already made this link between Christianity and this shift in the subject's relation to fantasy as it relates to the big Other. Such a traversing forfeits the familiar discomfort of subjection to the big Other, instead taking responsibility of the Other's desire as the subject's cause.[54] For Žižek, this transition is succinctly articulated in the crucifixion scene. The cry of dereliction becomes the secret hope of Christ. Jesus announces the possibility of not only escaping the rule of the Father, but also escaping a subjectivity where enjoyment is predicated on the Father's role as big Other.[55]

Žižek's move here is crucial. Rather than "smuggling atheism into Christianity," as suggested by Johnston, Žižek is playing out the atheistic core already found in Christianity. This affinity between Žižek's treatment of Christianity and theology in the mode of the analyst's discourse draws out a pre-existing affinity between liberation theology and the work of Ernst Bloch. Bloch, who anticipates much of Žižek's Hegelian reading of Christianity, was an important resource for liberation theology's early formulations. These formulations tend to draw on works such as *The Spirit of Utopia* or *The Principle of Hope*, but Bloch also wrote *Atheism in Christianity*, in which he carries out an extensive reading of the Bible and Christian theology in order to demonstrate an enduring materialist and atheist form of Christianity.[56] Bloch holds that "the

53. Fink, *Lacanian Subject*, 72.

54. See Ed Pluth, *Signifiers and Acts* (Albany: State University of New York Press, 2007) 98; Fink, *Lacanian Subject*, 72.

55. Slavoj Žižek, *The Puppet and the Dwarf: The Perverse Core of Christianity* (Cambridge: MIT Press, 2003) 171.

56. Ernst Bloch, *The Spirit of Utopia*, trans. Anthony A. Nassar (Stanford: Stanford University Press, 2000); Ernst Bloch, *The Principle of Hope*, vol. 1, trans. Neville

point to be made . . . against all pseudo-enlightenment which sees religion as a spent force caught between the alternatives Moses or Darwin . . . is this: the counter-blow against the oppressor is biblical . . . and that is why it has always been suppressed or distorted."[57]

For Bloch, Christianity is composed of two tendencies, the "On-high" (master and university discourses) and "From-below" (hysteric and analyst's discourses). Those who operate from On-high work to cover up and explain away the gaps and fissures in which those "From-below" can locate themselves. For Bloch, the Bible is the constant struggle between these two forces and the task of theology is to carry out the "detective work" of biblical criticism. His interaction with religion is a demonstration of carrying out an immanent critique of Christianity which lodges in these gaps like an explosive which destroys the discourses of the On-high, freeing the From-below to rebuild from the rubble.

We mention Bloch here for two reasons. First, we now have constructed a bridge from Lacan to Žižek to Bloch to theology in the mode of the analyst's discourse. Running through their work we see a parallel set of themes: rejection of the imposition of structures of domination whether they be psychoanalytic, material, political or theological; the need for this rejection to occur through an immanent critique; and an acknowledgment that the "end" of this work is not the arrival of a fullness or completion, but the freedom that comes from the awareness of the inherently fractured and incomplete nature of existence.

Second, Bloch, more than Žižek, emphasizes the possibility of carrying out this rigorously immanent critique.[58] The emphasis on the nature of this critique comes from a respect for the demands of liberation theology. As a theological discipline, it often met with scepticism or rejection from Marxism more generally. In response, liberation theology has called for a more open engagement. In particular Segundo has challenged what he sees as Marxism's inconsistent treatment of religion. While religion is one of several ideological apparatuses, to use Althusser's phrase, it alone is treated as purely erroneous and requiring immediate rejection. The state for example, while destined to wither away, plays a role in the revolutionary

Plaice, Stephen Plaice, and Paul Knight (Cambridge: MIT Press, 1995); Ernst Bloch, *Atheism in Christianity: The Religion of the Exodus and the Kingdom*, 2nd ed. (New York: Verso, 2009).

57. Bloch, *Atheism in Christianity*, 13.

58. While Žižek does draw on theological resources (especially in his engagement with John Milbank) Bloch works through a much broader swathe of theological literature. See Slavoj Žižek and John Milbank, *The Monstrosity of Christ: Paradox or Dialectic?* (Cambridge: MIT Press, 2009).

process. At its simplest, Segundo's objection is to the position that the rejection of religion is "a *precondition* for the revolution rather than an *effect* of the revolution."[59] From Segundo's perspective, this misses the opportunity for religion to play a role in the formation of a revolutionary consciousness.[60] "Instead of 'abolition,' one would expect Marx to have talked about 'changing' religion so that it might accentuate and eventually correct the situation being protested against."[61]

Segundo's remarks in regard to Marxism, in the present context, can be extended to include politically oriented materialist philosophies in general .In response to their objections, Segundo is calling for something like Bloch's reading of Christianity. Marx's objections are posed to religion externally. His "act of will to abolish religion is not an act of will from within theology itself, an act of will that cold signify a change in the way of treating problems theologically. It is rather an abandonment of them."[62] What Segundo is hinting at, what Bloch does and what all theology in the mode of the analyst's discourse requires is precisely the act within theology which signifies this change and is, in effect, the abolition of the impulse to liberation from the forms of theology which have previously characterized it. While admittedly taking this change further than Segundo would support, our effort here is to explore what this change would include if it were to have the two goals of "changing the situation" and doing so through an internal theological act.

Further, for Lacan this is the only chance for a real revolution. As Bracher summarizes,

> Operating from the position of an analyst with regard to culture means reading the various, mutually disjoint and even contradictory discourses of a culture in order to reveal the *a*, unconscious fantasy, cause of desire, which operates from behind the façade of the master signifiers and the entire signifying apparatus. By exposing the real that the system of signifiers, and particularly the master signifiers, fails to grasp, one can interpellate subjects to an activation of their alienated condition, their non-identity with their master signifiers, and thus create an impetus for the production of new master signifiers.[63]

59. Juan Luis Segundo, *Liberation of Theology*, trans. John Drury (Maryknoll, NY: Orbis, 1976; reprint, Eugene, OR: Wipf & Stock, 2002) 59. Although it is not clear from this passage, it is important to note that Segundo is not advocating the abolition of religion.

60. Ibid., 16.

61. Ibid., 17.

62. Ibid., 18.

63. Bracher, "On the Psychological and Social Functions of Language," 126.

Materialism and the Fate of Theology

This understanding of theology goes against a recent trend in philosophical discourse to insist on the importance, if not priority, of establishing a rigorously atheist materialism.[64] In relation to Lacan, the best formulation of this impulse is found in the work of Adrian Johnston, especially his essay on Lacan and the challenge of secularizing materialism.[65] While agreeing with much of Johnston's argument, we take issue with one of the key aspects of his treatment of religion, namely defining religiosity as that which "appeals to the supposed existence of some sort of extra-physical, immaterial dimension of transcendent (ultra-)being."[66] While this particular essay reacts against religion insofar as it is described by this definition, his work here and elsewhere clearly relies on this as the definition of religion as such.[67] In response, he advocates a Lacanian atheism, one in which the subject "acknowledges the non-existence of the big Other and the absence of anything all-powerful at the foundation of existence," an understanding of atheism which resonates with the analyst's discourse and that which we find in Žižek and Bloch.

Two points are raised by contrasting the argument offered here with Johnston's demand for an atheist materialism. First, he is correct to reject attempts at "theological materialism."[68] What is found in Žižek and Bloch is a materialist theology. In Bloch's framing what needs to be eradicated is not theology as such, but superstition. "The question here is not of giving the death-blow to fantasy as such, but of destroying and saving the myth in a single dialectical process, by shedding light upon it. What is really swept away is real superstition."[69] Bloch here reminds us, indirectly, that the end of analysis is not the abolishing of fantasy. For Lacan, it is only the pervert who thinks she has escaped from fantasy. Rather, to combine Bloch and Lacan is the establishment of a new fantasy, one which dispenses with superstition. The name for theology in the mode of the analyst's discourse is thus materialist theology.

64. For example, Christopher Watkin, *Difficult Atheism: Post-theological Thinking in Alain Badiou, Jean-Luc Nancy and Quentin Meillassoux* (Edinburgh: Edinburgh University Press, 2011) and Martin Hägglund, *Radical Atheism: Derrida and the Time of Life* (Stanford: Stanford University Press, 2008).

65. Johnston, "Conflicted Matter."

66. Ibid., 167.

67. See in particular Adrian Johnston, "Hume's Revenge: À Dieu, Meillassoux?" in *The Speculative Turn: Continental Materialism and Realism*, ed. Levi Bryant, Nick Srnicek, and Graham Harman (Victoria: re.press, 2011).

68. Ibid., 97.

69. Bloch, *Atheism in Christianity*, 27.

Second, there is a key difference between philosophical arguments for atheism and the task of materialist theology. The latter, to the extent that it seeks to incorporate the hystericization of the master's discourse found in liberation theology, functions in the service of a liberatory impulse, rather than remaining focused on theoretical elaborations of that impulse. Most of this essay has focused on employing Lacan to move past impasses within liberation theology. Here, however, liberation theology offers a corrective to forms of philosophical discourse which claim political significance. Liberation theology insists on thinking with the oppressed, not on their behalf. There is a sense in which theory submits to the tests of praxis. That is not to say the ultimate validity of any particular theory is finally its ability to manifest in a praxis at a given point in time, but it is to insist that theory must be done with the possibility of praxis as an essential goal.

For example, Žižek's cutting critiques of the master signifiers of our age—capital, liberalism, inclusion, and so on—has produced a great deal of knowledge. Yet, for all the exposing of the contingency of these master signifiers, his work never makes the turn beyond this interrogation. Pointing this out, just as with liberation theology, is not necessarily a criticism. Indeed liberation theology posits different levels of the task of liberation. While configuration may vary between different liberation theologians, Leonardo and Clodovis Boff's model of popular, pastoral, and professional is typical. There are those engaged in direct action and community organisation, those who lead communities and offer counsel, and those who provide necessary theoretical reflection on those actions and leadership.[70] Given this division, there is nothing to require that Žižek move beyond his interrogations. Nonetheless, until such a quarter turn occurs, we never move from the analysis of an inadequate situation to the production of something new. Moreover, we should not confuse the work of theory with the struggle of praxis. Politically oriented strands of current materialist philosophy are quick to denounce the corrupting influence of religion. While those denunciations bear elements of truth, liberation theology reminds us that if the choice is between philosophical precision and political action, the latter is usually to be preferred.

Conclusion

This essay has focused on understanding liberation theology through Lacan's four discourses, staging the quarter turn from liberation theology to a materialist theology. This drive to bring about the latter while preserving

70. Boff and Boff, *Introducing Liberation Theology*, 11–22.

the legacy of the former is to affirm the conclusions of the materialist theologian Roland Boer, namely, that liberation theology has brought together Christianity and Marxism in admittedly fruitful dialogue, but stops at the level of polite conversation. Theology, having engaged with the political, now must take this engagement to its "dialectical extreme." This brings about "not a going back to theology . . . but a theology beyond the initial opposition, one that is the next step, thoroughly politicised and materialised."[71]

Liberation theology begins a process of questioning those master signifiers upon which rest the authority of ecclesial institutions and the theologians which back them. That process of questioning must push on, shattering those signifiers. As Bloch concludes in his *Atheism in Christianity*,

> the ideologies and illusions, the mythologies and theocracies of ecclesiastical Christianity should by now have run their day, along with the fixed, transcendent, stationary In-the-highest of a world beyond all cares. True Marxism has no time for all that, but takes true Christianity seriously—too seriously for just another grey and compromising dialog. When Christians are really concerned with the emancipation of those who labor and are heavy-laden, and when Marxists retain the depths of the Kingdom of Freedom as the real content of revolutionary consciousness on the road to becoming true substance, the alliance between revolution and Christianity . . . may live again—this time with success.[72]

71. Roland Boer, *Criticism of Heaven: On Marxism and Theology* (Chicago: Haymarket, 2009) 451.

72. Bloch, *Atheism in Christianity*, 256.

11

By the Grace of Lacan

Marcus Pound

A notion as precise and articulate as grace is irreplaceable where the
psychology of the act is concerned, and we don't find anything equivalent in classic academic psychology. Not only doctrines, but also the
history of choices ... they demand all of our attention in their own
register and mode of expression.[1]

Introduction

GRACE HOLDS AN ABIDING fascination for Lacan.[2] Notice his admonition
in the opening quotation to its treatment from within its own "register," i.e.,
theology. This is a concern repeated in *Seminar VII* when he critiques the
anthropological category of "religion" in the name of religion "in the true
sense of the term—not of a desiccated, methodologized religion, pushed
back into the distant past of a primitive form of thought, but of religion as
we see it practised in a still living, very vital way."[3] In a different context,

1. Jacques Lacan, *The Seminar of Jacques Lacan, Seminar VII: The Ethics of Psychoanalysis, 1959–1960*, ed. Jacques-Alain Miller, trans. Dennis Porter (London: Routledge, 1999) 171.

2. I thank Marika Rose for her helpful discussion on this point.

3. Jacques Lacan, *The Seminar of Jacques Lacan, Seminar XI: The Four Fundamental
Concepts of Psychoanalysis*, ed. Jacques-Alain Miller, trans. Alan Sheridan, (London:
Vintage, 1998) 7.

when Lacan introduces grace in *Seminar XVI*, he does so somewhat ruefully in regard of theological rigor: Grace is "something about which we no longer even know how to speak."[4] And when chastising the psychoanalytic community in his 1953 "Rome Report" he contrasts their failure to "frame subjective problems" with the rigor "that structured the old quarrels about Nature and Grace however confused they might have been."[5] Indeed, he felt so strongly about this that following the publication of the "Rome Report" in *Écrits*, some thirteen years after its initial presentation, he directed his seminar audience to this very point: it is to grace that "instead of a thousand other futile occupations, psychoanalysts should turn their gaze."[6]

Theologically speaking, grace is traditionally if broadly understood as the supernatural gift of God, thereby implying not simply a giving, but also the benevolence of the giving as well as the gift, and hence thanksgiving. That these classical themes are not taken up by Lacan may suggest that he was less concerned with the "register of expression" than indicated. Yet as I argue that Lacan showed a deep commitment to the way grace delineates human relations, drawing on the classical distinction between a given truth to be realized and a revelation of truth. So while he does not entertain different theological positions regarding grace, it is the very fact of a revelation of grace that counts for him.

Lacan's comments on grace are scattered across his corpus and do not form a systematic whole, however, his reading of Pascal's wager from *Seminar XIII: The Object of Psychoanalysis*, and *Seminar XVI: From an Other to the other* provides a particularly pertinent source of reflection given Lacan's claim: "how can we, even for an instant, when it is a matter of game imagined by Pascal's pen, neglect the function of grace, namely, that of the desire of the Other."[7]

In what follows I want to take Lacan's treatment of Pascal as the means to explore the importance he attaches to grace. While my discussion principally revolves around Pascal's wager, I shall use the divisions: knowledge, the o-object, and enjoyment to guide my initial enquiry. Taken together, these areas form the relevant locus of subjective relations, relative to the

4. Jacques Lacan, *The Seminar of Jacques Lacan, Seminar XIII: The Object of Psychoanalysis, 1965–1966*, trans. Cormac Gallagher. Unpublished. 9.2.66, Lecture x, 5.

5. Jacques Lacan, *Écrits*, trans. Bruce Fink (New York: Norton, 2006) 218. In *Seminar XX* he commends in particular the rigor of Aquinas: "it's awfully well put together." Cf. Lacan, *The Seminar of Jacques Lacan, Seminar XX: Encore, 1972–1973*, ed. Jacques-Alain Miller, trans. Bruce Fink (New York: Norton, 1999) 114.

6. Lacan, *SXIII*, lecture x, 6.

7. Jacques Lacan, *The Seminar of Jacques Lacan, Seminar XVI: From an Other to the other, 1968–1969*, trans. C. Gallagher. Unpublished, 29.1.69 lecture ix, 10.

phase of Lacan's work on Pascal. In this way I am able to relate the wager back to the structure of subjectivity. I then explore the role of grace and revelation as it relates to Lacan's excurses on Exod 3:11: God's utterance at Sinai. What transpires is that grace not only names a theological problem, but the central problematic of subjectivity, and the platform for Lacan's critique of philosophy.

I begin with Lacan's methodological considerations on the treatment of theology within his work.

Against Apologetics

Given the initial comments from Lacan on grace, one should begin by recognizing Lacan's insistence that his treatment of theological ideas or history not be confused with the "position of religious apologetics."[8] Indeed, he goes to some lengths to stress this very point. For example, when discussing time spent reading a little around Pascal and Jansenism, he quickly adds that this was "naturally not to inform myself about Jansenism"[9] and continuing, "I will not say anything more about what is involved in my relationship to it, it would be too good an opportunity to precipitate yourself into the historical or biographical determinations of my interests."[10] Lacan displays here a clear reticence to identify with the religious dimension.

Such reticence recalls similar expressions of concern on the part of Lacan about over-speculating the relationship of his work to theology. For example, speaking some three years prior he says "Things have in fact got to the point that, having let slip recently in one of the interviews that I spoke to you about, that I had got my taste for commentary from an old practice of the scholastics, I asked them to take it out. God knows what people would have deduced from it (*laughter*)."[11]

One way to read Lacan on this matter is in terms of the methodological focus he brings to bear upon psychoanalysis. Where previously the direction of treatment was oedipal in direction; i.e., exploring what Cormac Gallagher calls "the banality of childhood experiences that are supposed to explain the subject's current behavior,"[12] his focus shifts to the very "structure

---

8. Lacan, *SXVI*, lecture xxii, 2.

9. Ibid., lecture viii, 2.

10. Ibid.

11. Jacques Lacan, *The Seminars of Jacques Lacan, Book XIV: The Logic of Phantasy*, trans. Cormac Gallagher. Unpublished. 7.12.66 lecture vi, 4.

12. Gallagher, "From an Other to the other: An Overview," *The Letter* 21 (2001) 1–27, 10.

of the subject itself."[13] As Gallagher points out, Lacan's engagement with Pascal falls within this post-Oedipal period from the late 1960s to early 1970s.[14] During this period Lacan was confronted by a new audience that included philosophers and anthropologists as well as training analysts, theologians, and the like. As such he began to recast psychoanalysis in the language of contemporary logic and set theory, drawing for example, upon the work of Frege, Bertrand Russell, Cantor, and Pascal. In doing so he claimed to develop a formal logic, the first of such to supersede Aristotelian logic to the extent it introduced a new conceptual object, the o-object, or *objet petit a*: the dispositional object by which enjoyment is measured and to which I shall return.[15]

This shift in focus was accompanied by a coterminous shift in how the clinic should operate: the oedipal clinic gives way to the clinic of the real. In the clinic of the real, what matters is the structure of the subject as it stands in relation to knowledge, enjoyment, and the o-object. As Lacan says,

> It is not enough to match the interpersonal relations of an adult with the second biography that we take to be original, that of his infantile relations. . . . It is not enough to discover a simple homology by going into the past with someone who comes to tell us about his present-day relations. . . . This quite often only conceals the question from us, the one we analysts should really question ourselves about . . . the style of presence in which each of these three terms knowledge, enjoyment and o-object were effectively presented to the subject.[16]

In other words, we should not be led by the theology in Lacan's work to posit something about Lacan as such; rather, we should ask: what can we learn structurally about the subject by recourse to theology.

In the following sections I will take Lacan's three terms (knowledge, enjoyment and the o-object) as a means to organize Lacan's reading of the wager and the role of grace therein.

13. Ibid.

14. Gallagher, "From Freud's Mythology of Sexuality to Lacan's Formulae of Sexuation," *The Letter* 38 (2006) 1–9, 7.

15. Ibid.

16. Lacan, *SXVI*, lecture xxi, 7—8.

Knowledge

In the "Rome Report" of 1966, an amended footnote by Lacan indicates that it is through his encounter with Pascal that he is "forced . . . to take the whole thing up again [grace] in order to reveal the inestimable value it conceals for the analyst."[17] The suggestion here is that the demand to take grace seriously indicates something specific about what grace offers conceptually for psychoanalysis. Indeed, during the course of *Seminar XVI* he boldly claims in enigmatic fashion that "the measure, in which Christianity interests us, I mean at the level of theory, can be measured precisely by the role given to Grace."[18] Grace is the point of contact between Christianity and psychoanalysis, and hence any discussion between the two disciplines must start with grace.

For Pascal the question of grace was colored by his Jansenist leanings which, following the Calvinist line, emphasized the depravity of human nature and hence the necessity of a divine and predestined grace. Yet, because of sin humans cannot discern the will of God in regard of their own salvation, or indeed what one should do to achieve that salvation. Henri Gouhier[19] claims that predestination is the axiomatic basis of Pascalian vision of the world,[20] and Lacan informs his listeners that it is Gouhier he has been consulting.

So, when Lacan says that grace concerns the function of "the desire of the Other," the implication is that our inability to discern the will of God because of sin is the model of the subjective relation, and the obscurity of the desire of the Other. And because Pascal's wager addresses the problem of the Other, albeit the existence of the Other, Lacan is able to map the question of desire onto the wager.

I will now take up Lacan's reading of Pascal's wager. While collated under the rubric *Penseés*, Pascal's wager was written on a quite separate piece of paper, and it is this slip of paper that Lacan begins with. For those unfamiliar, the slip upon which the wager was written bears irregular crease marks, and obtuse lines dissecting the page. The wager itself is written at varying degrees to the page with lines are crossed out, and paragraphs inserted. It is, as Lacan points out, as if it were kept in a pocket close to his

17. Lacan, *Écrits*, 266 n. 14.

18. Lacan, S*XVI*, lecture viii, 3.

19. Lacan, S*XIII*, lecture ix, 4. Henri Gouhier was the president of the exam board that oversaw the defense of Michael Foucault's main thesis in 1961.

20. John McDade, "The Contemporary Relevance of Pascal," *New Blackfriars* 91 (2010) 185–96.

heart—recalling another piece of paper found stitched into lining of Pascal's doublet following his death.[21]

The other piece of paper Lacan refers to is Pascal's "Memorial," a small scrap recalling the night of his mystical conversion, the so-called "night of fire"[22] in which Pascal records his encounter with the "God of Abraham, God of Isaac, God of Jacob, not of philosophers and scholars. Certainty, certainty, heartfelt, joy, peace. God of Jesus Christ."[23]

The suggestion here is that the wager and the Memorial are related to the extent that in both cases a step is taken by Pascal, away from an Other—the God of the philosophers—toward the "other" God; *from an Other to the other*:

> For Pascal the question is settled. Another little piece of paper sewn more deeply than in a pocket, under a lining, "not the God of the philosophers but the God of Abraham . . . of Isaac and of Jacob" shows us the step that has been taken, and that what is at stake is not at all the supreme being.[24]

To translate this into the philosophical parlance of Heidegger, what is staged here as far as Lacan is concerned is the theological critique of onto-theology. And it is the theological critique of philosophy that serves Lacan as a "correlate" to the questioning of truth in the unconscious.[25]

To clarify this correlation one should recall the background events to *Seminar XVI*.[26] Student protests were in full swing, advancing a critique of the University for its role in the commodification of knowledge. Although Lacan famously spoke out against the movement he also voiced his sympathy with it. He too was concerned with the status of knowledge, and in particular with knowledge as it pertains to the field of psychoanalysis. The barb of Lacan's critique is aimed at the self-assuredness of the Cartesian cogito which works on the basis of what can be known. In this way, it precludes the possibility of the Freudian claim: "I do not know." In other words, psychoanalysis does not concern knowledge as much as the failure of knowledge:

> This truth which is the one that we question in the unconscious as creative failure of knowledge, as the original point of the desire to know, is the schema that comes from a knowledge

21. Lacan, *SXVI*, lecture vii, 3.

22. John Cole, *Pascal: The Man and His Two Loves* (New York: New York University Press, 1995) 105.

23. Francis Coleman, *Neither Angel Nor Beast: The Life and Work of Blaise Pascal* (New York: Routledge, 1986) 60.

24. Lacan, *SXIII*, lecture iv, 6.

25. Lacan, *SXVI*, 23.4.69. 12–14.

26. Gallagher, "From an Other to the other," 1–27.

238 Theology after Lacan

condemned never to be in a way anything but the correlate of this failure. . . . Do we not sense here at least one of the essential correlates of what is put forward in our epoch about a so-called end of philosophy?[27]

As the above suggests, Pascal's critique of the God of the philosophers serves in advance of Lacan's critique of unconscious knowledge, and hence Lacan uses Pascal as a means to develop a way of speaking which takes into account precisely the "failure of knowledge," or as Gallaher puts it: "to hint at the presence of a truth, at the revelation of an o-object in a way that conventional academic teaching is unable to do.[28] For this reason, Lacan resists identifying the God of Pascal with the "*imaginary* plane" precisely because "it is not the god of philosophers; it is not even the god of any knowledge. We do not know, writes Pascal, either what he is, or of course, even if he is."[29] Pascal belongs to the plane of the real.

Said otherwise, the God of the philosophers correlates to "this Other" the "locus where knowledge is established in *the subject supposed to know*";[30] "This big Other is One."[31] However, as Lacan is quick to remind his audience, the Other "is not unrelated to the fact that there is a God of Abraham, of Isaac and of Jacob."[32]

The key phrase in the above is "not unrelated." The double negative affirms a link, albeit through the negative. We become subjects to the extent we are interpolated into the symbolic (the Other). The symbolic is particularized for each subject. The "Other" is the locus in which/out of which speech is constituted. Lacan's point then is that because the field of the Other stands in advance of the subject "you cannot escape, you are already on board; this is what the signifier *supports*, everything that we grasp as subject, we are in the wager."[33]

This is one way to interpret Lacan's rendering of Freud's *Wo Es war, soll Ich warden* [where it/id was, I/ego shall become]: "It is there, in the Other, that there is the unconscious structured like a language."[34]

All of this is, for Lacan, by way of grasping Pascal's initial point, against those who might say "he who chooses heads and he who chooses tails are

---

27. *Seminar XVI*, lecture xvii, 12–14.
28. Gallagher, "From an Other to the other," 8.
29. *Seminar XVI*, lecture x, 7 (emphases mine).
30. Ibid., lecture xxii, 7.
31. Lacan, *SXV*, lecture xxii, 4.
32. Lacan, *SXVI*, lecture xxii, 3.
33. Lacan, *SXIII*, lecture x, 6.
34. Lacan, *SXVI*, lecture xiv, 11.

equally at fault, they are both in the wrong. The true course is not to wager at all." On Lacan's reading, it is because the field of the Other stands in advance of the subject that "you cannot escape, you are already on board; this is what the signifier *supports*, everything that we grasp as subject, we are in the wager."[35]

In this way the wager recalls Lacan's excursus on the *forced choice* from *Seminar XI*, and allows a more persistent thread to surface in Lacan's work: the question of subjectivity is posed in terms of a dilemma, a wager, a game as such.[36] In *Seminar XI*, it is the highwayman's question that provides the clue to the subject's status: "Your money or your life!" As Lacan argues, the dilemma poses a false dichotomy as if there was a choice between two things (hence the use of the disjunctive "or"). However, as Lacan explains, there is no choice: "Your money or your life!" If I choose the money, I lose both. If I choose life, I have life without the money, namely, a life deprived of something."[37] To put this into psychoanalytic terms we can draw upon Adrian Johnston's bold rendering: "Your *jouissance* or your life!" In choosing life, the subject forfeits *jouissance* (i.e., castration—we cannot have the man or woman of our dreams); however, if the subject chooses *jouissance*, then he forfeits his very life and hence the promise of *jouissance* (i.e., if the subject does get to sleep with the man or woman of his dreams, s/he quickly discerns that the transitory experience of sex "isn't it!"[38]

In sum, it is not a question of *not* wagering; rather we *must* choose if we are to count as subjects. And the wager as Cleo puts it "records the fact that it is impossible to escape the above alternative and that it is our real; that we live, act and think only within this alternative which is our real."[39] In other words, existence *is* a matter of wager, *the absolute wager*. So it is not just that we must wager, but that the qualitative experience of the real testifies to a subjective position that amounts to a wager:

> The matter [of the wager], what could be its matter, is the radical wording that is the formulation of the real, as it can be conceived and as it can be touched with one's finger, that is not conceivable to fancy another limit of the knowledge as the stopping point where we are only concerned with this: with something

35. Lacan, *SXIII*, lecture x, 6.

36. Lacan, *SXI*, 203–15.

37. Ibid., 212.

38. Adrian Johnston, "The Forced Choice of Enjoyment: *Jouissance* between Expectation and Actualization," http://www.lacan.com/forced.htm.

39. Jean-Pierre Clero, "Lacan and Probability," http://www.jehps.net/Decembre2008/Clero.pdf.

indivisible, that whether it is, or not. In other words, something that falls in the province of heads or tails . . . The absolute real, on this little page, is what is expressed as heads or tails.[40]

And because the wager is what defines existence, Lacan introduces a qualification of the real not encountered anywhere in *Écrits*: "The absolute real."

To sum up the preceding discussion, it can be argued that for Lacan, grace principally belongs to the theological discourse, not the philosophical, to the extent it concerns not knowledge as such, but non-knowledge; i.e., an encounter with the real. The real names a quality of existence, which the wager brings into focus. And it is what the wager brings into focus that matters, because the wager defines the structural position the subject is faced with. Hence, given the wager, it is not a matter of choosing as such; to recognize the dilemma of the wager is to already *be graced*; i.e., to have chosen in one sense.

To draw a upon a theological analogy, to posit freedom as a realm of autonomy in which we might freely and therefore lovingly choose God is to misrecognise freedom as a sphere of autonomy—free of God as such; because if God gives freedom that we might choose him, then the very possibility of freedom is already a sign of God. Similarly for Lacan, we misrecognise the wager if we interpret it as a choice for God/the Big Other; the very possibility of the wager is already to be interpolated into the Big Other; to have already been chosen and to experience the uncertainty of grace.

The O-Object

If we must wager, what are the stakes? Lacan translates the stakes Pascal identifies as "infinity or nothing," to which he also refers to as a "formulation of the real."[41] In effect Lacan reads the wager in the manner one might develop the negative of a polaroid. So for Lacan the emphasis within his rendering of the wager falls not upon winning infinity, but losing "nothing." For Lacan, it is not simply that we have nothing to lose by wagering, but rather, we risk losing precisely this "nothing." Lacan's point is "nothing is not nothing," rather "it is something that can be put on the scales, and very

40. Lacan, *SXVI*, lecture viii, 4–5.
41. Lacan, *SXIII*, lecture lx, 8.

specifically at the level we have put it in the wager."[42] In Lacanese, "what is at stake is the absolute real"[43]—God *as the Nothing*.

The real can mapped in terms of subject and the Other. To take the latter first: As Lacan says, when we say "I wager that God exists or" we introduce this referent—the Other or the big Other which is marked by the bar of castration and which "reduces him [the subject] to the alternative of existence or not, and to nothing else."[44] The Other is situated within the symbolic, it stands for what is both constitutive and yet empty. In this way, Lacan is able to relate the Other to the function of a name: *The Name of the Father*, "a singular form . . . to carefully locate at the level of the wager."[45] Lacan's point is that a Name, while pivotal in establishing a discourse, "depends precisely on the fact that after all, you can never know who the father is. You can always look, it is a question of faith."[46] In other words, every discourse invites a wager on the Other which orders the field and yet remains unknown.

As Lacan points out, this is what makes Pascal's wager distinct from the usual type of wager. Whereas traditionally one wagers against another partner, what is at the stake in the case of Pascal's is the existence *of* the partner, which arises at the point one designates the "function of lack."[47] In other words the wager amounts to a "*fore*-throw," made in the hope of God who is "here" yet is never "there."[48]

Taken from the perspective of the subject, lack is encountered in terms of the o-object. The symbolic is the cultural means of subjectification. The "o" object locates the subject in terms of desire, and its relation to an Other, because the "o" arises within the field of the Other. In other words, it is through the process of becoming Other that we meet the o-object; in the process, something—the "o"—"falls away," and thereby establishing the subject as desiring subject, not unlike the cotton reel in Freud's fort da [gone/there] game.

For Freud the game was the means to master the loss of the mother. For Lacan however the game stages the basic linguistic/phonic distinction which gives rise to symbolic life: it is the instantiation of the subject through

---

42. Lacan, *SXVI*, lecture viii, 12–13.

43. Ibid., 5.

44. Lacan, *SXIII*, lecture x, 8.

45. Lacan, *SXVI*, lecture viii, 5.

46. Ibid., lecture ix, 14.

47. Lacan, *SXIII*, lecture x, 6.

48. Louis Armand, "Symptom in the Machine: Lacan, Joyce, Sollers," http://www.lacan.com/sympmach.htm.

the division of language, during which a small object falls: the object cause of desire or o-object:

> I am introducing the question here, to this always fleeting, always hidden object, to what is after all hope or despair the essence of our desire, to this unnamable, ungraspable, unarticulatable object and, nevertheless, that Pascal's wager is going to allow us to affirm . . . the (o) as cause of desire and value which determines it, is what is involved in the Pascalian stake.[49]

So on the one hand the "absolute" wager concerns the Other (the subject supposed to Know), and more specifically the existence of the Other; on the other the wager also "incarnates . . . the object lost for the subject in every engagement with the signifier."[50] To further draw out the implications in terms of grace and the o-object, we need first to understand how all of this bears on enjoyment.

Enjoyment

Desire and enjoyment are "linked to the division of the subject."[51] In tackling the question of enjoyment, Lacan turned to Pascal's game-theory. As Lacan notes, first: game (*jeu*) in French also implies enjoyment; second, Pascal makes enjoyment the stake of the wager when he warns that an "infinity of infinitely happy lives" is to be lost.

The problem out of which modern game theory grew was initially posed by Luca Pacioli (1445–1517), the subject of Pascal's exchange with Fermat. It concerned how to divide fairly the stakes of a game in the case that the game is interrupted with hands yet to be dealt.[52] Notice how the problematic begins with a chance (*hazard*) encounter, an instance of what Lacan calls the "real *qua* impossible" or *tuché*.[53] The aim is to avoid annulling the game and returning the initial shares, or simply awarding the share to the existing winner. Pascal's triangular display of binomial coefficients solves this problem and in doing so offers an oblique commentary on the status of knowledge, enjoyment, and the subject.

The philosophical import of Pascal's triangle is that, given an indefinite series (the chance disruption of the game), one can nonetheless

---

49. Lacan, *SXIII*, lecture ix, 8–9.
50. Ibid., 10–11.
51. Lacan, *SXVI*, lecture vii, 10.
52. Ibid., lecture viii, 5.
53. Lacan, *SXII*, lecture ix, 9; Lacan, *SXI*, 52–64.

discern and master a hidden order. To translate this into psychoanalytic terms: if psychoanalysis concerns not what can, but what cannot be known; i.e., the creative failure of knowledge within the unconscious, then it is the science of the discernment of that relationship to failure within the symbolic that is mastered. In other words it is the "process of discernment" that one masters.[54]

It is however the occurrence of the Fibonacci sequence within Pascal's triangle that provides the metaphor for the o-object and its relation to enjoyment. Recall that the structure of subjectivity includes a loss, not in the sense of the loss of an original unity; rather loss is original and constitutive. Should one presume an original enjoyment untainted by law, then the question of enjoyment turns upon its recuperation. However, if loss is original then what we seek to recuperate "has nothing to do with enjoyment, but with its loss."[55] Lacan introduces a name for this loss in relation to enjoyment: *surplus enjoying*:

> Namely, what responds, not to enjoyment but the loss of enjoyment in so far as from it emerges what becomes the cause conjugated by desire for knowledge and this animation that I recently qualified as ferocious that proceeds from *surplus enjoying*.[56]

Žižek provides perhaps the most succinct cultural example to flesh out this experience: caffeine-free diet Coke. "We drink the Nothingness itself, the pure semblance of a property that is effectively merely an envelope of a void." Subsequently, "the more you drink Coke, the more you are thirsty."[57] Žižek describes the "key to this perturbation" as "the surplus-*jouissance*," the *objet a* which exists (or rather insists) in a kind of curved space in which, the more you approach it, the more it eludes your grasp (or, the more you possess it, the greater the lack).[58] This is the real of enjoyment.

What then of the irrational number or "golden mean"[59] manifest in the fibonnaci sequence? It serves as an "equation of the symbolic process";

---

54. Or as Jean-Pierre Clero puts it: "there is a sort of indefinite series, but whose order of terms can be mastered. Psychoanalysis is not the knowledge of the psychical depths: it is the detection and precise spotting of the order of psychical acts, in their symbolic inscription which can be ignored by the imaginary of the signified." Cf. Clero, "Lacan and Probability".

55. Lacan, *SXVI*, lecture vii, 10.

56. Ibid., 11.

57. See http://lacan.com/seminars3.htm.

58. Ibid.

59. Lacan, *SXX*, 48.

it expresses the relation of the subject qua o-object to the Other.[60] As Levi Bryant points out, the advantage of this mathematical rendering is that it refuses any notion that o-object is a residue from some pre-symbolic. Rather, it is an internal relation, the property of a structural operation.[61] Hence Lacan claims that in an analogical way that the golden mean "playing on proportion . . . steals away what is approached about enjoyment along the path of *surplus enjoying.*"[62]

Grace and Revelation

Lacan tells us that key to enjoyment and the o-object is repetition: the "original point [genesis of the "o"] that makes of repetition the key of a process about which the question is posed."[63] The "o" is the excess that sets repetition, the search for the lost object, in motion. Lacan does not cite his earlier discussion from *Seminar II* on Kierkegaard and repetition, but the link is illuminating as it provides one of Lacan's earliest reflections on grace.

For Kierkegaard, repetition addresses the dilemma of selfhood: how does one reconcile the contingent nature of self-hood over time with its apparent unity? Plato's doctrine of recollection attends to this problematic by positing the transmigration of the soul: the soul is immortal and over the course of its transmigrations neither loses nor gains knowledge; learning is simply a matter of recollecting; i.e., finding out what we already know.[64] Lacan however endorses Kierkegaard's view that Christianity introduces something which upsets the easy recourse to truth: sin.

> Sin is from then on present . . . and it is by no longer following the path of reminiscence, but rather in following that of repetition, that man finds his way . . . so you can see the meaning of man's need for repetition. It's all to do with the intrusion of the symbolic register.[65]

60. Shingu Kazushige, *Being Irrational: Lacan, the Objet a, and the Golden Mean,* trans. and ed. Michael Radich (Tokyo: Gakuju Shoin, 2004) 98.

61. See http://larval-subjects.blogspot.co.uk/2006/11/rough-and-tumble-theory.html.

62. Lacan, *SXVI,* lecture viii, 14.

63. Ibid., lecture x, 1.

64. For an account of recollection, see Plato, *Meno,* trans. W. Guthrie (Middlesex: Penguin, 1981).

65. Jacques Lacan, *The Seminar of Jacques Lacan, Seminar II: The Ego in Freud's Theory and Technique of Psychoanalysis, 1954–1955,* trans. S. Tomaselli (New York: Norton, 1991) 87–88.

Recollection, argues Lacan, is structured along the imaginary axis: it is a dyadic relation between the knower and what is known, such that one may know "wholly." According to this model, knowledge is as a "mirage," we draw from knowledge conclusions which affirms our desires rather than challenge them. In this way we can draw a link from recollection to the mirror stage. However, the symbolic introduces a "third term" into the dyad: an Other which disrupts the unity of imaginary relations; thereafter repetition becomes the search for "*l'objet foncièrement perdu*" (the fundamental lost object).[66]

The significant point for Kierkegaard is that it is only by grace (i.e., revelation) that we know we are in sin in the first place. Something has to come from without to disrupt the imaginary unity of self-knowledge.

For this reason, Lacan's characterizes Kierkegaard's split between paganism and Christianity as "the difference between the pagan world and the world of grace,"[67] prefiguring his work in *Seminar XVI* when he insists on "the difference between philosophical discourse, whatever it may be, and what we are introduced to by this nothing other than is distinguished by starting from repetition."[68]

In *Seminar XVI*, this Kierkegaardian line comes into focus when Lacan, in reflecting on the difference between the philosophical and theological/psychoanalytic tradition says "What distinguishes the God of the Jews, the one designated as being at the origin of monotheism, was not some development that the One was subsequently able to make," what distinguishes him is that "this god that is in question designates himself by the fact that he speaks."[69] Philosophy tries to derive truth from Logos, and we can derive Truth from Logos because we are ourselves graduations of the Divine Logos—what Lacan calls the "development of the One," the metaphysical presumption which makes for recollection. In Lacanese, this puts us on the path of the imaginary.

In Christianity however the Logos is revealed directly, placing it within the order of the real, the point of contact between Christianity and psychoanalysis. And to underscore the point, Lacan turns not only to the fact of God speaking, i.e., revelation, but also *what is revealed*.

66. Lacan, *Écrits*, 45.
67. Lacan, *SII*, 87–88.
68. Lacan, *SXVI*, lecture x, 6.
69. Ibid., lecture xxii, 4. See also Lacan, *SXIII*, lecture x, 8.

The Real Name of the Father

Lacan's reflections on God's revealed speech is initially occasioned by reference to Pascal in his "Introduction to the Names-of-the-Father" Seminar (1963):

> The God who made himself known to Abraham, Isaac, and Jacob did so using the Name by which the *Elohim* in the burning bush calls him, which I have written on the blackboard. It is read as follows: *El Shadday*.[70]

As Lacan explains, conventional translators of the Septuagint tended to push the direction of interpretation into the categories of onto-theology, which Lacan equates with the imaginary. What this misses is the link between God's utterances at the bush from Exodus (Exod 3:14): אֶהְיֶה אֲשֶׁר אֶהְיֶה (*Ehyeh Asher Ehyeh*)[71] with the Tetragrammaton: YHWH (היה); "the name I do not pronounce." In this way he acknowledges first: the Rabbinic link made between the Tetragrammaton and *Ehyeh Asher Ehyeh* (YHWH is the third person singular imperfect of the verb "to be" suggesting simply "He is," or "He will be"; i.e., the meaning of *Ehyeh Asher Ehyeh*).[72] Second, in a move which precipitates his claim as to the impossibility of the sexual relationship, he posits "the untranslatability of the Hebrew God into Greek metaphysics:"[73] To draw on the work of Kenneth and Julia Reinhard Lipton: the Greek translation pushes the interpretation of *Ehyeh Asher Ehyeh* in the direction of a statement of predication or identity (e.g., "A=A"). By contrast, the oral repetition allows for an "incomplete semanticization of God's name, thereby crystallizing its "nonsensical character." In other words, the Name cannot be taken as a declaration of existence and especially substance; rather it is the "creative, legislative, and descriptive, instating within the apparently simple form of the statement a God otherwise than Being."[74]

And for this reason Lacan was able in his Seminar on *Identification*, to challenge the prevailing consensus on Freud's final text *Moses and Monotheism*. Instead of attributing the argument to the work of a dwindling mind, he argued that, "the fact that he [Freud] ended his discourse on Moses and the

---

70. Jacques Lacan, "Introduction to the Names-of-the-Father Seminar," in *Television: A Challenge to the Psychoanalytic Establishment* (New York: Norton, 1999) 81–96, 90.

71. Ibid., 90–91.

72. See http://www.jewishencyclopedia.com/articles/11305-names-of-god.

73. Kenneth Reinhard and Julia Reinhard Lupton, "Revelation: Lacan and the Ten Commandments," http://www.jcrt.org/archives/02.1/reinhard_lupton.shtml.

74. Ibid.

way he did it, leaves no doubt that the foundation of Christian revelation is indeed therefore in this grace relationship.[75]

During *Seminar XIII*, the original context of Lacan's discussion of Pascal, and following a further reference to the revelation of God's name at the burning bush, Lacan makes the following remark:

> Now this indeed is what is recognizable in the original message through which there appears in History the one who changes both the relationships of man to the truth and of man to his destiny, if it is true—one could say that I have been dinning it into you for some time—that the advent of Science, of science with a capital S—and since I am not the only one to think what Koyré has so powerfully articulated—this advent of Science would be inconceivable without the message of the God of the Jews.[76]

Alexandre Koyré's masterpiece *From the Closed World to the Infinite Universe* challenged the positivist assumption at the heart of historiographers of science; i.e., that the development of science follows a linear and progressive path of unfolding truths towards a final given truth.[77] Rather, in the manner now associated with Thomas Kuhn, one must understand the way knowledge works within a given paradigm; i.e., the sets of relations which allow knowledge to work the way it does. Hence Koyré's contention that the "rise and growth of experimental science is not the source, but, on the contrary, the result of the new theoretical, that is, the new metaphysical approach to nature that forms the content of the scientific revolution of the seventeenth century."[78]

Koyré's influence helps to explain why Lacan so deliberately engaged with theology. If psychoanalysis was to advance, then one must attend first and foremost to the metaphysical/theological paradigm within which such a science was conceived.

Grace and Revelation

Returning then to Pascal, the wager should be contextualized within the order of theology rather than philosophy, by which is meant, a discourse of grace and hence revelation; i.e., a discourse of the real. This is neatly

75. Jacques Lacan, *The Seminars of Jacques Lacan: Seminar IX, Identification 1961–1962*, trans. C. Gallagher. Unpublished, 14.3.62, lecture xiii, 126.

76. Lacan, *SXIII*, lecture x, 136.

77. See Alexandre Koyré, *From the Closed World to the Infinite Universe* (Radford, VA: Wilder, 2008).

78. Alexandre Koyré, *Newtonian Studies* (London: Chapman Hall, 1968) 6.

exemplified by Pascal's approach to grace which, fashioned by predestination, figures the question of revelation. If revelation were simply bold and extrinsic then humanity would know God in a direct way, but if God remains a mystery are we consigned to ignorance? Pascal offers an alternative:

> All appearance indicates neither a total exclusion nor a manifest presence of divinity, but the presence of a God who hides Himself. Everything bears this character.... He must not see nothing at all, nor must he see sufficient for him to believe he possesses it; but he must see enough to know that he has lost it. For to know of his loss, he must see and not see; and that is exactly the state in which he naturally is.[79]

What we have here, as John McDade highlights, is a dialectic of "seeing and not seeing" which reflects a *double-caesura*: the ignorance of the human mind through sin, and "the even darker mystery of the predestination of some to sight and others to blindness." God's will is obscure, and yet we must wager.[80] The double-caesura stands as the problematic in which the subject of psychoanalysis is conceived; the inconsistency on side of an Other and the inconsistency on the side of the other. And grace stands for the problematic of the relation.

Had Lacan spent more time on Pascal, he may have also developed his reading of the o-object and enjoyment in tandem with Pascal's scheme of progressive revelation within history according to which the "progressive disclosure of God [is] in direct proportion to the degree of divine concealment";[81] in other words, the more God is disclosed, the more obscured God becomes. God is initially both hidden and disclosed within nature, the disclosure of whom, Pascal argued is discernible only to some pagans. However, when God is more directly disclosed through the Incarnation, he is equally more hidden to the extent that neither pagan nor Jew, but only the Christians—be they heretical or otherwise—may discern God. And when he is most disclosed in the Blessed Sacrament he is most hidden, so that only Catholics can see him.

Does Pascal's scheme not highlight the real qua enjoyment through its curved space in which the more one approaches God the more God eludes one's grasp (or, the more you possess it, the greater the lack)?

However, one should note, as highlighted by John McDade, God's hiddenness for Pascal, as the Other is for Lacan, "is not of the order of God's

79. Blaise Pascal, *Pensées*, http://www.bartleby.com/48/1/8.html.

80. McDade, "Contemporary Relevance of Pascal," 189.

81. Ibid., 190.

mysterious and transcendent essence"[82] as one might expect within the works of Gregory of Nyssa or St. John of the Cross; rather, it belongs to the tradition of *Deus absconditus*: God's will to deliberately withhold from us something of God: the desire of the Other.

As Žižek points out, this makes for an "uncanny subject" who in responding in human relations must do so via a "third," a "terrifying" and impenetrable enigma who demands something of the subject which remains opaque nonetheless. Indeed, he goes as far as to suggest that "for Lacan, we do not have to evoke God to get a taste of this abyssal dimension; it is present in every human being."[83] Žižek may be right, we don't have to evoke God to appreciate this dimension, but we may have to invoke the theological heritage of the West to account more generally for the central structure of the Western subject in Lacanian terms.

Conclusion

Returning then to grace, if it remains "irreplaceable," it is not because it offers one concept amongst others to "add" to the Lacanian corpus. Rather, it is because it stands as the principle structuring of subjectivity and the real of experience. Grace refers us back to a God/Other whom we must question in the manner of the unconscious, but a God/Other to whom we must respond nonetheless given the uncertainty of the Other. What establishes this relation principally is the God who speaks and as such with whom one must negotiate enjoyment through the fall of an o-object. The imperative to wager given by Pascal can therefore be read in tandem with Lacan's further reworking of Freud's "Wo Es war, soll Ich warden": "there, where he is, in his field, namely the Holy Land, there is no question of obeying anyone but him [i.e., the unconscious]."[84]

And perhaps for this reason it does not do to ask what theology looks like after Lacan, or whether theology is either desirable or possible after Lacan; rather, we should ask, what were the theological shifts that made Lacanian psychoanalysis possible in the first place?

82. Ibid., 189.

83. Slavoj Žižek, "How to Read Lacan: From *Che vuoi?* to Fantasy: Lacan with *Eyes Wide Shut*," http://www.lacan.com/zizkubrick.htm.

84. Lacan, *SXVI*, 13.11.68, lecture xxii, 4.

12

The Triumph of Theology

CLAYTON CROCKETT

IN HIS BOOK *THE Triumph of Religion*, Jacques Lacan provocatively claims that religion will triumph over psychoanalysis. "Psychoanalysis will not triumph," Lacan states, "it will survive or not." Furthermore, religion will triumph not only over psychoanalysis, but "it will triumph over many other things as well."[1] Religion is an incredible power to overcome that cannot simply be dismantled. Psychoanalysis is a tool, but it is also ultimately a symptom of the "malaise of civilization."[2] Analysis is only possible as a result of an "intrusion of the real."[3] Here analysis is a fragile and weak power in contrast to the power of religion, which is triumphant.

Lacan is not celebrating religion's triumph; he is lamenting it while acknowledging that it is inevitable. He distinguishes psychoanalysis from religion, and argues that psychoanalysis is not a religion. Psychoanalysis is also not a secularized form of religion, at least in Lacan's terms. It is not an updated and modernized form of confession, for example.[4] This acknowledgment of the triumph of religion is a result of the pessimism that marks Lacan's later work about the liberating potential of psychoanalysis. So how does Lacan's diagnosis of religion fit into our contemporary post-secular theological moment?

---

1. Jacques Lacan, *Le triomphe de la religion* (Paris: Éditions du Seuil, 2005) 79.
2. Ibid., 81.
3. Ibid., 82.
4. See ibid., 78.

Following Lacan we could say that theology, as a form of religious discourse, will always triumph. The triumph of theology is the defeat of secular
modernity, despite Lacan's insistence that psychoanalysis is a purely secular
discourse, even though his work is saturated with religious references. But
is theology's victory a pyrrhic victory? Extending and applying Lacan, I suggest that theology triumphs, but as ideology, not as theology itself.

Borrowing the language of Hegel, we could say that theology in itself
or *an sich* is pure ideology. In the Middle Ages, theology was Queen of the
sciences because it served as handmaiden to the King, or God. Theology is
deposed from this royal position during the course of European modernity
as God's sovereignty is displaced first onto an absolute monarch and then
onto the representative democracy of a people. Ernst Kantorowicz's influential study *The King's Two Bodies* shows the former transition, from the
sovereignty of God to the sovereignty of the King.[5] And in his book *Political Theology*, Carl Schmitt provocatively claims that "all significant concepts
of the modern theory of the state are secularized theological concepts."[6]
Political theology names the mutual co-implication of religion and politics.
Although Talal Asad does not completely agree with Schmitt's analysis of
secularization, Asad does accept that there is a structural interrelation between the concept of the secular and the idea of religion. In *Formations of
the Secular*, Asad claims that the secularization hypothesis no longer appears credible because scholars realize that "the categories of 'politics' and
'religion' turn out to implicate each other more profoundly than we thought,
a discovery that has accompanied our growing understanding of the modern nation-state."[7]

Today, political theology is one name for the return of the religion, and
the current incredulity of the secularization hypothesis. Theology animates
our politics, often in disguised form. Here we could think about Walter
Benjamin's scenario of the hunchback and the puppet, which Slavoj Žižek
renames as *The Puppet and the Dwarf*. In the first of his famous "Theses on
the Philosophy of History," Benjamin recounts the story of a puppet who
plays chess, secretly animated by a "little hunchback who was an expert
chess player" who would manipulate the puppet with strings.[8] The puppet

5. See Ernst H. Kantorowicz, *The King's Two Bodies: A Study in Mediaeval Political
Theology* (Princeton: Princeton University Press, 1957).

6. Carl Schmitt, *Political Theology: Four Chapters on the Concept of Sovereignty*,
trans. George Schwab (Chicago: University of Chicago Press, 2005) 36.

7. Talal Asad, *Formations of the Secular: Christianity, Islam, Modernity* (Stanford:
Stanford University Press, 2003) 200.

8. Walter Benjamin, *Illuminations*, trans. Harry Zohn (New York: Schocken, 1978)
253.

is identified with "historical materialism" by Benjamin, while the hidden hunchback is called theology. Historical materialism can triumph "if it enlists the services of theology, which today, as we know, is wizened and has to keep out of sight."[9] Theology secretly animates our politics, and it knows how to triumph, to win every time.

The problem is that the hunchback no longer keeps out of sight, but shows his ugly and misshapen form. The hunchback's deformity serves to distract from the workings of global capitalism, which pulls the strings. So in a way the situation is reversed, or rather, the hunchback himself is also a puppet, in the form of ideology, which is how theology manifests itself. Political theology means that the theology that takes political form is always already ideological, and this is what theology is in itself. Theology in itself triumphs, just as Lacan argues that religion will always triumph. But the triumph of theology is pure ideology.

At the same time, ideology does not exhaust theology. Returning to Hegel's famous schema, we can say that while theology in itself (which means "for us") is ideology—theology is ideological in symbolic terms, although it is pure fantasy in the realm of the imaginary—theology for itself is something entirely different. I suggest that theology for itself is energy. As we have discovered in the twentieth century with Einstein's famous equation, being is energy transformation.

I understand energy in terms of the philosophy of Gilles Deleuze and nonequilibrium thermodynamics. Energy is what Deleuze calls intensity in *Difference and Repetition*, and it is intensity that propels repetition, which is always repetition of difference rather than identity. Deleuze says that "intensity is difference, but this difference tends to deny or cancel itself out in extensity or underneath quality."[10] Energetic intensity seems to cancel difference, but at the same time it is difference, because it is the differential energy that drives repetition. Good sense is thermodynamic in conventional terms; "it goes from the side of things to the side of fire: from differences produced to differences reduced."[11] This apparent reduction of differences creates the illusion of identity, and the transcendental illusion of entropy as the dissipation and disappearance of energy. Although we cannot call energy a form of consciousness, the intentionality of energy transformation is what drives existence in its becoming. Entropy and intentionality are two

9. Ibid.

10. Gilles Deleuze, *Difference and Repetition*, trans. Paul Patton (New York: Columbia University Press, 1994) 223.

11. Ibid., 225.

sides of the same process, and both lead to the generation of difference and complex self-organization.

How can entropy be related to self-organization? Isn't entropy the opposite, the loss of organization and order in the form of information? According to Eric Schneider and Dorion Sagan, entropy should be reconceptualized in terms of gradient reduction. In their book *Into the Cool*, they restate the famous second law of thermodynamics as "nature abhors a gradient."[12] Whenever there is a gradient differential, such as temperature, pressure and so on, nature works to reduce the gradient as quickly and efficiently as possible. Usually this process appears as a tendency to proceed from order to disorder, but in special cases and quasi-stable systems not at equilibrium, this entropic gradient reduction produces complex organization. Schneider and Sagan give examples of Bénard cells and Taylor vortices, but the simplest example is a "storm in a bottle." If you attach two soda bottles together at their openings and stand it so that liquid fills one of the bottles, and then turn it over, the liquid will inefficiently flow from one bottle to the other. But if you twist the bottle, this organizes the flow of the liquid so that it empties much more quickly. The gradient reduction (or entropy) organizes the system under the right nonequilibrium conditions and creates a situation of complexity. What is even more striking is the existence of hysteresis, a kind of memory, in physical systems. Systems "remember" previous states and return to them more easily and more frequently than systems that have never been organized.[13] This is the communication of what Deleuze calls intensity.

In *Difference and Repetition*, Deleuze says that "intensity affirms even the *lowest*; it makes the lowest an object of affirmation."[14] Energy flows from high to low or from hot to cool in its dissipation of entropy and pursuit of gradient reduction. "Everything goes from high to low, and by that movement affirms the lowest: asymmetrical synthesis."[15] The asymmetrical synthesis is the production of differences by means of repetition, which is a kind of entropy that both cancels out differences as extensity and preserves difference as intensity.

How can we call energy theology? I am suggesting that theology names what is ultimately real-energy, and this is the manifestation of theology for itself, *für sich*. In its intentional intensive becoming, theology

12. Eric D. Schneider and Dorion Sagan, *Into the Cool: Energy Flow, Thermodynamics and Life* (Chicago: University of Chicago Press, 2006) 6.

13. See ibid., 129.

14. Deleuze, *Difference and Repetition*, 234.

15. Ibid.

becomes not conscious but self-organized, or autocatakinetic. Theology is energy; it is the energy that drives existence in its infinite iteration. Energy is directional due to thermodynamics. Thermodynamic entropy provides time with an arrow, but this arrow is not simply from order to disorder, requiring counter-intuitive notions of negative entropy to produce life as an exception. Entropy more correctly understood is gradient reduction, which in special nonequilibrium cases produces complex order. Life is a very special and unique situation of energy. Building on the thought of Asad, Ananda Abeysekara claims that religion itself is life. It is impossible to fully separate or translate the essence of religion into something other than life itself, even though that is what we do as thinkers and scholars. According to Abeysekara, the "translation of that life into an articulatable knowledge about oneself is possible only for someone who theorizes and interprets a life in which one becomes a spectator to what one is/does."[16] Theory is a further entropic disorganization of life, but it manifests a complexity of its own when sustained by thermodynamic energy flows.

Ordinarily theology is seen as parasitic on religious life, as a form of linguistic discourse. But understanding theology as energy frees us from this conception and allows us to see that theology for itself is deeper than religion. Religion is a form of life, a concrete manifestation of theological energy. Intensive theology drives the process in thermodynamic terms, which desires the reduction of gradient differentials in the most efficient manner possible. Cellular life offers an incredible stability that allows efficient gradient reduction to proceed in a controlled manner for a limited period of time.

If theology in itself and for us is ideology, and theology for itself is energy, then what is theology in and for itself? Theology *an und für sich* is (psycho) analysis. Life splits itself into life lived and that spectator or theorist who observes life, as Abeysekara points out. This splitting of life into observer and observed is the genesis of psychoanalysis, even if the science has to wait until the apostle Freud comes on the scene. We require the analytic ability to think, comprehend and discern. The contemporary situation of theology after Lacan is this: the supplement of Lacanian psychoanalysis makes theology in and for itself, a coming to consciousness as divided between a triumphant theological orthodoxy allied with neo-liberal capitalism, and a non-triumphalist theology that conceals itself in the interstices of being, the intensive energy that produces individuating differences.

---

16. Ananda Abeysekara, "The Un-translatability of Religion, the Un-translatability of Life: Thinking Talal Asad's Thought Unthought in the Study of Religion," *Method and Theory in the Study of Religion* 23 (2011) 267.

Even if God is dead, religion still triumphs in the modern world as capitalism. In an unpublished fragment from 1921, Walter Benjamin analyzes "Capitalism as Religion." Benjamin claims that capitalism is a cult distinguished by three aspects: it is a pure cult with no dogma; it operates constantly, and there are no weekdays; and finally, it creates a feeling of guilt rather than atonement in its practitioners. We could quibble with parts of Benjamin's analysis, but what is more interesting is his radicalization of Max Weber's thesis about Protestant Christianity and the rise of capitalism. Benjamin says that "the Christianity of the Reformation period did not favor the growth of capitalism; instead it transformed itself into capitalism."[17] The continuity between Christianity and modern Western culture has become much more evident over the last few decades.

Christianity transforms into modern capitalism. Today corporate capitalism is triumphant, but its victory is pyrrhic too. We are reaching real limits to growth in terms of energy resources, and capitalism does not function without growth and cheap energy. The crisis and imminent breakdown of capitalism is reviving more traditional forms of religion, which is why political forms of religion are flourishing. In a more subtle sense, what Lacan calls the one true religion (Romanized Christianity) functions to sustain the beating heart of the West, even in its deconstructed mode, as Jean-Luc Nancy points out. Nancy claims that "Christianity is inseparable from the West," even if Christianity is the form of religion that deconstructs itself and thereby overcomes religion as religion.[18] So religion triumphs either way, with or without capitalism. Even if the West loses, another religion, such as Islam, will win, even if Islam cannot be the one true religion in Western terms.

What can psychoanalysis do? Psychoanalysis offers tools to understand this process. It consists of a form of theology that becomes in and for itself, which means that even though it claims a distance and a perspective, psychoanalysis is still implicated in all of these issues. Psychoanalysis does not directly analyze God as such, but focuses its attention on the concept of the Other. What is the Other? And more importantly, what if the Other does not exist? That is the idea that Lacan's later work suggests, and Slavoj Žižek and Lorenzo Chiesa develop some of the theological implications of the Lacanian Other in its unavoidable monstrosity.

17. Walter Benjamin, "Capitalism as Religion," in *Selected Writings*, vol. 1, 1913–1926, ed. Marcus Bullock and Michael W. Jennings (Cambridge: Harvard University Press, 1996) 290.

18. Jean-Luc Nancy, *Dis-enclosure: The Deconstruction of Christianity*, trans. Bettina Bergo, Gabriel Malenfant, and Michael B. Smith (New York: Fordham University Press, 2008) 142.

In *The Monstrosity of Christ*, with his response to John Milbank, the British theologian of Radical Orthodoxy, Žižek takes issue with Milbank's affirmation of a paradoxical love manifested in phenomological terms that despite its paradoxicality nevertheless points to a transcendent source that can only be articulated with a "Catholic metaphysics of participation."[19] Žižek takes the radical implications of the incarnation and crucifixion of Christ more seriously, claiming that "for me, there is no transcendent God-Father who discloses himself to us, humans, only in a limited way."[20] Žižek endorses the radical theologian Thomas J. J. Altizer, "whose vision of the death of God retains a properly apocalyptic shattering power," as opposed to John D. Caputo, whose weak God "appears much too aseptic, lifeless, bloodless, lacking the properly religious passion."[21] The death of God in Lacanian terms means that "there is no big Other," which is "the true formula for atheism."[22]

So long as the big Other exists, there is the Symbolic order, which is founded on the Name-of-the-Father. The Symbolic order provides the Law, which is a kind of social unconscious that structures our rituals and beliefs. Here Law is associated stereotypically with Judaism in a Freudian-Lacanian reading: "the problem of shofar—the voice of the dying father rendered in the Jewish ritual by the low ominously reverberating sound of a horn—is that of the rise of the Law out of the Father's death."[23] Something of the Father has to survive to sustain and perpetuate the Law, but this is what Christianity does away with in the Crucifixion, according to Žižek. For Christianity, the cry of Christ on the cross is the cry of the Father to Himself, for his own death and self-sacrifice.

The problem with this radicalized version of Christianity is that it is impossible to maintain, because the Law is always smuggled back in, along with the transcendent Father. This problem mirrors the problem that Lacan faces in his famous Seminar VII, where he still retains a kind of faith in the big Other as Law-of-the-Father that sustains the symbolic order. But Žižek says that "the true formula of atheism is not 'God is dead,' but 'God is unconscious.'"[24] Lacan shifts away from the big Other and abandons the Law-of-the-Father after 1960, and this has important consequences for

19. Slavoj Žižek and John Milbank, *The Monstrosity of Christ: Paradox or Dialectic?*, ed. Creston Davis (Cambridge: MIT Press, 2009) 123.

20. Ibid., 235.

21. Ibid., 260. This is a misreading of Caputo, as I explain in my essay "Monstrosity Exhibition," *Expositions: Interdisciplinary Studies in the Humanities* 4 (2010) 114–22.

22. Ibid., 297.

23. Ibid., 296.

24. Ibid., 297.

human belief. If the fundamental conception of atheism is "God is dead," then everything rests on the intentional, conscious and prepositional belief, whether it be belief in God, Nation, Love, or whatever. But if the formula for atheism becomes "God is unconscious," then the real issue is less one's intentional beliefs, but how one's beliefs are structured, which is indirectly by relation to the big Other who believes for me. If there is no big Other, then God is not the Other, but God is strictly speaking unconscious.

How do we have and sustain beliefs if the big Other does not exist? Belief in God becomes the belief in belief, the belief that someone else believes, and that that belief is healthy, meaningful and providential, and wards off nihilism and social anarchy, even if "I" do not have the faith to believe. Žižek says "to be truly an atheist, one has to accept that the big Other doesn't exist, and act upon it."[25] But how can one act according to the nonexistence of the big Other without being or appearing insane? Is not the rejection of the symbolic order a form of madness? At the end of *The Monstrosity of Christ*, Žižek elaborates his ethical materialism that in its rejection of morality necessarily appears monstrous. Discussing characters from the novel *The Notebook* by Agota Kristof, Žižek argues that the world would be a better place if "sentimentality would be replaced by a cold and cruel passion."[26]

This cold and cruel passion is what Lacan calls *jouissance*, which is the problem of the big Other's nonexistence after Seminar VII. *Jouissance* is not pleasure, but pleasure taken to an extreme, and in Seminar VII, so long as the big Other function as a kind of super-ego, the duty to be truthful to one's desire provides a radicalization of the problem Lacan sets up between Kant's absolute moral law and Sade's absolute perversion. The ultimate embodiment of *jouissance* in Seminar VII is Antigone, and it is her rejection of the symbolic order in favor of her commitment to *jouissance* that Lacan admires, even though it leads to her death. But this rejection is too atheistic, in the first sense of "God is dead"; or rather, it is not atheistic enough.

In order to better understand the implications of the rejection of the big Other, and the idea that "God is unconscious," I turn to Lorenzo Chiesa's account of this problem, which he discusses at the end of his excellent book on Lacan, *Subjectivity and Otherness*. According to Chiesa, in Seminar VII "Lacan definitely thinks that the Pauline dialectic between the law and desire . . . can be overcome by a radical transgression carried out by the superegoic law itself."[27] The ethics of psychoanalysis, exemplified by Antigone's

25. Ibid., 299.

26. Ibid., 303.

27. Lorenzo Chiesa, *Subjectivity and Otherness: A Philosophical Reading of Lacan* (Cambridge: MIT Press, 2007) 175.

sublime desire for death, avoids the twin dangers of Kant (Law) and Sade (Pleasure/Lust), even though all three indicate an extremity of *jouissance* that reaches beyond the Symbolic. "Antigone's act is at the root of psychoanalysis,"[28] but Antigone's pure desire is radical destructive, because it is the desire for death as such, and it is still related, albeit negatively, to the big Other.

Chiesa traces the shift of Lacan beyond Seminar VII following his abandonment of the big Other as guarantee of the symbolic order. There is no Other of the Other, which means that the symbolic is ungrounded; it floats. According to Chiesa, "in his late work Lacan progressively acknowledges that 'inherent' *jouissance* is, in a radical sense, the only possible *jouissance*."[29] Inherent *jouissance* is caught up with Lacan's formulation of an *objet petit a*, or a little bit of an other that metonymically symbolizes the subject's desire. The *jouissance* of object *a* "is a remainder of the Real which tears holes in the symbolic structure."[30] We never have access to the Real as Real, even in Lacan's late work, but only as already symbolized and imagined. Here desire and drive converge, and "the drive supplies a partial 'masochistic'satisfaction of unconscious desire precisely through the dissatisfaction of *jouis-sans*," the play on words that indicates that *jouissance* is fundamentally lacking for a subject. The lesson of Lacan's late work, despite his provocative speculations about woman's *jouissance* and God, is that we are all screwed, because we can only achieve very provisional and partial satisfaction by recognizing that we are stuck within the very dialectic of law and love that Lacan attempted to transcend in Seminar VII. Even though the Law has no ground or support, it still functions by means of object *a*, and this lack structures desire in an unavoidable way that constrains the subject even as she possesses limited means of affirming this lack in love. This is very sad, pitiful even, because the acknowledgment that God is unconscious here means that atheism itself is *jouis-sans*, without joy. Just play with your object *a* and your X-Box and get whatever little satisfaction you can, and your atheism can justify your lack of any moral scruples. Is this what Žižek's coldness and cruelty really amounts to?

But there is another possibility, associated with the name of Joyce. As Chiesa explains, in Seminar XXIII Joyce "abolishes the symbol" by means of "'his identification with the *sinthome*' (as the naming of one's Real)."[31] The *sinthome* refers to "the emergence of J (A barred)," which concerns "the *naming* of the Real and the 'marking' of *jouissance*."[32] The A refers to the big

28. Ibid., 176.
29. Ibid., 183.
30. Ibid., 184.
31. Ibid., 188.
32. Ibid.

Other (Autre), which is barred or nonfunctioning, and J (A barred) indicates an overlapping of Real and Imaginary without the Symbolic. The *sinthome* involves the production of one's symptom as symbolic, but it evades and avoids the "Name-of-the-Father." Joyce is paradigmatic of this possibility, because the symbolic does not function normally for him; "his paternal metaphor was defective; it had to supplemented by the writer."[33] For Chiesa the only truly liberating possibility in Lacan's late work, then, is not the mystical embrace of feminine jouissance, but the ability to manifest one's *jouis-sens* by writing it without any paternal support. As Chiesa concludes: "the name 'Joyce' is a 'singular universal': Joyce reaches a substitutive version of the Name-of-the-Father—thus individualized and anti-ideological by definition—precisely by writing his *jouis-sens*."[34]

What does this mean? Chiesa advocates constructing a new Master-Signifier for politics using the name Marx, and this politics would accord with a later Lacanian ethics of psychoanalysis. I will come back to Marx below, but for now let's go back to the Pauline dialectic of law and love. Basically, what if we take the name Paul in the same way as Lacan understands Joyce, as a singular universal? Paul writes the dialectic, and he is able to write the dialectic only because Christ comes to supplement his defective paternal metaphor. Furthermore, the only way to evade or overcome the Pauline dialectic is to repeat Paul, to be a new St. Paul.[35]

Theologically, that means to truly take responsibility for atheism. To become a *sinthome* means to take the place and write from the place where God is unconscious, to becomes one's own father and write and re-write the symbolic. As Lacan says in Seminar XX,

> The Other, the Other as the locus of truth, is the only place, albeit an irreducible place, that we can give to the term 'divine being,' to call him by his name. God (*Dieu*) is the locus where, if you will allow me this wordplay, the *dieu*—the *dieur*—the *dire*, is produced. With a trifling change, the *dire* constitutes *Dieu*. And as long as things are said, the God hypothesis will persist.[36]

---

33. Ibid., 190.

34. Ibid.

35. See the sequel to *The Monstrosity of Christ* featuring the same cast of characters—Creston Davis, John Milbank, and Slavoj Žižek (plus a cameo by Catherine Pickstock): *Paul's New Moment: Continental Philosophy and the Future of Christian Theology* (Grand Rapids: Brazos, 2010).

36. Jacques Lacan, *The Seminar of Jacques Lacan, Book XX: On Feminine Sexuality, the Limits of Love and Knowledge, 1972–1973 (Encore)*, ed. Jacques-Alain Miller, trans. Bruce Fink (New York: Norton, 1998) 45.

God is here identified with the locus of the Other, but where does God come from and how is God produced? From the region where the Real and Imaginary intersect, that is, J (A barred). To simply accept God as the big Other or Name-of-the-Father or guarantee of the symbolic order is to commit idolatry, because it is to reify the symbolic as real. But the "God hypothesis" persists in spite of our atheism, because we are speaking beings, which is why Nietzsche said that we still believe in God because we have faith in language, and why Lacan says that religion will always triumph over psychoanalysis. God is unconscious, and must be written into being as *jouis-sens*, which is the task of a truly radical theology, a theology that would be in and for itself. As Lacan concludes, "that is why, in the end, only theologians can be truly atheistic, namely, those who speak of God."[37]

The question remains, even if we are truly theological atheists, how does the symbolic patriarchal and capitalist order continue to function without the guarantee of the Other? Chiesa suggests, but does not develop, the idea that something like Lacan's reading of Joyce could be possible with Marx, that we could refashion a new Marxist Law. But the problem is that Lacan already realizes that this is impossible in Seminar XVII.

In *Living in the End Times*, Žižek argues that the events of May 1968 in France and elsewhere expressed "the crisis of a certain form of university discourse" and "the rise of a new 'spirit of capitalism.'"[38] Lacan's Seminar XVII, "The Other Side of Psychoanalysis," is given in 1969–1970, during the year following the insurrection of May '68. In this seminar, Lacan elaborates on four radical discourses: the master's discourse, the hysteric's discourse, the analyst's discourse, and finally and most crucially, the university discourse.[39] The university discourse is a discourse of knowledge that is derived from the slave's perspective, as presented in Hegel's famous discussion of the master-slave dialectic in the *Phenomenology of Spirit* and then developed by Marx into a revolutionary proletarianism. Lacan aligns Marx with the slave's perspective and with the creation of a kind of university discourse on knowledge in France and modern Europe.

The master does not want to know how something functions; he only cares that it works. The slave, from Hegel and Marx's perspectives, better understands the master's desires, and "it is clear that the master's desire is the Other's desire, since it's this desire that the slave anticipates."[40] Much

37. Ibid.

38. Slavoj Žižek, *Living in the End Times* (London: Verso, 2010) 355.

39. Jacques Lacan, *The Seminar of Jacques Lacan, Book XVII: The Other Side of Psychoanalysis*, trans. Russell Grigg (New York: Norton, 2007) 20–21.

40. Ibid., 38.

of the seminar concerns the interaction of the master's discourse and the university discourse, in the context of the liberation of revolutionary desire in 1968. The fantasy of university discourse is that it becomes unhinged from the slave's particular perspective, and wants to be "knowledge that speaks all by itself," which is the unconscious.[41] By virtue of the institution of the university as a medium, the "master's knowledge is produced as knowledge that is entirely autonomous with respect to mythical knowledge, and this is what we call science."[42]

So scientific knowledge functions as a universal knowledge at the level of the social unconscious insofar as it perpetuates and mediates the master's knowledge as reflected by the slave. The crisis of the university in 1968 is that this knowledge begins to crumble and fray, due to changing political, economic and environmental conditions, including the first real jolts of a limit on cheap energy. Knowledge has to be reconstructed and resituated, and the university discourse requires a new master to reflect its unconscious knowledge as scientific fact. The result is corporate neo-liberalism, in which as Žižek explains, "the hierarchical Fordist structure of the production process was gradually abandoned and replaced with a network-based form of organization founded on employee initiative and autonomy in the workplace."[43] As Deleuze points out in his "Postscript on the Societies of Control," societies based on discipline transform themselves into societies of control, where regulation and constraint is internalized.[44] This new spirit of capitalism appropriates the liberating energies of autonomy and egalitarianism expressed in the revolts of 1968 and presents itself "as a successful libertarian revolt against the oppressive social organizations of corporate capitalism *and* of 'really existing' socialism."[45] At the same time, money serves less as a marker of production and shifts to one of consumption and financialization of the economy as debt is compounded, beginning at the perimeters of the global economy and gradually spreading inward.

This new situation requires a new kind of knowledge, and a new kind of university, which is the transformation that Lacan is theorizing. Truth begins to fade, as simulation and virtual reality expand. Truth is ultimately impotent, and "the impossible is the real."[46] The effect of truth is the col-

41. Ibid., 70.

42. Ibid., 90.

43. Žižek, *Living in the End Times*, 355–56.

44. See Gilles Deleuze, "Postscript on the Societies of Control," *OCTOBER* 59 (1992) 3–7.

45. Žižek, *Living in the End Times*, 356.

46. Lacan, *SXVII*, 165.

lapsing of knowledge, or at least a specific form of knowledge that must be constantly revised as the process of production of knowledge speeds up. Lacan claims that "what is frightening about truth is what it puts in its place," which is the locus of the Other.[47] As any determinate truth fades, so does the position of the Other, which is seen to be non-existent. Analysis tracks this inexistence of the Other and the transition to another form of knowledge, which is associated with *objet petit a*, the little other. Lacan concludes that "the more your quest is located on the side of truth, the more you uphold the power of the impossibles which are those that I respectively enumerated for you last time—governing, educating, analyzing on occasion. For analysis, in any case, this is obvious."[48]

Lacan's analysis is not obvious to all readers, but I think he is showing how the appeal to the master's discourse remains constant despite the crisis and transformation of the university discourse about truth. This is why he is so skeptical and pessimistic about the movements for liberation and the events of '68 to which Alain Badiou remains faithful as an event even though he recognizes the outcome as the victory of unfettered neo-liberal capitalism.[49] Lacan argues that capitalism is based on a very solidly established master's discourse, which concerns the ability to count surplus *jouissance*, or what Marx calls surplus value. Once surplus value or *jouissance* becomes calculable, "this is where the accumulation of capital begins."[50] Surplus value combines with capital to produce liberal capitalism, and even though we no longer believe in capitalism as such, we still believe in and desire *jouissance*, which insofar as it is countable produces enormous profits for corporations that invest in this *jouissance*.

In a sense, capitalism kills God because the value of money as symbol of surplus *jouissance* replaces God as the highest value in the modern world.[51] With the more recent transition to neo-liberal capitalism, we simply give up the belief in an Other whose Law sustains and maintains the world in its truth, and knowledge is cut loose from the Other to float free, just as currency does after the abandonment of the gold standard by Richard Nixon in 1971. How does this still work? The master's discourse only concerns that it work, not how it works or can be understood. The slave's understanding drives the university's discourse, but it is always

47. Ibid., 187.

48. Ibid.

49. See Alain Badiou, *The Communist Hypothesis*, trans. David Macey and Steve Corcoran (London: Verso, 2010) 44.

50. Lacan, *SXVII*, 177.

51. See Philip Goodchild, *Theology of Money* (Durham: Duke University Press, 2009).

derivative of the master's. The hysteric imagines that she can cut out the master, but this is an illusion. The analyst can comprehend what is going on, but he cannot change it, because religion or capitalism under the sign of the master will always triumph.

Or will it? Yes and no, because everything turns on the little *a*. After making his point about the countability of surplus *jouissance*, Lacan asks, "Don't you feel, in relation to what I said before on the impotence of conjoining surplus value with the master's truth, that ground is being won here?"[52] On the one hand, Lacan is absolutely pessimistic about the revolutionary desire for justice that fuels the events of May '68. These revolutionaries are unable to recognize what is really going on, and this desire miscarries, resulting in a brutal neoliberalism sugar-coated in a jargon of liberating authenticity. On the other hand, this unavoidable miscarriage itself is significant for Lacan, and there is a power of psychoanalysis to understand it. Early in the Seminar, Lacan "state[s] the psychoanalyst's position in the following terms. I have said that it is substantially made from the object *a*."[53] Toward the end of the Seminar, he claims that "what is happening here, as the *a*, the *a* in living form, miscarriage that it is, displays the fact that it is an effect of language."[54] The *objet petit a* is an effect of language that miscarries. This means that "there is in every case a level at which things do not work out."[55] This little *a* as a sign of things not working out is our only hope, because the movement of *a* is entropic.

At a certain moment in time, *a* shakes free from A. The other is released from the Other. This shift is not liberating, because capitalism works even more efficiently without the guarantee of the Other, and the loss of the Other provokes a severe reaction on the part of neo-fundamentalist religions. The *a* circulates in and as capital, and it is completely extensive with late modern corporate capitalism. But that does not mean that there is no intensity. The movement of *a* does not stop, and its circulation does not maintain a stable equilibrium. Lacan understands this situation from the standpoint of speech and language, but that does not mean that these effects are not real. Everything is based on the notion of repetition, the repetition of *a*. According to Lacan, "the signifier becomes articulated, therefore, by representing a subject for another signifier. This is our starting point for giving meaning to this inaugural repetition that is repetition directed

52. Lacan, *SXVII*, 177.
53. Ibid., 42.
54. Ibid., 178.
55. Ibid.

at *jouissance*."[56] This inaugural repetition is the repetition of the other, *a*, which is masked by the repetition of the same, a repetition of identity that is grounded in and by the non-existent Other.

Deleuze calls inaugural repetition a repetition of difference in *Difference and Repetition*. In this inaugural repetition Lacan explains that "there is a loss of *jouissance*. And it is in the place of this loss introduced by repetition that we see the function of the lost object emerge, of what I am calling the *a*. What does this impose on us? If not this formula that at the most elementary level, that of the imposition of the imposition of the unary trait, knowledge at work produces, let's say, an entropy."[57]

Entropy is the result of repetition, but it is not simply a loss. We transpose what Deleuze calls the transcendental illusion of entropy onto existence when we signify, because signification appears to be extensive with reality. But this is too symbolic, for both Deleuze and Lacan. The energy that produces *a* as an effect is an intensive power that makes differences.

So we are misled to think that the liberation of *a* from the clutches of *A* will save us. Here is another form of ideology, a triumph of what Lacan calls religion. But that is not the last word of Lacan, nor is it the only form of theology, even if that is what is most evident. He says:

> If it's one's wish that something turn—of course, ultimately, no one can ever turn, as I have emphasized enough—it is certainly not by being progressive, it is simply because it can't prevent itself from turning. If it doesn't turn, it will grind away, there where things raise questions, that is, at the level of putting something into place that can be written as *a*.[58]

We cannot make it turn for our purposes in a progressive direction, away from exploitation and injustice, but nonetheless it turns and grinds in its entropy. This entropy appears entropic, that is, as a loss of order, only if we view it solely from the standpoint of human language and signification. But thermodynamics is not just loss of order as heat or information; it is the most efficient means of gradient reduction that produces complexity in systems not at equilibrium when sustained by energy flows.

What Lacan calls *a* is the pivotal position from which to analyze contemporary capitalism, and it is this *a* that drives French theory in the late 1960s and 1970s.[59] As with so many elements of French post-structuralism,

56. Ibid., 48.
57. Ibid.
58. Ibid., 179.
59. The change in Derrida's *différance* is made by a little *a*.

Heidegger opens the way, as Catherine Malabou explains in her study *The Heidegger Change*. In her provocative and original interpretation of Heidegger, Malabou claims that his philosophy produces the fantastic as an effect of the real by means of change, exchange, transformation or metamorphosis. She tracks the central "triad of change" encapsulated in three German terms—*Wandel*, *Wandlung*, and *Verwandlung*—as they animate Heidegger's work.[60] In the middle of this extraordinary book, Malabou fastens on what Heidegger calls the "little," or in French, *le petit(e)*. Fantastic change happens not via the large or colossal, but through the little, and "ultra-metaphysical thought is coming to grips with this little."[61]

The little is of course the *a*, although Malabou does not make this connection to Lacan explicit. She does, however, draw a connection from Heidegger to Deleuze and Guattari, who are also theorists of the little who produce the fantastic in philosophy as an effect of the real. According to Malabou, "there is, in effect, something entirely little in and for philosophy, an entirely little world within the world; as Deleuze and Guattari say with such pertinence and lucidity, there is a becoming minor of sense."[62] So what if we take this little in other than literal terms? The little *a* is not simply a microscopic thing, but it is an almost imperceptible change wrought by signification, energy and entropy that distorts our world just the slightest bit. And what if, underneath the superficial polemics between Deleuze and Guattari and Lacan, they are engaged in a similar project in the 1970s, that is, theorizing the little *a*? The minor of Deleuze and Guattari is the *petit* of *a*, and Deleuze and Guattari conduct an experiment in philosophy with *Capitalism and Schizophrenia* to see whether or not they can shake *a* free from capitalism. Lacan is ultimately right; they cannot. But despite this inability to liberate *a*, it does not simply stay fixed. It continues to turn, move and grind. This *a* has to be understood in energetic, economic, political and ecological terms, not simply linguistic and psychoanalytic.

We are running out of energy flows to sustain our post-industrial way of life, especially the cheap energy provided by the extraction of fossil fuels. This entropy will produce destruction but it will also liberate new energies and provide unforeseen structures of organization that may not be human. Earth is sustained by thermodynamic processes of nuclear radiation, generating magnetism and electricity that in turn allow for liquid water and life, most importantly bacteria. These entropic processes do not begin on earth,

60. Catherine Malabou, *The Heidegger Change: On the Fantastic in Philosophy*, trans. Peter Skafish (Albany: State University of New York Press, 2011) 2.

61. Ibid., 180.

62. Ibid., 183.

but are the result of dissipative processes and explosions of stars. That is the long view, and our lives are very short in relation to that of the earth, the sun and the universe. But this energy is also a kind of theology for itself, even if it is not *for* us. We are also emergent object(s) *a*.

So psychoanalysis is both a form of reflection and a form of life, and it will not triumph. But it is not nothing, and the insights of psychoanalysis are incredibly valuable. Lacan says provocatively that "if there is any chance of grasping something called the real, it is nowhere other than on the blackboard."[63] I am suggesting that psychoanalysis does not uncover the truth of theology, but it is itself a complex form of theology in and for itself that is worked out in thought, speech and writing, not simply in the streets.

Lacan is right. Psychoanalysis as theology in and for itself will not triumph. Theology in itself will always triumph as ideology, religion, or as the master's will to power. Theology for itself will not triumph, but it will continue as entropic intensity. It will survive, even if psychoanalysis does not. To paraphrase Mallarmé's famous poem, theology as a throw of the dice will never abolish the chance of its being otherwise, because *a* is always other and because it is an effect of entropic intensity.[64]

63. Lacan, *SXVII*, 151.

64. See Quentin Meillassoux's rereading of this poem in *The Number and the Siren: A Decipherment of Mallarmé's Coup de dés*, trans. Robin Mackay (Falmouth: Urbanomic, 2012). This is a powerful and provocative interpretation, and Meillassoux concludes that the *Coup de dés* is a "christic crystallization of Chance. As Christal of Nothing- ness." As that which "makes no longer *being*, but the *perhaps*, the first task—the task to come—of thinkers and poets" (222). I do not agree, however, on the necessity of number, that "Number (and it alone) escapes from the effects of Chance" (165).

Contributors

Tina Beattie is the Director of the Digby Stuart Research Centre for Catholic Studies at Roehampton University. Her doctoral research was on the theology and symbolism of the Virgin Mary, drawing on the psycho-linguistic theory of Luce Irigaray as a resource for the analysis of Christian writings on Mary and Eve in the early church and in recent Roman Catholic theology. Her thesis formed the basis of her book *God's Mother, Eve's Advocate* (2002). Tina is a regular contributor to *The Tablet* and to the online journal *Open Democracy*.

Lorenzo Chiesa is Professor of European Thought at the University of Kent (UK) and one of the initiators of the Materialism and Dialectics collective. His publications include *Subjectivity and Otherness: A Philosophical Reading of Lacan* (2007) and *The Italian Difference* (2009) (coedited with Alberto Toscano). More recently, he edited *Italian Thought Today: Bio-economy, Human Nature, Christianity* (2011), *Lacan and Philosophy: The New Generation* (special issue of *JEP European Journal of Psychoanalysis*, 2012), and translated Giorgio Agamben's *The Kingdom and the Glory* (2011). He is currently completing two new volumes: *For Lacan: Science, Logic, Politics* (2013) and *Der Möglichkeitspunkt der Freiheitsfunktion. Essays zu Politik, Ästhetik und Psychoanalyse* (2012).

Clayton Crockett is Associate Professor and Director of Religious Studies at the University of Central Arkansas. He is the author of four books, including *Radical Political Theology: Religion and Politics after Liberalism* (2011), and most recently *Deleuze Beyond Badiou: Ontology, Multiplicity and Event* (2013). He has also edited or coedited a number of books, including (with Slavoj Žižek and Creston Davis) *Hegel and the Infinite: Religion, Politics and Dialectic* (2011).

Mario D'Amato is an Associate Professor in the Department of Philosophy and Religion at Rollins College. His area of research is in Buddhist philosophy, with a special focus on the translation, interpretation, and analysis of Sanskrit Buddhist doctrinal texts from the Yogācāra school of Buddhist philosophy. He published a study and annotated translation of the fourth-century CE Buddhist treatise *Distinguishing the Middle from the Extremes* (2012), the coedited volume *Pointing at the Moon: Buddhism, Logic, Analytic Philosophy* (2009), as well as articles on Buddhist thought in the *Journal of the International Association of Buddhist Studies, Journal of Indian Philosophy, Journal for Cultural and Religious Theory, Semiotica,* and other journals. He also regularly teaches a course on Psychoanalysis and Religion.

Creston Davis is the director of the The Global Center for Advanced Studies and Professor of Philosophy at the Institute of Social Sciences and Humanities. He has coedited or coauthored a number of books, and he is an editor of the book series Insurrections: Critical Studies of Religion, Politics, and Culture, for Columbia University Press.

Adrian Johnston is a Professor in the Department of Philosophy at the University of New Mexico at Albuquerque and an Assistant Teaching Analyst at the Emory Psychoanalytic Institute in Atlanta. He is the author of *Time Driven: Metapsychology and the Splitting of the Drive* (2005), *Žižek's Ontology: A Transcendental Materialist Theory of Subjectivity* (2008), and *Badiou, Žižek, and Political Transformations: The Cadence of Change* (2009), all published by Northwestern University Press. He has three books forthcoming: *Self and Emotional Life: Merging Philosophy, Psychoanalysis, and Neurobiology* (coauthored with Catherine Malabou); *Adventures in Transcendental Materialism: Dialogues with Contemporary Thinkers;* and *The Outcome of Contemporary French Philosophy: Prolegomena to Any Future Materialism, Volume One* (the first installment of a trilogy forthcoming from Northwestern University Press).

Katerina Kolozova is Director of the Institute in Social Sciences and Humanities-Skopje and a Professor of philosophy, sociological theory and gender studies at the University American College-Skopje. She is also a Visiting Professor at several universities in the former Yugoslavia and Bulgaria (the State University of Skopje, University of Sarajevo, University of Belgrade, and University of Sofia, as well as at the Faculty of Media and Communications of Belgrade). In 2009, Kolozova was a visiting scholar at the Department of Rhetoric (Program of Critical Theory) at the University of California, Berkeley. Kolozova is the author of *The Lived*

Revolution: Solidarity with the Body in Pain as the New Political Universal (2010), *The Real and "I": On the Limit and the Self* (2006), *The Crisis of the Subject* (with Judith Butler and Zarko Trajanoski, 2002), *The Death and the Greeks: On Tragic Concepts of Death from Antiquity to Modernity* (2000), and editor of a number of books from the fields of gender studies and feminist theory, including one with Svetlana Slapshak and Jelisaveta Blagojevic: *Gender and Identity: Theories from/on Southeastern Europe* (2006). She is also the editor in chief of the *Journal in Politics, Gender and Culture Identities*, a member of the editorial board of Punctum Books, and a member of the Non-Philosophical Society (ONPHI) and AtGender (The European Network for Feminist and Gender Studies).

Thomas Lynch is a PhD student at Durham University and a lecturer at the University of Roehampton. His work focuses on the role of religion in the philosophy of Hegel, liberation theology, and non-theistic forms of theology.

Marcus Pound is a Lecturer in Catholic Studies, and Assistant Director of the Centre for Catholic Studies, Durham University. He has taught at Bristol University, Birkbeck College London, and Nottingham University, and has published widely on Lacan, Žižek, and theology, including *Theology, Psychoanalysis and Trauma* (2007), and *Žižek: A (Very) Critical Introduction* (2008).

Carl Raschke is Professor of Religious Studies at the University of Denver, specializing in Continental philosophy, the philosophy of religion, and the theory of religion. He is an internationally known writer and academic, who has authored numerous books and hundreds of articles on topics ranging from postmodernism to popular religion and culture to technology and society. His latest book, titled *The Revolution in Religious Theory: Toward a Semiotics of the Event* (2012) , looks at the ways in which major trends in Continental philosophy over the past two decades have radically altered how we understand what we call "religion" in general. His previous two books—*GloboChrist* (2008) and *The Next Reformation* (2004)—examine the most recent trends and in paths of transformations at an international level in contemporary Christianity.

Kenneth Reinhard is Associate Professor of English at the University of California, Los Angeles. He is coauthor of *The Neighbor: Three Inquiries in Political Theology* (2006) and *After Oedipus: Shakespeare in Psychoanalysis* (1993), and author of *The Ethics of the Neighbor in Religion* (forthcoming).

Noëlle Vahanian is Associate Professor of Religion and Philosophy at Lebanon Valley College, a small liberal arts college in central Pennsylvania. She is the author of *Language, Desire, and Theology: A Genealogy of the Will to Speak* (2003). Her forthcoming book is titled *The Rebellious No: Variations on a Secular Theology of Language.*

Slavoj Žižek is "the most dangerous philosopher of the West." His most recent books include *Less Than Nothing: Hegel and the Shadow of Dialectical Materialism* and *The Year of Dreaming Dangerously*, both published in 2012.

Bibliography

Aeschylus. *Eumenides*. Edited by Alan H. Sommerstein. Cambridge: Cambridge University Press, 1989.

———. *Eumenides*. Translated by Ian Johnston. http://records.viu.ca/~johnstoi/aeschylus/oresteiatofc.htm.

Alexander, Franz. "Buddhistic Training as an Artificial Catatonia." *The Psychoanalytic Review* 18.2 (1931) 129–45.

Althusser, Louis. "Ideology and Ideological State Apparatuses." In *Lenin and Philosophy, and Other Essays*, translated by Ben Brewster, 126–86. New York: Monthly Review Press, 1971.

Aristide, Jean-Bertrand. *In the Parish of the Poor: Writings from Haiti*. Translated by Amy Wilentz. Maryknoll, NY: Orbis, 1990.

Badiou, Alain. *Being and Event*. Translated by Oliver Feltham. London: Continuum, 2005.

———. *Ethics: An Essay on the Understanding of Evil*. Translated by Peter Hallward. London: Verso, 2001.

———. *Theory of the Subject*. Translated by Bruno Bosteels. London: Continuum, 2009.

Becker, Ernest. *The Denial of Death*. New York: Free Press, 1973.

Blanchot, Maurice. *The Infinite Conversation*. Translated by Susan Hanson. Minneapolis: University of Minnesota Press, 1993.

———. *The Step Not Beyond*. Translated by Lycette Nelson. Albany: State University of New York Press, 1992.

Bloch, Ernst. *Atheism in Christianity: The Religion of the Exodus and the Kingdom*. Translated by J. T. Swann. 2nd ed. London: Verso, 2009.

———. *The Principle of Hope*. Vol. 1. Translated by Neville Plaice, Stephen Plaice, and Paul Knight. Cambridge: MIT Press, 1995.

———. *The Spirit of Utopia*. Translated by Anthony A. Nassar. Stanford: Stanford University Press, 2000.

Boer, Roland. *Criticism of Heaven: On Marxism and Theology*. Chicago: Haymarket, 2009.

Boff, Leonardo, and Clodovis Boff. *Introducing Liberation Theology*. Maryknoll, NY: Orbis, 1996.

Bracher, Mark. "On the Psychological and Social Functions of Language: Lacan's Theory of the Four Discourses." In *Lacanian Theory of Discourse: Subject, Structure and*

Society, edited by Mark Bracher et al., 107–28. New York: New York University Press, 1994.

Brown, Norman O. *Life Against Death: The Psychoanalytical Meaning of History*. Middletown: Wesleyan University Press, 1959.

Butler, Judith. "The Pleasures of Repetition." In *Pleasure Beyond the Pleasure Principle: The Role of Affect in Motivation, Development, and Adaptation*, edited by Robert A. Glick and Stanley Bone, 259–75. New Haven: Yale University Press, 1990.

———. *Precarious Life: The Power of Mourning and Violence*. London: Verso, 2006.

———. *Psychic Life of Power: Theories in Subjection*. Stanford: Stanford University Press, 1997.

———. *Undoing Gender*. New York: Routledge, 2004.

Chiesa, Lorenzo, and Alberto Toscano. "Ethics and Capital, *Ex Nihilo*." *Umbr(a): A Journal of the Unconscious: The Dark God* (2005) 9–25.

Clément, Catherine. *The Lives and Legends of Jacques Lacan*. Translated by Arthur Goldhammer. New York: Columbia University Press, 1983.

Congregation for the Doctrine of the Faith. "Instruction on Certain Aspects of the 'Theology of Liberation.'" In *Liberation Theology: A Documentary History*, edited by Alfred T. Hennelly, 393–414. Maryknoll, NY: Orbis, 1990.

———. "10 Observations on the Theology of Gustavo Gutiérrez." In *Liberation Theology: A Documentary History*, edited by Alfred T. Hennelly. Maryknoll, NY: Orbis, 1990.

Conze, Edward. *Buddhist Thought in India*. Ann Arbor: University of Michigan Press, 1962.

Crownfield, David. "Extraduction." In *Lacan and Theological Discourse*, edited by Edith Wyschogrod, David Crownfield, and Carl A. Raschke, 161–69. Albany: State University of New York Press, 1989.

———. "Summary of Chapter 1." In *Lacan and Theological Discourse*, edited by Edith Wyschogrod, David Crownfield, and Carl A. Raschke, 35–38. Albany: State University of New York Press, 1989.

D'Amato, Mario. "Buddhism, Apophasis, Truth." *Journal for Cultural and Religious Theory* 9.2 (2008) 17–29.

———. "The Semiotics of Signlessness: A Buddhist Doctrine of Signs." *Semiotica* 147.1 (2003) 185–207.

———. "Why the Buddha Never Uttered a Word." In *Pointing at the Moon: Buddhism, Logic, Analytic Philosophy*, edited by Mario D'Amato, Jay L. Garfield, and Tom J. F. Tillemans, 41–55. New York: Oxford University Press, 2009.

Deleuze, Gilles. *Expressionism in Philosophy: Spinoza*. Translated by Martin Joughin. New York: Zone, 1990.

Derrida, Jacques. *Aporias*. Translated by Thomas Dutoit. Stanford: Stanford University Press, 1993.

———. *Specters of Marx: The State of Debt, the Work of Mourning, and the New International*. Translated by Peggy Kamuf. New York: Routledge, 1994.

Descartes, René. *Meditations on First Philosophy*. Translated by Donald A. Cress. Indianapolis: Hackett, 1993.

Dolar, Mladen. "At First Sight." In *Gaze and Voice as Love Objects*, edited by Renata Salecl and Slavoj Žižek, 129–53. Durham: Duke University Press, 1996.

Dostoevsky, Fyodor. *Notes from Underground*. Translated by Richard Pevear and Larissa Volokhonsky. New York: Vintage, 1993.

————. *Notes From Underground and The Double*. Translated by Ronald Wilks and Robert Louis Jackson. New York: Penguin Classics, 2009.

Epstein, Mark. *Thoughts Without a Thinker: Psychotherapy from a Buddhist Perspective*. New York: Basic Books, 1995.

————. "Beyond the Oceanic Feeling: Psychoanalytic Study of Buddhist Meditation." In *The Couch and the Tree: Dialogues in Psychoanalysis and Buddhism*, edited by Anthony Molino, 119–30. New York: North Point, 1998.

Fink, Bruce. *A Clinical Introduction to Lacanian Psychoanalysis: Theory and Technique*. Cambridge: Harvard University Press, 1997.

————. *The Lacanian Subject: Between Language and Jouissance*. Princeton: Princeton University Press, 1995.

Freud, Sigmund. "Overview of the Transference Neuroses." In *A Phylogenetic Fantasy: Overview of the Transference Neuroses*, edited by Ilse Grubrich-Simitis, translated by Axel Hoffer and Peter T. Hoffer, 5–20. Cambridge: Belknap Press of Harvard University Press, 1987.

Freud, Sigmund. *The Standard Edition of the Complete Psychological Works of Sigmund Freud*. Edited by James Strachey, in collaboration with Anna Freud, assisted by Alix Strachey and Alan Tyson. London: Hogarth, 1957–1974.

————. "Beyond the Pleasure Principle." In *SE 18:1–64*.

————. *The Future of an Illusion*. In *SE 21:1–56*.

————. "Mourning and Melancholia." In *SE 14:237–58*.

————. *New Introductory Lectures on Psycho-Analysis*. In *SE 22:1–182*.

————. "On Narcissism: An Introduction." In *SE 14:67–102*.

————. "On Transience." In *SE 14:303–7*.

————. *Project for a Scientific Psychology*. In *SE 1:281–397*.

————. "Recommendations to Physicians Practicing Psycho-Analysis." *SE 12:109–20*.

————. "Thoughts for the Times on War and Death." In *SE 14:273–302*.

————. *Totem and Taboo*. In *SE 13:1–162*.

————. "The Uncanny." In *SE 17:217–56*.

————. "The Unconscious." In *SE 14:159–215*.

Green, André. "L'originaire dans la psychanalyse." In *La diachronie en psychanalyse*, 41–85. Paris: Les Éditions de Minuit, 2000.

Gutiérrez, Gustavo. *A Theology of Liberation: History, Politics, and Salvation*. London: SCM, 2001.

Hägglund, Martin. "Chronolibidinal Reading: Deconstruction and Psychoanalysis." *The New Centennial Review* 9 (2009) 1–43.

————. *Radical Atheism: Derrida and the Time of Life*. Stanford: Stanford University Press, 2008.

Hallward, Peter. *Damming the Flood: Haiti, Aristide, and the Politics of Containment*. London: Verso, 2007.

————. "'One Step at a Time': An Interview with Jean-Bertrand Aristide." In *Damming the Flood: Haiti, Aristide, and the Politics of Containment*, 317–45. London: Verso, 2007.

Hanly, Charles. "Ego Ideal and Ideal Ego." *International Journal of Psychoanalysis* 65 (1984) 253–61.

Haraway, Donna. "Ecce Homo, Ain't (Ar'n't) I a Woman, and Inappropriate/d Others: The Human in a Post-humanist Landscape." In *Feminists Theorize the Political*, edited by Judith Butler and Joan Scott, 86–100. New York: Routledge, 1992.

————. *Primate Visions: Gender, Race, and Nature in the World of Modern Science*. New York: Routledge, 1989.

Hegel, G. W. F. *Lectures on the Philosophy of Religion: The Lectures of 1827*. Edited by Peter C. Hodgson. Translated by R. F. Brown, Peter C. Hodgson, and J. M. Stewart, with H. S. Harris. Berkeley: University of California Press, 1988.

————. *Logic: Part One of the Encyclopedia of Philosophical Sciences*. Translated by William Wallace. Oxford: Oxford University Press, 1975.

Heidegger, Martin. *Being and Time*. Translated by John Macquarrie and Edward Robinson. New York: Harper, 1962.

Hennelly, Alfred T, ed. *Liberation Theology: A Documentary History*. Maryknoll, NY: Orbis, 1990.

Hobbes, Thomas. *Leviathan*. Edited by C. B. Macpherson. New York: Viking Penguin, 1985.

Horney, Karen. *Our Inner Conflicts: A Constructive Theory of Neurosis*. New York: Norton, 1945.

International Theological Commission. "Theology Today: Perspectives, Principles, and Criteria." *Origins: CNS Documentary Service* 41.40 (2012) 641–60.

Johnston, Adrian. "A Blast from the Future: Freud, Lacan, Marcuse, and Snapping the Threads of the Past." *Umbr(a): A Journal of the Unconscious: Utopia* (2008) 67–84.

————. "Conflicted Matter: Jacques Lacan and the Challenge of Secularizing Materialism." *Pli: The Warwick Journal of Philosophy* 19 (2008) 166–88.

————. "Hume's Revenge: À Dieu, Meillassoux?" In *The Speculative Turn: Continental Materialism and Realism*, edited by Levi Bryant, Nick Srnicek, and Graham Harman, 92–113. Victoria: re.press, 2011.

————. "Intimations of Freudian Mortality: The Enigma of Sexuality and the Constitutive Blind Spots of Freud's Self-Analysis." *Journal for Lacanian Studies* 3 (2005) 222–46.

————. "Nothing Is Not Always No-One: (a)Voiding Love." *Filozofski Vestnik: The Nothing(ness)/Le rien/Das Nichts*, edited by Alenka Zupančič, 26.2 (2005) 67–81.

————. "Sigmund Freud." In vol. 3 of *The History of Continental Philosophy*, edited by Keith Ansell Pearson. Chesham, UK: Acumen, 2009.

————. *Time Driven: Metapsychology and the Splitting of the Drive*. Evanston: Northwestern University Press, 2005.

————. "The Vicious Circle of the Super-Ego: The Pathological Trap of Guilt and the Beginning of Ethics." *Psychoanalytic Studies* 3.3 (2001) 411–24.

————. *Žižek's Ontology: A Transcendental Materialist Theory of Subjectivity*. Evanston: Northwestern University Press, 2008.

Kant, Immanuel. *Anthropology from a Pragmatic Point of View*. Translated by Victor Lyle Dowdell. Carbondale: Southern Illinois University Press, 1978.

Kee, Alistair. *Marx and the Failure of Liberation Theology*. London: SCM, 1990.

Kotsko, Adam. "Žižek's Work since *The Parallax View*." *IJŽS Special Issue: Žižek's Theology* 4.4 (2010). http:// Žizekstudies.org/index.php/ijzs/article/view/272/365

Lacan, Jacques. "Aggressiveness in Psychoanalysis." In *Écrits: The First Complete Edition in English*, translated by Bruce Fink, 82–101. New York: Norton, 2006.

————. "Aristotle's Dream." Translated by Lorenzo Chiesa. *Angelaki: Journal of the Theoretical Humanities* 11.3 (2006) 83–84.

————. "Desire and the Interpretation of Desire in *Hamlet*." Edited by Jacques-Alain Miller. Translated by James Hulbert. *Yale French Studies* 55/56 (1977) 11–52.

———. "The Direction of the Treatment and the Principles of Its Power." In *Écrits: The First Complete Edition in English*, translated by Bruce Fink, 489–542. New York: Norton, 2006.

———. "Kant with Sade." In *Écrits: The First Complete Edition in English*, translated by Bruce Fink, 645–68. New York: Norton, 2006.

———. "*L'étourdit.*" In *Autres écrits*, edited by Jacques-Alain Miller, 449–95. Paris: Éditions du Seuil, 2001.

———. "*Le symbolique, le imaginaire et le réel.*" In *Des noms-du-père*, edited by Jacques-Alain Miller, 9–63. Paris: Éditions du Seuil, 2005.

———. "*Le triomphe de la religion.*" In *Le triomphe de la religion précédé de Discours aux catholiques*, edited by Jacques-Alain Miller, 67–102. Paris: Éditions du Seuil, 2005.

———. "The Mirror Stage as Formative of the *I* Function as Revealed in Psychoanalytic Experience." In *Écrits: The First Complete Edition in English*, translated by Bruce Fink, 75–81. New York: Norton, 2006.

———. "On a Question Prior to Any Possible Treatment of Psychosis." In *Écrits: The First Complete Edition in English*, translated by Bruce Fink, 445–88. New York: Norton, 2006.

———. "Position of the Unconscious." In *Écrits: The First Complete Edition in English*, translated by Bruce Fink, 703–21. New York: Norton, 2006.

———. "*Radiophonie.*" In *Autres écrits*, edited by Jacques-Alain Miller, 403–47. Paris: Éditions du Seuil, 2001.

———. "The Signification of the Phallus." In *Écrits: The First Complete Edition in English*, translated by Bruce Fink, 575–84. New York: Norton, 2006.

———. "The Subversion of the Subject and the Dialectic of Desire in the Freudian Unconscious." In *Écrits: The First Complete Edition in English*, translated by Bruce Fink, 671–702. New York: Norton, 2006.

Lacan, Jacques, The Seminars:

———. *The Seminar of Jacques Lacan, Book II: The Ego in Freud's Theory and in the Technique of Psychoanalysis, 1954–1955*. Edited by Jacques-Alain Miller. Translated by Sylvana Tomaselli. New York: Norton, 1988.

———. *The Seminar of Jacques Lacan, Book III: The Psychoses, 1955–1956*. Edited by Jacques-Alain Miller. Translated by Russell Grigg. New York: Norton, 1993.

———. *Le Séminaire de Jacques Lacan, Livre IV: La relation d'objet, 1956–1957*. Edited by Jacques-Alain Miller. Paris: Éditions du Seuil, 1994.

———. *Le Séminaire de Jacques Lacan, Livre V: Les formations de l'inconscient, 1957–1958*. Edited by Jacques-Alain Miller. Paris: Éditions du Seuil, 1998.

———. *Le Séminaire de Jacques Lacan, Livre VI: Le désir et son interprétation, 1958–1959*. Unpublished typescript.

———. *The Seminar of Jacques Lacan, Book VII: The Ethics of Psychoanalysis, 1959–1960*. Edited by Jacques-Alain Miller. Translated by Dennis Porter. New York: Norton, 1992.

———. *Le Séminaire de Jacques Lacan, Livre VIII: Le transfert, 1960–1961*. Edited by Jacques-Alain Miller. 2nd corrected ed. Paris: Éditions du Seuil, 2001.

———. *Le Séminaire de Jacques Lacan, Livre IX: L'identification, 1961–1962*. Unpublished typescript.

———. *Le Séminaire de Jacques Lacan, Livre X: L'angoisse, 1962–1963*. Edited by Jacques-Alain Miller. Paris: Éditions du Seuil, 2004.

_____. *The Seminar of Jacques Lacan, Book XI: The Four Fundamental Concepts of Psychoanalysis, 1964*. Edited by Jacques-Alain Miller. Translated by Alan Sheridan. New York: Norton, 1977.

_____. *Le Séminaire de Jacques Lacan, Livre XIII: L'objet de la psychanalyse, 1965–1966*. Unpublished typescript.

_____. *Le Séminaire de Jacques Lacan, Livre XIV: La logique du fantasme, 1966–1967*. Unpublished typescript.

_____. *The Seminar of Jacques Lacan, Book XIV: Logic of Phantasy*. Translated by Cormac Gallagher. Unpublished manuscript/

_____. *Le Séminaire de Jacques Lacan, Livre XV: L'acte psychanalytique, 1967–1968*. Unpublished typescript.

_____. *Le Séminaire de Jacques Lacan, Livre XVI: D'un Autre à l'autre, 1968–1969*. Edited by Jacques-Alain Miller. Paris: Éditions du Seuil, 2006.

_____. *Le Séminaire de Jacques Lacan, Livre XVII: L'envers de la psychanalyse, 1969–1970*. Edited by Jacques-Alain Miller. Paris: Éditions du Seuil, 1991.

_____. *The Seminar of Jacques Lacan, Book XVII: The Other Side of Psychoanalysis, 1969–1970*. Edited by Jacques-Alain Miller. Translated by Russell Grigg. New York: Norton, 2007.

_____. *Le Séminaire de Jacques Lacan, Livre XVIII: D'un discours qui ne serait pas du semblant, 1971*. Edited by Jacques-Alain Miller. Paris: Éditions du Seuil, 2007.

_____. *Le Séminaire de Jacques Lacan, Livre XIX: . . . ou pire, 1971–1972*. Unpublished typescript.

_____. *Le Séminaire de Jacques Lacan, Livre XIX: Le savoir du psychanalyste, 1971–1972*. Unpublished typescript.

_____. *The Seminar of Jacques Lacan, Book XX: Encore, 1972–1973*. Edited by Jacques-Alain Miller. Translated by Bruce Fink. New York: Norton, 1998.

_____. *Le Séminaire de Jacques Lacan, Livre XXI: Les non-dupes errent, 1973–1974*. Unpublished typescript.

_____. *Le Séminaire de Jacques Lacan, Livre XXII: R.S.I., 1974–1975*. Unpublished typescript.

_____. *Le Séminaire de Jacques Lacan, Livre XXIII: Le sinthome, 1975–1976*. Edited by Jacques-Alain Miller. Paris: Éditions du Seuil, 2005.

_____. *Le Séminaire de Jacques Lacan, Livre XXV: Le moment de conclure, 1977–1978*. Unpublished typescript.

La Rochefoucauld, François, duc de. *Maxims*. Translated by Leonard Tancock. New York: Penguin, 1959.

Laplanche, Jean, and Jean-Bertrand Pontalis. "Fantasy and the Origins of Sexuality." In *Formations of Fantasy*, edited by Victor Burgin, James Donald, and Cora Kaplan, 5–34. New York: Methuen, 1986.

Laruelle, François. *Introduction au non-marxisme*. Paris: Presses Universitaires de France, 2000.

_____. *Philosophie et non-philosophie*. Brussels: Pierre Mardaga, 1989.

Libânio, João Batista. "Hope, Utopia, Resurrection." In *Mysterium Liberationis: Fundamental Concepts of Liberation Theology*, edited by Ignacio Ellacuría and Jon Sobrino, 716–27. Maryknoll, NY: Orbis, 1993.

Macey, David. *Lacan in Contexts*. London: Verso, 1988.

Mejido Costoya, Manuel Jésus. "Beyond the Postmodern Condition, or the Turn to Psychoanalysis." In *Latin American Liberation Theology: The Next Generation*, edited by Ivan Petrella, 119–46. Maryknoll, NY: Orbis, 2005.

——. "Theology, Crisis and Knowledge-Constitutive Interests, or Towards a Social Theoretical Interpretation of Theological Knowledge." *Social Compass* 51. 3 (2004) 381–401.

Milbank, John. "The Double Glory, or Paradox Versus Dialectics." In *The Monstrosity of Christ: Paradox or Dialectic?*, by Slavoj Žižek and John Milbank. Cambridge: MIT Press, 2009.

——. *Theology and Social Theory: Beyond Secular Reason*. 2nd ed. London: Wiley-Blackwell, 2005.

Molino, Anthony. "Zen, Lacan, and the Alien Ego." In *The Couch and the Tree: Dialogues in Psychoanalysis and Buddhism*, edited by Anthony Molino, 290–304. New York: North Point, 1998.

——, ed. *The Couch and the Tree: Dialogues in Psychoanalysis and Buddhism*. New York: North Point, 1998.

Moncayo, Raul. "The Finger Pointing at the Moon: Zen Practice and the Practice of Lacanian Psychoanalysis." In *Psychoanalysis and Buddhism: An Unfolding Dialogue*, edited by Jeremy D. Safran, 331–63. Boston: Wisdom, 2003.

——. "True Subject Is No-subject: The Real, Imaginary, and Symbolic in Psychoanalysis and Zen Buddhism." *Psychoanalysis and Contemporary Thought* 21 (1998) 383–422.

Muller, John P. "Psychosis and Mourning in Lacan's *Hamlet.*" *New Literary History* 12.1 (1980) 147–65.

Oliveros, Roberto. "History of the Theology of Liberation." In *Mysterium Liberationis: Fundamental Concepts of Liberation Theology*, edited by Ignacio Ellacuría and Jon Sobrino, 3–32. Maryknoll, NY: Orbis, 1993.

O'Regan, Cyril. "Žižek and Milbank and the Hegelian Death of God." *Modern Theology* 26.2 (2010) 278–86.

Parker, Robert. *Miasma*. Oxford: Clarendon, 1983.

Petrella, Ivan, ed. *Latin American Liberation Theology: The Next Generation*. Maryknoll, NY: Orbis, 2005.

Pluth, Ed. *Signifiers and Acts*. Albany: State University of New York Press, 2007.

Pound, Marcus. *Theology, Psychoanalysis, Trauma*, London: SCM, 2007.

Powers, John, ed. and trans. *Wisdom of Buddha*. Berkeley: Dharma Publishing, 1995.

Pfister, Oskar. "The Illusion of a Future: A Friendly Disagreement with Prof. Sigmund Freud." Edited by Paul Roazen. Translated by Susan Abrams. *International Journal of Psycho-Analysis* 74.3 (1993) 557–79.

Rank, Otto. *Beyond Psychology*. New York: Dover, 1958.

——. *The Trauma of Birth*. New York: Dover, 1993.

Roudinesco, Elizabeth. *Jacques Lacan: An Outline of a Life and a History of a Thought*. Translated by Barbara Bray. Cambridge: Polity, 1999.

Rubin, Jeffrey B. *Psychotherapy and Buddhism: Toward an Integration*. New York: Plenum, 1996.

Safouan, Moustapha. *Pleasure and Being: Hedonism from a Psychoanalytic Point of View*. Translated by Martin Thom. New York: St. Martin's, 1983.

Safran, Jeremy D., ed. *Psychoanalysis and Buddhism: An Unfolding Dialogue*. Boston: Wisdom, 2003.

Schelling, F. W. J. "Philosophical Letters on Dogmatism and Criticism." In *The Unconditional in Human Knowledge: Four Early Essays (1794–1796)*, translated by Fritz Marti, 156–218. Lewisburg: Bucknell University Press, 1980.

Segundo, Juan Luis. *Liberation of Theology*. Translated by John Drury. 1976. Reprint, Eugene, OR: Wipf & Stock, 2002.

Smith, Christian. *The Emergence of Liberation Theology: Radical Religion and Social Movement Theory*. Chicago: University of Chicago Press, 1991.

Sophocles. *Oedipus at Colonus*. Translated by F. Storr. Cambridge: Harvard University Press, 1912.

Spinoza, Benedict de. *The Ethics*. Translated by R. H. M. Elwes. Project Gutenberg, 2003. http://www.gutenberg.org/etext/3800.

Suler, John R. *Contemporary Psychoanalysis and Eastern Thought*. Albany: State University of New York Press, 1993.

Suzuki, D. T., Erich Fromm, and Richard De Martino. *Zen Buddhism and Psychoanalysis*. New York: Harper and Row, 1960.

Taylor, Mark C. *Erring: A Postmodern A/Theology*. Chicago: University of Chicago Press, 1984.

———. "Refusal of the Bar." In *Lacan and Theological Discourse*, edited by Edith Wyschogrod, David Crownfield, and Carl A. Raschke, 39–53. Albany: State University of New York Press, 1989.

Thompson, Joe. "Psychology in Primitive Buddhism." *The Psychoanalytic Review* 11 (1924) 39–47.

Torres, Camilo. *Revolutionary Priest: The Complete Writings and Messages of Camilo Torres*. Edited by John Gerassi. Translated by June de Cipriano Alcantara et al. London: Cape, 1971.

Verhaeghe, Paul. "From Impossibility to Inability: Lacan's Theory on the Four Discourses." In *Beyond Gender: From Subject to Drive*, 17–34. New York: Other Press, 2001.

Vernant, Jean-Pierre, and Pierre Vidal-Naquet. *Myth and Tragedy in Ancient Greece*. Translated by Janet Lloyd. New York: Zone, 1990.

Waldron, William S. *The Buddhist Unconscious: The Ālaya-vijñāna in the Context of Indian Buddhist Thought*. New York: RoutledgeCurzon, 2003.

Watkin, Christopher. *Difficult Atheism: Post-theological Thinking in Alain Badiou, Jean-Luc Nancy and Quentin Meillassoux*. Edinburgh: Edinburgh University Press, 2011.

Wilden, Anthony. *Speech and Language in Psychoanalysis*. Baltimore: Johns Hopkins University Press, 1981.

Williams, Paul. *Mahāyāna Buddhism: The Doctrinal Foundations*. New York: Routledge, 1989.

Winquist, Charles. "Lacan and Theological Discourse." In *Lacan and Theological Discourse*, edited by Edith Wyschogrod, David Crownfield, and Carl A. Raschke, 26–38. Albany: State University of New York Press, 1989.

Wyschogrod, Edith, David Crownfield, and Carl A. Raschke, eds. *Lacan and Theological Discourse*. Albany: State University of New York Press, 1989.

Žižek, Slavoj. "The Abyss of Freedom." In *The Abyss of Freedom/Ages of the World*, edited by Slavoj Žižek, with material from F. W. J Schelling, 1–104. Ann Arbor: University of Michigan Press, 1997.

————. "*Da Capo senza Fine.*" In *Contingency, Hegemony, Universality: Contemporary Dialogues on the Left,* by Judith Butler, Ernesto Laclau, and Slavoj Žižek, 213–62. London: Verso, 2000.

————. "Death and the Maiden." In *The Žižek Reader,* edited by Elizabeth Wright and Edmond Wright, 206–21. Oxford: Blackwell, 1999.

————. *For They Know Not What They Do: Enjoyment as a Political Factor.* 2nd ed. London: Verso, 2002.

————. *The Fright of Real Tears: Krzysztof Kieślowski Between Theory and Post-theory.* London: British Film Institute, 2001.

————. "How to Read Lacan: From *Che vuoi?* to Fantasy: Lacan with *Eyes Wide Shut,*" http://www.lacan.com/zizkubrick.htm.

————. "'I Do Not Order My Dreams.'" In *Opera's Second Death,* by Slavoj Žižek and Mladen Dolar, 103–225. New York: Routledge, 2002.

————. "'I Hear You with My Eyes'; or, The Invisible Master." In *Gaze and Voice as Love Objects,* edited by Renata Salecl and Slavoj Žižek, 90–126. Durham: Duke University Press, 1996.

————. *In Defense of Lost Causes.* London: Verso, 2008.

————. *The Indivisible Remainder: An Essay on Schelling and Related Matters.* London: Verso, 1996.

————. *Iraq: The Borrowed Kettle.* London: Verso, 2004.

————. "Kant as a Theoretician of Vampirism." *Lacanian Ink* 8 (1994) 19–33.

————. *Le plus sublime des hystériques: Hegel passe.* Paris: Points Hors Ligne, 1988.

————. *Less Than Nothing: Hegel and the Shadow of Dialectical Materialism.* New York: Verso, 2012.

————. *The Metastases of Enjoyment: Six Essays on Woman and Causality.* London: Verso, 1994.

————. *On Belief.* New York: Routledge, 2001.

————. *The Parallax View.* Cambridge: MIT Press, 2006.

————. *The Plague of Fantasies.* London: Verso, 1997.

————. *The Puppet and the Dwarf: The Perverse Core of Christianity.* Cambridge: MIT Press, 2003.

————. *The Sublime Object of Ideology.* London: Verso, 1989.

————. *Tarrying with the Negative: Kant, Hegel, and the Critique of Ideology.* Durham: Duke University Press, 1993.

————. *The Ticklish Subject: The Absent Centre of Political Ontology.* London: Verso, 1999.

Žižek, Slavoj, and John Milbank. *The Monstrosity of Christ: Paradox or Dialectic?* Cambridge: MIT Press, 2009.

Zupančič, Alenka. *The Ethics of the Real: Kant and Lacan (Wo Es War).* London: Verso, 2000.

————. "Philosophers' Blind Man's Buff." In *Gaze and Voice as Love Objects,* edited by Renata Salecl and Slavoj Žižek, 32–58. Durham: Duke University Press, 1996.

Index

a/theology, 6, 278
Abelard, Peter, 62
Abeysekara, Ananda, 254
Adorno, 19
Aeschylus *Eumenides*, 137, 271
ain sof, 160
Alexander, Franz, 72–73
Althusser, Louis, 211n1, 227, 271
    and sexual relation and God, 161
Altizer, Thomas, 10, 256
Antigone, 8, 257–58
Aquinas, Thomas, 34–57
    and Avicenna, 41
    and creation, 49–50
    and incarnation, 51
    One and the many, 42
Aristide, Jean Bertrand, 215, 271
Aristotle, 30, 34, 43–45
    and creation, 37–39, 40
    and unmoved mover, 40, 44
Armstrong, Louis, 207, 210
Asad, Talal, 251, 254
Atman, 71, 75–76, 192
automaton, 126, 140, 147

Badiou, Alain, 14, 147
    and *Ethics*, 145
    and Event, 143, 151
    and feminine *jouissance*, 160n11
    and fidelity, 146
    and Frege, 156
    and infinity, 154n4
    and Lacan, 12
    and multiplicity, 150–51
Barth, Karl *analogia entis*, 59
Beattie, Tina, 12, 267
Becker, Ernest, 103, 271
Benjamin, Walter, 165, 251–52, 255,
    278
Blanchot, Maurice, 105, 271

Bloch, Ernst, 226–29, 231, 271
Boer, Roland, 231
Boff Clodovis, 213n5, 230
Boff, Leonardo, 213n5, 230
Bouyer Mohammad, 205–6
Bracher, Mark, 218, 220, 221, 224n46,
    228, 271
Brahma, 192
Brown, Norman, 103, 271
Buddhism, 84
    anātman, 71, 75–77
    and meditation, 78–79, 81
    and *samādhi*, 72, 75
    and semiotics, 80, 82
    and *śūnyatā*, 80, 82
    Buddha, 13, 73, 75, 81n36
    Yogācāra School, 13, 77, 80, 81, 82,
        84, 268
Butler, Judith, 13, 103n49, 117,
    125, 127, 128–30, 124,
    142–45, 147–48, 269, 272

Calvin, John, 60
Calvinism, 236
Camus, Albert *Myth of Sisyphus*, 3–4
Cantor, Georg, 156, 157
Caputo, John, 256
Catherine of Siena, 56
Chernyshevsky, Nikolai, 3
Chesterton, G. K. 23
Chiesa Lorenzo, 14, 257–59
Christ, 9–13, 44, 51–52, 54–56, 163,
    194, 214, 226, 237, 256, 259
    and Oedipus, 13, 129–35
    Pro me, 59
Christianity
    and atheism, 226–29
    and capitalism, 213, 252–55
    and despair, 202–3

Christianity *(cont.)*
  and Marxism, 131, 213–14,
    227–28, 231
  and Neo-Platonic influences, 161
  obscenity of the flesh, 38
  true religion, 39, 193, 197–98, 255
Clement, Catherine, 6
Cogito, 19–33
Conze, Edward, 80n34
Costoya, Mejido, 212, 215–18, 222,
    226, 276
creation exnihilo, 36, 38, 47, 49–50
  andnumbers, 156
Crockett, Clayton, 15, 267
Crownfield, David, 7, 11

D'Amato, Mario, 13
De Martino, Richard, 73, 278
Death of God, 2, 5, 9, 10, 14, 121,
    193–94, 202, 256–57
Deleuze, Gilles, 145n40, 208, 252–53,
    261, 264–65, 272
Dennet, Daniel, 20–21
Derrida, Jacques, 65, 272
  and *cogito*, 22–24, 26–29
  and *différance*, 6, 264
  and Hegel, 117
  andnegative theology, 6
  and Žižek, 12
  hauntology, 110–11
  radical atheism, 13, 88–89, 91,
    93–94, 97, 104–5, 112,
    115–16, 229
  Spectres of Marx, 110,111, 272
Descartes, 12, 22, 23–24, 27–30,
    104m, 272
Deuteronomy, 154
discourse of the analyst, 222–26
discourse of the hysteric, 220–22
discourse of the master, 218
discourse of the university, 218–20
Dolar, Mladen, 92, 115n97, 157n8,
    272
Dostoyevsky, Fyodor, 121, 123
  Notes from Underground, 1–4

Ehyeh Asher Ehyeh, 246
entropy, 252–54

Epstein, Mark, 76, 273
Erikson Eric, on Luther, 67–68
Exodus, 36, 47, 48, 54, 246

Fink, Bruce, 2, 7, 36–37, 40, 83, 221
feminine
  and feminine masochism, 202, 204
  and God, 162
  and *jouissance*, 166–91
  and lack, 43
  and phallic *jouissance*, 166–91
  critique of Lacan, 56
  formula of sexuation, 55, 153–54,
    159, 160n11, 164
  mystical *jouissance*, 14, 40, 45,
    54, 56, 162, 167, 169, 171,
    177n47, 179, 183, 186,
    18–190, 259
  not-all, 14, 55
Foucault, Michel, 12, 19–33
  and Derrida, 27–30
  Discipline and Punishment, 20, 26,
    29n20
  History of Sexuality, 25
  Language, Counter–Memory,
    Practice, 26
  Madness and Civilization, 23,
    26–30
free association, 93
Frege, Gottlob, 156, 235
Freud, Sigmund
  and atheism, 88, 90–95, 121, 123
  and *Buddhism*, 72–73, 77–79
  and Cartesian subject, 197
  and *das Unheimliche*, 118
  and death, 102, 103
  and death drive, 21, 84
  and fort-da, 195, 241
  and Judge Schreber, 32
  and morality, 101
  and *Nachträglichkeit*, 93, 117
  and paranoia, 25
  and progress, 87
  and religion, 197
  and sovereign exception, 152
  and talking cure, 64–65
  and temporality, 95–100, 123
  and the female body, 38

and the *id, ego, superego*, 68
and the linguistic turn, 63
and the oceanic, 192, 273
and the psyche, 77
and theology, 35
and trauma, 83
and *verdrängnis*, 67n11
and *Wo Es war, soll Ich warden*,
238, 249
Freud: works by
"Beyond the Pleasure Principle,"
72, 173
Civilization and Its Discontents,
192
"Drives and Their Vicissitudes," 97
Future of an Illusion, 87, 88, 106
Moses and Monotheism, 246
"Mourning and Melancholia,"
97–99, 111, 273
"On a Question Prior to Any Pos-
sible Treatment of Psychosis,"
112n86, 114n94, 275
"On Narcissism: An Introduction,"
97–99, 273
"On Transience," 95–99, 123, 273
"Recommendations to Physicians
Practicing Psycho-Analysis,"
78n29, 273
"Repression," 97
"Thoughts for the Times on War
and Death," 97, 100–102
Totem and Taboo, 121
"The Uncanny," 103n48, 118n103,
273
"The Unconscious," 97, 100
Fromm, Erich, 73, 278

Gallagher, Cormac, 8, 234, 235
Gilson, Etienne, 34, 35, 40–41, 47, 49
God
and absent lawgiver, 45
and capitalism, 262
and created in image, 59–60
and *deus ex machine*, 1
and divine *logos*, 68
and Divine Simplicity, 41
and feminine *jouissance*, 166,
184–91

and forgiveness, 65
and kenosis, 9, 10
and matter, 50
and modernity, 45
andnegative theology, 11
and *objet petit a*, 69
and occasionalism, 31–32
and relational, 59
and the Death of God, 2, 5, 9, 10,
14, 121, 193–94, 202, 256–57
and thename of, 48
as sovereign subject, 14
evil God, 28, 32
false God, 2
is an atheist, 9
non-copulative, 57
of Exodus, 36, 41
the unknowable, 39
unconscious, 121
unmoved/prime mover, 44, 48
Goodchild, Philip, 262
grace
and Lacan, 14–15, 34, 232–49
and revelation, 244–48
Green, Andre, 119, 273
Gregory of Nyssa, 249
grief, 127
Guattari, Felix, 265
Gutierrez, Gustavo, 213, 214

Habermas, Jürgen, 212
Hadewijch, Saint, 167
Hägglund Martin, 13, 88–124
Hallward, Peter, 215n13
Hanly, Charles, 76, 273
Haraway, Donna, 129–40
Hegel, G. W.
and dialectics, 103
and ideology, 251–52
and infinity, 117–19
and *kenosis*, 9
and Lacan, 12
and *Lectures on Philosophy of History*, 21
and madness, 19–33
and master/slave, 218, 260
andnight of the world, 23–25
and parallax, 85

and religion, 71
Heidegger Martin, 70, 265, 274
"being-towards-death," 101, 105
and *Überwindung*, 63
onto-theology, 237
Hennelly, Alfred, 214n9, 274
Hirsi Ali, Ayaan, 205–6
Hisamatsu Shin'ichi, 73
Hobbes, Thomas, 104, 274
Hollywood, Amy, 35
Holsinger, Bruce, 35
homo sacer, 133
Horney, Karen, 73

Incarnation, 56, 59, 135, 194, 248, 256
Irigaray, Luce, 56

Jacobi, F. H. 212
Jesus, 12, 51, 60, 129, 131–32, 163, 165, 184, 193, 199, 226, 237
Johnston, Adrian, 13, 224, 229, 239, 268
Juan, Don, 170, 171n19, 184, 190
Jung, Carl, 73

Kant
and freedom, 19–33, 101
and Sade, 258
Kantorowicz, Ernst, 251
Kee, Alister, 212
kenosis, 9–10
Kierkegaard, 11–12, 53, 202–3, 244–45
Kolozova, Katerina, 13
Kotsko, Adam, 9, 274
Koyré, Alexandre, 247
Kristeva, Julia, 14, 24, 194–96
Kristof, Agota, 257

Lacan, Jacques
and ego-ideal, 77
and "The Triumph of Religion,"
15, 87, 88, 193, 195, 196–200, 250–266
and *"there is no sexual relation,"*
120, 154
and alienation, 33

and *après-coup*, 93, 116
and Aquinas, 34–57
and *automaton*, 126
and between-two-deaths, 116
and Buddhism, 73–86
and Catholicism, 57, 233–35
and *das Ding*, 66–67, 107, 108, 114
and formula of sexuation, 152, 156, 180–81
and grace, 232–49
and James Joyce, 258–59
and Kierkegaard, 11–12, 53
and *lamella*, 118
and *manqué-à-être*, 107
and master's discourse, 158, 163
and Monotheism, 161
and mysticism, 53–54
and ontology, 40
and *Parmenides*, 156–58
and Pascal, Blaise, 232–49
and Plato, 40
and political theology, 163–65
and racism, 158
and repetition/recollection, 244–45, 263–64
and Saint Thomas, 162
and sexual difference, 43–44
and the body, 46–47
and the exception, 153–54
and the four discourse, 211–31
and the sexual relation and God, 161
and the soul, 39
and the true formula of atheism, 121
and *Todestrieb*, 106
and traversing the fantasy, 200
and *tuché*, 126
and *Vorstellungen*, 119
and *Wo Es war, soll Ich warden*, 79
Desnoms-du-pere, 115n97, 272
desire/drive, 11–12
Works by (excluding Seminars):
"Aggressiveness in Psychoanalysis," 115, 274
"Aristotle's Dream," 103, 106, 274
"Desire and the Interpretation of Desire in *Hamlet*," 99n38,

112n82, 113n88, 273
"Kant with Sade," 74, 224n47,
275
"*L'étourdit*," 103n49, 191n89, 275
"*Le symbolique, le imaginaire et le
réel*"
"*Le triomphe de la religion*," 88n5,
197, 198n13, 250n1, 275
"Position of the Unconscious," 113,
275
"*Radiophonie*," 103n49, 115n97,
275
"The Direction of the Treatment
and the Principles of Its
Power," 90n12, 108n67, 275
"The Mirror Stage as Formative of
the *I* Function as Revealed in
Psychoanalytic Experience,"
115n97, 275
"The Signification of the Phallus,"
108n68, 275
"The Subversion of the Subject and
the Dialectic of Desire in the
Freudian Unconscious," 75,
108n68, 119n104, 275
and Zen, 73–75
Lactans, Virgo, 57
Libanio, Joao Batista, 222n43
Liberation theology, 212–17, 220–31
Life Is Beautiful, 205
Luther, Martin, 13, 58–70
and *Commentary on Galatians*,
60–61
and *Deus Absconditus*, 69
and Gospel and Law, 60–62
and *sola fide*, 65
revelation of Law, 60
Lynch, David, films, 25
Lynch, Thomas, 13

Macey, David, 7, 8
Malcolm Bowie, 35
Malebranche, Nicholas, 30, 32
Marxism, 75, 140, 227, 259, 260
and Christian Marxism, 131
and religion, 212–15, 227–28, 231
and surplus value, 153, 220, 262
Mary, Mother of God, 183, 275

Matrix, 32, 33
McDade, John, 248
Meister Eckhart, 51
Mejido Costoya, 216n14, 276
Mejido, Manuel, 212, 215–17
Milbank, John, 219, 256
Miller, Jacques-Alain, 8, 166
Molino, Anthony, 73
Moncayo, Raul, 73–74
Muller, John, 99

Nancy, Jean-Luc, 255
Napoleon, 32
Nietzsche, Friedrich, 23, 27, 56, 64,
94, 260
Nishida, Kitarō, 73

O'Regan, Cyril, 9
Object petit a, 11, 15, 66n11, 69, 73,
119, 197, 217–19, 224, 225, 235,
258, 262–63
Oedipus, 13, 42, 121, 129, 182, 224
Oedipus at Colonus, 133–36, 139
Oliveros, Roberto, 214

Parker, Robert, 134n18
Pascal, Blaise, 8, 233–38, 240–43,
246–49
Paul (Saint) 55, 59
Peirce, Charles Sanders, 79
Philippe, Julien, 197
Petrella, Ivan, 216n14
Pfister, Oskar, 88
Parmenides, 151, 156
Pluth, Ed, 226n54, 277
political theology, 10, 14, 150–65,
251–52, 267
Pontalis, Jean-Bertrand, 119
Green, Andre, 119
post-structuralism, 8, 11, 64, 67, 70,
129, 264
Pound, Marcus, 14, 53

Rank, Otto, 103
Raschke, Carl, 6, 12
Reformation Theology, 59
Regnault, Francois, 158
Reinhard, Ken, 14

andneighbour love, 154–55, 159
revelation, 233–34, 238, 244–48
revelation, progressive, 248
Rhapsody in Black and Blue, 207, 210
Robbins, Jeffrey, 207–8
Robocop, 21
Roettgen Pieta, 57
Rose, Marika, 233
Roudinesco, Elizabeth, 8n20
Rousseau, 19
Reformation, *sola Scriptura*, 65–66
Rubin, Jeffrey, 79n79
Regnault, Francois, 35

Safouan, Moustapha, 115n97
Sagan, Dorion, 253
Saussure, Ferdinand, 79
Schelling, F. W. J. 23, 101
Schmitt, Carl, 14, 152, 153, 162, 251
Schneider, Eric, 253
Segundo, Juan Luis, 59
sexual jouissance, 168–73
Shakespeare, William *All's Well That
    Ends Well*, 206
Sophocles, 121, 133–38
Spinoza, Benedict de, 143–46
St. John of the Cross, 249
St. Theresa of Avila, 167, 183
Suzuki, D. T. 73

talking cure, 64–66
Taubes, Jacob, 151
Television, 30
theology and materialism, 229–30
Thompson, Joe, 72
Torres, Camilo, 215
tuché, 126, 140, 147, 242
Taylor, Mark C. 6, 7, 10
traverse the fantasy (theological sig-
    nificance) 2, 5. 9. 14, 15, 25, 165,
    200, 224–25

Usual Suspects, 122

Vahanian Noelle, 14
Van Gogh, Theo, 205
vanishing mediator, 21
Vernant, Jean-Pierre, 132

Waldron, William, 77–78, 278
Watkin, Christopher, 229n64, 278
Wilden, Anthony, 7, 278
Winquist, Charles, 6
Wittgenstein, Ludwig, 27, 63
Wyschogrod, Edith, 6

Yogācāra, 13, 80–84

Žižek
    and atheism, 9, 256–57, 260
    and Christ, 226
    and cyberspace, 32
    and *das Ding*, 108
    and death of God, 202, 204, 255,
        256
    and Ernst Bloch, 226–27, 229
    and female masochism, 202
    and inter-passivity, 209
    and Job, 9
    and Judaism, 55
    and Kierkegaard, 202–3
    and Lacan, 9–12
    and liberation theology, 14, 211–32
    and love, 55–56
    and Milbank, 219, 256
    and Mohammad Bouyeri, 205–6
    and neo-liberalism, 261
    and political theology, 10, 251
    and surplus enjoyment, 243
    and the abyss, 249
    and the critique of ideology,
        211–12
    and the fall, 22
    and the undead, 92, 116, 118, 119
    and Thomas Altizer, 256
    and traversing the fantasy, 225
Zupančič, Alenka, 119, 149

Lightning Source UK Ltd.
Milton Keynes UK
UKOW02f0749311014

240865UK00002B/43/P